Dieppe

TRAGEDY TO TRIUMPH

Dieppe

TRAGEDY TO TRIUMPH

Brigadier General Denis Whitaker
DSO and Bar, CM, ED, CD
Shelagh Whitaker

McGraw-Hill Ryerson
Toronto   Montreal

Dieppe: Tragedy to Triumph

First published in 1992 by
McGraw-Hill Ryerson Limited
300 Water Street
Whitby, Ontario, Canada
L1N 9B6

  2 3 4 5 6 7 8 9 0 DWF 1 0 9 8 7 6 5 4 3 2

Canadian Cataloguing in Publication Data
  Whitaker, W. Denis
    Dieppe : tragedy to triumph

  Includes bibliographical references and index.

  ISBN 0-07-551385-4

  1. Dieppe, Raid, 1942.   2. World War, 1939-1945 -
  Canada.   I. Whitaker, Shelagh.   II. Title.

  D756.5.D5W45 1992   940.54'21425   C92-094471-X

All inquiries regarding the motion picture or other dramatic rights for this book should be addressed to the author's representative, MGA Inc., 10 St. Mary Street, Suite 510, Toronto, Ontario M4Y 1R1. Representations as to the disposition of these rights are strictly prohibited without express written consent and will be vigorously pursued to the full extent of the law.

Interior design: Dianna Little

Printed and bound in Canada

104906

This book is dedicated to fellow veterans of Dieppe and to the strong and unified Canada for which you fought. Your country stands proud for your sacrifice which made such an important contribution to victory in World War Two.

CONTENTS

LIST OF ABBREVIATIONS

AA	Anti-Aircraft
A/TK	Anti-Tank
ADC	Aide de camp
AFV	Armoured Fighting Vehicle
AP	Armour Piercing
COO	Chief of Combined Operations
CIGS	Chief of the Imperial General Staff
CO	Commanding Officer or Combined Operations
COS	Chiefs of Staff
CRA	Commander Royal Artillery
CRE	Commander Royal Engineers
FOO	Forward Observation Officer
GOC	General Officer Commanding
HE	High Explosive
HQ	Headquarters
LCA	Landing Craft Assault
LCF	Landing Craft Flak
LCM	Landing Craft Mechanized
LO	Liaison Officer
LCP	Landing Craft Personnel (R Boat)
LCT	Landing Craft Tank
LMG	Light Machine Gun — (Bren)
LSI	Landing Ship Infantry
MG	Machine Gun
MGB	Motor Gun Boat
ML	Motor Launch
OP	Observation Post
PA	Personal Assistant
RAF	Royal Air Force
RAP	Regimental Aid Post
RCAF	Royal Canadian Air Force
RCA	Royal Canadian Artillery
RCE	Royal Canadian Engineers
RT	Radio Telephony
SAPPER	Engineer
SGB	Steam Gun Boat
VCIGS	Vice-Chief Imperial General Staff
25-Pdr	Field Artillery Gun
WT	Wireless Telegraphy

CAST OF PRIMARY CHARACTERS

(ranks and titles as of 1942)

GREAT BRITAIN:

Sir Winston Churchill: Prime Minister and Minister of Defense
Chiefs of Staff Committee:
  General Sir Alan Brooke, Chief of the Imperial General Staff (CIGS)
    and chairman of the Chiefs of Staff Committee
  Sir Dudley Pound, Admiral of the Fleet
  Sir Charles Portal, Marshal of the Royal Air Force
  Lord Louis Mountbatten, Chief of Combined Operations
  Major General Sir Hastings Ismay, Chief of Staff to the Minister of
    Defence (Churchill's representative on the Chiefs of Staff)
Field Marshal Sir John Dill, Churchill's representative on the Joint Chiefs
  of Staff in the United States

UNITED STATES:

Franklin D. Roosevelt: President
General George C. Marshall, Chief of Staff of the United States Army
Brigadier General Dwight D. Eisenhower, Deputy Chief of Staff of the
  United States Army
Admiral Ernest King, Chief of U.S. Naval Operations
Henry Stimson, Secretary of War
Mr. Harry Hopkins, President Roosevelt's advisor

RUSSIA:

Joseph Stalin, Chairman of the Council of the People's Commissars of the
  Union of Soviet Socialist Republics
Vyacheslav M. Molotov, People's Commissar of Foreign Affairs

CANADA:

The Right Honourable Mackenzie King, Prime Minister of Canada
General Andrew McNaughton, Commander 1st Canadian Army
Lieutenant General Harry Crerar, Commander 1st Canadian Corps
Major General John Hamilton Roberts, General Officer Commanding
  Second Canadian Division

INTRODUCTION

In summertime, the ten o'clock sailing of the Newhaven ferry arrived at the French port of Dieppe shortly after five p.m.

As the boat neared the harbour, passengers crowded the rails, relishing their first glimpses of their holiday destination. Inevitably, the splendour of the immense white cliffs rising starkly out of the green Channel waters inspired gasps of delight.

To the eager tourists, it was like a huge marzipan confection, sliced cleanly through so that the chalk bluffs took on hues of pinks and purples in the reflections of the late afternoon sun. As far as the eye could see, there was this long skyline of white cliffs, with sheer drops down to narrow, rocky coves bordering the sea. Atop the headlands, verdant meadows promised a gentler, pastoral Normandy.

A young woman at the railing stood apart from the holiday makers. She was a student: she wore jeans, carried a knapsack. She was a Canadian: her kit had a maple leaf blazoned on its back.

She was weeping silently.

The man beside her was many decades her senior. He was, probably, a veteran. He wore a Canadian regimental blazer. His eyes were also misted as he gazed — for the second time in his life — at the magnificent, and terrifying, white cliffs of Dieppe.

Maple leaf saw maple leaf, and both sensed the instant kinship born between fellow countrymen far from home.

"Were you there, at the Dieppe raid, in 1942?" she asked. "You were, weren't you. You have the same look in your eyes that my father gets when he speaks of the raid — a mixture of anger, bewilderment and utter sadness.

"Look up at those cliffs. A handful of men with machine guns perched away above us could kill the hundreds of people here on the ferry in minutes. We'd be defenceless. It must have been like that for you, when you landed that morning, and suddenly fire opened up at you from all sides.

"You didn't stand a chance, you and your friends. You must have felt like rats trapped in a cage, with gunfire mowing you down from every direction.

"How could it have happened? How could they send thousands of you — my God, you were all just my age! — into that trap? Why?"

On August 19, 1942, 10,000 men from the British and Canadian navy, army and air force mounted a five-hour raid against the French port of Dieppe. Tactically, the raid failed. Of the 5,000 Canadian infantry, 65 percent were casualties, with nearly 1,000 killed. Two thousand men were marched off to prisoner-of-war camp. The losses to the Royal Navy were severe; the RAF and RCAF had 108 planes shot down and 60 pilots lost. Most survivors concluded that the enemy had been alerted.

For 50 years, historians have sought the reasons behind the raid: *Why* was it mounted? *How* could the high command endorse such a seemingly faulty plan? *What* were the *real* behind-the-scenes objectives?

How? why? Those words sent the authors on a decades-long search through a trail of records that had been buried, and to interviews that had been lost — or never sought. They led us to men whose military experience was learned from command positions on the battlefield, and to historians whose expertise was gleaned from years of patient archival sifting. We found scores of veterans — many of whom had been asking the same questions — whose experiences at Dieppe have surely entitled them to have a voice.

Ours is one opinion — one we believe in fervently. There have been many others proffered over the years; doubtless, more will come in print in the future. This endless search for pieces of the puzzle is what gives history its vitality.

With this book we demonstrate that there can, finally, be an acceptance of the reality of Dieppe as an important element in the Allied Grand Strategy.

That makes the losses just a little easier to bear for those of us who were there.

PROLOGUE

I awakened to a stab of early morning sunlight searing my eyelids.

My batman, Corporal Mino, peered through the tent flap, letting in more of that punishing light. "Sir, wake up!"

I sat up groggily in my cot. Christ! I was a mess. I was still wearing my battledress, filthy, streaked in grime and dried blood. Threads hung where I had impulsively torn off my captain's pips just before going into battle. There was a two-day stubble on my chin. My hands were scraped raw, my fingernails blackened.

My head throbbed. God, I'd put down a lot of fast shots of rum. I recalled getting off the boat and being trucked somewhere with a lot of other guys — all of us in a daze. They gave us a sandwich, a cup of tea, then more belts of that rough navy rum than I could remember.

The grounds of Arundel Castle had seemed eerily quiet, almost ghost-like, in the filtered rays of moonlight when I had got back. The last time I'd seen it, two days before, six hundred men had been milling around their tents, exchanging rude jibes, stuffing gear into rucksacks, collecting up photographs of the girlfriend, examining personal weapons, scrounging cigarettes. Exercise Ford, we had been told . . . *another* bloody two-day training scheme.

In the midst of the confusion, a fleet of lorries had rolled up to the gates. The troops, clambering aboard, had grumbled coarsely about having to wear heavy battledress and hobnailed boots on a warm summer's afternoon.

How many of my friends were now floating dead in the English Channel, washed out by the tides, their bullet-ridden bodies weighted down by those hobnailed boots?

A lone officer had stood at the gates to see us off. It was my close friend, Captain Jervis O'Donohoe, the assistant adjutant, left behind to take charge of the abandoned headquarters.

When I arrived back at camp two days later, alone, Jervis walked towards me. Is there no one else coming back? he asked, tears gleaming in the half-light. I had no heart to talk about that day, or about our friends who had been killed or taken prisoner.

Then I tumbled into bed, still in battledress, and slept until my batman roused me.

"Sir, sir, you must get up! Admiral Mountbatten has ordered you to attend a debriefing in London two hours from now."

I peered groggily at the anxious corporal. "Bugger off," I growled. "An admiral doesn't ask a captain's advice."

"But sir," my batman insisted, "you're all that's left. You're the senior officer in the battalion. In fact, they said you were the only unwounded officer *of the whole brigade* who came back from the beaches. There aren't many left — a few here in hospital, the rest dead or captured in France, and a handful who never landed. So you're it, sir."

The whole impact of Dieppe exploded in my brain at these words. There had been over 100 officers in my brigade. There were scores of officers my rank or senior to me: captains by the bushel, majors, lieutenant colonels — were they all gone?

———————

Room 21 in Montagu House was not far from the War Office. The Combined Operations debriefing had begun when I finally got to London. On the platform of the conference room, I recognized the Dieppe military commander, Major General Roberts — his face bore a gaunt, stricken look — and the two senior Canadian officers, Lieutenant Generals McNaughton and Crerar. I assumed that the two men beside Admiral Mountbatten were the air and naval commanders of the operation. The rest was a sea of brass: naval, army, and air force commanders, senior men from Combined Planning.

There were few other familiar faces. I saw one or two officers from 6th Brigade, an acquaintance from the South Saskatchewan Regiment, and a major with the shoulder patches of the Queen's Own Cameron Highlanders of Canada.

But where in hell were the 4th Brigade representatives? Was there no one from the Royal Regiment; no one from Les Fusiliers Mont-Royal?

General Roberts was finishing his report. "I am inclined to question whether tactical surprise was achieved." he said. "It is evident that the German gun crews were standing by with all defence posts manned when the first wave of troops came in."

Mountbatten shrugged off the comments impatiently. "You have to take into account that a state of alert was normal at dawn, and that the condition of weather and tide might have increased the state of alert," he said.

I stood up. My mind reeled. So surprise had never even been possible? "Yes, Captain," an imperious voice addressed me. "Identify yourself, please."

"Captain Denis Whitaker, Admiral Mountbatten. Royal Hamilton Light Infantry."

"Right, Whitaker. Now, we have already established that secrecy and tactical surprise were maintained in the Dieppe raid. The fact that the lights were still on at the lighthouse, the slow entry of the Luftwaffe into the battle, the success of the commandos on the right flank: these are all convincing evidence of this.

"Please inform this hearing as to your impressions."

"Sir, I landed on the main beach. When I interrogated a German prisoner at the casino, he boasted, 'We have been waiting for you for a week!' "

"Sit down, Captain Whitaker. I do not believe the enemy was forewarned. I want constructive comments — not excuses."

I thought, "What's going on? Yesterday we laid on a raid whose success depended on surprise. Today they tell our military commander that no surprise had been possible anyway. And they tell me to shut up.

"What are they doing to him? To me? To all my friends who are dead on the Dieppe beaches or sitting right now in German prisoner-of-war camps?" The whole raid now seemed so incongruous.

What is the real story behind Dieppe?

———

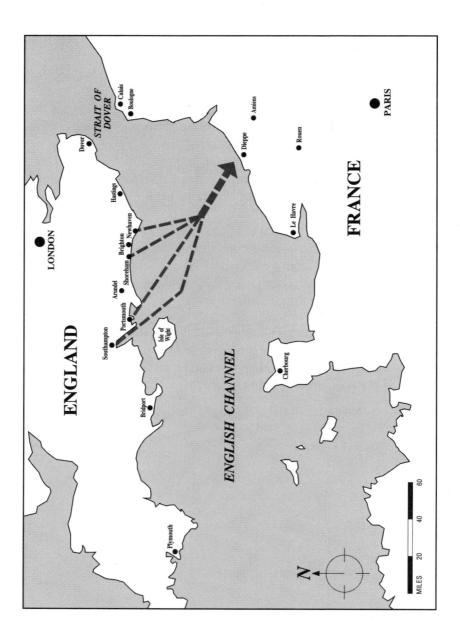

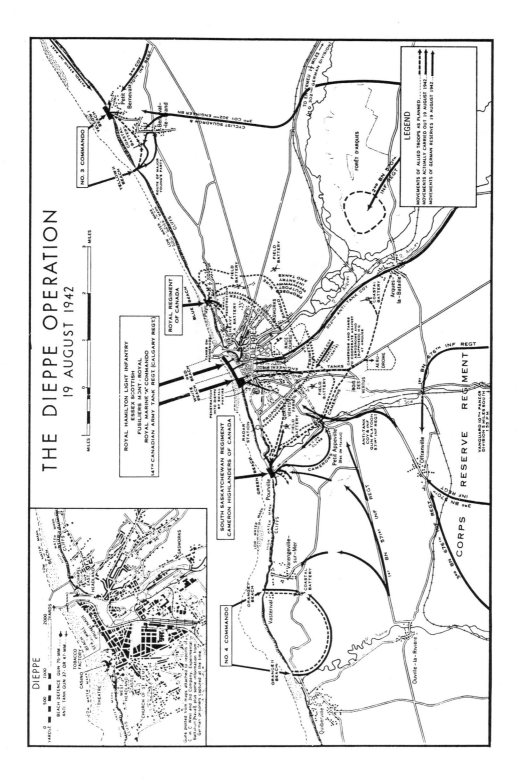

THE DIEPPE OPERATION
19 AUGUST 1942

ROYAL HAMILTON LIGHT INFANTRY
ESSEX SCOTTISH
FUSILIERS MONT-ROYAL
ROYAL MARINE "A" COMMANDO
14TH CANADIAN ARMY TANK REGT (CALGARY REGT)

ROYAL REGIMENT OF CANADA

SOUTH SASKATCHEWAN REGIMENT
CAMERON HIGHLANDERS OF CANADA

NO. 3 COMMANDO

NO. 4 COMMANDO

LEGEND

MOVEMENTS OF ALLIED TROOPS AS PLANNED
MOVEMENTS ACTUALLY CARRIED OUT 19 AUGUST 1942
MOVEMENTS OF GERMAN RESERVES 19 AUGUST 1942

MILES
0   1   2   3

DIEPPE

YARDS   0   500   1000   2000

BEACH DEFENCE GUN 75-MM.
ANTI TANK GUN 37- OR 47-MM.

Guns plotted from maps attached to report of
C in C West and 3rd Company. Experimental
Battalion (Naval) plus some information from
German prisoners captured at the time.

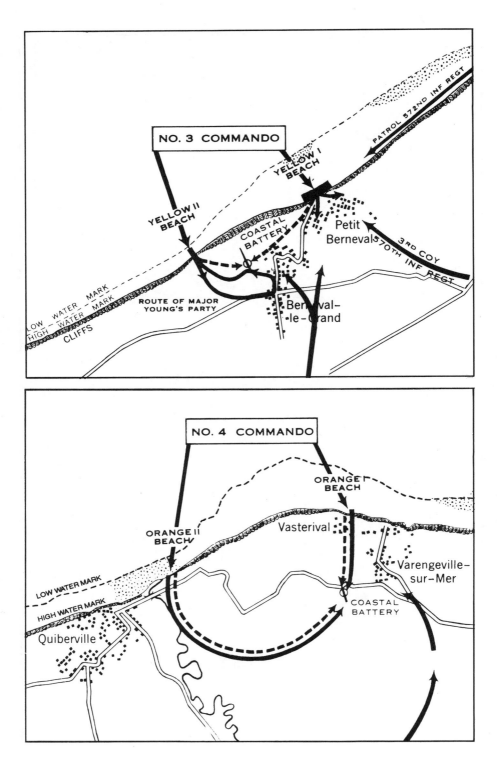

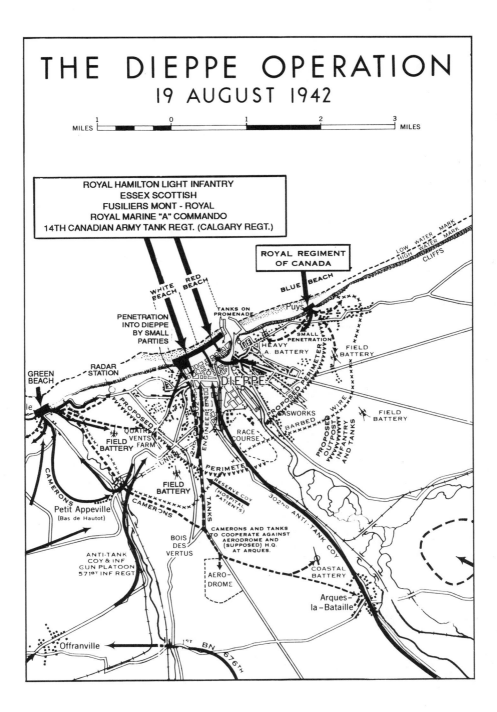

THE DIEPPE OPERATION
19 AUGUST 1942

MILES | 1   0   1   2   3 | MILES

ROYAL HAMILTON LIGHT INFANTRY
ESSEX SCOTTISH
FUSILIERS MONT - ROYAL
ROYAL MARINE "A" COMMANDO
14TH CANADIAN ARMY TANK REGT. (CALGARY REGT.)

ROYAL REGIMENT
OF CANADA

LOW WATER MARK
HIGH WATER MARK
CLIFFS

WHITE BEACH
RED BEACH
BLUE BEACH
Puys

PENETRATION
INTO DIEPPE
BY SMALL
PARTIES

TANKS ON
PROMENADE

SMALL
PENETRATION

HEAVY
A. BATTERY

FIELD
BATTERY

GREEN
BEACH

RADAR
STATION

DIEPPE

GASWORKS

FIELD
BATTERY

PROPOSED PERIMETER

PROPOSED OUTPOST WIRE
BARBED WIRE
INFANTRY
AND TANKS

le

QUATRE
VENTS
FARM

FIELD
BATTERY

RACE
COURSE

CAMERONS

PROPOSED

TUNNEL

ENGINEER END

PERIMETER

FIELD
BATTERY

RESERVE COY
(HOSPITAL
PATIENTS)

302ND ANTI-TANK CO.

Petit Appeville
(Bas de Hautot)

CAMERONS

TANKS

CAMERONS AND TANKS
TO COOPERATE AGAINST
AERODROME AND
(SUPPOSED) H.Q.
AT ARQUES.

ANTI-TANK
COY & INF
GUN PLATOON
571ST INF REGT

BOIS
DES
VERTUS

AERO-
DROME

COASTAL
BATTERY

Arques-
la – Bataille

Offranville

1ST BN 676TH

PART

1

AUGUST 19, 1942

CHAPTER

1

POINT OF NO RETURN

The battle for Dieppe began at 0124 hours on August 19, 1942, in a small room in the top storey of a remote house on the Sussex coast.

The radar officer on the graveyard shift at Beachy Head picked up echoes of an enemy convoy heading from Boulogne to Dieppe — dead in the path of the Anglo-Canadian assault force of 6,000 men. He alerted the Commander-in-Chief Portsmouth, Admiral Sir William James. Three minutes later, James relayed the warning to Operation Jubilee's naval force commander, Captain John Hughes-Hallett, on the command ship, the destroyer H.M.S. *Calpe*. The warning went unheeded. *Was it not received?*

In the wardroom of the *Calpe*, the Canadian in charge of the military operation, Major General Hamilton Roberts — unaware of the threat — peered at his watch. It would soon be 0300 hours: officially, the point of no return. In minutes, the landing ships would be at their allotted positions 10 miles off the coast of France, ready to lower their assault landing craft (LCAs) into the Channel waters. Already, the small boats were swinging from davits as troops clambered aboard, clumsy under their 60-pound burdens of weapons, grenades and ammunition.

The tank landing craft (LCTs) and small wooden R boats (unarmed landing craft personnel) had made the uncomfortable crossing and were now bobbing here and there, waiting for the final run-in to begin.

Unaware of the impending disaster, the assault force of 4,961 officers and men of the Second Canadian Infantry Division, and 1,057 British commandos and 50 U.S. Rangers, sailed serenely south through the calm Channel waters. It was a warm night, moonless. In 13 separate groups, the 237-ship flotilla had steamed without incident through the quarter-mile-wide paths being cleared by the mine-sweepers, and assembled off the French coast to make their final approaches. All was in darkness, silent except for the hum of the engines, the gentle slap of water on the hulls, and the murmur of men bemused by the battle ahead of them.

For Hughes-Hallett, it was a heady experience to go into action — his first action as a captain — in the greatest amphibious operation since Gallipoli. The sight of hundreds of ships and craft filling the horizon had a "certain dream-like quality" after so many months of planning.[1] The flotilla was manned by 3,000 British sailors. There were eight destroyers as well as a variety of crafts such as gunboats, flak ships, converted Channel ferries put to use as troops carriers, and a vast number of landing craft for personnel and armour.

———■———

At 0244 hours, two south-coast radar stations once more picked up the German convoy's echo. By now it was clearly on a collision course with the Dieppe raiders. Again, Admiral James urgently signalled the command ships: unidentified vessels were on a direct line with them.

Still the flotilla forged ahead.

Several other of the destroyers in the flotilla also intercepted the warning. They had not sighted enemy vessels on their radar screens and were perplexed. But they maintained an uneasy silence, believing that the *Calpe* would take charge.[2]

Strangely, the man to whom this vital intelligence was sent, Captain Hughes-Hallett, did nothing. *Had he not received the signals? Why was he not acting upon them?*

———■———

There would be no sleep for Major General Ham Roberts that night. Although he turned in for a brief rest, it was only to lie awake, tossing on the narrow berth and — for the hundredth time — mentally reviewing the plan of attack. There was reassurance in the fact that it was the plan of Lieutenant General Bernard Montgomery, and that it had received strong votes of approval by Canada's senior officers, Generals Andrew McNaughton and Harry Crerar.

In a few hours, 10 separate units would force landings on eight different assault points. But if any one of them failed, he reflected, the entire operation was in jeopardy.

First there were the four surprise attacks planned at "nautical twilight," just before dawn. Two commando units were assigned to take out the heavy six-gun batteries on Dieppe's extreme flanks: No. 3 Commando's objective, the battery codenamed Goebbels, was at Bernaval, eight miles east of the port. No. 4 Commando's objective was the "Hess Battery" — the second of the enemy's heavy six-gun coastal batteries — on the heights overlooking the chic seaside resort of Varengeville, six miles to the west. Like Goebbels, it had the potential to drive off or destroy the British flotilla escorting the Dieppe raiders. Each of the gun positions was held by a force of more than 100 Germans.

The hope was that this pair of commando hit-and-run pincer attacks would catch them by surprise.

While the Allied force steamed to the attack, the two officers and 130 men who manned Naval Artillery Battery No. 813 in Varengeville, which the British had codenamed Hess, slept peacefully. Their commander had ordered them out on manoeuvres all day on August 18, and the men had tumbled into their beds, exhausted, when they finally returned to base late in the evening. The last thing on the minds of the German battery troops was any fear of an attack. Each of the six guns was set in concrete in entrenched gun pits some 25 feet in diameter, connected by communication trenches. They were protected from attack by a ring of machine gun posts and by the dual-purpose flak guns mounted in a high tower.[3]

It wasn't so much the batteries that were worrying him, General Roberts was thinking. The British commandos were confident and experienced men. While those guns were a threat to the flotilla, an even bigger threat to the assaulting troops was the enemy guns on the headlands overlooking the harbour and the main beach of Dieppe.

To silence these, Robert had also ordered two additional flank forces to land half an hour prior to the main attack, still in pre-dawn darkness, and to launch surprise attacks on two villages just outside of Dieppe. The Royal Regiment of Canada — with a company of about 100 men from the Canadian Black Watch under command — would land at the village of Puys in the east; and the South Saskatchewan

Regiment would attack Pourville to the west of the port. After over-running the beach defences each battalion would climb the heights and attack those worrisome enemy installations on the east and west headlands that harboured the deadly guns.

The Royals had the key task; the guns that were their main objective commanded all movement on the main beach. It all depended on surprise. If they could get ashore in darkness, before the Germans became aware of the attack, they should have a reasonable chance of succeeding in their vital mission.

———————

At 0230 hours, the enemy that Roberts hoped to catch napping was very much awake. Hauptmann (Captain) Richard Schnösenberg had just returned to his billet in Puys and was relaxing in a hot shower, looking forward to a few belated hours' sleep. It had been a long night for the commanding officer of the 3rd battalion, 571st Infantry Regiment. Ever since the commander of 302 Division, Major General Conrad Haase, had posted his army commander's Order of the Day the week before, all battalions and their artillery and naval units had been on the alert.

> The ANGLO-AMERICANS will SOON be forced to TAKE SOME KIND OF ACTION IN THE WEST. I have REPEAT-EDLY given the troops this news, and request you to REPEAT my orders AGAIN AND AGAIN in order to ensure that these thoughts BECOME AN OBSESSION. HE OR WE! That's the slogan for all! You WILL WILLINGLY AND BRAVELY do your duty!
>
> Long live our PEOPLE, our COUNTRY, OUR FUHRER, ADOLF HITLER![4]

General Haase knew what he was doing, Schnösenberg thought approvingly. The 302 Infantry Division had been responsible for the defences of the Dieppe sector since April 1941. Two years' construction, using concrete fortifications, land mines, machine gun posts concealed in caves in the cliffs overlooking the beaches, triple coils of barbed wire, flak-gun emplacements, and with full knowledge of the ground, had made them impregnable. Haase had divided the sector into three strongpoints (*stutzpunkt*): Dieppe East, the Puys area which was the responsibility of Schnösenberg's battalion, Dieppe South —

the town and its port — and Dieppe West, extending to the heights above the village of Pourville.

With satisfaction, Schnösenberg reviewed the practice alert he had held that night for his infantry battalion. "The navy has given us times which are favourable for a landing," he had warned his men at the drill. "One of these includes tomorrow, the 19th of August, when dawn combines with high tide. You must keep an increased level of vigilance."

Schnösenberg's sector included a considerable section of the interior plus two miles of coastline. It began at the eastern jetty of Dieppe's harbour and the headlands overlooking the port, and extended two miles along the bluffs to the village of Puys.

It had once been an artist's dream, Puys. The narrow beach, ringed by sheer chalk cliffs some 200 feet high, had inspired painters, musicians and writers for centuries. Debussy had enjoyed its pleasant summers; Alexandre Dumas had often visited his son there and had died in his large white house on the Puys headland.

War had driven away the artists. There would be no more strangers coming to Puys, not if Richard Schnösenberg had anything to say about it. Puys had now become a defender's dream instead. A 12-foot concrete seawall densely covered with coils of heavy barbed wire extended across the entire beach, blocking its only exits: two flights of concrete steps leading to a footpath and a country lane.

Under command, Schnösenberg also had several companies of naval and air force personnel to man defensive weapons. Machine gun positions on the bluffs controlled the beach. The villas along the heights benignly overlooked the tiny cove, giving no hint of their deadly function. Schnösenberg was especially pleased with the fortification of the white house on the cliff — Dumas' house, many decades ago, so they said. Its windows concealed concreted slits, through which automatic weapons controlled every inch of the beach as well as its sea approaches. His camouflage people had cleverly disguised the concrete pillbox in front of it as a pretty little summer house.

From Puys, it was a short stroll along the bluffs to the headlands overlooking the port of Dieppe. On this four-kilometre perimetre, Schnösenberg had strategically positioned two heavy machine gun detachments to augment the artillery batteries in discouraging any landing attempt by the enemy. On the east headland overlooking the harbour entrance and the main Dieppe beach and promenade, his 12th

Field Company had 12 heavy machine guns sited carefully to rain crossfire over the entire area. Firing at the amazing rate of 1,200 rounds per minute — ten times the speed of any British automatic weapon — they could hold back the whole English army, he figured.

Schnösenberg was vigorously towelling off when his adjutant came in:

"Captain! Outside, it seems to be a little different than usual — more noise."

Schnösenberg rang the naval station 50 metres from his command post: "What's up out there?"

"*Ach*," was the reply, "don't get yourself worked up; it means nothing at all. At 0500 hours a German convoy should arrive in Dieppe harbour and probably they're banging around out there with the enemy speedboats."

Reassured, Schnösenberg was again preparing for bed when his adjutant once more burst in. There had been a renewed warning of the disturbance at sea. "So," Schnösenberg said gruffly, "if you won't let me sleep, then we'll throw the whole battalion out of its beds and call a morning alarm exercise."[5]

For Lieutenant Walter Höpener, the duty officer at Schnösenberg's 12th Field Company command post, the night had passed peacefully. His men standing watch at each machine gun (MG) post had reported nothing strange, despite the warnings of the danger of an enemy attack. They grumbled about being ordered out of their beds for the long alert. "Apparently, sleeping is over for the night," Höpener observed sourly.[6]

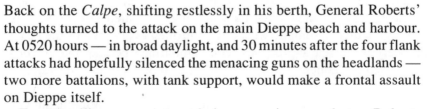

Back on the *Calpe*, shifting restlessly in his berth, General Roberts' thoughts turned to the attack on the main Dieppe beach and harbour. At 0520 hours — in broad daylight, and 30 minutes after the four flank attacks had hopefully silenced the menacing guns on the headlands — two more battalions, with tank support, would make a frontal assault on Dieppe itself.

From intelligence reports and air reconnaissance photos, Roberts could conjure a mental picture of a picturesque port tucked into the valley of the River d'Arques. Tourist hotels and restaurants lined the long esplanade. As the village had expanded inland, shops, houses, municipal buildings and one or two fine old churches had been built along the steep cobbled roads that led away from the sea towards the high ground behind the little town. The hotels overlooked the wide promenade and beach — much like Brighton or Hastings, he thought. With its casino and pitching greens and the cinder paths where families could stroll and dogs could run, this playground had made Dieppe popular as a seaside resort for centuries.

Within minutes of the attack, he thought grimly, it would become a deadly killing ground.

The battle plan divided the beach into two sectors: the Royal Hamilton Light Infantry (RHLI) would go in on the right and attack the western half near the casino, under the shadow of the castle. This was codenamed "White Beach." The Essex Scottish Regiment would land at "Red Beach," on the eastern end abutting the harbour jetty.

It was a daring plan, this frontal attack, Roberts mused. He remembered how rival factions from the navy and army had hotly debated the concept of an assault across an open, defended beach. The navy — specifically, Combined Operations chief Lord Louis Mountbatten and Captain Hughes-Hallett — had argued that they stick to flank attacks where they would have a better chance of surprising the enemy. But the army — principally Lieutenant General Montgomery — had insisted on a plan that combined flank and frontal. The tanks, Monty contended, *had* to go in frontally. They would have too far to go, and over several troublesome streams, if they landed on the flanks.

Better, he had argued, to send them in on the main beach, in daylight, half an hour after the flank assaults had knocked out the guns, and then count on an extra umbrella of support from naval guns and RAF fighter-bombers. Monty had won the argument; the Canadians under Roberts' command had inherited this predetermined plan — this gamble. But could they pull it off? he wondered.

Roberts remembered being struck with dismay when he was first presented with the plan. "It won't work," he thought grimly. "Not at any price could we put our tanks in on those beaches." But what other alternative was there? If tanks were to be used at all, they had to be used frontally.[7]

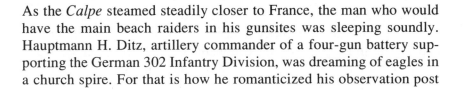

As the *Calpe* steamed steadily closer to France, the man who would have the main beach raiders in his gunsites was sleeping soundly. Hauptmann H. Ditz, artillery commander of a four-gun battery supporting the German 302 Infantry Division, was dreaming of eagles in a church spire. For that is how he romanticized his observation post overlooking the main Dieppe beach. "I found it right by the Gulf Hotel on a rock pushed out on the bluff like a shoulder!" he had enthused to the Luftwaffe officer whose billet he shared. "It fell straight into the sea [from] about 85 metres high. It was the most beautiful [observation] post which I had ever had as a soldier at the front. We settled there and the whole world lay deep under our feet."

From his "eagle's nest," Ditz had a panoramic view of the area he was defending: "In front of us lay the sea. To the right, however, we looked directly onto the crescent-shaped beach of Dieppe which stretched to the breakwater of the harbour entrance. It was a stone beach about 100 metres wide which was closed off from the town by a concrete wall of about two metres high. On the wall were hefty barbed-wire obstacles. Between this and the facades of the houses in the town was an esplanade of about 200 to 300 metres of green lawn. Close to the edge of the town was a ditch which had been dug out for the beach [infantry] company."

Just a few days earlier, Ditz had been ordered to set up a close-combat gun position as added defence against a beach assault. He found the perfect site: a smugglers' cave "blackened with smoke" that overlooked the beach on the west side. His gun crew were "delighted," he noted.

"If only they had suspected what was in store for them, they would certainly have been less enthusiastic."

Ditz had gone to bed that night rather complacently. It had been a pleasant day, sunny and warm with a calm sea. His infantry battalion commander, Captain Ullrich, had even suggested that the men clamber down to the beach for a swim. One of the local Dieppoise matrons, sympathetic with the homesick troops and grateful for their help with the harvest, had brought over a cake for tea. Ullrich had courteously invited the civilians to enjoy a swim too.

It would be the last swim permitted to civilians until the end of the war.

Dieppe was a good posting; infinitely better, Ditz mused, than the Russian front. Even after the Luftwaffe air reconnaissance had warned his intelligence section in early August of "suspicious clusters" of what might be landing craft in the rivers of south England, it had not been so bad. Since then, an "alarm level No. 2" had been ordered.

Ditz felt he had been lucky to secure such an excellent billet. He had a room in Dieppe's once-fashionable Gulf Hotel up on the headlands, which had been built, he was told, for the "sports-loving English." The Luftwaffe officers who shared the billet had mysterious assignments in a nearby structure. Even Ditz had no idea that it was one of the top-secret German radar installations.

"At midnight, I was awakened by a 1st Lieutenant of the Air Force Communications company. He told me that his people thought they had noticed movements of ships. They were, however, still so far away and still so unclear, they could be banks of fog. Since they lay out of reach of my guns anyway, I lay down to sleep."

Ditz slumbered on, undisturbed by any notions of an aggressor getting very far on *his* beach. The British may come soon, he had repeated to himself in nightly litany, but they won't survive *my* guns.[8]

——■■■——

General Roberts knew there was no thought that his two frontal battalions could surprise the enemy. His ace-in-the-hole was his tanks. In the history of amphibious assaults, no one had ever before tried to land armour. It had been stressed to him by General Montgomery that getting the tanks into the town was the key factor to the attack. Wasn't that why he, Roberts, had been persuaded to cancel the bombing attack? It had been pointed out that bombs make rubble — and rubble stops tanks.

Roberts had seen to it that his infantry would have armoured support from the moment they set foot on the beaches. He had 58 brand-new Churchill tanks at his disposal. The first 9, along with nearly 100 engineers charged with detonating the beach obstacles that might block armour and infantry, would land with the first wave. The remainder were scheduled to land in successive waves at short intervals afterwards.

The infantry had orders to penetrate the defensive crust of the beach defences as quickly as possible and get into town. The tanks would help get them there, and support them until he gave the "Vanquish" signal to all his forces to withdraw.

——■■■——

Major General Conrad Haase, commander of 302 Division, had also been concerned about the possible use of armour in an invasion by the British. From his headquarters in Evermeu, a village a few kilometres inland from Dieppe, Haase had ordered some months ago that tests be conducted using their own German tanks on the Dieppe beach. The results had been encouraging. The tank treads had either sunk into the shingle, or they had become clogged. Haase reported to his corps commander that he had in Dieppe a natural antitank obstacle: the sharp stones that formed its beach.

Although it was concluded that tanks would never land at Dieppe, Haase made doubly sure. Hefty concrete antitank barricades still guarded the entrance to every street into town. He ordered that an antitank ditch be freshly dug across the beach.[9]

Roberts' main concern focussed on two potential problems. The first was the danger that the inexperienced naval crews would be as inaccurate in landing the troops in battle as they had been in the rehearsals. He had voiced this fear in the wardroom to Lieutenant Dan Doheny, Second Canadian Division liaison officer: "We'll be all right if only the navy puts the troops ashore at the right places and at the right times." Doheny thought to himself, prophetically, as it turned out, "The general is stressing the point once too often. I'm starting to get worried about it myself, now."[10]

Roberts' second concern was whether there was a sufficient weight of fire support for the troops. He had been assured of support for the attack by the naval and air force commanders — Captain Hughes-Hallett and Air Vice Marshal Sir Trafford Leigh-Mallory. But was it enough? he worried. The Royal Navy's eight Hunt-class destroyers would escort the infantry force and its 237 vessels across the Channel. But he'd heard some of the seamen scoff at the destroyers, calling them "ersatz" because they were smaller than normal. And while eight sounded impressive, only half, each with just four 4-inch guns, were available for direct fire support of the two battalions attacking the main beach frontally.

He recalled with some bitterness the flat refusals the force commanders had received from Combined Operations planners when they had asked for more guns, or more powerful battleships, to cover the men. Don't make waves, they had been told. This raid has been ordered from the "highest quarters" — Churchill himself, it had been implied.[11]

It had been the same with the air force. Originally, sorties by 150 heavy bombers had been planned. These could have flattened the town the night before the attack. But Roberts had been persuaded by the air force to cancel them. They argued that their chances of finding their targets and smashing the gun batteries at night were virtually nil. Even if they did hit the town, there was the problem of the rubble. Besides, Bomber Command had been reluctant to commit its aircraft to support infantry.[12]

Leigh-Mallory's Fighter Command had committed a force of 800 aircraft including more than 600 Spitfires, 24 Hurricane fighter-bombers, 24 medium bombers (Blenheims and Bostons), 48 Army Cooperation Mustangs for reconnaissance and 36 Blenheims to lay smoke. But the task of the majority of the aircraft was to fight an attrition battle with the Luftwaffe and to protect the flotilla. Only a few would support the infantry, and only briefly.

Would all this supply that "extra umbrella of support" to get the infantry across the beaches past the enemy defences?

———————

The "fortress" (as it would come to be described) that awaited the attackers bore little resemblance to the idyllic resort of General Roberts' imagination. Hitler had recently appointed his brilliant minister of war productions, Professor Albert Speer, to strengthen coastal defences. The results were already evident: an elaborately reinforced "Iron Coast" would present formidable obstacles to any invader.

At Dieppe, the hotels and buildings facing the beach and the casino were now fortified, and had sniper posts on the roofs. Sandbagged pillboxes had been established to cover all approaches to the main beach with enfilade fire. An immobilized French tank with a 75-mm gun was embedded in concrete at the eastern end of the beach, and would provide fire across the esplanade. Anti-aircraft guns had been sited on the casino roof and on the cliffs behind. Two more 75-mm guns were mounted in a concrete embrasure in front of the castle. Also on the west headland, mortars had been sited to inflict devastating fire on the seafront. Speer had specified that the caves that perforated the face of the cliff be carefully transformed into gun positions; the artillery could be hauled out on tracks when required. The work, begun in May, had been pretty well completed by July, except for finishing the demolition of the casino when they had run out of explosives.

Behind the beach, in the twin headlands, more gun positions had been established. The artillery batteries had been programmed to bring immediate defensive shell fire concentrations on all areas of the beach and esplanade.

If any enemy set foot on the beach, he would be cut down by lethal crossfire: from the caves in the cliffs overlooking the beach, from the buildings in the town, from the headlands towering over him on each side and the pillboxes on the beach — and even from the jetty behind the attacker.

Thick coils of barbed wire some six or seven feet deep and the concrete seawall blocked the beach exits. On the east side, five rows of dragons'-teeth closed an 80-metre gap between the cliff and the seawall.[13]

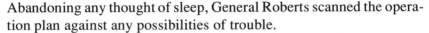

Abandoning any thought of sleep, General Roberts scanned the operation plan against any possibilities of trouble.

Pourville, a sleepy little village just west of Dieppe, was the designated landing place of the South Saskatchewan Regiment — the SSR. The battalion was allotted 30 minutes to establish a bridgehead, which would include seizing the town, its headlands and Quatre Vents Farm. The Queen's Own Cameron Highlanders would then advance through them and link up with tanks from the Calgary Tank Regiment in an attack on the airfield several miles inland behind the town.

When Roberts' two battalions on the frontal attack had broken through the beach defences and captured Dieppe, their objectives were to consolidate with the flank battalions to complete the mopping up. The RHLI would attack west across the headlands, destroying enemy positions on the cliffs, and then join forces with the SSR. The Essex, meanwhile, would capture the harbour and then loop eastward along the headlands to hook up with the Royal Regiment. When the harbour was secure, the Royal Marines, acting as "cutting out" party, could remove the invaluable German invasion barges from the harbour.

The village of Pourville may have been sleepy, but its defenders were not. The town — really just a collection of houses, a church, one touristique inn and a small cafe or two — lay in a valley at the mouth of the Scie River just four kilometres west of Dieppe. It hadn't been necessary to fortify Pourville. While it was outside the *stutzpunkt* sector of defended Dieppe, the headland that towered over the eastern edge of the town was an extension of the fortified Dieppe bluffs. The artillery and MG posts such as the battery of which Captain Ditz was so proud would produce withering fire on any aggressor attempting to capture that headland.

At Quatre Vents Farm there was also an engineer unit of 571st Regiment. Demolitions of possible targets in case of an invasion, like the factory smoke stacks and the casino, had been their particular responsibility. These were nearing completion. An officer of the regiment, Lieutenant Siegfried Butzert, remembered one of the first alerts of pending invasion that his unit had been given, back in June, when assault ships had been sighted by the Luftwaffe near Portsmouth and Southampton. There had been practice alarms at least once a week ever since.

On the night of August 18, a state of increased alarm was again ordered. The sappers, forming part of the infantry defences, had dug and fortified slit trenches, ready to intercept any attackers. An immediate reinforcement unit, positioned deeper in the Scie Valley, was Sergeant Mosel's well-equipped bicycle platoon.[14]

General Roberts had one reserve battalion — Les Fusiliers Mont-Royal (FMR) — to be called into the battle wherever he thought it could reinforce success. Later — six hours later, by the plan — it would take up defensive positions and hold off any enemy counter-attacks while the assault force withdrew through them.

Intelligence reports had been reassuring. The region was lightly held by one infantry battalion of the 110 Infantry Division, supported by some 500 divisional artillery. There were no infantry troops on either side of the town and only a total of 1,400 poor quality German troops in the area. The beaches in the vicinity were "suitable for landing Infantry and Armoured Fighting Vehicles."[15]

Against one battalion of Germans, Roberts was pitting his assault force of six battalions of infantry, plus the commandos and the tank regiment. The entire operation was to be of "one-tide" duration with reembarkation at 1100 hours. They only had to hang on for five to six hours — surely possible against the weak enemy force he had been assured was holding Dieppe. Overall, Roberts thought with growing confidence, the odds of pulling off a successful raid were in his favour.

The intelligence on which General Roberts was depending had badly misinformed him. The defending enemy force was not one *battalion* of the 110th, with headquarters in Arques-la-Bataille. The 110th, in fact, had been at the Russian front throughout the war. In actuality, the defending force was one *regiment*, or three battalions, of the 302nd Division, headquartered not at Arques but at Envermeu.

Nor was it the weak force that he had been led to believe. As well as bringing 302nd up to strength that month with an additional 2,500 men, its commander, General Haase, had ensured that there were ample reinforcements just a few hours' distant. He had the corps and army reserve battalions to call on. As well, one of the Wehrmacht's most powerful tank formations, 10 Panzer Division — a first-class fighting formation and up to strength in men and equipment — was in Amiens, fewer than 40 miles from Dieppe. It could be moved up in four hours. There were three other divisions that Hitler had recently moved from Russia to Northern France to bolster their reinforcements in case of a prolonged British attack: Leibstandarte S.S. Adolf Hitler, and S.S. Division Das Reich, as well as one parachute division.

"It is important to have as many mobile reserves as possible in order to be able to support strongpoints and initiate immediate counter-attacks against enemy troops that may have landed in between these strongpoints," Haase had stressed.[16]

———————

0300 hours: The point of no return.

As Roberts watched, hundreds of small LCAs crammed with kitted-up infantrymen were lowered silently into the water from the mother ships. This was the moment of commitment. Now he could not call off the attack.

One of the 13 sub-groups of the flotilla had made an uncomfortable crossing in 32 unarmed plywood R boats: each craft crammed with 20 tense, black-faced men. In the lead gunboat, Lieutenant Colonel John Durnford-Slater, No. 3 Commando leader, and Captain Roy Murray, the U.S. Ranger commander, had set the pace for their force of 460 men. Herding the vulnerable craft ahead were an armed motor launch and a flak landing ship. But the two destroyers they believed were their escorts were still six miles away, having been given no such instructions to form close detail support.[17]

Four landing craft had already turned back with engine trouble. The remainder swept onwards, oblivious to the fact that their group was in the exact path of the enemy convoy.

On the *Calpe*, Roberts silently thanked his stars that the flotilla had navigated the long-dreaded minefields so effortlessly. The navy had been magnificent. So far, the 70-mile crossing had been uneventful; the enemy suspected nothing. The surprise element that was so vital to the assault seemed intact. Roberts had no inkling of brewing disaster.

General Roberts was not aware of it, but he was being cosseted from any hint of trouble. Hughes-Hallett had not passed on the warnings from Portsmouth to him, although the two men had been together aboard the *Calpe* for much of the night.

———————

The German Port Commandant of Dieppe didn't like the look of the weather report. High tide 0403 hours; low tide 1056 hours; wind velocity 2 SSE; visibility 700 metres. It spelled danger to him — the conditions were ideal for an attack by sea. He wasted no time in issuing a "threat of danger" alert.

At the port entrance, Harbour Protection had its boats standing off port on routine patrol. They had been signalled to expect one of their convoys that had sailed from Boulogne at 2000 hours, and was due to arrive at Dieppe at approximately 0330 to 0400 hours. There would be five motor vessels escorted by a mine-sweeper and two submarine-chasers. Tugboat 32, with navy pilot Hederich and tug commander Sonderfuehrer (Boatswain) Achtermann aboard, was ordered to escort the convoy into the harbour.

At 0350 hours, the signal station reported to the Port Commandant that a naval engagement was in progress about four nautical miles from port. It was assumed that a small fight had erupted between the German convoy and British naval forces. A routine matter, they thought. Further observation was ordered.[18]

———————

0347 hours: Roberts peered anxiously into the darkness from *Calpe*'s bridge. A brilliant flare suddenly sliced through the black night and arced across the skies some miles to the east. It was a warning from one of their destroyers that something was going wrong. Then he heard sharp gun fire. "For God's sake, what is going on out there?" he demanded.

Major General Roberts would wait hours and even weeks before receiving an answer to his question, and a host of other questions that erupted as the whole terrible day unleashed its awful consequences on this man who stood — and remained — in the dark on HMS *Calpe* off the coast of France.

———

On 20 August 1942 — the day after the Dieppe raid — Captain Hughes-Hallett admitted that "a report had been received from the Admiralty of two [German] vessels on passage to Dieppe.... It was learned subsequently that they had entered Dieppe at about 0330."[19]

This has not proven to be truthful. At 0400 hours the tug commander (Sonderfuehrer) was still standing off port waiting for the convoy, as he had been ordered by the German port commander. No convoy had arrived before this time, or even arrived afterwards, as evidenced by the port commander's subsequent statement concerning ships in port during the Dieppe battle: "No seagoing formations were present in the port."[20]

In a written post-Dieppe report several weeks later, Hughes-Hallett changed his story. He denied receiving any of the warnings. He claimed that running into the convoy was just a "chance encounter," and a "thousand to one" occurrence of which he had no knowledge and which therefore he could not have prevented.[21]

He said he was convinced that the subsequent battle with the trawlers "had not prejudiced tactical surprise."[22] The German 81st Corps' report disagreed. "The entire coast defence system was alerted," it stated. At Puys, and at Dieppe, the guns were waiting.[23]

In trying to cover up, Hughes-Hallett was evidently not aware that General Crerar, meanwhile, had demanded an inquiry to explain the navy's lack of response to the alleged signals. Crerar asked the Chief of Combined Operations, Lord Louis Mountbatten, to investigate the matter.

Mountbatten formally acknowledged in writing that signals *had* been received by Hughes-Hallett — at about the same times, and with the same warnings of the imminent presence of a German convoy. But, the CCO said lamely, *that* convoy was a *different* convoy and "had nothing to do with the German vessels met at 0350 hours."[24]

Following Mountbatten's admission and Hallett's conflicting account, a cloak of silence and denial has fallen forever on the subject.

———

The battle for Dieppe began on August 19, 1942. But it had its *real* beginnings back in April in mass rallies from Trafalgar Square in

London to Madison Square Garden in New York. There, tens of thousands of war-beleaguered citizens from two continents demanded a second front.

PART

2

APRIL 1942

CHAPTER

2

SECOND FRONT NOW!

The "invasion season" in England officially opened in the middle of April. Britons, tensed against the expected German invasion since the fall of France in 1940, knew that from spring until fall, weather conditions would be ideal for a full-fledged enemy assault on their shores.

In the first two-and-a-half years of the war, civilians plodding by foot to work, or caught in interminable queues, turned anxious glances south towards the Channel horizon, as if behind every cumulus cloud and murky wave there lurked a German invader.

The south-east coastal resorts, just a few hours' distant from German-occupied France, were under special surveillance. Travellers there required a special police permit; there were few takers. The prospect of beaches full of barbed wire and mines, and hotels full of khaki was disheartening. The joys of a day at the seaside had lost their appeal. The British were too busy fighting for their lives.

The nation geared up for the expected enemy assault.

In one of his first speeches after taking office, on June 17, 1940, Prime Minister Winston Churchill had promised, "We shall defend our island home" — and a million men and women had quickly responded.[1] The Home Guard, some of them men in their 80s, or 15-year-old schoolgirls, stood defiantly on hilltops, pitchforks at the ready to repel the "Nazi hordes."

But the volunteer Home Guard wasn't going to be enough to save Britain. On September 11, 1941, the government declared that everyone between the ages of 18 and 41, male or female, was conscripted into some form of national service. (Strangely, government legislation singled out young chorus girls as being essential to defence — creating some awkward gaps in the chorus lines of dance hall stages!)

A government-published pamphlet, *If the Invader Comes*, exhorted people to "hide your food and your bicycles. Hide your maps. See that the enemy gets no petrol."[2] Roadblocks were erected, some as crude as broken-down vehicles or cement posts positioned at key intersections. Signposts were ripped out and place names on shops, buildings and war memorials were painted over or defaced. The rhododendrons — for which England was justifiably famed — now lay squashed behind concrete pillboxes housing machine guns and antitank weapons. A total blackout was enforced. Civilians as well as military were under orders to carry gas masks at all times. Even the ringing of church bells was forbidden — except on special occasions to celebrate victories such as El Alamein. For five years they would become a warning of invasion instead of a call to worship.

Hitler, however, reversed his strategy. Instead of tanks and infantry he sent his Luftwaffe to England. The RAF had fought off the daylight raids and won the Battle of Britain in the summer of '40. But now in the fall and winter Hitler sent over his night bombers. The wail of air-raid sirens became a nightly occurrence over the cities and towns of Great Britain; 43,000 civilians were killed in these attacks.

The Blitz spared no place and no person. Buckingham Palace was bombed on three occasions. London took the brunt, enduring 76 consecutive nights of intensive bombing. The East End was virtually flattened. St. Paul's Cathedral stood as its seventeenth-century architect, Christopher Wren, had originally dreamed, a splendid monument that was the focal point of the City of London: he could not have envisioned that it would be thousands of tons of explosives, causing a wasteland of rubble, that would create this isolated splendour.

Although St. Paul's survived intact, one-and-a-half million private homes in London alone were destroyed or damaged. Whole blocks of magnificent old buildings in London's historic squares were pounded into rubble. Others were grim hulks, windows boarded up, ornamental brass railings long since scrapped for salvage. Uncounted other homes had survived the bombs only to succumb to the bitter cold of two winters; evacuated owners returned to find their homes ruined by burst pipes.

Later, the Luftwaffe bombers came back for the morale-smashing "Baedeker Raids," so called because pages from these famous travel guides were supposedly taped to their bombsights. This deliberate and spiteful destruction of historic monuments in defenseless towns and villages was topped off by German fighter bombers attacking helpless civilians all across Southern England in "tip and run" raids.

The winter of 1942 seemed to unload every possible hardship, every conceivable military disaster on the struggling Britons. Just as they pulled themselves up from one knockout blow, another loomed ahead.

The Russians were fighting for their lives in Eastern Europe. The Germans were defeating British troops in North Africa. In the Battle of the Atlantic, Allied merchant navies had suffered the loss of hundreds of thousands of tons of supplies and more than 100 ships.

In another theatre of war, a new enemy threatened: the Japanese. Launching their offensive at Pearl Harbor in December 1941, they quickly gained total control of the Pacific in both sea and air. The Americans and British were pushed back from the Philippines, the Dutch East Indies, the Solomons, Burma and New Guinea. The fall of Singapore on February 15th, with the humiliating surrender of 60,000 ill-organized British troops to just 5,000 Japanese, is still considered the most devastating military loss in the history of Great Britain. Morale plunged even further when the Japanese sank the British capital ships *Repulse* and *Prince of Wales*. These disasters brought home to the people the realization that Allied military and naval superiority had been swept away.

Perhaps the most damaging blow to morale had been the infamous "Channel dash" — the impudent escape from Brest to Kiel on February 12th of two large German battleships, *Scharnhorst* and *Gneisenau*, through the Straits of Dover. The galling fact that they had "strolled right past Britain's front yard in broad daylight" — straight through the English Channel, without interference by the RAF! — was described in *New Yorker* as a "moral knockout."[3]

The Russian ambassador to Britain, Ivan Maisky, gloated publicly about the "astounding impotence of [the British] defences, which had shouted so loudly about special vigilance along the southern shores of the country."[4]

Back home, the blitz — terrifying and demoralizing as it had been — had given way to a new impact of war: the helpless feeling of inaction.

After Dunkirk, Churchill had rallied the British. His passionate "blood, toil, tears and sweat" oratory had brought out the tough courage of the people. Even at the worst of it, there had been a sense of being able to do something: dig out rubble from a bombed house, mount a rooftop vigil, pile sandbags around buildings. The Brits loved a fight; they were never more buoyed up and resolute.

But now they faced a new reality. In this most desperate of winters, in the midst of this most desperate of wars, the bad news amassed by military disasters was only eclipsed by a grim domestic scene. Hardships and shortages, and the ever-growing casualty lists published in the daily newspapers, created a new feeling of helplessness. An unprecedented cold spell with below-zero temperatures had been devastating. Families huddled beside a single flicker of warmth from kitchen cook stoves. Coal was rationed and in such short supply that coal dust and even cinder paths were sieved for precious granules. People learned to make their own fuel out of coal dust mixed with cement and water. A visitor would bring a lump or two of coal as his contribution to the evening.

The Ministry of Fuel produced a veritable barrage of warnings and advice against wastage of coal or gas. Central heating was forbidden in offices, hotels and flats. Private householders had to be content with heating just one room, perhaps rotating so that friends and neighbours shared a single fireside. "Serve raw or unheated food," they were advised. "Burn low wattage bulbs. Paint a solid black line five inches from the bottom of the tub to limit your hot water."

When Eleanor Roosevelt visited Buckingham Palace in 1942, she, too, had to wriggle to the bottom of the tub to get sudsed up. "There was a plainly marked black line in my bathtub above which I was not supposed to run water," she wrote. "The restrictions on heat and water and food were observed as carefully in the royal household as in any other home in England."[5]

The disastrous losses of merchant ships in 1941 escalated in 1942 by over a million tons when the German U-boats gained control of the western Atlantic. Petrol for automobiles became nonexistent for pleasure driving. Even the essential use of automobiles was strictly supervised; a deviation by a mile or two was subject to prosecution.

Civilian travel by any means was frowned upon. By the spring of 1942, even the traditional Easter exodus of holiday-makers had settled into a bizarre reversal worthy of a headline in a London newspaper.

On Tuesday, April 7th, the *Express* trumpeted: "London was Holiday Resort Number One: The All-day Queue. Londoners found a new Number One holiday resort yesterday for the 'official day off' — London. The government had asked them not to go away, and they did not go away. They Eastered in town — by the hundred thousands. Railway stations, which in pre-war Easters were stiff with perspiring holiday-makers and their baggage, were almost deserted."[6]

There were critical shortages in nearly every day-to-day item; a rationing scheme was finally imposed on food, clothing and fuel. The 66-coupon basic ration would provide an occasional necessity but no luxuries for family dinners or wardrobes for the foreseeable future. A man on basic clothing ration could buy one pair of socks every four months and a sweater every five years. Newspaper columns were full of tips about transforming the ubiquitous spud into a gourmet dish, or remaking a tired and threadbare frock — or curtain — into a smart new outfit. Cosmetics and toilet articles were vanishing.

Women were getting frumpy, and they knew it. Even A.P. Herbert was compelled to observe in *Punch*:

> I see a day, before we win this war,
> When razors — and cosmetics — are no more;
> When whiskered bishops will unite in joy
> The paintless maiden with the bearded boy.[7]

Other shortages appeared. After the fall of Malaysia, rubber was in short supply; pharmacies hung signs saying "No more hot water bottles." Without petrol, people couldn't drive to work. Walking wasn't much better: they couldn't get rubber for their shoes. They couldn't drown their sorrows: beer was plentiful for the troops but getting more and more scarce for civilians. What was available was grossly watered down. Hard liquor could be found only in bars. Cigarettes became a coveted item. And to cap it all, they often couldn't even read about how wretched they were; newsprint was in short supply too. For their one penny, the English received all of the world and national news compacted into a flimsy four-page daily paper.

Milk, eggs, meat and tinned foods were rationed; luxury imported foodstuffs such as chocolate, condensed milk, tinned salmon and olive oil were disappearing from the shelves. A home-cooked meal was produced only after endless queues at the shops — so time-consuming that factories started letting women out for an hour in mid-morning to get to the top of the queues.

Substitutes abounded, usually with dismal results. Britons weren't starving, but as they tucked into a bilious piece of grey-coloured "National" bread or some evil-smelling morsel of unspeakable fish, they couldn't resist the occasional wistful thought of the traditional steaming Sunday prime rib, or even a homely platter of eggs and bacon. These traditions would have to wait until peacetime.

People were discouraged from frivolous dining out by the imposition of a five-shilling maximum on restaurant charges. There were only certain days when meat, fish and poultry were offered. Restaurants, forced to abide by an 11 p.m. curfew, went into a tailspin and flooded the Ministry of Food with confused queries. Railway snack bars wondered if the late traveller must starve. The newspapers had a field day: "Austerity Goes on the Menu: But Eleven PM Curfew Puzzles Hotels."[8]

New expressions crept into the British vocabulary — and stayed there: "You've had it," meaning you've used up your ration coupons; "browned off" — the colour referring to army khaki and the meaning reflecting the soldier's general disgruntlement; and "bull," a universal reaction to pompous officialdom.

Yet none of these intrusions or deprivations was seriously resented by the people. They viewed rationing as the fair way to share out what little they had left, and made the best of it with traditional gutsy British humour.

A large tin of Spam, costing a month's coupon ration and considered a great delicacy, would make canapés for a splendid wedding reception. A child's birthday cake could be concocted from a mixture of flour, dried eggs and custard powder. Decorations were scarce, but drops of ordinary candle wax were dyed and worked into decorative shapes. "My, oh my," the inventive mother would glow, "never was such excitement seen as at the cake properly decorated. The tots were not as jubilant as the adults: we had given Adolf an extra cock in the snoot as our little ones were not missing a thing on their birthdays."[9]

It was precisely that "extra cock in the snoot for ol' 'Itler" for which the British yearned. Clearly, Mr. Churchill wasn't levelling with them. And what was most baffling was why he wasn't *doing* something, lashing out, using the increasing air superiority that Britain's factories had managed to achieve, to get back at Adolf. Hope — the hope Churchill had instilled in the early war years through his courage, leadership and inspired oratory — was vanishing. The people viewed each fresh disaster as a promise broken. Singapore will hold, Churchill had assured them; Rommel will be booted out of the Western Desert; our troops will never be thrust from Malaysia — all ended as empty prophecies.

A Gallup Poll indicated that half of the British people were dissatisfied with the government's conduct of the war. Members of the Cabinet were echoing the public's cries for action.[10] They were all sick and tired of being on the defensive.

"It appears that the British people can't or won't recognize the existence of any substitute for a genuine, slap-up opening of a land offensive on the Continent," journalist Mollie Panther-Downes reported from London in her weekly *New Yorker* column.[11]

The people's growing sense of frustration at the inactivity — and above all, the monotony of the war — was seized upon by Stalin as a heaven-sent opportunity to launch an intensive public relations campaign that would compel his western allies to launch a second front in 1942.

Just prior to the outbreak of war, the infamous Molotov-Ribbentrop non-aggression pact had allied Russia on the side of the Germans, allowing Hitler freedom to attack Poland and giving Russia carte blanche to seize the Baltic states. Soviet Foreign Minister Vyacheslav Molotov — who was to play a key role in Stalin's relationships with Churchill and Roosevelt in 1942 — was the pact's architect in 1939.

The alliance collapsed when Hitler unleashed his sudden invasion of Russia (Operation Barbarossa) in June of 1941. The Germans forecast a Soviet defeat within 8 to 10 weeks. Hitler had reason to be optimistic; at the beginning of the campaign he had 205 divisions, of which 145 were available for the Russian front.

Initially, the Wehrmacht attack devastated the Russians. German panzer divisions penetrated deep into Soviet territory and by November were closing in on Moscow.

But when 30-below-zero Fahrenheit temperatures heralded the onset of the bitter Russian winter, the advance faltered on Moscow's outskirts. Even the oil in the tanks froze. Expecting a swift victory, the Germans had stockpiled winter clothing for only 20 percent of the force. Of their three-and-a-half million fighting force, 743,000 had become casualties by December.

As winter progressed, the Russians rallied courageously, forcing the Germans back at many points. By spring, both sides were reeling. Millions of soldiers and civilians died of wounds, or of cold and starvation during the harsh winter. Recently released Russian army casualty figures reveal that three million troops were killed in the first six months of the war. Yet the conflict was still unresolved; Hitler prepared for a new spring offensive.

Desperate, Stalin turned to the west for help. He demanded "the earliest possible opening of a second front in Northern France, for the purpose of diverting at least 40 German divisions from the Eastern front."[12]

In the Allied nations, a groundswell of emotion grew in response to Stalin's appeal. Second-front mania swept Britain. From Speakers' Corner in Hyde Park to Sauchiehall Street in Glasgow, outraged citizens protested that Russia was doing all the work and taking all the punishment, while the British were doing nothing. At Trafalgar Square tens of thousands of frustrated Britons demonstrated in mass rallies demanding a cross-Channel attack against the Germans: "Let's have action, not just words!" they clamoured — "a second front to smash that bastard Hitler."

The Russian dictator had powerful backing for his campaign. "There was a widespread, if ill-informed, agitation, fostered by persons whose political opinions lay far to the left," British historian, Stephen Roskill, contended.[13] But the pro-Russian enthusiasm went far beyond that. Almost overnight, people who had traditionally regarded Russia with suspicion and hostility now viewed her sympathetically as an ally.

The Communist party in Britain launched a membership drive and surprised itself by almost doubling its objective. Ambassador Maisky, receiving an unprecedented one hundred social and diplomatic invitations in a single month, noted that the British seemed to have more admiration for Russian military commanders than for their own. "The prestige of the Red Army has grown to a colossal extent," he said. "All speak of it with delight. Half-jokingly, half-seriously, some of my acquaintances here are asking, 'Couldn't we get a couple of your generals on loan?' "[14]

Media and pub-level criticisms spilled over into the House of Commons. Bill O'Connor, the popular "Cassandra" whose column in the tabloid *Daily Mirror* delighted millions, found the issue tailor-made for his favourite target: the government. It was a splendid excuse for many factions to campaign against the Conservative prime minister.

In February the "Battle of Winston Churchill" gripped the floor.

Churchill demanded, and got, a vote of confidence from the house. But criticisms still abounded about the government's reluctance to go on the offensive.

The Chief of the Imperial General Staff (CIGS), General Sir Alan Brooke, singled out Lord Beaverbrook and his sensational newspaper, the *Daily Express*, to note impatiently in his diary,

The Beaverbrook press [is] influencing public outlook in the direction of a Western Front. Albert Hall meetings, Trafalgar Square meetings, vast crowds shouting for immediate help for the Russians.

Many seem to imagine that Russia had only come into the war for our benefit! Certainly very few of them realize that a premature Western Front could only result in the most appalling shambles which must inevitably reduce the chances of ultimate victory to a minimum. What can we do with some ten divisions against the German masses? Unfortunately, the country fails to realize the situation we are in.[15]

Churchill backed him up, protesting that Britain had neither the manpower nor the logistical strength to make a cross-Channel assault. He was "not prepared to give way to popular clamour for a second front in 1942 in view of the strong military arguments against such an operation."[16]

But Ambassador Maisky countered this with a lecture on good housekeeping. Russia's allies had plenty of "troops, tanks, planes and arms" to launch a second front in 1942, he argued. They were just being overly cautious. "One cannot wait until the last button has been sewn on the tunic of the last soldier," he mocked.[17]

Churchill and Brooke might have withstood this enormous lobby from their British and Soviet critics. But when Stalin's second-front agitation moved westward to the United States, their stance became more precarious. Where they could dismiss their own pressure groups, they could not afford to disregard the influence that the American voting public had on its leaders — political and military — or the spillover effects of this influence on their British allies.

The prime arsonist in fanning second-front fervour in America was Max Aitken, a tough little scrapper from a small town in Canada. As a young man, Aitken had parlayed a series of financial deals (some, according to his biographer, of "borderline" integrity) into a modest fortune in Canada.[18]

In 1910 he moved to Britain and became involved in the two consuming passions of his life: politics and money. His slogan was "work without stopping"; by World War Two the credo had gained him proprietorship of a number of businesses, including the derelict *Daily Express*, which he propelled into a powerful publication. King George V appointed him to a peerage, and the homely, brash young man with the rasping Canadian accent, not yet 40 years of age, took the name of a New Brunswick fishing stream and became Lord Beaverbrook.

In the first two years of the war his efforts as Minister of Aircraft Production contributed a lot towards saving his adopted country from annihilation. Beaverbrook dramatically bolstered the production of fighter planes, enabling the RAF to repel the Luftwaffe. He became a hero of the Battle of Britain.

His methods were sometimes more flamboyant than effective. His "pots to planes" campaign inspired millions of Britons to offer up everything from kitchenware to golf clubs and even their precious ornaments to be melted down for the cause. Unfortunately, "the Beaver" hadn't determined before the fact that the minuscule amount of high-grade aluminium to be found in this sort of scrapage made the sacrifices unnecessary.

In a more successful crusade, he induced individuals to contribute to the "Spitfire Fund." A school boy with his precious sixpence could buy a rivet; a rugger group could send in 20 guineas and own part of a bomb; a small town — after strenuous fund-raising — might have its name on a Spitfire plane.[19]

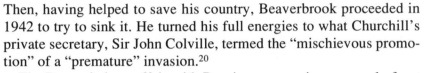

Then, having helped to save his country, Beaverbrook proceeded in 1942 to try to sink it. He turned his full energies to what Churchill's private secretary, Sir John Colville, termed the "mischievous promotion" of a "premature" invasion.[20]

The Beaver's love affair with Russia was a curious anomaly for a man who published a conservative newspaper and counted Winston Churchill as his oldest and closest friend. It began with a trip to Moscow in September 1941, where he was captivated by Stalin's persuasive call for a second front.

Soon afterwards, he kicked off this new campaign with a memo to Churchill parroting Stalin's urgings for an attack on France. "Plans should be made forthwith for a raid of a major nature on one of the ports of northern France," he urged his boss.[21] The words would haunt him for the rest of his life; they planted the first seeds of an idea that would take the lives of many of his beloved countrymen.

Recapturing his Battle of Britain charisma, the Beaver again became something of a folk hero to a restless nation. He used the editorial pages of his *Daily Express* to encourage mass meetings across Great Britain. He hosted large dinners, using the gentler persuasions of champagne and *pâté de foie gras* to spread the second-front propaganda to highly placed personages who were influential with Churchill and his ministers.

"If ever there was a one track mind it is Max's," sighed one of his colleagues resignedly.[22] But Ivan Maisky, a frequent dinner guest, was delighted to have the pro-Russian Canadian on side in such a powerful way.

In February 1942, Beaverbrook resigned from Cabinet, giving as an excuse his recurring asthma. In Brooke's opinion, "the greatest blessing of all was to be rid of Beaverbrook."[23]

Had he but known the trouble that was brewing in the very near future by unleashing the Beaver, he might have wished him back.

The next month, Beaverbrook went to America as Churchill's semi-official representative for war production — an endorsement that would backfire uncomfortably on the prime minister. The Canadian found that Stalin had completed his ground work here as well. Like Maisky, the Russian ambassador to the United States, Maxim Litvinoff, was publicly demanding a second front in France.

Beaverbrook was gratified to learn that President Roosevelt, the American military and the civilian populace were already enthusiastic for a second front. "The President has come to the conclusion that an Anglo-American invasion of Western Europe should become the strategy of 1942," he reported happily.

On April 23rd, Beaverbrook — Britain's most powerful media person and publisher — addressed America's most powerful media group, the Bureau of Advertising of the American Newspaper Publishers' Association. He reckoned his message would have international exposure — and explosion. Preparing the speech in Miami, he turned to his secretary, "[Churchill] won't like it, will he?" he ventured. And then, like a naughty schoolboy, he grinned, "The President will like it, though."[24]

Churchill indeed would not have appreciated his old friend's devious efforts to commit Britain to a definite second-front commitment. The Beaver's talk would later be described as "the most enthusiastically pro-Soviet speech ever delivered in the United States"[25]: "Communism under Stalin has produced the most valiant fighting army in Europe . . . the best generals in this war," the stocky Canadian told the Americans. "Strike out to help Russia! Strike out violently — strike even recklessly!" he exhorted dramatically.

Then this mischievous — some even said dangerous — little man carried Stalin's seeds of dissension one step further. Claiming to be an authority because of his former position as Britain's war production head, Beaverbrook glibly fibbed, "How admirably Britain is now equipped in weapons of war for directing such an attack upon Germany, I well know."

"A second front in western Europe would provide an opportunity to bring the war to an end here and now," he concluded.[26]

In the resulting media furor, the second front became a by-word for peace. "Anxious millions forthwith believed what they wanted to be told," reported *Time* magazine. "The Beaver's call sweeps America," gloated the *Express*. "There is mounting eagerness both in this country and in the U.S. to pass from defence to offense," echoed the London *Times*.[27]

Rallies in Madison Square Garden and in Washington erupted in Beaverbrook's feverish wake. Captain Harry Butcher, Eisenhower's naval aide, read no less than three editorials from American newspapers in a single day, all urging a second front: "I believe the editorial writers . . . little know what a cost, probably what a futile cost, is involved in a second front now."[28]

The battle cry was picked up by other leftist organizations around the world. In Canada, huge crowds rallied in hockey arenas like Maple Leaf Gardens and the Montreal Forum. A publication of dubious origin went so far as to call second-front opponents "sinister fifth columnists" who "formed a powerful opposition to the offensive strategy."[29]

Stalin's public relations campaign had succeeded beyond his wildest dreams. The fires originally lit under the frustrated Britons had not swayed the prime minister and his Cabinet. They had steadfastly refused to be pressured by public opinion into premature action. That hardly mattered to the crafty Soviet. He was convinced that the second-front concept would ricochet across the Atlantic and that Roosevelt, with an eye to a looming election, would have to respond to popular demand. A top-secret document on the Russian front, prepared by the deputy director of Air Intelligence, concluded that "the Allies have promised to relieve German pressure by opening a new theatre of war this year which will divert considerable German forces from the Eastern Front."[30]

Americans wanted action. As Stalin had foreseen, their elected leaders seized upon the second-front crusade. Adapting it to their particular needs, they threw it back at Churchill. And while the prime minister might have shrugged off his own people, he could not afford to ignore the demands of his American allies. The outcome of the war, and even the peace to follow, depended on the coalition remaining intact.

Second-front fever thus rebounded from America back to Britain to become the bugbear that dominated Anglo-American decision-making for the coming months. In May an estimated 60,000 attended a demonstration in Trafalgar Square. "Jerry's going to get it now!" they cried.

The second-front obsession of a wily Canadian with the name of a fishing stream had become blown up and distorted, even to a point that the Allied strategic philosophies were affected. What many Britons viewed as Beaverbrook's "unholy alliance" with left-wing politicians would have a huge influence in determining the course of the war.[31]

CHAPTER

3

CHURCHILL AND THE CHIEFS

Beaverbrook, Maisky and their left-wing supporters would have been encouraged to know that the second front they had been demanding had become the focus of a constant stream of meetings in the murky subterranean cabinet war rooms of the British Chiefs of Staff.

The Chiefs — the most highly ranked staff officers from each of the three military services — were the most powerful military group in Great Britain. But in these dark hours of 1942, they were stymied. They feared they were on the brink of losing the war and their American and Russian allies were pressuring them into a suicidal strategy — an assault on France — that could be the culminating blow in this year of "hideous calamity."

This triumvirate had enormous seniority and experience. Their decisions determined Britain's actions throughout the war. The Chiefs were empowered to appoint and give directions to commanders-in-chief in all the war theatres, and to advise the Cabinet on strategy. More importantly, they bridged the gap between political and military decision-making — what Lieutenant General Sir Hastings Ismay facetiously termed the "frocks" and "brasshats."[1]

The Chiefs of Staff (COS) committee had been in existence since 1923, so when war broke out the system needed only to be cranked up to high gear to become a smooth-running machine for the higher direction of war. The engine was finely tuned, but it still depended on a skilled driver: Winston Churchill. As military assistant secretary to the War Cabinet throughout the war, Lieutenant General Sir Ian Jacob saw Churchill on an almost daily basis and accompanied him to major strategy conferences such as the one at Moscow in August 1942 that would play such a vital part in the mounting of the Dieppe assault. Jacob considered Churchill the indispensable head of state. "At various times, people thought the war not well conducted, but this was

37

based on ignorance as to how a country operates in wartime," he commented to the authors. "Anyone as close as I was realized what a disaster it would have been if Winston were pushed out. He was the only man who had the courage, the guts, the determination and the knowledge to carry through the war."[2]

The Chiefs have been described as a "band of brothers" and although the personnel sometimes changed, the spirit of their fraternity never did. There were only two ways to resolve a major personality conflict with the prime minister: a chief could be fired or he could resign. Usually they found less dramatic safety valves with which to cope with the clashes that were inevitable among strong-willed men: the Chiefs went fishing. Without Churchill.

The essential arbitrator and soother of ruffled personalities for this group was Lord Ismay, military secretary to the War Cabinet and Churchill's representative on the Chiefs of Staff.

The tall and broad-shouldered Ismay dominated any gathering with his calm but forceful manner and gracious wit. He had a rounded head and large brilliant eyes that had earned him the nickname of Pug for, as Churchill's secretary John Colville explained, "he looked like one and when he was pleased one could almost imagine he was wagging his tail."[3] Ismay attended every COS meeting, and if he was not always wagging his tail he was at least content that, in this committee of elitists, with a huge potential for dissension from within and resentment from without, such calamity was averted by his efforts. Joan Astley, who ran the War Cabinet's Secret Information Centre under Ismay's direction, remembered him as "a marvellous oilcan-smoother."

"He held the balance between the prime minister and the service chiefs, presenting the views of each to the other with clear-headed verity and simplification of divergencies."[4]

The Chiefs met every morning at 10:30 and often in the evenings as well. Although not a member of the COS, in his dual capacity as prime minister and self-appointed minister of defence, Churchill often presided over these meetings, sitting on a large wooden chair, his corpulence fittingly framed by a huge map of the world that took up most of the wall behind him.

Across the baize-covered table, a dashing figure in the light blue uniform and rank badges of a Marshal of the Royal Air Force, Sir Charles Portal would run a hand absently through wisps of brown hair and, as usual, reserve his comments. Churchill considered Air Marshal Portal the ablest of his three Chiefs.

A First World War ace of considerable audacity, Portal never lost his pilot's abilities of shrewd judgement and great daring. Now 48, the Air Chief was 10 years younger than the committee chairman, General Sir Alan Brooke, and nearly 20 years junior to Churchill and Admiral Pound. Tall and lean, he had an aquiline face and shrewd eyes.

Portal was more absorbed in machines than in men. He had none of the loquacious wit of Churchill and Brooke and was the committee's most taciturn member: "The principal exception to Churchill's inability to work with the reticent," as Colville put it. Joan Astley recalls that it was his cool detachment, even in the face of criticism, that made him the most easily understood of the Chiefs by his American counterparts.

Portal was not in the least interested in the frivolous or unimportant, and cared nothing for material comfort. Mrs. Astley remembered that he "preferred a bench to a feather bed, a hunk of cheese to a soufflé." Each midday, he would alight from his Rolls-Royce at the Traveller's Club on Pall Mall, eat his inevitable solitary luncheon with total indifference to his food or surroundings, and leave without having exchanged a word with anyone. But while he said little, he carried huge responsibility which he bore with great determination and courage.[5]

In the darker blue of the Navy sat the Admiral of the Fleet, the ailing Sir Dudley Pound (who would succumb to a brain tumour in 1943). He may have seemed ponderous and somnolent; but his deep-set observant eyes missed nothing. Churchill had great ties of loyalty to "the old admiral," who had served under him in the Admiralty.

Immaculately turned out in khaki uniform, with the dark good looks of his Irish forefathers, was the third member of the committee: its chairman, General Sir Alan Brooke, Chief of the Imperial General Staff. The CIGS, as he was commonly known, would sit back listening, spectacles eased off, weary eyes half-closed, as if he were "viewing in his mind the whole picture."[6]

General Sir David Fraser wrote in his definitive biography *Alanbrooke*: "To be chief advisor to a genius demands a certain genius of its own sort, and Alanbrooke possessed it."[7]

Brooke was renowned as a military strategist. A gunner who served in the field in the First World War, he established himself as an authority in artillery doctrine and went on to become, in General Fraser's words, "the outstanding soldier of his generation." He was capable of quick assessment and incisive decision-making.

But Brooke was the victim of his Celtic origins and Gallic upbringing: he was impatient, peppery, quick tempered, frank to the point of brutality, intolerant of stupidity, and uncompromising when his beliefs were challenged. It was in his relations with the American Chiefs of Staff whom he met at about that time that Brooke was at his most abrasive. They were in awe of his international reputation of icy self-control. His abrupt manner and tactlessness "jarred" them. They did not understand his "machine gun" way of speaking and they disliked his aloof demeanour.[8]

Yet he was capable of profound emotions. "He was a great man and a whole man," Fraser considered. "He could love and be moved, as well as fight and decide. He had passion and compassion as well as strength and will."[9] Wedded to war, he limited himself to a visit each Sunday with his beloved wife and their two young children. His safety valve, besides his fishing rod, was the nightly letter and diary he wrote for her. In a quiet hour before retiring, he unleashed into his diary all the suppressed frustrations and anguish from a war that he hated and feared they were losing, and his profound weariness from the effort to save it.

On March 31 he confided his sense of despair to his diary: "During the last fortnight I have had for the first time since the war started a growing conviction that we are going to lose the war. . . . It is all desperately depressing."[10]

At times, Brooke despaired at Churchill's impatience and refusal to acknowledge the immense amount of detail, logistical and operational, that had to be sorted out when the practicality of one of his ideas was being examined by the Chiefs. Churchill at the same time could become wildly frustrated by Brooke's lack of "imaginative leaps of reasoning." Ismay cited an instance when Brooke had been insufferably rude and unyielding as a result of Churchill's mercurial behaviour.

"The Prime Minister says he can't work with you and that you hate him," Ismay reported to the CIGS. "Hate him?" said Brooke. "I don't hate him. I *love* him. But the first time I tell him I agree with him when I don't will be the time to get rid of me, for then I will be no more use to him."[11]

"I know of no major matter in which Mr. Churchill decided to take a line which was opposed to Brooke's advice," Lord Ismay stressed. In every case of dissension, they "argued themselves into agreement."[12]

But it was an exhausting ordeal for a man who was under extraordinary pressure and "viciously overworked." By the beginning of March 1942, Brooke seemed to General Kennedy, his director of military operations, to be "wilting a little . . . showing signs of wear and tear."[13]

Churchill, as minister of defence, often met the Chiefs of Staff with no one else present. In that role, he was responsible for the entire military side of the war: strategy, operations and resources. They found him a mass of contradictions; at once exasperating and endearing. General Jacob stressed that although Churchill was not above using his persuasive skills to try to get his way, he never actually prevailed over the Chiefs' military judgement. "He had some very long arguments with them — usually on strategic matters; but in the end he would not overrule them. Ever!"[14]

Historian A.J.P. Taylor confirmed that "those who stood up to him — for example Brooke — were able to resist his urgings."[15] If he gave the Chiefs a direct order *of which they approved*, they would carry it out. In other circumstances, they became skilled at manoeuvring around it, sometimes quietly countermanding an order, other times steering the prime minister towards more acceptable alternatives. Churchill's obsession with a raid on Norway was case in point: when he instructed Andrew McNaughton to proceed with an outline plan for it, Brooke gently took the Canadian aside and put a subtle damper on it. General McNaughton cooperated in the charade. He wired Mackenzie King not to allow Canadian troops to serve in Norway, should Churchill request it.[16]

Ever the orator, one of Churchill's most powerful tools of persuasion was the word "pray," which he used, historian Basil Liddell Hart recalled, "like a jockey showing the whip to a laggard racehorse."

For all his dignity, Churchill's mannerisms were bizarre. His signature dress of the one-piece coverall-like siren suit gave him the appearance of a rather fat child in play clothes. His energy was notorious — but he made no effort to synchronize his work schedule with that of his associates.

Late into the night, while they yearned for sleep, he would hold compulsory court. Mornings would find his colleagues at their desks early while Churchill was served breakfast in bed by his valet, Inches: orange juice from a tin (he abhorred it freshly squeezed); then a cooked English breakfast followed by a "weak" (three-ounce) scotch and soda, always Johnny Walker Red, which he sipped over the next four hours, nude and still under the covers, as he conducted the affairs of state. "His minutes streamed out daily in all directions," Liddell Hart wrote, "urging that obstacles be overcome, that red tape should be cut, that excuses should not be accepted."[17]

His official biographer, Martin Gilbert, noted that "if the news was good he bounced up and down like a small boy with joy — if the news was bad he would slowly slide down pulling up the sheet till his face was hardly visible, as though to keep out the bad news."[18]

The remarkable strength of his captainship over a tottering empire has never been in serious dispute. "No Englishman who lived through 1940 can regard him dispassionately," Taylor observed. "A long catalogue of impatient blunders can be drawn against him. But the fact remains that he won the Second World War."[19]

Churchill had a profound faith in democracy. He had won the Battle of Britain by harnessing British courage and determination into a national defiance of Hitler. But he did not consider himself obliged to pander to the whims of the populace. They were amateurs in this business and must trust him to do whatever was expedient in *his* judgement to win the war.

In the spring of 1942, this was demonstrated by his stubborn refusal "to give way to popular clamour for the opening of a second front in Europe."[20]

Churchill's bravery was monumental. He thrived on physical danger and loved adventure; war itself was an adventure — a drama. With the fascinated historian's eye, he loved to watch it unfold as on a Shakespearean stage. He could not resist confronting its physical perils; his preferred vantage point for an air raid was an exposed upper-storey balcony.

To the despair of his director of military operations, General John Kennedy, "he was inclined to be a great gambler in his strategic notions, while I was not."[21]

At a time when there was a very real possibility that Britain might not survive, Winston never panicked or lost faith. And he had the inner courage that enabled him to overcome periods of profound depression: the "Black Dog," he would call these.

Yet he couldn't face criticism; he hated making mistakes and shrank from blame. Taylor described the occasion when Churchill shrugged off strenuous advice (by the then CIGS, General Sir John Dill, and others) to bolster the defences of Singapore. He then tried very hard to cast the responsibility elsewhere when it was captured. "My advisors ought to have told me," he said in lame excuse. "Well, I am sorry to say that the records show his advisors told him, and Churchill pushed their warnings aside," Taylor wrote in rebuttal.[22]

For all his personal courage, Churchill dreaded a replay of his First World War nightmare: a bloody war of attrition in the trenches. Yet his position on casualties never wavered over two world wars: he was prepared to accept them if by doing so a greater number would be spared.

"Importance of results would justify severe loss," he had cabled his naval commander at Gallipoli.[23] "A military attack is not ruled out simply because a fifth of the soldiers may be shot on the way," Churchill informed Ismay 27 years later.[24]

In the spring of 1942, Churchill created a fourth permanent seat in the Chiefs of Staff committee and appointed Lord Louis Mountbatten, Chief of Combined Operations, to fill it.

Combined assault melded the skills of all three services (Navy, Army and Air-Force) into an integrated force of all arms in amphibious operations. It had come a long way in the decades since the concept of amphibious assault was first put to modern use by Britain in World War One — then with the simplistic objective of combining the efforts of the navy and the army to put a soldier ashore on alien land.

Neither Britain nor the United States had attempted an opposed amphibious landing for many decades: the British at Gallipoli and the Americans in the Civil War. The disaster at Gallipoli, in 1915, with its 252,000 casualties, was one of its first tests. Winston Churchill, as First Lord of the Admiralty, was the architect behind the Dardanelles strategy. Although he was badly let down by his military and naval commanders, he considered the operation "a legitimate war gamble," and for the rest of his life his fascination with the strategy of amphibious assault never wavered.[25]

In World War Two, Churchill seized upon the raiding concept following the Dunkirk evacuation in 1940. He saw it as one way the British could take early offensive action against Germany. The first commando raid — a defiant swoop on the French coast in June of 1940 — was staged the day after Hitler had signed an armistice with France, gloating that Britain had been driven forever from the continent of Europe.

That June raid was marked by amateurism and poor results. The 120 commandos landed briefly but were unable to take any prisoners. When they returned to Britain, they ran into a suspicious coastal guard who thought they were deserters. While this was being sorted out, their boat was refused entry into the harbour and they became violently ill, first from the high seas and then from the rum they had swigged to alleviate seasickness. The dispirited and disreputable-looking commandos were finally arrested as deserters and spent the night in jail.

After that wretched beginning, the skill of the raiders improved and British raiding capability expanded. Commando headquarters grew proportionately, but not fast enough or imaginatively enough to suit the impetuous prime minister. That is why in 1941 Churchill appointed Mountbatten to replace the aging and arch-conservative Sir Roger Keyes as "technical advisor." A few months later, Mountbatten was named chief of Combined Operations.

Mountbatten's first task as Combined Ops' chief was to plan a series of raids on the European coast — an essential prerequisite to the second front for which their allies were clamouring. Sir John Peck, Churchill's private secretary of the time, recently outlined the objectives of the raids to the authors:

> (a) intelligence getting; (b) specific targets e.g. St. Nazaire; (c) training in all aspects of combined operations in preparation for the main invasion of Europe; (d) sustaining morale in Occupied Europe (e) tying up German forces which could otherwise be transferred to the S.E. Europe–Mediterranean–Middle East–Africa theatres. Their ultimate objective was the planning of a full-scale invasion of Europe.[26]

This was a challenging promotion for the confident, polished 41-year-old cousin of the king. His career was spiralling. In less than three years he had risen from captain (of a destroyer that was sunk from under him — it was the third such occasion), to commodore and advisor to Combined Operations, to acting vice admiral and overall commander of Combined Ops.

The other Chiefs had been puzzled when Churchill created an unprecedented fourth place on their COS committee. Why, they wondered, was it necessary to make him a full-time member when he had been contributing to it satisfactorily enough as a frequent consultant for some months? As Philip Ziegler, Mountbatten's biographer noted, "[Brooke] felt that Mountbatten was doing a good job at Combined Operations and had no particular objection to the titles with which he was to be adorned, but it seemed to him that his membership of the Chiefs of Staff Committee was a waste of time."[27]

An additional time-waster, when he took his seat with the group, was what General Jacob remembered as his "most maddening habit of chasing every hare." Jacob himself had been on the receiving end of this penchant of Mountbatten's, and he remembered the Chiefs being infuriated by it.

"Brooke was one of those people who liked to finish up the business and get going. But just as he'd be folding up his papers with a 'Right, then, we're off,' up would pipe Mountbatten: 'Excuse me, sir, but there is one point I want to raise.' This would be about half a dozen marines or something. You could see Brooke scowling away, getting very angry. But Mountbatten didn't seem to realize when and how to deal with these things. He could not avoid mixing up the trivial with the important. That was one reason he didn't always get on very well with the Chiefs of Staff."[28]

Brooke himself noted that "Mountbatten considered that he was there to express his views on all subjects, most of which he knew nothing about." The CIGS admitted that in keeping the young admiral on track he was consequently "ruder than I cared to be as Chairman."[29]

In Mountbatten's favour was his youth. He was replacing a 70-year-old of First World War vintage. General Jacob recalled how encouraging it was to see the prime minister appoint a young and vigorous man to the important job of organizing combined assaults. Raids could be an important element to the British comeback.

"Originally, when he took office, Winston appointed men to key positions whom he had known in the first war," Jacob noted. "It was a mistake. So when he chose Mountbatten everyone thought it was a good move. He appealed very much to Winston because he was brave, courageous, put off by nothing.[30]

From the beginning, Mountbatten's style and verve attracted him to the prime minister. The maverick in them both sparked a bond between the 67-year-old prime minister and his young protégé: a love of drama, a flair for the audacious, a gift of charm and persuasiveness. They shared a careless courage that had seen Mountbatten haul survivors out of oil-slicked Mediterranean waters and into his rubber dinghy while being strafed by enemy aircraft, and then lead a chorus of "Roll Out the Barrel" as they watched their ship go down.

The same disregard for personal safety made Churchill by far the most daring of the three Allied heads of state during those early war years as he blithely traversed hostile seas and skies — the latter a perilous venture even in peacetime — on his several trips to America,

Canada, North Africa and Russia. He was the first British prime minister and the only head of state ever to cross the Atlantic to America in wartime.[31]

Mountbatten's imagination, like Churchill's, leaned towards bizarre contrivances. He often found an eager accomplice in the prime minister. "The more outrageous the methods used, the more he [Mountbatten] relished them," Ziegler noted.[32]

On one occasion, Mountbatten became fascinated with the idea of making a type of craft out of shatterproof ice. To prove his point, he turned up at a Chiefs of Staff meeting with two lumps: one of ice and the other of pykecrete. Carefully depositing his load on the boardroom table, he startled the sedate committee by pulling out his revolver and firing three shots at each object. Bullets ricocheted wildly around the room; one even nicked the leg of the U.S. Chief of Naval Operations, Admiral King. A terrified orderly, who had heard rumours of Anglo-American dissention, raised the alarm, "Quickly, come quickly, the Chiefs of Staff are firing at each other!"[33]

Churchill was considered equally mad for his equally eccentric inventions. His love of gadgetry declared itself even in World War One when he persuaded the Cabinet to endorse his latest brainchild: "White Rabbit Number 6." This was to be a monstrous 80-foot-long earth-eating tank, capable of cutting a six-foot-deep trench at the rate of one mile per hour. It was presented as an ingenious means of penetrating enemy lines and taking him by surprise. Churchill never did explain how a 130-ton beast thrashing about cross-country could achieve surprise.

At worst, these inventions created a harmless outlet for Churchill's "demonic energy and extraordinary imagination." At best, they generated several valuable innovations.[34]

As far back as 1917 he had become intrigued with the concept of creating an artificial harbour that would allow assaulting ocean craft to land troops and supplies on enemy shores. Even then, Churchill obviously realized the perils of attacking a defended port. In May of 1942, still pursuing the idea, he cautioned Mountbatten that "the piers *must* float up and down on the tide. . . . Let me have the solution worked out. Don't argue the matter." The final product, *Mulberry*, became an essential element in the success of D-Day in 1944.[35]

Mountbatten wasted no time in tackling his new challenge, which was to execute raids on German-held territory and prepare for the ultimate invasion. Under his prolific authorship, a veritable laundry-list of proposed raids were offered for the Chiefs' endorsement. Ten were carried out; many more were cancelled, sometimes by weather but often because the Chiefs did not rate the rewards as being worth the risks.

The Chiefs' difficulty with Mountbatten's proposed operations was to sort out the practical from the impractical. Here the bonding between the prime minister and his protégé became a little more worrisome.

Whenever Mountbatten disappeared in the direction of Chequers for a weekend with Churchill, or to the Savoy or the Other Club to share a leisurely dinner, there was a collective holding of breath by the Chiefs and their principal advisors.

"Dickie's visits [to Chequers] were always dangerous moments and there was no knowing what discussions he might be led into or what he might let us in for," Brooke wrote, underlining the frustrations that inspired the Chiefs' frequent need to escape to the fishing streams.[36]

"Winston wanted action everywhere at all times," General Jacob recalled. "He felt the right thing to do was to take a thousand — or ten thousand — men, make an awful mess and come away. As if it were easy. But it wasn't easy.

"I don't think there was any objection to the policy of raids — whether to do any raiding at all. I'm quite sure that everybody felt we must get more experience; we had to do everything possible to improve our technique in these matters.

"The disagreement would be whether any particular operation was worth doing."[37]

Many of the raids that were concocted in the first half of 1942 by Mountbatten and his staff — very likely with some enthusiastic coaching from his mentor — were not considered practical or workable by the Chiefs. Their skill and vigilance in examining the proposals averted many potential disasters. Mountbatten found their caution exceedingly frustrating. He complained vehemently to an associate at the "incredible mass of obstruction which he [had] to overcome for every one of his projects."[38]

These raids were all small in concept but of great importance to British morale. They were directed at such targets as the temporary disruption of enemy shipping at Vaagso in Norway and at the capture of a German radar installation at Bruneval on the Normandy coast by a force of paratroops and navy. Tabled for future consideration were commando assaults on targets such as Bayonne, Alderney, Paris, Cherbourg and northern Norway.

The raid on St. Nazaire was acclaimed their most notable success. In March 1942, an assault force blew up a German dry-docks in France — a potential docking or repair basin for the battleship *Tirpitz*.

The cost was terrible: 79 percent of the commandos and 52 percent of the naval force was killed or captured. Yet so starved were the British for a success of any sort that although almost two-thirds of the force was lost, public morale soared.

Responding to second-front pressures, the Chiefs of Staff authorized in April a policy of raids "to be undertaken in the summer of 1942 on the largest scale that the available equipment will permit."[39]

It was also hoped that besides harassing German ground forces, raids could be "bait to bring on air battles" with the Luftwaffe. The fisherman instinct in them would appreciate that. Air Marshal Portal's major problem had been the inability of the RAF to entice the Luftwaffe into an attrition battle on British terms.

The German Focke-Wulf 190s, superior to the Spitfires, had refused to fight unless they had a tactical advantage. They continued to frustrate Fighter Command's daylight offensive over Europe by inflicting heavy damage when they had the advantage and by ducking out when they didn't.[40]

The Chiefs speculated that sea raids and an air offensive would force the enemy to shift more of his focus from Russia to France. The raids, Brooke said, were "part of our 'Second Front' campaign."[41]

There is little to suggest — except in token references like this — that any other elements of this so-called Second-Front "campaign" by the Chiefs of Staff existed. Perhaps even then Brooke viewed raids as a substitute second-best to hush up the second-fronters — a sop to his insistent allies.

CHAPTER

4

A MODICUM OF DUPLICITY

The distance between Trafalgar Square and the House of Parliament is barely a half-mile. At one end, Nelson's Column looms 185 feet into the historic London skyline, dominating the square. Four huge lions guard the column's base. Twin fountains flank it.

For hundreds of years, Trafalgar Square has been the traditional gathering place for fiery political rallies, the sounding box for disgruntled Britons. The slightest ground wave emanating from Trafalgar vibrates the half-mile down the length of Whitehall to erupt at Parliament Square. In Britain at least, public opinion does not have far to travel to make an empire tremble.

Sandwiched between these two squares like so many seismographs are the offices of state, among them the Ministry of Defence, the Cabinet Office and the official residence of the prime minister, 10 Downing Street. By 1942 this hub of all wartime decision-making had yielded to the pounding of Hitler's air raids and gone underground to protect the prime minister and his Cabinet and staff. A bombproof concrete slab three feet thick and reinforced with steel separated the men of war from the act of war.

This top-secret headquarters on Great George Street, off Whitehall, consisted of a complex warren of rooms capable of accommodating 2,000 men and women. Working underground like moles, they relied on a primitive wooden weather indicator board to inform them if the weather outside was wet or dry, cold or hot. A sign proclaiming "windy" was posted as a tongue-in-cheek indication that a heavy raid was in progress.

There were board rooms where the prime minister, the Chiefs of Staff, and the War Cabinet Secretariat met; and in the sub-basement, cubicles with camp cots where they could sleep. (Many preferred to brave the raid: the presence of rats, the ever-burning electric lights, and the constant hum of ventilation machinery were not conducive to rest.)[1]

Blue-uniformed Royal Marine guards manned the entrance: a gas-proof steel door opening to a flight of stone steps that led down to the War Cabinet Rooms.

The centre had full communications, including power generators and radio. The Map Room was staffed around the clock by highly qualified retired officers, who were linked to key ministries by colour-coded telephones. Even when bombs crashed around them and anti-aircraft artillery fire chattered incessantly, the night-and-day conduct of war was pursued without pause.

In the Transatlantic Telephone Room — a tiny subterranean cell once used as a broom closet — Churchill could speak privately over scramblers directly to President Roosevelt in the White House. However, it was not as private as either man believed: it is now known that from March 1, 1942, until July 1942, when the British detected it, the Germans had succeeded in unscrambling the radio-telephone link between London and Washington. They were eavesdropping on many of the conversations the two heads of state were holding that spring, including one, on May 5, 1942, which alerted Hitler to the Allied plans for a second front.[2]

On a mild April evening in 1942, two men, both Americans, strolled down Whitehall toward the secret Cabinet rooms. Turning into King Charles Street, they paused to savour a glimpse of green lawns of St. James's Park and the display of fragrant narcissi and daffodils that bordered the walks. Harry Hopkins mused, "It's only when you see that country in spring that you begin to understand why the English have written the best goddam [sic] poetry in the world."[3]

In the distance, from Trafalgar Square, they could hear an excited crowd rallying for a second front. It was an encouraging sound to two Americans who were lobbying hard for exactly that among the strategists in London. Their arrival had been heralded by London's media.

April 9th, Thursday: General Marshall here with Harry Hopkins, declares: 'U.S. Army will expand in Europe.'

General George C. Marshall, Chief of Staff of the United States Army, and Mr. Harry Hopkins, President Roosevelt's principal production advisor, arrived in London yesterday and drove straight to see Mr. Churchill.[4]

Roosevelt had sent Hopkins and Marshall to London on a top-priority mission — to promote "Modicum," the new American proposal to focus Allied strategy on Europe in 1942 and 1943.

It was early days for transatlantic air travel. The Modicum party travelled on a Pan Am Clipper that lost an engine on its first lap to Bermuda. The next lap, to Northern Ireland, took 20 hours. Four days after departing from Baltimore, the frustrated party finally reached London, where they headed straight for Chequers.

Hopkins was emaciated, and so frail that he required frequent blood transfusions, but he still had the mental vitality and quick wit that had won him many friends in the international echelons of political leaders. In appearance he looked like anything but a dignified emissary. General Sir Hastings Ismay would recall that "he was deplorably untidy. His clothes looked as though he was in the habit of sleeping in them, and his hat as though he made a point of sitting on it. But we were soon to learn that in that sickly frame there burned a fire which no flood could quench."[5]

Although he had no official status, Hopkins was probably Roosevelt's closest friend and advisor. When he remarried in 1942, Roosevelt insisted that the newlyweds take up residence in the White House — despite his wife's reservations. Eleanor Roosevelt did not share her husband's enthusiasm for Hopkins, who was the son of a harness-maker and seemed to her to be overimpressed by high-flying "artificial society." She never questioned his loyalty but felt he lacked political prudence and was "not so wise a friend to Franklin."[6]

The president chided her. "I need what Harry has to give and I need him here at the House," he insisted. And although his friend's illness often made him an "unreasonable and irritable" house guest, Hopkins remained a fixture both as Roosevelt's confidant at the White House and as his liaison officer at Allied strategic meetings.

Roosevelt's strong tendency to by-pass the army's professional strategists in favour of amateurs like Hopkins did not endear the president to his regular advisors in military affairs. They were jealous of Hopkins' influence.[7]

Hopkins viewed himself as something of a marriage broker between Roosevelt and Churchill. In that capacity he had become one of the most influential men in the world, as well as one of the most popular and welcome visitors abroad. When Hopkins heard he was returning to London he couldn't resist teasing his old friend Winston about the chilliness of ill-heated British homes, including even the stately

Chequers. On his way to London, he had cabled, "Will be seeing you soon so please start the fire."[8]

But it would be Hopkins who would kindle a fire under his British friends.

Walking briskly beside him, George Marshall loomed tall, robust and every inch a dignified career officer. Roosevelt's Chief of Staff was a Virginian, exhibiting all the graciousness and charm of his heritage. As the author of the Modicum memorandum, he had come to London to sell it to the British.

For some time now, Marshall had been concerned that American resources were being squandered as a result of the urgent demands of its allies for more and more supplies and men. Marshall passionately believed that the United States had to focus relentlessly on a single objective. That objective, he was convinced, had to involve a direct attack against the Germans across the Channel in France. And that attack must take place soon, before Russia was defeated and the Germans were able to turn all their power on the West. Marshall was certain that he could raise a citizen army of one million Americans within a year to launch that assault.

In 1941 he had added a new staff officer to his War Plans Division, a bright young colonel named Dwight Eisenhower, who was eager for action and would soon become an apostle to Marshall's creed. By year's end he would be a general officer and Marshall's Deputy Chief of Staff.

"We've got to go to Europe and fight," Eisenhower noted vehemently in his diary in January 1942. "We've got to begin slugging with air at West Europe, to be followed by a land attack as soon as possible. We've got to quit wasting resources all over the world."[9]

Marshall soon convinced Roosevelt of the wisdom of the proposed new strategy outlined in the Modicum memo. The United States had four main needs and Modicum addressed all of them specifically: the Americans would be able to stop dribbling away their resources. They would mobilize American troops for immediate action against the Germans. This would not only assist the Russians, but perhaps most importantly in this election year, build up American morale.

Covertly, this plan of Marshall's had a fifth, and very strong, point in its favour: it would take the strategic initiative out of Churchill's hands and enable the U.S. to dominate Allied policy-making.[10]

Unhappily, an atmosphere of internal suspicion, jealousy, and political intrigue was permeating the American military headquarters in Washington. The army resented the navy's influence. Both services were afraid of continuing domination by the British — whose strategy, they thought, was too often directed with an eye to preserving the British Empire rather than with winning the war.

Hopkins laid the groundwork in his memo to the president in March: "I doubt if any single thing is as important as getting some sort of a front this summer against Germany." Roosevelt had indicated his tentative agreement with this in an earlier note to Churchill: "I am becoming more and more interested in the establishment of this new front this summer, certainly for air and raids. . . ."[11] Beaverbrook's visit to Washington in April had stoked the fire very effectively.

The American ambassador to London even tipped off the Russians. "I can give you a pleasant piece of news," he murmured to Ivan Maisky, at a reception, drawing the Soviet ambassador into a secluded corner. Roosevelt and Marshall, he told him, were advocating "immediate action" by the United States and Britain for an invasion of northern France, even if "our British friends do not fully agree."[12]

The strategy's code name sounded misleadingly trivial. Both Marshall and Hopkins were keenly aware that their mission to sell Modicum was one of the most important of the war; their objective was to establish once and for all the grand strategy that would defeat Hitler.

Hopkins and Marshall arrived at the secret entrance to the underground war office, where Royal Marines led them down a long passage to a stout door. A guard peered out through a bulletproof slit of glass before letting them enter. Inside, chairs were lined uniformly around long trestle conference tables. This was the Cabinet Room, the largest room in the underground offices and, despite the air conditioning, the dankest. Stale cigar smoke hung like a pall.

General Brooke welcomed the visitors. It was the first meeting of the two Chiefs of Staff. Even a seasoned statesman like Marshall must have had some anticipatory qualms about confronting Brooke, who was already a legend for his brilliant rescue of the British forces in France in June 1940.

Although Brooke and Marshall were unlike in personality, their careers as professional soldiers had run on parallel lines for more than 40 years. Both had fought in France in the First World War, although Marshall had been a staff officer and Brooke a gunner in the field.

Both were career officers who had made solid progress up the difficult, congested between-wars ladder. Each now served as Chief of Staff to a national head of state who obstinately insisted on taking an active part in setting the war's strategy — and neither head of state was always competent regarding military matters. (Roosevelt in particular was totally without military experience.)

It was in philosophy that the pair differed fundamentally. Brooke certainly agreed with his American counterpart that top priority had to be given to attacking Europe and taking the heat off the Russians. But he was too skilled and experienced a military man to forget the heavy odds the Allies would face if they opened a second front too soon; and he well knew how meagre the Allies' resources still were, compared with those of the Germans.

Brooke and the other British Chiefs were absolutely adamant that Nazi-held France must not be attacked until the Germans were considerably weakened and the Allies were strong enough to stay there.

They believed that the only way to defeat Hitler was to encircle him with a ring of bases from which they could attack the Continent. This would gradually weaken and disperse the enemy while giving the Allies time to build up their own strength.

Uncharitably, the Americans mocked this crucial British strategy as "periphery-pecking."[13]

Now the two generals squared off: Marshall, the gracious but determined Virginian, and Brooke, the obstinate Anglo-Irishman. They were undertaking one of the most challenging tasks of their lives: somehow they must find a common solution that would satisfy two nations whose essential interests were miles apart.

On April 9, Marshall confidently presented his strategy. The Americans, he proposed, would begin at once to pour all their resources into the United Kingdom (Operation Bolero) in preparation for a powerful cross-Channel assault in the spring of 1943 (Operation Roundup). In all, 48 divisions would be employed, 18 of them British and 30 American, manned by the million men of Marshall's instant army. The attack, which would be supported by 5,800 combat aircraft, would go in on a six-division front between Le Havre and Boulogne.

To this master plan Marshall attached a rider, which he called Operation Sledgehammer. This would be a more limited cross-Channel emergency operation. Employing just 2 American divisions and 10 British, it would be staged later in 1942 if the Russians were on the verge of defeat or if the Germans showed signs of collapse. In Marshall's view, this would be a sacrifice "in the common good."[14]

Finally, Marshall added, the Americans wanted "repeated commando-type raids all along the coast not only for the purpose of harassing and confusing the enemy but, even more importantly, to give our own troops combat experience. Hopkins interjected that "the American political and military leaders and the people were all agreed on one point: *Our men must fight!*"[15]

The Americans stressed that the British Chiefs of Staff must make an immediate and unqualified decision confirming their acceptance of the plan. Roosevelt was not going to transfer one million American troops to British soil for mere "sightseeing."[16]

On April 12, Churchill cabled Roosevelt, expressing his "entire agreement in principle with all you proposed" in the "masterly document."[17]

In the following days, representatives of the two countries met a number of times to discuss the proposals. The Chiefs expressed some concerns — though no firm objections — to the Sledgehammer proposal. Brooke said that if Britain were forced to launch an assault across the Channel in 1942, it could only be "on a small scale."[18]

Marshall grew frustrated with the inconsistent response and complained to his deputy in Washington that "everybody was agreeing with him 'in principle' but 'held reservations regarding this or that.' "[19]

But he cast aside his doubts when, at 10:30 p.m. on the night of April 14, the Defence Committee met with the American delegates at the Cabinet war rooms. Churchill opened the meeting by saying that the "momentous proposal" brought over by Marshall and Hopkins had now been "fully discussed and examined by the Staffs," and that he had "no hesitation" in cordially accepting the plan. Its conception, he enthused grandly, was in accord with the "classic principles of war — namely, concentration against the main enemy."

Churchill expressed his delight that the Allies would be on the offensive at last, and that the two nations "would march ahead in a noble brotherhood of arms."

He followed up this meeting with an effusive cable to Roosevelt:

Former Naval Person to President Roosevelt. 17 April, 1942: "We whole-heartedly agree with your conception of concentration against the main enemy . . . we cordially accept your plan . . . Broadly speaking, our agreed programme is a crescendo of activity on the Continent, starting with an ever-increasing air offensive . . . and more frequent and large-scale raids, in which United States troops will take part."[20]

The prime minister ended by assuring his American counterpart that complete unanimity existed concerning the Modicum proposals.

The Americans were delighted. "[Now] we won't be just thrashing around in the dark," Eisenhower rejoiced. It was "a real meeting of minds," Hopkins reported jubilantly to his chief.[21]

In truth, it would prove to be not so much a meeting of the minds as a resounding collision between two opposing views. Marshall's proposition had alarmed and stunned the British. Although his plan obviously suited the American strategy of concentration of forces, it clashed in every important way with the British peripheral approach.

The minutes of the meeting contain no record of Brooke raising any British criticism. All along, though, he had privately dismissed the cross-Channel proposals, Sledgehammer and even Roundup, as over-confident pipe dreams: poorly conceived and certain to lead Britain as well as America to disaster. In his view, the American planners had not taken into account the shortage of essential landing craft that would cripple an invasion like Sledgehammer; or the problems of laying on an attack beyond the Allies' range of air cover; or the fact that British military strength would be totally sapped by the inevitable heavy losses; or even the difficulties that inexperienced American troops would have in facing battle-hardened Germans.

What amazed him was that Marshall had not even considered what he would do once he got his army ashore. "I asked him, do we go west, south or east after landing? He had not begun to think of it."[22]

Brooke admired the American's charm but disparaged his strategic skills. "Marshall does not impress me by the ability of his brain," he wrote in his diary. "It is not possible to take his castles in the air too seriously. . . . In many respects he is a very dangerous man."[23] Marshall, equally unimpressed, compared Brooke with his predecessor and confided to Hopkins that "[Brooke] may be a good fighting man but he hasn't got Dill's brains."[24]

When the British stated their "entire agreement in principle with all you proposed," the Americans believed that Modicum had been accepted at full and face value. It did not occur to them that their allies privately viewed it as a list from which they could arbitrarily select some items but not others. Nothing in the whole-hearted acceptance by the Defence Committee warned the Americans that the British harboured any reservations; or that the Chiefs' agreement was essentially directed at the 1943 proposals but not those of 1942; or that, in other words, Bolero/Roundup was acceptable but Sledgehammer was not.

Sledgehammer deeply disturbed them: Brooke regarded it as an "unlikely adventure" and Ismay was "frankly horrified."[25]

"Our Chiefs were dead against Sledgehammer from the beginning," General Jacob recalled.[26] So why did they conceal their opposition?

General Sir David Fraser summed up the intrinsic differences in national character that led to the Americans' fateful misconception and its repercussion: "It is a British characteristic to find a formula of agreement in order to preserve some sort of unity in an organization, while postponing a crunch of opinion until real decisions on action have to be taken. It is an American characteristic to take at literal value the written word."[27]

When Churchill told Roosevelt, "We whole-heartedly agree with your conception of concentration," was he merely postponing a confrontation? Or did his hypocrisy stem from motives "a good deal less than honest"? American strategists would conclude the latter.[28]

General Ismay foresaw trouble. As Churchill's representative on the Chiefs of Staff, he attended every COS meeting and was now regarded by the service Chiefs as a trusted, straightforward and indispensable member. He was appalled at the duplicity of his fellow Britons in endorsing policies they had no intention of carrying out. He noted in his diary his profound regret that the British did not express their views "more frankly": "No doubts were expressed; no discordant note struck . . . Our American friends went happily homewards under the mistaken impression that we had committed ourselves to both Round-up and Sledgehammer. This was destined to have unfortunate results . . . and lay at the root of many future misunderstandings."[29]

Even before the American Clipper took off next day, their British hosts had begun nibbling away at the Modicum menu.

In the weeks to come, two of the Modicum agreements would be eroded away: Sledgehammer discarded and the 1943 invasion shelved.

Ironically, their hypocrisy over Modicum had saddled Britain's ablest warriors with an unbearable burden. The Chiefs absolutely *had* to keep their American allies onside; but not at the expense of sacrificing 10 of their own divisions.

They now had to concoct a plausible "out."

CHAPTER

5

A VERY POLITICAL WAR

Just when Roosevelt and Stalin and the media-fanned second-front advocates were starting to breathe hard down the necks of the British Chiefs, Ottawa's politicians were exerting a great deal of pressure on the same men to get Canadian troops into action.

"It is a tragic coincidence," a British historian all too accurately observed, "that Mackenzie King's political requirement concurred with the Chiefs of Staff's requirements."[1]

Canada declared war on Germany on September 10, 1939, just days after Britain had done so. The ties of loyalty that bound the offspring to the mother ruled out any possibility of neutrality. Hitler had not yet openly declared his malevolent intentions, and the world would have no inkling of his attitude to Jews till much later. Canadians were prepared to go to war because of their ties to Britain and because Hitler's invasion of Czechoslovakia, Austria, and Poland was generally and deeply resented.

Three months later, the all-volunteer Canadian Expeditionary Force sailed for England.

Between then and 1942, William Lyon Mackenzie King, prime minister of Canada, "fat, devious and dull," had a very comfortable war.[2]

King had been trying, with some success, to wage a war of "limited liability."[3] His wartime military policy contained an almost untenable contradiction: he wanted to have his cake (i.e., to bask in the impression of making an all-out war effort) and eat it too (i.e., to keep his promise not to inflict conscription for overseas service on the country).

There was little about Canada's war effort that did not sooner or later reduce itself to the question of conscription. Historically, that issue had always been the high explosive underlying Canadian politics, mainly because it always deepened the divisions between English and French Canadians. If national unity was to be preserved in this war, avoiding conscription was vital — at least until there was sufficient public approval for it.

King had vowed that Canada would participate in Hitler's war as a united country. "Unity is the thing!" he cried. And unity became King's mission, his obsession. He believed that only he could keep the country together. Any divisiveness would have been a terrible comment on his leadership.

His other obsession, of course, was the electorate. A man who placed so much importance on psychic symbols — the position of hands on the clock, for example — could never ignore the even more powerful symbolism of electoral defeat in a by-election. King's eye never strayed far from the voting public.

The impact of King's two obsessions on Canada's military involvement was enormous. The country's military efficiency would be eroded by political pressures.

King placed his trust in the man he had appointed as commander of the Canadian forces overseas, Lieutenant General A.G.L. "Andy" McNaughton. A distinguished scientist and Canada's most celebrated soldier, McNaughton seemed the country's best hope, not only as field general but also as guardian of the national interest. He was, like King, an ardent nationalist who believed that keeping Canada's forces together, under Canadian command, would enhance his country's international prestige. Dispersing the Canadian Corps and placing it under British control would, he was certain, seriously undermine Canada's still-struggling sense of nationhood. As long as he had anything to say about it, Canada's army would stay just that — *Canadian*, in every respect.

So McNaughton was more than happy to keep his troops occupied with the defence of the United Kingdom, awaiting real action — but only, he stressed, as an entire entity against the Germans in Europe. They were to be used, in his evocative phrase, to form a "dagger, pointed at the heart of Berlin."[4]

This kind of rhetoric exhilarated Canadians. The press could always count on McNaughton for a provocative quote to liven up domestic headlines. The tall, lean general "had a commanding presence and made an imposing figure with his iron grey hair, piercing eyes and bushy eyebrows." He made good cover and the media took full advantage of that fact.[5]

However, General Brooke, who had served with McNaughton in the First World War, was to be less impressed with his old commander as the war continued. In his view, McNaughton was "not gifted with the required qualifications as a commander" and had "been worked into the position of a national hero by the Canadian press."[6]

It did not take long for King's *bête noir*, conscription, to wobble his comfortable war. With the conflict in Europe becoming more and more threatening, many of the public and press to whom he so slavishly pandered began lobbying for complete mobilization of Canada's manpower.

Pressure came, too, from his Cabinet and specifically from his minister of defence, Colonel James Layton Ralston. As early as 1940, the army had been calling for men to come forward and help fulfill their country's commitment to defend England's south coast against the expected German invasion.

To achieve this, Canada's military objective was to raise an overseas army of two corps. The fledgling force began with the newly created First Canadian Corps, initially consisting of just the First Canadian Division. Some six months later, the Second Canadian Division was added. This still left another corps of several more divisions to raise.

In August 1941, Lieutenant General Harry Crerar, Chief of the General Staff, had pointed out to McNaughton that this number was feasible, without interfering with essential industry and other home activities: "Our departmental appreciation indicates that manpower is available to maintain a Canadian army of eight divisions, of which two will be in Canada, for a period of over six years from now." A little over four months later, the Canadian Cabinet approved the scheme.[7]

The hitch, which Crerar had spelled out, was that the army could meet its objectives only if the government took "the steps required to get those numbers in the Services." By this time the line-ups at recruitment centres were getting drastically short.

More volunteers were needed. But young Canadians were deciding that there wasn't much glamour in joining an army that was sitting around in England, digging trenches and manning pillboxes. The air force, for example, had more appeal.

Ralston, a man with an overwhelming sense of duty, was deeply concerned about this dwindling enlistment rate. There was one sure way to increase it: Ralston asked the government to invoke conscription for overseas service. King would hear none of it and threatened to resign unless the issue was dropped.[8]

Ralston then changed his tactics. If conscription was out, maybe recruiting would be given a boost if the troops saw some action. Ralston informed King that the Corps' garrison duties in England "accounted for the degree of apathy evidenced by the public," and also "prevented enthusiasm from being aroused in regard to the recruiting campaign." Could the Canadians not be given a chance to meet the enemy? Perhaps in the Middle East?[9]

But combat would result in casualties, and consequently more manpower shortages, which in turn would raise the ugly spectre of conscription again. The prime minister exploded at Ralston's suggestion: "I refuse to countenance anything of the kind. I do not feel that any government has the right to take the lives of men for spectacular purposes."[10]

The truth was, those defensive duties allocated to his overseas divisions suited Mackenzie King's war policy to a tee. "We owe it to our men to seek to protect their lives," he would repeat, taking refuge in sanctimony to justify his opposition.[11]

Finally, King was forced to back down. In June 1940, he compromised by introducing the *National Resources Mobilization Act*, the infamous NRMA. This gave the government the right to conscript soldiers, but just for home defence. Only volunteers would be considered for military service overseas.

It was conscription without teeth, designed by King primarily to get Ralston and the English-Canadian media off his back. But it didn't work out as intended: pro-conscriptionists, many of them from English Canada, soon realized that the "Zombies" — as NRMA troops were soon dubbed — would be able to stay home while the volunteers were giving up their lives. The mayor of Montreal and passionate Quebec nationalist, Camillien Houde, urged all Quebec men to resist. He was interned for the rest of the war for sedition.

Initially, Canada's military forces were hardly worth the fuss. The gesture of sending an Expeditionary Force overseas in 1939 had more sentimental than practical value. Historically, when required to be warlike, Canada had proved her ability. But in the Depression-ridden political climate of the 1930s, King, "the inveterate army-hater," had sustained such a "determined opposition to the Militia" that Canada was woefully unprepared for conflict.[12]

Canada's prewar militia reserves amounted to a mere 51,000 "Saturday night" soldiers, airmen, and sailors. The Permanent Force had 4,261 all ranks. There were exactly four anti-aircraft guns, five mortars, 82 Vickers machine guns, 10 Bren guns, and two light tanks in the entire Canadian army. Transport was scarce. Even after mobilization, supplies were so short that there weren't enough steel helmets for the men, and uniform jackets did not even match the pants. At one point the ranks were told that they could only receive an issue of new socks if they produced the old ones — washed — to prove they were beyond repair.[13]

Still, the country's efforts to mobilize were impressive. In September 1939, almost 60,000 Canadians lined up at recruiting depots to volunteer for active duty. The First Canadian Division sailed for England in December. By February 1940 it was 23,000 men strong, though largely untrained. This was the nucleus of an army of Canadian volunteers that would grow to 125,000 by the end of 1941 — and to double that number by D-Day.

Denis Whitaker

How do you learn to drive a Bren carrier when you haven't got any carriers? On a double-decker London bus, of course! That was the solution my superiors came up with for me during the summer of 1940.

My battalion, the Royal Hamilton Light Infantry, Second Canadian Infantry Division, was mobilized in September 1939. I was 24 years old, a graduate of Canada's Royal Military College, and in those days I think I was more interested in playing football than in playing soldier. I was appointed to command the Bren Carrier Platoon. A Bren carrier was a tracked vehicle armoured against small-arms fire such as rifles and machine guns. It was capable of moving across country at high speed. The carrier platoon's fighting establishment was supposed to consist of 13 carriers, each with a crew of three (driver, gunner and commander), and each carrying one Bren gun. A carrier platoon at full strength was capable of producing an extremely high volume of fire power and could be moved rapidly to a strategic point during a battle.

During the first winter of the war in Canada, our total equipment consisted of one diagram of a single Bren gun.

Because we had no carriers in Canada, I was sent in advance to Britain to learn how to operate them. This was in June 1940, shortly after Dunkirk, and I found that much of the British equipment — including those still-mythical carriers — had been lost in France. The need for driving and maintenance instruction was so important that arrangements were made for us to take a mechanic's course, using buses at the London Transport Board shop in Chiswick.

This was a pleasant suburb of London on the Thames and a fascinating way to spend a summer. I must have done something right: the next year I was privileged to give my regiment's colonel-in-chief, King George VI, his first ride in a Bren Gun Carrier. It's not often a young Canadian lieutenant gets to chauffeur a king — I'm glad he didn't realize that I learned my skills driving a London bus!

By August of 1940, my regiment and the rest of Second Canadian Division had arrived in England and I rejoined my unit. We still had little gear — weapons, vehicles or equipment — other than our uniforms. Few of us had had any training; none had battle experience. The First Division in particular, many of them raw recruits who were sent over months ahead of us with absolutely no training, must have seemed a rag-tag, ill-disciplined lot.

The gunners recall their field artillery regiments arriving in England to find weapons so scarce that "the men went about their gun drill using crudely constructed sawhorses as guns."[14]

The Army Tank Brigade, in Canada waiting to be shipped overseas, was equipped by the ingenuity of Major General F.F. "Fighting Frank" Worthington, known as the "Father of the Armoured Corps." Quite illegally, "Worthy" finagled a deal with the Americans to purchase 265 WWI Renault tanks which they had sold to junk dealers for scrap iron. The tanks cost $120.00 — each.[15]

A good many of Canada's early volunteers were casualties of the Great Depression. They had joined up "to get off the streets" or for the security of "$1.30 and three squares a day."[16] They probably hadn't reckoned on sharing the British ration. Brussels sprouts, national wheat loaf, canned herring — known to some as "sewer trout" — powdered eggs, and minute portions of tough mutton all made unappetizing appearances on the soldiers' mess tins.[17]

At first, the infantry battalions and artillery regiments were stationed at Aldershot in Hampshire. Aldershot's barracks, which were as old as the Boer War, offered little cheer and no central heating to keep out the frost of the unusually cold first winters. The gunners remember huddling around small open grates over a few small lumps of coal. Many didn't realize that they were receiving a larger fuel allowance than the British troops — or the British civilians, for that matter.[18]

The misery was relieved to some extent by the distractions. The men had a little money in their pockets and no responsibilities. The work was interesting, the sports were terrific, and the pubs weren't all that bad either.

Not many of us had been in England before, and we found it a beautiful country. The people were hospitable; we were often invited to their homes. Many of the men had British girlfriends, and some of them became Canadian war brides. Movies were shown regularly. The film, *49th Parallel*, starring Laurence Olivier, was shown to all ranks at the Ritz Theatre in Seaford. It was about the hunt for a group of German sailors who had escaped from a damaged submarine in Hudson Bay and were trying to cross wartime Canada to seek refuge in the United States, which was still a neutral country when the movie was made. The Mounties, of course, tracked them down.[19]

The Knights of Columbus, Salvation Army, Canadian Legion, YMCA, and Red Cross organized a number of hospitality centres for us. They arranged concerts and sports events, and provided tea and biscuits for soldiers on exercises. They also provided a wide range of educational courses. Best of all, they even arranged home stays for those on leave, which gave homesick Canadian lads a taste of family life.

Dances were one of the most popular distractions. To the men of the Calgary Tanks, these twice-weekly events were a highlight. They weren't much fun for the organizers; The Knights of Columbus described them as a thankless task. First they had to find a suitable hall, usually in a small town unaccustomed to hosting hundreds of men in uniform. Then they had to find decorations, prizes, and an orchestra. Their most formidable challenge was to find dancing partners who were "suitable and of high standard," with whom the troops could jive and shag without inhibition. Finally, they had to find a way to transport these maidens to — and especially *from* — the dances.[20]

In 1941, 56,000 Canadian soldiers saw in the English New Year with varying degrees of sobriety, and with equally varying degrees of exuberance, nostalgia and downright homesickness.

Many men of the RHLI posted to Hastings on the Channel coast, fondly remember the Royal Thirteens, the Rileys' dance band which provided the music for "Midnight 1941," a celebration and pageant in that seaside town.[21]

Gradually, the soldiers grew accustomed to the British way of life. As a carrier officer, I was sometimes assigned to lead night convoys, so I quickly received what the Queen's Own Cameron Highlanders of Canada described as "a speedy indoctrination into living without lights." I once made a mistake in my map reading and led over 60 vehicles down a blind alley. Extricating them was an unforgettably embarrassing experience.

We got into a lot of accidents while learning to drive on the left. Night driving was particularly hazardous. To avoid observation by enemy aircraft, headlights were blacked out except for one-inch circles that allowed only a dot of light to show the way. At the rear of each vehicle, a very small light illuminated a tiny white patch painted on the undercarriage. These were supposed to prevent rear-end collisions. They didn't. "Driving through a heavy fog demanded a new quality of skill in the drivers and map reading of the officers," the South Saskatchewans recalled.[22]

The hospital wards were overflowing with Canadian motorcyclists. "It will be easy to eradicate the Canadian army," Lord Haw Haw, the German propagandist, taunted us one evening in his radio broadcast. "Simply issue every soldier with a motorcycle and turn him loose."

Britons and Canadians drew closer together. We shared the hazards and discomforts of the Blitz. We viewed with enormous excitement and pride the courage of British and Canadian pilots during the Battle of Britain. We endured together the air raids, the blackouts, and the food and fuel shortages — these were some of the things that showed Canada's soldiers how difficult life was for ordinary citizens.

A Calgary Tank sergeant had a poignant experience while posted at Seaford on the south coast. The defence forces had been suffering frequent incendiary raids by enemy Junkers 88s. The coast bristled with defences: "barbed wire entanglements, sand-bagged gun emplacements, and helmeted people racing to their posts at the guns." One afternoon, several men from his battalion visited a Bofors gun crew they had gotten to know. Most of that crew were young women from the Auxiliary Territorial Service.

> The girls knew their jobs and could get their gun unlimbered and ready for action within seconds of the first wail of the Air Raid sirens. When we got there it was immediately obvious that something was wrong. A lone German fighter plane had sneaked in through the mist, almost on the water, and opened up with machine guns. The [crew] dived for their gun . . . and got it into

action. The plane was gone before they got more than a clip of shells off. But then the gun aimer sighed and slumped in her chair, dead. She had been shot by a stray bullet.[23]

This kind of day-to-day heroism by the British inspired everyone's admiration.

It didn't take us long to shake down. Basic training at the platoon and section levels, and route marches and inspections, were all the order of the day. And the various units finally received their equipment. An enemy invasion seemed inevitable. "The grim atmosphere of emergency spurred all ranks to a new level of personal effort," the Royal Hamilton Light Infantry history noted.[24]

By December 1940, the Second Canadian Division was considered ready for a new role. We took over the defence of the Channel coast. It was a miserable winter — it rained, it snowed. Everything froze, including ourselves. Many of us were living more or less in the open on the South Downs in unheated barracks and unused factory buildings, or under canvas.

During most of 1940 and 1941, routine training consisted of route marches and fitness drills, range firing of rifles and Bren guns to improve accuracy and speed, and communications practice by radio telephony.

We dug trenches, erected wire obstacles, laid minefields, and practised manning our defences in minimum time. Frequent exercises, staged night and day at battalion, brigade, or division level, focussed on coastal defence, sometimes against imaginary German paratroops dropped on strategic sites. Infantry units held the beaches or counterattacked with mobile units held in reserve.

The Saskatchewans found that their slit trenches had to be camouflaged against German reconnaissance, particularly if they had been dug into the white chalk of the South Downs. "The chalk had to be carried away and disposed of," the SSR noted.

It was in this area that they unearthed three skeletons. It turned out that these had probably been undisturbed since the Battle of Lewes in 1264. "Sad to relate, before the English authorities could retrieve and preserve the ancient relics, parts of the skeletons and teeth had been distributed as souvenirs."[25]

By the end of 1941, there were three infantry divisions, one army tank brigade and one armoured division in the U.K. Supporting troops for each division consisted of artillery regiments, reconnaissance regiment, engineer units, medical corps, signals corps, army service corps, ordinance corps and provost corps.

Our units were becoming fitter and we had learned to use our weapons with effect. Above all, we had achieved a military bearing and a pride of regiment.

In the spring of 1942, Mackenzie King was faced with the first — and by far the lesser known — of Canada's two conscription crises. The growing cry in favour of conscription for overseas duty inspired the prime minister to concoct yet another ploy to quiet Ralston and the criticisms from English Canada. Ralston had wanted a straight non-partisan vote in the House. King settled on a national plebiscite to determine the nation's wishes. (He had discovered on investigation that a plebiscite was less binding than a referendum.)

Are you in favour, he asked the voters, of releasing the government from its commitment not to send conscripts overseas?

Yes, said 64 percent of all Canadians. But *non*, said 76 percent of Quebeckers. In other words, King was still trapped by his national quandary. He resolved his political dilemma only temporarily — with a single phrase that would cling to and muddy Canada's war effort for the next two years: "Not necessarily conscription but conscription if necessary."[26] He plucked the phrase from the lead sentence of a six-week-old editorial in the *Toronto Star* on the eve of his critical wrap-up speech.

So, he *could* send the conscripts overseas, but only when *he* decided it was "necessary." With this fancy verbal footwork King had talked his way out of a tight position. However, in doing so, he lost a great deal of credibility with his pro-conscription voters. By the spring of 1942, the behind-the-scenes factions influencing King's military policies were giving him more cause for concern than ever. Even abroad, he was inspiring little respect.

Despite all his posturing, King never *had* achieved much credibility with his military allies. When the United States entered the conflict and the war intensified, Canada lost her status as Britain's "most powerful ally"; she now lagged behind as the "lightweight in Anglo-American affairs."[27]

His War Cabinet was not consulted or even advised when Britain and the United States formed the powerful Combined Chiefs of Staff. This new supercommittee was created to determine the direction of the war and the employment of all Allied troops, including Canada's. King only found out about it in the morning newspaper.

The first summit meeting between Churchill and Roosevelt was held in the waters off Newfoundland in August 1941. Those arrangements were made without King's knowledge; he was not even informed of them until Churchill was en route to the meeting.[28]

Preserving Canada's international status was an obsession for General McNaughton, who antagonized his British colleagues by crusading endlessly on this point. He was absolutely determined to protect Canada's international prestige and went to every possible length to keep her army intact. All of this would result in bitter confrontations between McNaughton and his boss in the Cabinet, Ralston.

It was no secret that, for a number of reasons, McNaughton had a vendetta going with Ralston. While the latter wouldn't rock the political boat, the King-McNaughton caveat on action was causing him real trouble.

The two men even disagreed on conscription. McNaughton was as profoundly against conscription as King himself. Ralston saw conscription as the most practical way to bolster the dwindling numbers of recruits for overseas duty. Whitehall was perplexed by this divisiveness in the Canadian family.

However, Ralston's political fortunes were about to improve. King was discovering that the static role of the Canadian troops, which up to a point had helped him politically, was beginning to cause him a number of serious problems. The media's reports of idle troops were making a bad recruitment situation worse. This in turn was increasing the demands on him to send the conscripts overseas. The country was being split down the middle while King juggled his two armies — the conscripts at home and the volunteers abroad.

Denis Whitaker

Meanwhile, in England, one of King's armies was striving to learn its trade.

Early in 1942 the general training policy of the Canadian army began to shift slowly from one of training in the defensive role to one of offensive action in preparation for an eventual invasion of Europe.[29]

We had by then come under the operational command of Lieutenant General Bernard Montgomery, Commander South-Eastern Army: SECO, as it was known. Montgomery's belief — which he prescribed to all those under him — was that effective defence required a strong "offensive mentality." One of his disciples was Lieutenant General Crerar, who assumed acting command of the Canadian Corps in late 1941. Crerar circulated a letter to all commanding officers stating that "before the next three months have elapsed the Canadian Corps must be capable of meeting every requirement of battle." A good exercise, Crerar stressed, should test the administration as well as the tactical efficiency of a unit or formation.[30]

At about this time a new form of basic infantry training was introduced: battle drill. This was a major change that became the medium to revitalize all training at lower levels. Battle drill utilized the basic principle of fire and movement at a greatly accelerated pace. This had been a basic and recognized principle dating back to the First World War where one element, the infantry, moved forward while another element, the artillery, supplied covering fire. Now speed had become a key factor.

Battle drill at the section and platoon level taught all ranks to appreciate a battle situation quickly, to issue brief orders and then to swing immediately into an attack. Everything was done at top speed in open country. Each section was divided into two groups: a Bren gun group of two men and a rifle group of five. The section commander would give an order: "Enemy machine gun, line of my arm (pointing) two hundred yards — Bren give covering fire — GO!"

The rifle group then took off at top speed in a wide flanking movement to attack the enemy position. Meanwhile the Bren gun would give covering fire by concentrating on the objective until the riflemen charged and captured it. Then the Bren group would run at top speed to catch up.

The battle drill routine — the guts of any infantry attack at any level — would be repeated over and over again through mud, hail or rain. It soon instilled basic infantry tactics and made the units physically fit.

The heightened emphasis on battle drill as an offensive tactic at the unit and formation level was accompanied by a tougher and more realistic individual training program. River crossing and night training were increasingly emphasized. A battle drill school was established at Bernard Castle in Yorkshire and every infantry officer attended it. The South Saskatchewan Regiment reported that

during the winter Majors McTavish and Mather and Captain Fritz attended the Canadian Army's new Battle Drill School. On their return and during a demonstration at which General Montgomery was in attendance, he asked many questions of Captain Fritz, who was in command of the company. During this question and answer session the husky red-haired Captain chewed a wad of gum incessantly. The ever proper General turned to the Colonel and asked him what that officer was chewing. The Colonel replied, with his fingers crossed, that it was chewing gum and that all Canadian and American athletes chewed gum because it was good for the wind, etc., etc. The General was very impressed and stated all soldiers should be chewing it.[31]

In addition, battle drill also involved unarmed combat and training in other skills similar to those taught at British commando units. It required fast, clear thinking on the part of the NCOs and officers, enhancing the excellent physical fitness in all ranks.

The officers and men of Les Fusiliers Mont-Royal found out quickly that their new commanding officer was a maniac for fitness. Lieutenant Colonel Dollard "Joe" Menard was only 29 years of age — the youngest battalion commander in the Commonwealth — when he was appointed C.O. of the FMRs in the spring of 1942. This caused considerable dismay among all ranks. They knew little about him; he was a major from another regiment and did not even come from Montreal. A career officer, the young broad-shouldered giant — standing six-feet two-inches tall — had served in the Indian Army for three years after graduating from Royal Military College of Canada.

The men called him "l'outsider," but not for long. Immediately after assuming command, he intensified training for the battalion, setting an example by his own vitality that soon won his men over.

By 1942, the Second Division had one other battalion commander from the Permanent Force: 30-year-old Lieutenant Colonel Johnny Andrews, from the 14th Army Tank Battalion. He was a small man with a large and total dedication to the role of armour.

"Civilian soldiers" commanded five of the six infantry battalions that would fight at Dieppe. Lieutenant Colonel Fred Jasperson, a lawyer from Windsor, was C.O. of the Essex Scottish. A stockbroker named Bob Labatt commanded the RHLI, as his father had done in the First World War.

Montgomery had decided to unload a number of the Canadian battalion commanders — many of them of First World War vintage — whom he considered too old for active command. Their replacements were young men in their thirties. Lieutenant Colonel Hedley Basher of the Royal Regiment would be replaced by his younger second-in-command, Douglas Catto, a Toronto architect. The Queen's Own Cameron Highlanders of Canada would have a one-time radio repairman, Lieutenant Colonel Alfred Gostling of Winnipeg, in command. The South Saskatchewans also had a new commanding officer: 32-year-old Cec Merritt, a lawyer and accomplished athlete from Canada's west coast.

Back in Canada, Mackenzie King was being warned that Canada's image might well be tarnished by his cautious policies concerning the "idleness" — as it was viewed in Canada — of her infantry forces overseas.

The Department of External Affairs went so far as to tell him that Canadian influence in the postwar world would suffer "if her troops did not fight."[32]

Increasingly, Canadians were becoming tired of King's all-talk, no-action approach to the war. Criticism about the Canadian army's continued inactivity was coming from every quarter now. Newspaper editorials and opposition MPs seized on the growing call for action.

"It seems an awful thing to say," a senior officer at CMHQ remarked at the time to historian Colonel Charles Stacey, "but the people of Canada are calling out for blood." [33]

King had two ways open to soften the manpower crunch: he could send the Canadian volunteers into action in the hope of bolstering recruitment, or — and he did not consider this a viable option — he could order the conscripts overseas and into active duty. To save his political hide, he took the former approach. The volunteers, he informed Whitehall in an abrupt about-turn in August 1941, could now serve in any theatre of war.[34]

At around the same time, Cabinet gave McNaughton the authority "to undertake minor raids and operations without the necessity of obtaining Cabinet authority in each case." They later took out the word "minor."[35]

The players were now on the field. All they needed was a coach, a starting time, and an opponent.

Lieutenant General Crerar, a Permanent Force officer and a graduate of Canada's Royal Military College, now stepped forward. Crerar was a fine administrator, precise in thought and immaculate of person. He was an "exponent of military orthodoxy"; in other words, he was a stickler for official procedures.

While serving as a gunner in France during the First World War, Crerar had designed the largest, most intricate, and most successful creeping artillery barrage of the fighting in France: a three-day barrage at Canal-du-Nord that halted Germany's final advance in 1918. His distinguished career between the wars testified to his great competence as a staff officer.[36]

Of late, though, Crerar had been growing weary of Canada's war bureaucracy. He was beginning to feel that the fighting was passing him by. So far, his war had been all tea cups and paper clips. He was a soldier; not a politician. In 1940, as Chief of the General Staff, he had learned this the hard way when he got his knuckles rapped for naïvely assuring the British Chiefs of Staff that "he knew of no desire on the part of the Canadian government to discourage the use of its forces in any operation . . . no matter where the theatre might be." Embarrassingly, the prime minister hadn't even bothered to brief him to the fact that he, King, was "hostile" to sending Canadian troops to the Mediterranean, and that the Canadian public "would not be enthusiastic."[37]

But by 1942, King had changed his mind. He and Crerar now shared the same objective. Their motives, however, were vastly different: the prime minister wanted the troops under fire in order to gain popularity back home; Crerar wanted to command men in the field and see his corps in the fight. In his view the dagger of McNaughton's oft-quoted slogan was becoming "palsied through lack of use."[38]

Crerar doubted that McNaughton would lobby aggressively for Canadian action, and so took it upon himself to get the Canadians into battle. He now had, after all, the government's sanction.

He did not have to look hard for a likely operation and the opportunity to campaign for it — behind McNaughton's back.

On January 23, 1942, McNaughton left England for a three-month visit to Canada and the United States. Crerar, who had returned to England just before Christmas to assume command of Second Division, became acting corps commander in McNaughton's absence. It would prove to be the perfect opportunity for him to lobby the British hard for a taste of the sharp end. "This probably influenced the selection of Canadians to execute the raid [on Dieppe]," Colonel Stacey believed.

During February and March, Crerar "took advantage of being in command in McNaughton's absence . . . to urge Montgomery, Sir Alan Brooke and Mountbatten to give the Canadians opportunities in raids."[39]

Crerar was asking for much more than token participation; he was pleading that "a very high proportion of these prospective raids, if not the total, should be undertaken by detachments from the Canadian Corps."[40]

His personal battlegrounds became the Savoy for lunch with General Brooke, the Naval and Military Club — the familiar "In and Out" — for tea with General Montgomery, and Boodles or the Ritz for dinner with Mountbatten.

"Sunday, March 1: Comfortably and quietly spent at home. Crerar came to tea," was a not infrequent and somewhat plaintive Brooke reference to his activities on the only day of the week which he could spend privately with his wife and young children.

An avalanche of letters from Crerar and his BGS (Brigadier General Staff) Guy Simonds to Brooke, to Lieutenant General Paget (Commander-in-Chief Home Forces), to Montgomery and to other high officials engulfed them:

5 Feb 42: General Crerar to General Montgomery: "Possibility of Canadian Tps taking part in raids."

8 Feb 42: General Montgomery to General Crerar: Reply to above re availability of craft.

6 Mar 42: BGS, 1 Canadian Corps [Brigadier GG Simonds]: Notes re meetings held with DCIGS [Deputy Chief of the Imperial General Staff] re Canadian participation in raids.

10 Mar 42: BGS, 1 Canadian Corps: Notes re preliminary arrangements for training . . . in Scotland.

15 Mar 42: BGS, 1 Canadian Corps: General Paget approves arrangement for Canadian participation in raids.[41]

Meetings abounded. In plain truth, Crerar and Simonds probably made something of nuisances of themselves with their zeal.

Finally, on March 6, Crerar made Brooke the key convert in his campaign. It could be that he wore him down with rhetoric.

Soon after, Brooke leaned on Mountbatten, who had long been resisting Crerar's pressure. The Combined Ops Chief did not want the Canadians on board. His position was that it ran "counter to the policy"; that raids should be carried out by commandos; and that "army representation would take the form of 'dilution' of raiding Commandos." In the end, however, he backed down, saying that he "appreciated the special position of Canadian Corps and was agreeable to making an exception to policy in favour of a largely Canadian enterprise, providing [Paget] would also agree."[42]

Shortly before McNaughton returned to England, Mountbatten met with Crerar and Simonds. "Dieppe was specifically mentioned and Crerar urged that it should be undertaken by Canadian troops." Simonds reported: For reasons of military protocol, all three decided to keep quiet about the plans for the Canadians "until a request for Canadian troops had been formally made to General McNaughton."[43]

One month later, on April 30, Montgomery made that formal approach to McNaughton, now back in England as commander of First Canadian Army. If McNaughton was surprised to learn that Monty "had been pressed to agree to a composite British and Canadian force," and that "General Crerar had already been approached and had nominated the 2nd Division for the operation," he made no comment.[44]

He wasn't about to admit that he had been outfoxed by his own corps commander. It would have irreparably undermined his authority.

———————

Denis Whitaker

So many myths have persisted over the years about the Canadian troops in England during those early war years. The propaganda that the media and the government doled out to the Canadians back home in 1941 and 1942 — that *we* were the ones who wanted action, that *we* were bored and demoralized — is pure nonsense. *They* were the ones who were trying to justify action — action for action's sake. Action for votes. Canadian troops were *not* spoiling for a fight.

It *was* an awful and shocking thing to say—suggesting that the people of Canada were demanding the blood of the volunteer soldiers overseas. It was totally erroneous — a lie propagated by a sensationalizing press and manipulative politicians. As historian Desmond Morton wrote, "No one in touch with Canadian army morale ever believed that soldiers demanded blood-letting at Dieppe as a curb on their frustrations. In fact, Canadian discipline and morale in England were satisfactory by any reasonable standard."[45]

And it was an awful thing for Mackenzie King to do — after all his hypocritical talk about not allowing the lives of the men to be taken "for spectacular purposes" — to permit this myth to flourish so that he could then offer us up indiscriminately, like so many pork sausages, just to gain a few votes.

The myth that Canadian corps soldiers were howling for a fight has gone on for 50 years. Well-regarded military histories have perpetuated it: "the morale of the forces was suffering because of lack of opportunity for fighting."[46] Another: there was "forlorn and increasingly vocal resentment" as Canadians "languished at garrison duties in England." And still another: it was "common knowledge that the troops were browned off."[47]

As a platoon commander and later as a commanding officer, I can attest that we weren't "browned off." I don't believe the morale in the Rileys was suffering, nor was it in any other units I saw or heard about in England. Many veterans will corroborate this: for example, Major General Dan Spry, who commanded the Third Canadian Division, and Lieutenant Tom Taylor of the Royal Regiment who as a Dieppe POW surely qualifies as a specialist in troop morale.[48]

The men were keen. They may not have liked the 25-mile marches, but who does? There was a very positive side to the experience of being in Britain. There can be few veterans today who would not agree that living in England was a rewarding experience. Colonel Stacey, who researched the subject in depth, called the transformation of the Canadian soldier's relationship with the British people "remarkable" for its warm goodwill.[49]

We certainly didn't feel we were "languishing." We believed we were fulfilling a role. Our job was to defend England from enemy invasion. There was always that possibility of a German paratroop attack.

I can't remember a lot of crime. Sure, there were a few guys who didn't get back from leave on schedule, but there weren't a lot of criminal offences.

Another popular myth has to do with the fact that Canadian troops at Aldershot booed the prime minister when he addressed them in August 1941. Yes, they did boo him, and this has since been attributed to the restlessness and belligerence of the men who were there — and to the "morale problems," reports of which were so greatly exaggerated.

I was present that day. It was a very cold, wet afternoon. Many of us had travelled 50 miles or more to reach Aldershot on time, and we were assembled at the sports stadium, fortunately under cover of the grandstand. However, a special colour guard had been assembled, and was formed up in the open awaiting King's arrival. The prime minister was delayed by several hours and evidently did not bother to send word ahead. The guard and bands were kept standing in the belting rain all that time, soaked and cold. This cavalier treatment was what made the men so furious. When King finally arrived, they booed.

It was not from sagging morale, not from any fever-pitch for battle — it was just momentary anger at thoughtless treatment of soldiers. It quickly passed.

"I bring you greetings from your wives and loved ones," King began.

"But did you bring us any cigarettes?" a bold voice shouted from the back.

"I'll see that you get *lots* of cigarettes!" King, ever the politician, promptly retorted.

Whereupon he was cheered.

When we were posted to England — voluntarily giving up our homes, families, and employment — we thought we were serving our country. We never dreamed our sacrifice might actually be viewed by Canadian politicians as a period of idleness or dissipation.

If we'd been ordered to battle, anywhere, we would have gone, with determination and enthusiasm — as we did, to Dieppe. After all, we had volunteered to fight and we respected that commitment. But we certainly weren't agitating for it. It's all right for the press to criticize the fact that we hadn't seen much action — their lives weren't on the line. I sure wasn't pushing my neck out and saying I wanted to get shot at.

I was overseas for almost six years, and I think morale was pretty good all the way through, except perhaps when we were fighting in the fall of 1944 with untrained reinforcements. Then we again realized that the government didn't give a damn about us.

Morale would not have been as good if we had known then what we now know — that we were pawns being moved by political whim. We were there to help win a war — not to be vote-getters for Mackenzie King.

CHAPTER
6

ENEMY ATTACK!

At 0500 hours on March 24, 1942, a telephone call was relayed from Fourth Canadian Infantry Brigade to Langley Place, a large estate in the historic town of Hastings. The duty officer of the Royal Hamilton Light Infantry HQ picked up the receiver.

Two words flashed across the wire: AFLOAT FAIRLIGHT.

The duty officer snapped into long-rehearsed action. WARN SENIOR OFFICER AT LANGLEY PLACE, were his standing orders. Then: CONTACT COMMANDING OFFICER FOUR BATTALION COMPANIES AND CARRIER PLATOON STANDING TO IN FORWARD POSITIONS. JERRY was the single code word of warning.

All ranks, including personnel of unit headquarters, immediately manned their defensive positions. Within minutes, 3,000 men were on "Stand To." Fourth Brigade's commander, Brigadier Sherwood Lett, alerted Major General Hamilton Roberts at Second Division headquarters.

Meanwhile, the duty officer quickly called in the prescribed message to RAF HQ at Hastings and Coast Guard stations at Hastings and St. Leonards: RHLI CALLING: ENEMY SEABORNE RAID EXPECTED VICINITY OF FAIRLIGHT COVE. KEEP US INFORMED OF ANY SIGNS OF ENEMY.[1]

Intelligence personnel had warned the division that a concentration of German gliders was being massed on a French airstrip. Allied Photographic Intelligence, based largely on air reconnaissance, confirmed that a large fleet of shallow-water landing craft was assembling in the French Channel ports.

All battalions had been alerted that a German invasion or amphibious raid on the south coast of England was imminent. High tides were estimated to peak just before first light, ideal for an amphibious landing. The division's meteorology specialists had advised that the weather would be favourable for invasion.

At this point in the war, an attempted enemy raid or invasion was uppermost in everyone's mind. Canadian Corps was responsible for defending the 100 miles of vulnerable coastline in West and East Sussex. Responding to the warnings, Brigadier Lett had placed his three 4th Brigade battalions on stand-to under arms at action stations from 0430 hours to 0700 hours daily until further notice. Patrols were sent out. Every man was taut with expectation.[2]

By happenstance, the Canadian sector lay just over 60 miles across the English Channel from the Dieppe coast. We were defending a historic sector of England our ancestors had last defended in A.D. 1066. Our brigade headquarters was at Battle, where William the Conqueror had celebrated his victory against the Saxon King Harold.

Almost 800 years later we hoped that we would have better success against an invasion from France. There was a sense of the enemy being so close. From vantage points along the coast we could look across the Channel on a clear day and see the distant outline of Boulogne. We knew that Germans patrolling those cliffs were staring back at us with similar awe.

———————

Second Division, comprising three brigades — 4th, 5th and 6th — held this critical stretch of coastline. Of the 4th Brigade battalions, the Royals manned the beach defences from Winchelsea to Rye, the Rileys were posted farther west at Hastings and the Essex Scottish were in reserve at Battle some eight miles inland. The Calgary Tanks (14th Armoured Regiment) formed a mobile counterattack force at Battle. Of the 6th Brigade, the South Saskatchewan Regiment was based near Lewes. Here, defences faced inland against possible enemy glider and paratroop attacks. The Camerons and Les Fusiliers Mont-Royal were nearby at Newhaven. Our divisional artillery had sighted batteries so that fire could be brought down anywhere along 30 miles of beaches.[3]

The Rileys had been billeted in hotels and houses from St. Leonards, at the west end of Hastings, to Fairlight Cove to the east. The eight miles of coast between these points were its responsibility. Hastings was one of the original Cinque Ports of Norman days. On the sandstone cliffs above its Old Town loomed the ruins of England's first Norman castle. However, there wasn't much time for sightseeing. The battalion had worked hard at improving defences: digging, wiring and sandbagging. The commander, Lieutenant Colonel Labatt, had carefully prepared what he believed were impregnable defensive positions. (In his zeal he had infuriated the local fishermen by trying to prohibit them from beaching their boats on *his* coast.)[4]

Three Riley companies, each with more than 100 riflemen, were in forward positions defending the beaches with two platoons up and one back, all in close communication by number 18 radio sets. The fourth company and the carrier platoon were in reserve, acting in battalion counterattack role.

Each company had six light machine guns (Brens) sited to fire down the beaches in enfilade crossfire. Most guns were in concrete pillboxes. To thicken up the fire, two sections of medium machine guns from the Toronto Scottish Regiment were attached to us. Fire support, available on call, consisted of 3-inch mortars, 4.2-inch mortars, and the guns of 4th Field Regiment Royal Canadian Artillery (twenty-four 25-pounders). The battalion's antitank guns were also sited to cover the beaches.

During the days and nights of the invasion alert, supporting arms had been brought to immediate preparedness for defensive fire. All mobile counterattack forces had been placed on immediate call. We had been warned that the attack could include paratroops landing behind our beach defences. As well, the mortar-fire controllers and the forward observation officers of the 4th, 5th and 6th Field Regiments were set to call down defensive fire tasks wherever the enemy appeared.

In the months that the Royal Regiment had been stationed in the Winchelsea sector they had — like their sister battalions — erected impenetrable barriers against enemy invasion. They had installed heavy wire entanglements and tubular scaffolding to obstruct any attempt at approaching or traversing the shores. Large sections of the beaches were planted densely with antipersonnel mines (which had proved disastrous for any local dogs who persisted in escaping into the minefields).

———■———

At 0500 hours, the moment just before dawn known to sailors as nautical twilight, sentries covering the front at the Winchelsea beach/Fairlight Cove/Hastings sector reported sighting a flotilla of small craft about half a mile out to sea. Radar soundings confirmed their findings.

In split seconds the word went out to the RHLI headquarters: AFLOAT FAIRLIGHT. Infantry companies on stand-to were contacted by line: JERRY!

The company commanders swung into action. "Enemy assault craft approaching," they yelled. "Prepare to fire." The infantry readied their machine guns, antitank rifles and rifles.

The gunners from 4th Field Artillery were already firing concentrations on the approaching craft. Some of these received direct hits, spewing bodies into the cold sea, but most continued their advance to the beaches. Obviously the Germans had been depending on surprise to get through the beach defences, as there was no air bombardment and little fire support from the escort vessels.

As the enemy assault troops touched down, the Canadian infantry opened up with enfilade fire from their Bren guns. At the same time mortars plastered the beaches in their DF SOS tasks, which had been registered and tested for maximum accuracy. (Defensive Fire: Save Our Souls was the highest priority of fire.) The artillery 25-pounder shells were falling all along the beaches.

The enemy assault troops disembarked and rushed into a veritable wall of bullets and shell and mortar fragments. Some were hit before they were able to leave their craft. Bodies were piling up on the beaches. At first, no enemy was able to surmount the seawall or the barbed wire defences. Their sappers were being knocked out before they could get explosives forward.

The firefight continued. A few invaders got through the curtain of fire. They were able to penetrate the buildings behind Hastings and the cottages at Winchelsea Beach. However, the reserve Canadian platoons quickly rounded them up.

Throughout the early morning, the enemy remained pinned to the beaches, under continuous small-arms, mortar and shell fire. A few were able to get their MG-42s into action and these rapid-fire weapons, capable of firing at 1,200 rounds per minute, caused many Canadian casualties. The enemy's attempts to mount and fire their 80-mm mortars were frustrated by the accuracy of the Canadian snipers.

At 0930 hours, the German assault craft again approached the beaches to salvage what was left of the landing force. They were met by fire from all Canadian weapons. The remnants of the raiders who could, dashed for the craft. Many failed to make it. Those who did not get away were soon rounded up and made prisoners of war.

At 1015 hours, six hours after it had been kicked off with the codeword AFLOAT, Exercise Hill was completed.[5]

Although Exercise Hill was only a mock-up of an actual invasion, it was impressed upon the troops that this is what could happen, what they were being trained to defend against.

Throughout March and April, a number of similar exercises were arranged at brigade, inter-brigade and divisional level, usually with the participation of armoured and artillery units. Many, like Exercise Hill, took place at dusk or dawn — the time when things are inclined to happen in war. These training exercises were designed to simulate actual fighting conditions and tested every military skill: planning and administration, intelligence work, reconnaissance, scouting, communication, medical evacuation, mapping, field messing, sleeping arrangements, ammunition, petrol, food, supplies of all kinds, and liaison with the Home Guard. Each detail could make or break the success of the venture, based as it was on actual fighting conditions.[6]

In Exercise Flip, the riflemen from all battalions of the Second Division were sent on a 24-hour forced march over rough country. Next was a series of marches which increased in distance and speed until the battalions could travel ten miles in two hours with each man carrying 50 pounds of equipment and ammunition. After another four exercises — Flap, Flop, Beaver III and Beaver IV — the troops had been welded into first-class fighting units.

The final field exercise that spring, "Tiger," was staged by Montgomery himself. It involved the Canadian Corps and 12th British Corps in a gruelling eleven-day manoeuvre. More than 100,000 troops marched and fought over 250 miles. Monty had heard rumours that troops on previous exercises had been topping up their basic rations by stopping at pubs and shops, and hitching rides on lorries. This time he made sure it was a "no-frills" exercise. "By his orders the infantry were not allowed transport at any time," the artillery history noted. "To be able to boast 'I was on Tiger' marked the veteran who had slept in ditches in the rain, lived for days on bully beef and hard tack, and . . . marched in eleven days a distance which represented 'about the life of army boots on English roads.' "[7]

Denis Whitaker

Exercise Hill made its point: coastal assaults by the enemy on our heavily defended positions were bound to fail. We all wondered, if we

were so well prepared for a German attack, would not the Germans —
on the alert anyway because they expected a cross-Channel raid — be
just as well prepared for *our* attack?

Besides giving the troops a taste of actual battle conditions, Tiger
was a means to confuse the Germans as to our whereabouts. Second
Canadian Infantry Division had been sent instead on a "training
exercise" to the Isle of Wight.

For us, it was still make-believe. We didn't know it, but we were
preparing for the real thing: Dieppe.

And so were the Chiefs of Staff. The Anglo-American sparring up
to now had been mere dress-rehearsals for their *real* battle of strategy
that was imminent.

PART

3

MAY 1942

7

THE FISH, FLESH AND FOWL

The raid on Dieppe was parented by duplicity from within and pressure from without.

When Churchill and the Chiefs of Staff responded so positively to the Modicum proposals in April, promising Roosevelt and Marshall complete accord with their second-front strategy, they put themselves in an untenable position.[1]

Churchill had guaranteed a "crescendo of activity on the Continent."[2] The Americans thought they had a three-part deal — one that included Sledgehammer, the mini-invasion by mainly British troops on the French coast that summer, and a major build-up of Anglo-American forces focussed on a cross-Channel assault in 1943 (Bolero/Roundup).

But the British COS had neither the capability nor the intention of honouring their commitment to stage Sledgehammer. As General Jacob pointed out, the Chiefs were "dead against Sledgehammer from the beginning."[3]

This posed a serious dilemma for the British. They were in no position to tell the Americans in plain words that Sledgehammer was impossible. They *had* to go along outwardly with the pretence of planning it.

Meanwhile, they began quietly to hedge their bets. As a substitute, should it come to that, they had to be in a position to make a gesture that would placate the Americans with some kind of cross-Channel action instead. Dieppe would be the British ace-in-the-hole, the contingency plan they could produce if the Americans persisted in demanding Sledgehammer.

"While preparations [for Sledgehammer] should continue," Philip Ziegler noted, "there should also be plans made for a major raid which, by implication, would take Sledgehammer's place."[4]

Apparently sifting through their existing roster of small raids under consideration, Combined Operations planners selected one they felt could be adapted and expanded to fit the mandate: a "super-raid," large enough for the Chiefs to use as a substitute for Sledgehammer if need be — and certainly audacious enough for their boss, Mountbatten. They came up with a raid on the French port of Dieppe.

Hence the raid on Dieppe "almost immediately became an element in the programme agreed that month with Marshall and Hopkins."[5]

"Dieppe was offered up as the minimum we could get away with," Ziegler stated in an interview. "It was Churchill's outside chance. The British felt, we *must* get the Russians off our backs. If it works, we've lost nothing. If it doesn't work, we have at least demonstrated that a second front is not on."[6]

The metamorphosis from an earlier Dieppe plan to this later one had its beginnings in April 1942. The date coincides with Churchill's Modicum promises. It would be hard not to see a coincidence between the hypocritical commitment to Sledgehammer and the scramble to come up with a substitute.

The French port of Dieppe had been examined as a possible target as early as February 1942 — well before the concept of a "super-raid" was suggested. Dieppe was one of dozens of alternatives that Combined Ops had been considering that winter. All were designed as small-scale forays by an elite force of commando troops specially trained in amphibious warfare: the so-called "butcher-and-bolt" raids. Many never got to operational level.

Although no documents have been preserved that describe the original objectives of the proposed commando raid on Dieppe, it was probably meant to be a follow-up to the successful Bruneval raid in February, when a valuable German Würzberg radar installation was attacked and its critical components were brought back to Britain by a small force of paratroopers and naval personnel. This breakthrough into enemy radar posts must inevitably have inspired demands by British intelligence for more of the same. An important German radar base was located at Dieppe, on the cliffs just west of the town. Mountbatten's earlier plan for the raid — a flank attack by commandos — was surely focussed on that installation.[7]

In a recent search through contemporary war diaries, historian Nigel Hamilton, Montgomery's biographer, found evidence that confirms this. In February and March, Combined Operations Intelligence had lodged specific requests to army and navy sources for intelligence information on Dieppe.[8]

This bears out a little-known account of the original Dieppe plan that has been revealed by Colonel Brian McCool, then a major with the Royal Regiment of Canada. McCool had a unique second life as "corps raiding officer." On March 14 he was ordered to report to Second Canadian Infantry Division HQ for "special duties."[9]

"I was detached and sent for training to Scotland," McCool stated in an interview. He immediately began training for a small raid. The target was identified as Dieppe.

"Originally, Dieppe was geared to entail the Guards Brigade reinforced by the 8th Argylls. Later, the assignment was given to LCol Mike Rogers of 1st Commando, my old commander."[10]

Dieppe was better suited as a target for a compact raid, one that might employ five *hundred* men (rather than the five *thousand* that were sent) on a hit-and-run operation. Using the credo of Captain Hughes-Hallett, they would rely on "a little darkness, a lot of surprise." The other two essential ingredients for a successful raid would also have been provided in this earlier plan: mobility of movement and the carefully honed skills of the troops executing it.

A small band of commandos, in a surprise attack on the flank, would probably have captured the radar installation at Dieppe, and would have kept the enemy off-balance. Nothing more. It could have worked.

Major McCool pointed out, "Mountbatten's plan was a good plan. There were only five hundred men involved. But that was wiped out, and the job was given to the Second Canadian Division.

"Then the boys started to fiddle [it] away."[11]

It was probably at this point that Dieppe's conception as an effective and small military exercise changed into an operation on a grander scale that could serve as Sledgehammer's substitute. By being expanded, tarted up to become a mini-invasion, Dieppe lost out on those three essential winning ingredients: mobility, surprise and experienced assaulters.

The very topography of Dieppe that was so appropriate for a small sneak attack was highly unsuitable as a target for a large and cumbersome force.

The "boys who were fiddling [it] away" belonged to four separate factions, each with its own motives. First, Combined Operations wanted a raid that was large enough to satisfy the Chiefs' mandate and sound enough to secure their blessing. They had seen many of their plans shot down by the COS; they wanted this one to go.

Then the Chiefs, as we have seen, merely wanted a showpiece to impress and deter their allies, and to test their enemy.

The third element — the Canadian factor — was influenced by Crerar's wish to have his soldiers take part in the action — whatever action it might turn out to be.

It was the fourth faction — Home Forces — that created dissension, heightened already bitter inter-service jealousies and added yet another intrusive personality: Lieutenant General Bernard Law Montgomery.

General Paget, whose Home Forces included all British and Canadian divisions headquartered in Britain, had a large voice, though a quiet presence, in the military planning of the Dieppe project. He had the absolute authority to assign and govern the military troops involved with raids or invasions. Paget delegated the military responsibility for Dieppe to his South-Eastern commanding general, Montgomery.[12]

Hence, there were two teams: one from Combined Operations HQ, where Mountbatten still had accountability for the raids, and another from HQ Home Forces which appointed the military units taking part and had the authority to govern their actions.

———————

The time had come for Combined Operations commander Lord Louis Mountbatten to present the basic Dieppe plan to the Chiefs of Staff for their approval. It was called Operation Rutter.

The war had provided a giant step up for the King's cousin: from captain to commodore to member of the omnipotent Chiefs of Staff committee. Now he was responsible for the largest amphibious raid of the Second World War.

When Mountbatten first took over as technical advisor to Combined Ops in late 1941, there were 23 staff including clerical members, and some 5,000 commandos under training in Scotland. Within a few months, as his authority grew, COHQ had burgeoned into an establishment of 400 staff. Mountbatten himself described his rapidly mushrooming empire as "the only lunatic asylum in the world run by its own inmates."[13]

The Combined Ops headquarters was a modern building off Whitehall at 1A Richmond Terrace. Just a 10-minute stroll from the traditional clubs of St. James Street and the chic restaurants of Haymarket, the centre had become a mecca for Mayfair hangers-on. A somewhat shocked Lord Lovat described it as "honeycombed with rooms filled with every branch of the services, including the powder-puff variety, who looked elegant in silk stockings."[14]

The menagerie of oddballs employed for their scientific inventiveness gave COHQ the reputation as being "a resort of cranks and Communists."[15]

Mountbatten also left himself open to censure by indulging in a sort of aristocratic pork-barrelling by filling many of the key positions in his organization with friends from his prewar days of high living. One such throwback was his new intelligence chief, Wing Commander the Marquis of Casa Maury. Bobby Casa Maury was a wealthy sports car racer and glamour boy of the international set. His appointment to the specialized field of intelligence over the heads of capable career officers had been bitterly resented.

COHQ's intelligence section did not itself gather intelligence. It was, one senior officer said disdainfully, merely a "post box" for collecting pertinent data from a number of service agencies as required. Casa Maury's performance as gleaner and disseminator during his year or so as intelligence chief was more abysmal than expected. As a "postman" he was, in the words of Rutter's naval force commander, "utterly useless."

"Much intelligence was not officially shared and was sometimes obtained by chance," Rear Admiral H.T. Baillie-Grohman said scathingly.[16]

A key appointment to COHQ was Captain John Hughes-Hallett, Mountbatten's trim, dapper 40-year-old naval advisor and planning director whose tenacity — one might even say, obsession — with the job and whose supreme self-confidence were matched only by that of his boss.

His admirers attributed to him "a mind like a steel trap" that could unravel a complicated problem in seconds. "Once convinced of the rightness of his course he never gives up," they said. His detractors dubbed him "Hughes-Hitler." One unimpressed officer from a rival service branch noted sourly that, "his trouble was his conceit, just like all the breed at Combined Operations Headquarters."

This sort of inter-service jealousy had always existed, but it burgeoned rapidly when Combined Ops began stealing away the most talented officers of the army, navy and air force. It was to become a major hazard in the Dieppe raid.[17]

"Mountbatten was in a very difficult position," Lieutenant General Sir Ian Jacob recalled. "He was a colossal empire builder and his staff grew enormously. But he had to draw all his strength from existing forces. The service arms hated giving up resources to a third party and consequently he was opposed by people who didn't want things taken from them."[18]

This tri-service mêlée was a vast organization bursting with young soldiers, sailors and airmen intermingling and sometimes tripping over one another. Their mandate was to administer the technical and operational planning and training for amphibious assaults. So much was untried territory that everyone was an amateur.

This assortment of dilettantes and adventurers exasperated the skilled and dedicated elitists of the commando service such as Lieutenant Colonel the Lord Lovat, chief of Clan Fraser and commander of No. 4 Commando. What the austere and aristocratic "Shimi" Lovat saw at COHQ prompted him to dub it "H.M.S. Wimbledon: all balls and rackets."[19]

A more serious charge was levelled by Admiral Baillie-Grohman, who had just been appointed naval force commander of the Dieppe venture. To a dedicated and seasoned professional like Baillie-Grohman, the day-to-day chaos at COHQ was incomprehensible: "There were actually whole departments in COHQ which neither I nor my Staff had ever heard of, and which could have been of great assistance."[20]

On May 13, 1942, Brooke noted in his diary; "Main interest of morning's C.O.S. was examination of projected large-scale raid for vicinity of Dieppe."[21]

Mountbatten's presentation that day was the Chiefs' first opportunity to examine carefully and formally approve or reject the outline plan of the Dieppe raid. Until now, all of the planning had been executed jointly — and not always harmoniously — by the staffs of two departments: Combined Operations and Montgomery's South Eastern Command.

The outline plan that the Chiefs first saw stated:

"Intention.

A force of infantry, airborne troops and A.F.V.s [Armoured Fighting Vehicles] will land in the area of Dieppe to seize the town and vicinity. This area will be held during daylight while the tasks are carried out. The force will then re-embark. The operation will be supported by fighter aircraft and bomber action."[22]

Six battalions of infantry with engineers in support were designated for the raid along with airborne troops and a regiment of tanks.

As this figure correlated exactly with the number of available landing craft, the scope of the raid was obviously at maximum capacity to fit the "super-raid" requirement. A total of 237 ships, including eight destroyers, would support the assault.

As well, there would be strong support from the RAF. There were 60 squadrons of fighter planes to provide cover for the flotilla and engage enemy aircraft; and 150 high-level bombers and four squadrons of low-level bombers to plaster the town immediately before H-hour. The raid would be of "two-tide" duration — some 15 hours.

The advantages to using Dieppe as the target, Mountbatten pointed out, were mainly geographical. It was a port, and at that time it was believed that the capture of a port was an essential preliminary to a successful invasion. It was near enough to England (67 miles) that the assault force could cross the Channel entirely under cover of darkness. More importantly, it was within effective range of fighter planes, although their "loiter time" — that is, their period over target — would be a mere 10 minutes.

Besides harassing German ground forces, the raid might also lure the Luftwaffe into a major air battle. Both measures, it was hoped, would force the enemy to shift more of his air and land forces from Russia to defend his Channel flank. As well, the raid would test his defences before the inevitable invasion of France.

The disadvantages, as the Chiefs of Staff must have immediately realized, lay in Dieppe's topography.

Churchill had courted his Clementine there, perhaps clambering with her up the cliffs' precipitous paths to pick blackberries. Brooke, brought up in France, scrawled nostalgically in his diary, "Little did I ever think in the old days of my regular journeys from Newhaven to Dieppe that I should have been planning [a raid]."[23]

For hundreds of years, English tourists on summer excursions had taken the Newhaven-Dieppe ferry to France. They had gazed at the imposing headlands that commanded the approaches to Dieppe's harbour. They might well have remarked on the similarity of the unscalable French bluffs to the great sandstone cliffs that guarded long sections of England's southern coast.

As vacationers, they probably had been drawn to the shingle beaches that seemed so wide and inviting — until a closer inspection revealed them to be steeply graded and strewn with large, slippery rocks.

These features were surely going to cause difficulties for infantry and armour. Yet the Chiefs said "yes."

———■———

Several new characters now joined the mêlée at 1A Richmond Terrace. Three force commanders were appointed to represent what Montgomery's liaison officer, Goronwy Rees, irreverently termed the tri-service "fish, flesh and fowl" of Combined Operations' navy, army and air force. Their task was to add the detailed operational nuts and bolts to the plan. The Dieppe Raid would be under the joint command of these three men.

The "fish" was Admiral Baillie-Grohman, under whose veteran command Mountbatten had served as far back as in 1933. He was rushed back from the Middle East in late May to become naval commander of Rutter.

For "fowl," Air Vice Marshal Sir Trafford Leigh-Mallory, head of No. 11 Group, RAF, was appointed air force commander.

This pair must have seemed formidable in experience and weight to the third member of the triumvirate: Major General John Hamilton Roberts of Canada. Roberts, the "flesh" of Rees' analogy, was experiencing major career leaps: he had been newly promoted both to the rank and command of Second Canadian Division and was now appointed military commander of the Dieppe Raid.

Fifty-year-old "Ham" Roberts was a big man, tall and hefty, rock-like in physique and in temperament. He was not easily intimidated. As a junior officer with the Royal Canadian Horse Artillery in the First World War, he had been awarded the M.C. for valour at the Somme. In 1940, by then a lieutenant colonel, he had commanded a Canadian field regiment that landed at Brest as part of the British Expeditionary Force. The speed of the German advance alarmed the British and Roberts was ordered to return to England, destroying his guns and equipment so that they would not fall into enemy hands. This was a red flag to the bull-like Roberts.

The British commanding general, haggard and strained with the pressures of evacuating the British contingent, must have been startled when the upstart Canadian stormed into his office, flailing his fists and creating a furor over a mere 24 guns. But the artillery was Roberts' passion. He wasn't going to lose his guns. Heels dug in, he braved the general's fury and insisted that he be given the opportunity of rescuing them.

"You have two hours," the commander snapped. "Then your ship sails."

Roberts got his guns aboard with 30 minutes to spare — and used the extra time to snatch several more stray weapons that had been abandoned on the docks. That afternoon's work put Roberts in line for swift promotion to the rank of brigadier.

When Montgomery decided to replace the vintage Canadian battalion commanders with a younger breed, he gave Roberts the unpleasant task of firing them.

Roberts himself was an unwitting beneficiary of that carnage. Monty engineered the sacking of the aging Second Division commander, and then appointed Roberts as replacement. His first challenge was to transform a division of civilian soldiers, trained mainly in defence, into a crack unit in aggressive warfare. The disciplinary measures he imposed to achieve this proved the mettle of the man. On April 11, 1942, he was promoted to major general. A little over two weeks later he was placed in charge of the military force in the biggest raid of the war.

It was, perhaps, a case of too much, too fast, for a man with no infantry experience at all. Brigadier Stanley Todd, who in 1942 commanded an artillery field regiment in Roberts' division, notes:

> People don't realize that many of our professional soldiers were at the level of captains and majors when war broke out, and suddenly they became major generals. At his own level, General Roberts was a great soldier. Ham had been a gunner all his life, and when he was appointed GOC [General Officer Commanding] Second Division his gunner friends were delighted with his promotion. But we were slightly concerned as to his welfare in commanding an infantry division when he had no experience of infantry except in training camps.
>
> People said he was naïve from a tactical point of view, but I don't think he was naïve; he was just not knowledgeable. I don't remember Ham ever being sent on a staff course. He didn't have the experience to understand what he was getting into.
>
> It's probably understandable that some of the British professional soldiers tended to look down on the Canadians. They thought we were toy soldiers. They thought we had amazing men with amazing courage, no discipline and stupid officers.[24]

In early May 1942, in a mood of suppressed excitement, General Crerar briefed Roberts on the pending operation. A raid was going in at the end of June on the French port of Dieppe, he told him. His division had been selected to mount it.

For security reasons, Roberts was ordered to stay under cover in London until he was contacted by Combined Ops headquarters. A suite had been booked for him under an assumed name at the Mayfair Hotel.

Roberts was holed up for several days, forbidden even to make a telephone call. He was impatient to get started with the intensified training needed to prepare his men for their first encounter with the enemy. Finally, Montgomery summoned him and reviewed the entire operation. It was the first time Roberts had seen any details of the raid. The Canadians, he now learned, had inherited a made plan.

It was also made clear to Roberts that the project was not his to refuse. His son, Major John Roberts, then 22, had been posted to England at about this time. "My understanding in conversation with my father not long afterwards was that [Dieppe] had been offered to another division, but that it had managed to beg off. My father was told that Second Division was going to run the raid; that he had no alternative. The raid was wished on him. It was not of his making," Major Roberts stated flatly.[25]

Roberts senior must have known he was facing an awesome task. He would be working for the first time with senior British officers of the Royal Navy and the RAF in a major operation. His years in the Permanent Force between the wars had been spent in relatively obscure Canadian posts. He had not attended the British Army Staff College in Camberley where his British counterparts had been schooled in theoretical strategy and tactics, and where they also made the connections to the "old boys' net" that were so valuable to a career officer.

Perhaps Goronwy Rees best summed up the differences between the polished officers in Montgomery's command and the homespun Canadian. Roberts, he said, was "as rough and ready as Monty was fine and calculating."[26]

At first, Roberts must have been swept off his feet by the importance of the assignment and the prestige of those who were endorsing it. Later, as the plan began to evolve — or in point of fact, erode — he began to develop serious apprehensions. His confidence in his men of Second Division never wavered; but his confidence in the *plan* they were to carry out began to disintegrate.

One can only speculate on the turmoil in this man's mind as the doubts grew like tumours within him. All he could do now was hope that it would — somehow — work out.

———

Denis Whitaker

When can a soldier say no?

I believe that the Canadian government exerted unjustifiable pressure on its army and corps commanders, Generals McNaughton and Crerar, to get Canadian troops into action. Roberts became the scapegoat for Canadian prime minister King's anti-conscription obsession, and for the military ambitions of McNaughton, Crerar and Simonds.

It seems to me very unfair and unreasonable that a fine gunnery officer with no infantry experience was asked to direct the largest and most complex amphibious infantry assault of the war.

The excellent reputation he had earned over twenty-five years was thereby put at risk. We know that Roberts' initial reaction was enthusiastic. He would have been flattered that a plan designed by so experienced a commander as Montgomery should be entrusted to his operational command. Besides, he was a "soldier's soldier": he could never have brought himself to refuse this assignment and thus abandon the men of his division. His loyalty to and affection for those under his command must have convinced him that somehow, things would work out.

Lieutenant General William Anderson, RCA, one of Canada's most highly regarded and experienced general officers, concurred that Ham Roberts could not have said no.

Anderson, who was posted to England as General Crerar's personal assistant at about that time, remembers that "there was inference in some quarters that Roberts should have said 'This isn't a proper plan — it is unsound militarily — the Canadians won't do it,' or words to that effect.

"My view is that you have to put yourself back in the context of 1942. The British were fighting all over the world. The Canadian army had done bugger-all. We were still just training and training. The pressure was on that we had to get into action!

"In that context it would have been unthinkable for any Canadian to say, 'We won't do it,' or 'We shouldn't try this.' Ham was enough of a soldier to realize that an order's an order. He would not have been intimidated or overawed; he was a man of pretty sturdy principles who would not allow himself to be kicked around. But he would not compromise easily on things he thought were really important or against his principles.

"I felt here was a good honest soldier caught in the crosscurrents of opinionated people like Crerar, Montgomery, Paget and Mountbatten who were looking after their post-Dieppe interests."[27]

CHAPTER

8

THE MOLOTOV COCKTAIL

It was teatime on a sweltering May afternoon in Washington. The valet at 1600 Pennsylvania Avenue N.W. had welcomed the foreign guest to the prestigious Rose Suite and was routinely unpacking his suitcases when he encountered a strangely shaped package at the bottom of one of the bags. Puzzled, he ran his hand over it. The brown paper wrapping fell open to reveal . . . a large sausage.

Now thoroughly mystified, the valet searched further and found a hunk of black bread . . . and a pistol.

Vyachoslav M. Molotov had more need for the sustenance — Mrs. Roosevelt's White House cuisine being noted for its monotony — than he did for the gun. The Soviet People's Commissar for Foreign Affairs already held a powerful weapon at the heads of Churchill and Roosevelt: the threat of leaving them to fight Germany on their own.

His ammunition was powerful. The Red Army could not hold out against the Germans much longer. Seventy percent of Hitler's forces — some 150 divisions — were now concentrated on the Russian front. At that very moment their tanks were a menacing 80 miles from Moscow. The Americans and British *must* make a cross-Channel attack this coming summer. By 1943 it might well be too late.

Molotov told Roosevelt and his U.S. Chiefs of Staff of the horrible suffering of the Russians. Millions of soldiers and civilians had been killed, whole villages devastated. In one German-occupied town, only three houses had survived out of a thousand. The Germans looted everything they could get their hands on, seizing food and fuel and even carrying off livestock. The people had nowhere to live and nothing to eat. Scurvy was a severe problem.

Luxury items like sugar, fats and tobacco had almost disappeared. In Moscow, a man could make a tidy profit by selling puffs of the cigarette he was smoking to passers-by — at two roubles a drag.

It would be impossible for his country to last another year, Molotov insisted. If Russia should fall, he argued, the Allies would inevitably lose as well. Not only would a Nazi victory release a vast number of German divisions to turn their attention towards the west, but the Germans would also gain access to Russian oil in the Caucasus and the raw materials of the Ukraine. And, if they advanced even farther, they would control the Middle East oil and dominate the Suez Canal, opening up the possibility of Germany linking up with Japan at India.

Molotov had fired off his most potent shots. One round still remained: the implied threat that the Russians might sue for a separate peace with the Germans, just as the Bolsheviks had done with the Kaiser in 1918. He knew that the United States and Britain could not afford to lose Russia as an ally.

Molotov was shrewdly playing on the two Anglo-American soft spots: the dependence of the American government on popular opinion, which was pushing hard for action, and the disharmony that British duplicity over Modicum was fostering between the two countries.

He was very much aware that Churchill was deceiving Roosevelt in feigning to go along with a cross-Channel attack in 1942. Ambassador Maisky had already reported to him that Churchill had accepted Roosevelt and Marshall's Modicum proposals in their entirety, and was now engaged in the "systematic sabotage" of them.[1]

Molotov was equally aware that Roosevelt, too, was playing less than straight. The American president had gone behind Churchill's back by inviting the Russian foreign affairs minister to Washington to explore second-front possibilities. Roosevelt had not consulted or even informed London before the fact.[2] "The impression was left with me that Roosevelt really did want to meet Stalin alone, without Churchill," Ambassador Maisky had confided to Molotov.[3]

Before coming to Washington, Molotov nevertheless took it upon himself to stop off in Britain. Wartime security made this a complex operation. On May 20, the mysterious "Mr. Cocktail" — the British intelligence codename for Molotov — landed in Dundee and clambered aboard the prime minister's private train for London.

His suspicions were confirmed the next day when he and Maisky had a lengthy meeting with Churchill at 10 Downing Street. "The People's Commissar for Foreign Affairs . . . pressingly demanded the earliest possible opening of a second front in Northern France," Maisky later reported.[4]

Churchill had refused to commit himself, citing "alleged" excuses. There could be no major invasion that year, he told the Russian:

> Britain even together with the U.S.A., was not able in 1942 to organize an effective second front in France. They had not as yet a sufficient number of planes, landing craft and other military equipment. At best the cross-Channel operation is fraught with great risk. . . . There is much about it that is guesswork . . . the probability of extensive losses is very great.

Churchill's final prophecies were his gloomiest. "The waters of the Channel would be red with blood of our lads," he predicted. All that they could do in 1942, he added, was to "intensify to the maximum their air bombardments of Germany and prepare energetically for the invasion of Northern France in 1943."[5]

The next day, May 23rd, Brooke and Mountbatten spent three hours with Churchill intensely discussing the Dieppe raid and exploring the prospects for invasion. They were obviously perturbed by the squeeze they were in between Molotov's threats and Roosevelt's urgings.[6]

Molotov flew on to Washington, convinced that the British were now lukewarm about Sledgehammer. He was not impressed with their excuses about logistical shortages, speculating that the historic British suspicion of the communist regime was at the bottom of their reluctance. He wondered if there was not a resurgence of the old British dream that Germany and Russia could be "somehow played off against each other" until both countries were too weak to pose any problems to the British Empire.[7]

On May 27th, the British launched their first formal salvo to torpedo Sledgehammer. At the regular evening Chiefs of Staff meeting, Portal pointed out that deterioration on the Russian front might make it essential to undertake the operation "even at heavy cost to ourselves." General Paget settled the debate by insisting that "we could not put ashore more than 4,300 men, together with 160 tanks, in the first flight." Churchill agreed that it would be "looking for trouble" to try to force a bridgehead with such limited equipment.[8]

It would be another six weeks before Churchill would fully disclose to the Americans the Chiefs' secret thumbs down on Sledgehammer. But he hinted at it, very obliquely, in a cable he sent to Roosevelt the next day. Without suggesting that they were cancelling Sledgehammer, Churchill planted the seed for another venture, one that he vastly preferred. He urged the Americans to consider an operation against French North Africa instead.

Molotov's departure for the United States had provoked a collective sigh of relief from the British. The stubborn commissar, his hosts agreed, "had all the grace and conciliation of a totem pole."[9]

Privately Roosevelt and his Chiefs of Staff agreed with the assessment. After a few days of his company, the exasperated Americans dubbed him with the rather more inelegant epithet of "Stone Ass."[10]

And Stone Ass he remained as he relentlessly hammered in his point. "Molotov's English was limited to four words," Russian journalist Alexander Werth related: "Yes," "no" and "second front."[11] For three trying days in Washington the Soviet glowered sourly while his interpreter, V.N. Pavlov, pounded out his unyielding demand for a "straight answer" confirming their intentions.

Molotov was gambling that if he could get Roosevelt onside, it would put into operation a squeeze play between his two allies that would force Churchill to cooperate. The ploy worked.

On Sunday morning, May 31, Roosevelt called in his Chiefs of Staff and military advisors for an impromptu meeting.

"I want to read you a draft of a telegram I propose sending to Churchill," he started out cheerfully. "It will be the basis of a communiqué we will issue simultaneously."

Roosevelt's proposed cable horrified his planners. It stated that in view of the "precariousness" of the Russian situation, the United States was giving its pledge to Stalin that the Allies would stage a second front "in August."

"You can't say 'in August!' " an alarmed Marshall protested. After all, he reminded his boss, it was the British who would be mounting the assault and providing most of the ground forces. They would naturally resent being pinned down so precisely to its timing. Roosevelt reluctantly changed the last two words to "the fall of 1942."[12]

"You can't say 'in 1942!' " Marshall retorted again. He underlined their misgivings. Churchill's recent cable had imparted the first "danger signals" that the British were beginning to waver from their agreed course about launching Sledgehammer in 1942.[13]

But this time Roosevelt impatiently shrugged off the warning. It was better, he insisted, to lie to the Russians than to send them away without hope of support. "Encouragement, even when based on false premises, would stiffen the Soviet will," he blandly assured his Chief of Staff.[14]

Roosevelt's service chiefs had become totally frustrated by the haphazard way the American president went off on his own strategic tangent without consulting his military experts. They thought he was impulsive and disorganized, and had no system like Churchill's of holding regular meetings. "He is a rank amateur in all military affairs," complained one of Roosevelt's army planners."[15]

A good deal more than two words would be changed before the official communiqué was made public. So mesmerized was Roosevelt by Molotov's persuasiveness that he gave the Russian a virtual free hand to rephrase the communiqué to his satisfaction.

"Full understanding was reached with regard to the urgent tasks of creating a second front in Europe in 1942," became the Soviet-edited version which was released to the world.[16]

Armed with this fresh ammunition, Molotov packed up his pistol and returned to London to wave the memorandum smugly in Churchill's face. "We were not consulted about this wording," protested Anthony Eden, "and we could not have agreed to it, with its implication of a final pledge."[17]

But the British were trapped by their own duplicity. Had they not made exactly that commitment to the Americans at the Modicum conference? The Chiefs had no option but to capitulate. Reluctantly, they inserted that damning "full understanding was reached" clause in their own British-Russian communiqué, which would be released in tandem with the American one.

"We could not give the enemy the comfort of conflicting communiqués," Eden said.[18]

No amount of British backtracking could undo the damage of that dispatch. Churchill tried. He handed Molotov a private *aide-mémoire*, drafted by his Chiefs of Staff. It included the loophole clause that Roosevelt had been so unwilling to insert: while "preparations were being made for a continental landing in August or September 1942 ... we can give no promise in the matter."[19]

Stalin deliberately ignored Churchill's private rider, and focussed only on the Anglo-American assurances that a second front would be opened that year. When the joint Allied communiqués were made public a short time later, a huge public outcry of joy swept the free world.

In Russia, 1,200 deputies were flown from every distant part of the country to the Kremlin for a special meeting of the Supreme Soviet Assembly. It was the first gathering of this auspicious body since the beginning of the war. A Russian journalist described the startling transformation this influx made on drab, shattered, impoverished Moscow.

"There were many colourful oriental costumes and dresses in the front half of the floor. Many of the women wore bright scarves and sari-like dresses, and many men wore embroidered colourful caps, and many of the faces were Mongol, and others almost Indian-like."[20]

Pravda reported that Molotov's news of the "creation of a Second Front in 1942" was greeted by "stormy, lengthy applause" by the assembly.

"1942 must become the year of the enemy's final rout," the usually temperate newspaper crowed, becoming almost syrupy in its eulogizing. "Already the small children of France, looking across the misty sea, are whispering: 'There's a ship over there.' And the name of the ship is the Second Front."[21]

German propaganda broadcasts mocked Churchill's proclamation, implying that he was merely an American puppet. "He has always kept quiet about the fact that he himself had his own commander: a gentleman who is seldom referred to as such. You can guess who it is — Roosevelt.[22]

Churchill had manoeuvred himself into a corner in this round-robin of deception. It had begun when he stood silently by while Beaverbrook lied to the world that Britain was well equipped to stage such an invasion, when, in fact, assault landing craft were available to transport fewer than 5,000 troops.

The Russians seized upon this lie for their own propaganda. They built up even more second-front hysteria by repeating the inflammatory fabrication. "The U.S.A. and England had at their disposition a large body of armed forces and enormous military and technical reserves for waging war in Europe," the Russian people were informed.[23]

Next, the Chiefs matched Beaverbrook's craftiness with a double-dealing of their own. They pretended to the Americans at the Modicum conference in April that they would go along with their second front in 1942.

Finally, Roosevelt called the bluff of his "good friend" Churchill with a cunning exercise in diplomacy himself. He staged a *sub rosa* meeting with the Russians which he capped by issuing a public statement in both their names promising the Channel assault that year. Roosevelt knew he couldn't uphold that promise without British cooperation — and he knew the British wouldn't risk a confrontation by publicly backing out of their Modicum commitment. They *had* to go along with him.

The pressure of that festering boil, the second front, was causing an irreparable rupture in the Allied grand alliance.

For Churchill there was only one answer — a meeting with Roosevelt in Washington.

PART

4

JUNE 1942

General Andrew McNaughton: Holding a dagger at the heart of Berlin. (NAC)

Prime Minister Mackenzie King: Unity at any price. (NAC)

General Harry Crerar: Canadian catalyst for action. (NAC)

Churchill, Montgomery and Brooke. (Imperial War Museum)

Churchill and Eisenhower: Deadlock in London. (Personal collection: Terrance Macartney-Filgate)

Stalin (r.) and Molotov: Second front now! (USAMHI, Carlisle, Pa.)

U.S. Chief of Staff General George Marshall: Day of the Dupes. (USAMHI, Carlisle, Pa.)

Canadian General Hamilton Roberts: "History will exonerate me." (NAC)

Lord Louis Mountbatten (r.): "Churchill's dynamic protégé responds to a crescendo of activity on the Continent." (Personal collection: Terrance Macartney-Filgate)

Churchill, Roosevelt and Stalin: The Big Three. (USAMHI, Carlisle, Pa.)

R boats crossing the Channel to Dieppe. (NAC)

Landing craft mechanized (LCM) loading up for the assault. (NAC)

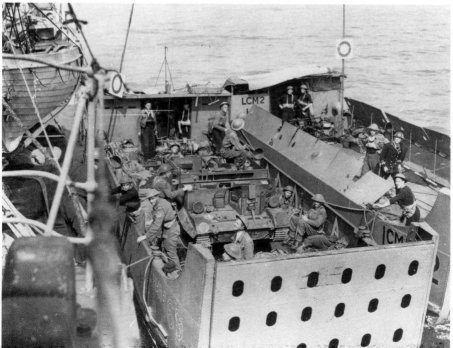

Piper Alec Graham pipes the Queen's Own Cameron Highlanders into the attack at Pourville. (Artist: Gordon Wilson)

Puys: Photo taken from German concrete pillbox on the headland. Royal Regiment troops assaulting this beach were mowed down by enfilade fire and grenades tossed from the cliff top. (Personal collection: Terrance Macartney-Filgate)

Royal Regiment beach at Puys: Most of the 207 dead were killed at this wall. (Personal collection: Terrance Macartney-Filgate)

View of Green Beach at Pourville, looking west. (Personal collection: Terrance Macartney-Filgate)

Esplanade and main beach at low tide after the battle. View is from castle on west headlands. Casino is to the right. It had been partially destroyed by Germans. (Personal collection: Terrance Macartney-Filgate)

Sandbagged German strongpoint behind the wall on the main beach. Note barbed-wire obstacle in background. (Personal collection: Terrance Macartney-Filgate)

One of the many concealed concrete gun positions in a cave in the west cliff. Note the bullet holes in the gun shield. (Personal collection: Terrance Mccartney-Filgate)

German infantry in esplanade slit trench that was attacked by the author. (Bundesarchiv, Koblenz)

Six-gun battery codenamed Hess at Varengeville, successfully destroyed by Lovat's Commando. Gun is a 155-mm French Filion. Note camouflage. (French Army photo)

A Boston medium bomber retires after dropping its load on Dieppe (top left).

Major Pat Porteous, VC, of 4 Commando. (Personal collection: Terrance Macartney-Filgate)

German NCO leads troops of 571 Infantry Regiment in rush to man defensive positions on headlands between Dieppe and Pourville. Mortar team bring up rear. (Bundesarchiv, Koblenz)

Commandos harass enemy in battery position while awaiting Lovat's main assault from behind. (Artist: Gordon Wilson)

Lovat's No. 4 Commando breaches the wire at Varengeville. (Artist: Gordon Wilson)

B Company of Royal Hamilton Light Infantry storms the casino. The company commander was killed in the attack. (Artist: Gordon Wilson)

Lieutenant Colonel Cec Merritt, VC, leads his men across the bridge at Pourville. (Artist: Gordon Wilson)

French firefighters putting out fire at Hotel Villa Bristol on the esplanade. Roof was destroyed, probably by bombing or shelling. German infantry in foreground are patrolling for wounded Canadians. The low wall with the iron fence was the furthest point of penetration by the author, where he crouched while enemy machine-gun fire swept the road. (Bundesarchiv, Koblenz)

"Blitz buggy" jeep loaded with high explosives for the sappers to breach the Dieppe wall. Most of the engineers were killed or wounded before they got to that point. Note bundle of chespaling for tanks. (French Army photo)

After the battle, a German Red Cross soldier investigates assault craft. Scout car "Helen" in foreground was used for signals. Beached LCT behind provided some protection from enemy fire for Canadian wounded. Tank in background was drowned when shell fire shattered the LCT's ramp. (French Army photo)

Beached LCT still smoking from direct hit. Disabled tanks and dead on main beach. U.S. Ranger Lieutenant Randall identified by American gaitors, lies nearest the tank. (Personal collection: Terrance Macartney-Filgate)

German soldiers walk past the Canadian dead after the battle. Note Lieutenant Ed Bennett's disabled tank "Bellicose" with its treads shot off. Beached LCT is in background. (Personal collection: Terrance Macartney-Filgate)

Churchill tank bogged down in antitank ditch. Note concertina wire obstacle. (Personal collection: Terrance Macartney-Filgate)

Canadian survivors boarding a destroyer from an LCA. (NAC)

Wounded Canadian prisoners being cared for by French nuns. (Personal collection: Terrance Macartney-Filgate)

The aftermath: Canadian dead and their weapons on main beach. (Personal collection: Terrance Macartney-Filgate)

A German photograph of wounded Canadian soldiers being marched off to POW camp. Lieutenant Fred Woodcock (c.), RHLI, was blinded in battle. (NAC)

Canadian prisoners marching down Rue de Sygogne behind the casino. Left front is RHLI Padre H/Captain John Foote, who was awarded the VC. The battalion doctor, Captain Wes Clair, is on the right. (Bundesarchiv, Koblenz)

Blindfolded German POWs are escorted back to England. (NAC)

Soldier of No. 4 Commando gives a light to U.S. Ranger Sergeant Alex Szima after the raid. Lovat's Commando wore woollen hats for the attack. (NAC)

CHAPTER

9

PRECIPICE AT HYDE PARK

Winston Churchill padded into his Hyde Park bedroom, pink and plump from a long soak in the tub, just as Franklin Roosevelt was wheeled in for a chat. Churchill seized a towel, waving off apologies for the intrusion: "The Prime Minister of Great Britain has nothing to conceal from the President of the United States."

When reminded of the incident shortly afterwards, he grinned mischievously, "the President himself would have been well aware that it was not strictly true."[1]

When attempts are made to assess Churchill's character as a wartime leader, it is too often forgotten that in peacetime he was a professional writer and historian. He always had an eye to the rhetoric of war.

His position was unique. As a politician and statesman he was in the process of *making* history; but at the same time, as a journalist, he was *recording* history in his mind's eye. And he knew for a certainty that in the not-too-far-distant future he would also be the first to be *writing* that history. A.J.P. Taylor observed that "he had been writing and living history for well over forty years, and no one was more anxious than he that all that he did and all that he said would be judged by the historians of the future. This must have influenced him, both consciously and unconsciously, particularly when he set out his arguments in memoranda which he knew would become historical documents."[2]

So it was that Churchill-the-politician, keen on maintaining good relations with his allies, approved the *public* release in early June of the joint communiqué promising Stalin his second front by year's end. And so it also was that Churchill-the-historian, with an eye to how he would look when he inevitably backed out of the deal, made sure that he covered his tracks by sending Stalin a *private* memo containing an escape clause: "we can give no promise in the matter."[3]

And so it was that at Hyde Park, Churchill-the-politician could toss off a witticism about the abiding trust in his relationship with his host. But Churchill-the-historian would cynically shrug off the incident, knowing that history would one day expose their real relationship.

Joke all he may, the pair truly did have plenty to conceal from each other; both had been double-dealing quite recently, first over Modicum and then over the Molotov affair. Despite this, they had established a curious camaraderie in the course of three long visits and frequent transatlantic chats in less than a year.

Harry Hopkins, who was with them more often than anyone else, believed that the bond was created because they were both in the same line of business: politico-military leadership on a global scale.

> They used to stroll in and out of each other's rooms. They established an easy intimacy, a joking informality and a moratorium on pomposity and cant — and also a degree of frankness in intercourse which, if not quite complete, was remarkably close to it. But neither of them ever forgot for one instant what he was and represented or what the other was and represented.[4]

Churchill alternatively viewed Roosevelt as a man of "infinite subtlety," or an "artful dodger," depending on how charitably he felt towards him at the given moment. The prime minister was prepared to use any tactic to get his way. "No lover ever studied every whim of his mistress as I did those of President Roosevelt," he once confided to Brooke.[5]

When he did get his way, however, he confessed to a more cavalier attitude: "That's the way we talked when we were wooing her. Now that she is in the harem, we talk to her quite differently."[6]

Roosevelt, in turn, alternately admired Churchill's tenacity — or wearied of his mulishness.

A small incident that underlined the insecurity of Churchill's relationship with the Americans took place soon after Churchill's plane set down at the little airport at New Hackensack, near Hyde Park. Roosevelt himself met him, driving a car — a small Ford especially designed for the disabled. The two men toured Roosevelt's estate where he proudly showed his visitor the dramatic landscape. The excursion gave Churchill some "thoughtful" moments.

He took me to the majestic bluffs over the Hudson River on which Hyde Park, the family home, stands. Mr. Roosevelt's infirmity prevented him from using his feet on the brake, clutch, or accelerator. An ingenious arrangement enabled him to do everything with his arms . . . I confess that when on several occasions the car poised and backed on the grass verges of the precipices over the Hudson I hoped the mechanical devices and brakes would show no defects.[7]

In June 1942, with the British Empire crumbling, Churchill found himself, not for the first time, poised politically at just such a precipice and at the mercy of American skill, industrial power, and cooperation. He needed the Americans in Europe. He hoped that their strategic brakes would not slip and that no American flaws or defects would imperil him.

The growing familiarity of the two men alarmed their Chiefs of Staff. For two days the pair had hibernated cosily at the Roosevelt family home, where the Hudson's cooling breezes did much to alleviate the June heat. Back in Washington, Brooke and Marshall, meeting at the Munitions Building, sweltered and privately stewed at what the bosses might be "brewing up together" — as if their chiefs were two mischievous lads at a school reunion rather than two heads of state debating the destiny of millions.[8]

Brooke and Marshall were the two most powerful and militarily skilled men in the world, yet they were subject to the whims of two mercurial leaders — "amateurs," at that.

Brooke, on round-the-clock call to Churchill — who wanted to know every detail of every operation — envied Marshall's freedom from constant interference by Roosevelt. But Marshall, who operated in a "haphazard" system and was seldom consulted by his boss, envied Brooke's close association with the prime minister. "He informed me that he frequently did not see {Roosevelt] for a month or six weeks," Brooke noted wistfully in his diary. "I was fortunate if I did not see Winston for six hours."[9]

Well they might worry about the antics of their chiefs. Churchill *did* want something: a clear and final "out" from Sledgehammer. Even Mountbatten, with his charismatic flair with Americans, had failed to achieve this on a visit earlier in the month, although he had underlined the problems convincingly to the president during a five-hour dinner session. The two men had discussed as a possible alternative the pending assault on Dieppe.

Marshall and Admiral King had been more than a little upset that Roosevelt did not invite them to sit in on the meeting. They were even more peeved when they learned that Roosevelt had responded to Mountbatten's eloquence with a compromise suggestion: a "sacrifice landing" to help the Russians.[10]

Brooke was not impressed by the suggestion when it was relayed to him. It was all very well for the Americans to talk about a sacrifice invasion to save the Russians, but most of the lives they were offering up were British.

And he was adamant against Sledgehammer: "like a rock," as his biographer Sir David Fraser put it. It would be "another and worse Dunkirk."[11] As corps commander of the British Expeditionary Force, it was Brooke who had masterminded the stunning evacuation of the bulk of the British troops in 1940. He had no intention of allowing 150,000 men — almost the last of Britain's manpower resources — to be trapped on the coast of France again. This time, they might not be as lucky. In total frustration, he noted in his diary that he "could not get either Marshall or Stimson (Secretary of State Henry L. Stimson) to realize that operations across the Channel in 1942 and 1943 were doomed to failure. We should go in with half-trained divisions against a superior number of war hardened German divs."[12]

Meanwhile, at Hyde Park, Churchill and Roosevelt had many private chats during their brief holiday from their military staffs. Roosevelt extended his hour of retiring to accommodate Churchill's legendary late-night pow-wows; Churchill made an effort to shut off the conversational taps earlier than his customary 3 or 4 a.m.

They would make themselves comfortable in the small den, with a fire in the grate in deference to Churchill's chronically cold hands, and debate into the night.

The prime minister of Great Britain cut a strange figure. Rippled in fat, he wore a siren suit tailored in red, blue, or black velvet, often topped by a dressing gown of coronation splendour that flapped in gold-and-crimson hue about plump velvet-slippered feet. His neck obtruded in corpulent layers to frame a pale, pudgy face. He would sit benignly, holding his inevitable cigar — often unlit — always with a large brandy or Johnny Walker Red Label at his elbow.

Across from him, Roosevelt would be urbanely turned out in an elegant smoking jacket, waving his cigarette holder for emphasis with a practised hand. The president spoke with a patrician accent and a sparkling wit. A paraplegic for more than 20 years — a result of poliomyelitis — he still gave off an air of irresistible vitality.

The talk at Hyde Park at first focussed on "Tube Alloys," the cover name for the research being conducted by both countries on the awesome potential of atomic energy.[13]

But inevitably the two men came back to Sledgehammer. Churchill had come to America troubled that Roosevelt was "getting a bit off the rails."[14] He wanted to curb his friend's impatience to land American troops in France by diverting him to another theatre of action — North Africa. He explained that by clearing Rommel's forces out of North Africa and thence Egypt, the Allies would gain free use of the shipping routes through the Mediterranean and the Suez Canal.

The Mediterranean, he reminded him, was the gateway to the "strategic centre of gravity" — the Persian Gulf.[15] If access to the Suez were closed to them, 15,000 miles and 45 days would be added to their communication links with the Gulf and with important parts of the British Empire.

Churchill's eloquence had some effect; Roosevelt was warming to the Mediterranean strategy. After all, Churchill was offering him the one thing he wanted most: action against the Germans — even if it wasn't in Europe. It is "very important to morale to give this country a feeling that they are in the war," he explained to the Englishman.[16]

But when they returned to Washington they met set-in-stone opposition from the military staff of both sides of the Atlantic. In fact, while the "amateurs" had been deciding a Mediterranean strategy in Hyde Park, the American and British Combined Chiefs of Staff — in this context, the "professionals" — had been forming an alliance based on exactly the opposite strategy. Fearing the worst from the Russian Front, they had drafted a joint proposal for the immediate consideration of their bosses. It was essentially a reaffirmation of the Bolero concept decided upon at the Modicum conference in April — namely, that all military concentration should be focussed on Europe. Marshall, Brooke, and the other Joint Chiefs had also agreed unequivocally that Operation Torch — as the North African invasion that Churchill was promoting so actively would come to be called — "should not be undertaken in the present situation."[17]

It was a curious reversal. The consensus on Modicum in April had been split straight down the middle, but on national lines — the United States versus Britain. Now, two months later, the split was on professional lines: the Chiefs of Staff of both countries had joined forces against their bosses.

Although Brooke saw the Mediterranean strategy — and the oil that its supply lines would open up — as an absolutely essential prerequisite to tackling the Germans head-on in Europe, he did not agree with Churchill about the timing. With the British suffering serious reverses in North Africa, it was too early to consider such an assault; this was a classic case of Churchill precipitously rushing his fences. But Brooke was equally disturbed, perhaps with justification, about what the motives of his American counterparts might actually be in pushing for a second front. He increasingly suspected, as did Churchill, that the Americans were out to "cripple the British empire regardless of the consequences."[18]

"I have not become the King's First Minister in order to preside over the liquidation of the British Empire," Churchill had stoutly declared.[19]

The way one analyst saw it, "Churchill and Brooke were committed to an imperialist strategy and Torch was an exercise in imperialism. But the U.S. was committed to an anti-imperialist strategy; Roosevelt was bitter about the empire. Brooke had to string the Americans along."[20]

This necessity to "string the Americans along" was acknowledged — though not relished — by British strategists. After all, the U.S. had the bulk of the money, the men and the matériel. However, it annoyed them that the Americans were capitalizing so blatantly on their position of strength, "seizing more and more power" so that they could "run the war from Washington." This especially rankled as Britain, alone for the first two years, had previously had full control of the war.[21]

Damaging self-interest, rather than concern about defeating Germany, was creating a power play between the two countries. The British Chiefs of Staff feared that the Americans were putting their ingrained political biases against the British Empire ahead of everyone's military needs.[22]

Marshall and his Chiefs harboured similarly uncomplimentary suspicions about the British motives. Torch, they pondered peevishly, was just one more example of the British using Roosevelt to hang on to their empire. As well, the American Chiefs thought the "defensive-minded" British had an ingrained repugnance for an invasion of France which would cause them to exaggerate their difficulties in order to get out of their commitment to the Russians.

Lieutenant Colonel Albert Wedemeyer, U.S. member of the Joint Staff Planners, was especially bitter about what he termed the British "elastic scruples." He reported that the British had 34 divisions available: they surely could have spared 6 or 8 if a desperation strike had been indicated.[23]

He feared they were being outmanoeuvred by the professional glibness of the British. As one historian put it, the Americans "suspected the British, rightly, of backing away from that [cross-Channel assault] in favour of Mediterranean operations for which military arguments concealed political purposes."[24]

Roosevelt's military staff was adamantly in favour of immediate cross-Channel action. That is why they were pushing Sledgehammer. The Middle East was their "last priority of all," Secretary of State Stimson had declared. Prophetically, Stimson warned that soon "the British would be howling for help there. We really should not give it to them . . . now is the time to stand pat."[25]

Clearly, there had to be some cross-Channel operation this summer. But it was a no-win situation for the Allies. If Russia was to survive the latest German offensive, Stalin would be furious if the Allies were to renege on the deal and he would possibly sue for a separate peace. Yet if Russia folded, the enemy would gather in strength on the western front, making it impossible to mount an invasion the next year.

So Sledgehammer had become the Americans' insurance policy to ensure that the Allied focus stayed where they wanted it: on France for 1942. Could they be persuaded to change their stance? That was the underlying reason for Churchill's visit.

Roosevelt's advisors were understandably worried that their boss might "jump the traces." Stimson warned his boss testily against considering Churchill's North African notion: "No new plans should even be whispered," he admonished. "When one is engaged in a tug of war, it is highly risky to spit on one's hands even for the purpose of getting a better grip."[26]

Colonel Wedemeyer observed with some bitterness, "With their ingrained habit of assuming authority, born of centuries of domination, the British naturally expected Washington to defer to whatever strategy was decided upon by their own military and civilian chiefs."[27] These suspicions made the American military hierarchy all the more determined to cling to Sledgehammer, if only to restrain wild diversionary efforts proposed by the British prime minister." Sledgehammer was becoming just that: a rather spiteful weapon the Americans were wielding to pound the British into reluctant acquiescence.[28]

Sadly, the two powers could not even fall back on their verbal skills to sort out the profound misunderstanding festering between them. They weren't even talking the same language. Though the words were the same, their meanings were often poles apart in interpretation. For example, when their transatlantic friends suggested that an item be "tabled" — with the British meaning of being entered on record for deliberation — the Americans got riled. They thought that meant that the motion was to be shelved or postponed.[29]

Air Marshal Sir Charles Portal, the air force element of the British Chiefs of Staff Committee, recalled an incident that graphically illustrated this linguistic confusion. Portal had been trying to make the point with the Chief of the U.S. naval staff, the crusty Admiral King. The American public could be *educated* to recognise the wisdom and necessity of the policy of concentrating first against the Germans before the Japanese.

"Admiral King retorted waspishly, 'I'll have you know that the American public is as well *educated* as the British.' "[30]

———

Sunday, June 21, a day when temperatures soared both in Fahrenheit and emotion — became known to the American and British Chiefs as the "Day of the Dupes." Their brief was ready for presentation to Churchill and Roosevelt: it stated clearly that priority must be given to building up strategic reserves in England. "Continental operations on a large scale at the earliest possible moment should be the principal offensive effort of the United Nations." A North African operation would be a meaningless diversion that would do nothing to help Russia and should not be undertaken in the present situation.[31]

Then an event occurred that wiped any thought of long-term considerations from the planners' minds. At 7:30 a.m., Roosevelt's naval aide, Captain John McCrea, had checked the White House map room for overnight cables. He then walked to the south entrance to meet Roosevelt and Churchill, who were just arriving by train from New York. "If anything important comes in, bring it to me immediately," the young aide had instructed the watch officer.

In fact, an urgent dispatch did soon come. The president glanced at it and said quietly to Captain McCrea, "Show this to Winston."

McCrea crossed the room and handed it to Churchill. The prime minister's pink cheeks "faded visibly," McCrea later remembered. "I can't understand it," the captain heard him gasp. "I simply can't understand it."[32]

In the pink slip of paper Churchill read, "Tobruk has fallen. Forces at our command in this theatre are inadequate to enable us to cope with the enemy."[33] The entire garrison of 25,000 men — a figure later revised to 33,000 — had surrendered to Axis forces of less than half that number.

It was a "body blow" for Churchill. The upset was as stunning as the seizure of Singapore the previous February when 85,000 British and Commonwealth troops had been taken prisoner by a small force of Japanese; as shocking as the loss of Crete, where in 1941 the British had been driven off the island by German paratroopers. Perhaps the most devastating thing of all was that Churchill knew from top-secret Ultra sources, the British intelligence system of intercepting and deciphering coded enemy signals, that Rommel's Afrika Korps had been severely short of fuel and ammunition.

Tobruk was on the Libyan coast near the Egyptian border. Its capture, besides opening the gate for Rommel to sweep eastward through Egypt to the Suez, put Britain's credibility on the line with her allies. The inevitable doubt had been planted: had the British troops lost their cutting edge?

General Ismay later described how the prime minister and his military advisors reacted to this "hideous and totally unexpected shock."

> The silence was broken by President Roosevelt. In six monosyllables he epitomized his sympathy with Churchill, his determination to do his utmost to sustain him, and his recognition that we were all in the same boat: "What can we do to help?"[34]

Brooke noted later:

> I cannot remember what the actual words were that the President used to convey his sympathy, but I remember vividly being impressed by the tact and real heartfelt sympathy which laid behind these words. There was not one word too much nor one word too little.[35]

Roosevelt immediately offered three hundred Sherman tanks and one hundred 105-mm self-propelled guns for the North African defenders — arms taken from his own divisions that he could ill afford to give away.

That evening in his bedroom, a shattered Churchill muttered to his physician, Lord Moran, "I am ashamed. I cannot understand why Tobruk gave in. More than 30,000 of our men put their hands up. If *they* won't fight . . . " and then stopped abruptly.

Churchill then made a curious aside that revealed how very vulnerable he was to any threats to his prestige at such a sensitive stage of negotiations with the Americans: "What matters is that it should happen when I am here." Clearly, he hated to lose Tobruk, but he hated most that it had happened in front of his allies.

Lord Moran prepared to spend the night with his patient, fearing that he might fall into one of the deep and prolonged depressions that had plagued him all his life. "Black Dog" was Churchill's name for this crippling disorder. "A mistake would get him down," Moran later said of these episodes, some of which lasted for months.

Instead, Moran glimpsed the stirring of combativeness. His patient was rallying from his initial slump. It was clear that Churchill had somehow found a way out of his terrible predicament. "Before I left his bedroom on Sunday," his physician noted, "Winston had refused to take the count; he got up a little dazed, but full of fight."[36]

Whitaker Commentary

We can only speculate on just what Roosevelt, Churchill and Brooke talked about on their last night together. However, we can make a reasonable assumption, based on the following observations:

Churchill's swift recovery from the news of Tobruk's fall was uncharacteristic. At first he was horrified and depressed, much as he had been after previous reversals in his life — after Gallipoli, for instance, and after the Singapore defeat. But from this episode he recovered almost immediately. Something had galvanized Churchill, and there is circumstantial evidence at least that it was the sudden realization that he could turn adversity to triumph by playing on Roosevelt's genuine sympathy.

Persuade your people to drop their insistence on Sledgehammer, he might have said. Convince them that Torch is the answer, especially now that our problems in North Africa have magnified.

In return, we'll stage a super-raid on France. It will be the first of its kind, a miniature invasion involving all the supporting arms. This could be enough to appease Russia. At least we would be demonstrating our willingness to fight, even though initially on a small scale.

You yourself talked of a sacrifice raid this summer, Churchill might have reminded Roosevelt. You told Molotov that if necessary you would be prepared to sacrifice the lives of 120,000 men this summer.[37]

The raid on Dieppe need not be a sacrifice to achieve our ends. It would test the enemy defences on the French coast as effectively with 6,000 men as Sledgehammer would with 150,000. It's ready to be mounted; troops are training for it as we speak. Because it is scheduled in two weeks' time, we can still prepare for a major invasion next year, having gained essential pre-invasion experience and knowledge.

Skilfully, persuasively, Churchill could have exploited the disaster into the personal triumph that Lord Moran was glimpsing. "He made use of the crisis as an argument for postponing the second front," his physician observed. "Without help from anyone, he has sustained the theme that only an invasion of North Africa can relieve the crisis.

"With our military prestige zero here, [Winston] dominated the discussions . . . He has not allowed the facts, damaging as they are, to handicap him. At this game, there is no one here of his own weight."[38]

Churchill, fighting for his life, would have had no difficulty describing to the president the consequences of the British defeat in North Africa. And he would have waved at Roosevelt a Washington newspaper that announced yet another devastating blow to their shared cause: Britain's House of Commons — with no little encouragement behind the scenes from his "friend" Beaverbrook — was challenging his conduct of the war with a call for a vote of censure on July 2, five days hence: CHURCHILL FACES STORMY SESSION WHEN HOUSE CONVENES. TOBRUK FALL MAY BRING CHANGE OF GOVERNMENT.[39]

Brooke would surely have added his weight to the argument. The CIGS had a great capacity to view issues in their broadest perspective as well as the strength of character to make tough, fast decisions for the sake of long-range benefits. Obviously, the British had to divert the Americans and Russians from Sledgehammer — a premature and dangerous second front. If they could persuade them to accept the Dieppe operation as a substitute, so much the better.

There had to be a trade-off — a compromise between the American demand for a Channel assault that courted disaster, and the British need for a North African operation to forestall disaster. The obvious approach was to offer a watered-down Channel assault immediately, followed by a major one in a year, in return for American support in North Africa.

Certainly, Brooke displayed some very uncharacteristic behaviour. For almost the first time in his career, he changed his mind abruptly on a matter of strategy.

Before the Tobruk crisis he had been dead against the Allies' switching their strategic focus to North Africa; yet by the time he returned to London a few days later, he was all for it. Even Sir David Fraser, Brooke's biographer, noted the "wavering." "He was seldom inconsistent, but this was an inconsistency."[40]

As long as his troops fought Germans, Roosevelt really didn't strongly care where they were "blooded." He too could see little alternative to Torch. Stalin had been promised a second front that year, no matter what: Dieppe could become their substitute for a second front. In fact, it would have to be.

———■———

Churchill left the White House in a confident mood. Although his armies had just been crushed and his leadership was in jeopardy, he had not panicked; nor had he slumped into a typical depression, as his physician feared. He had not run for home; instead, he went calmly on as if his problems were solved. The next day he flew to South Carolina, where he reviewed a demonstration of America's infantry, armour, and airborne at Fort Jackson.

On that "Day of Dupes," Marshall's memorandum was never even tabled. Instead, Lord Ismay diplomatically recorded a face-saving everybody-wins conclusion to the Anglo-American talks: An offensive in 1942 was essential. The build-up for Bolero would continue. Plans and preparations for cross-Channel operations would be pressed forward with "all possible speed, energy and ingenuity." But at the same time, an assault on North Africa (Gymnast/Torch) would be explored.[41]

———■———

On the night of June 25, the British contingent took off from Baltimore in their Boeing Clipper. To Brooke's amusement, the prime minister was dressed, as he had been on his departure from England, in his zip-suit and zip-shoes, "with a black Homburg hat on the side of his head and his small gold-topped malacca cane in his hand."[42]

As the flying boat lifted off from Chesapeake Bay, the travellers settled in for the 26-hour-long flight to Britain. Churchill and Brooke retired to the rear of the craft, where comfortable easy chairs had been installed. The stewards, already making up the berths amidships, knew their passengers' needs. On the outgoing journey, Churchill, when asked if he wanted high tea, had replied, "high whiskey."

The Englishmen now sank back thankfully with two large scotches — no ice this time — with what must have been a profound sense of relief that their visit to America was over.

Their drinks were finished, and their refills considerably lightened when Brooke glanced at the rotund figure beside him and recalled a prophetic moment seven days before as the pair were leaving for America.

> Suddenly, almost like Pooh Bear, [Winston] started humming "We are here because we are here — We are here because we are here!" This little song could not have been more appropriate. It was at a time when the Atlantic had not been so very frequently flown. We were both somewhat doubtful why we were going, whether we would get there, what we would achieve while we were there, and whether we should ever get back.[43]

Now the two leaders reflected quietly on the events of the past week. Had they achieved anything while they were there? The Americans were difficult to read. When Mountbatten had tackled Roosevelt three weeks earlier about the impossibility of a Channel assault in 1942, he had felt "quite sure that Mr. Roosevelt had at last accepted the British point of view." But it turned out that his impression was quite wrong. (Mountbatten's companion on that visit, Captain Hughes-Hallett, would recall that "the Prime minister had 'pulled our legs' about this, saying that 'it was not unusual for Ambassadors to fail in their missions, but they usually knew when they had failed!' ")[44]

Churchill and Brooke wondered if they, too, had been fooled by the president's courteous manner into thinking that the Allies had finally achieved a degree of harmony. Much rested on the president's ability to persuade his obstinate staff. For Roosevelt to pull off such a reversal in American strategy, against all the advice of his senior strategists, would be a minor miracle for Churchill, who in these circumstances was a determined David trying to subdue a rich and powerful Goliath. Which would it be? A Channel assault or French North Africa? Sledgehammer or Torch? He and his people would soon know the answer.

Churchill raised his glass in brave salute. He was returning to England to face on the one hand a military staff that didn't want a North African invasion, and on the other some insistent Members of Parliament who no longer wanted him to lead the country.

"Now for England, home, and — a beautiful row."[45]

CHAPTER

10

TIGHTEST LITTLE ISLAND

The small, diamond-shaped Isle of Wight is an enticing jewel that has attracted *overners* — "strangers from over the sea" — for more than 2,000 years.

The Romans called the island Vectis, and valued its benign climate as well as its strategic vantage points from which they could see predators plying their craft toward England. The Normans built a castle on the same high ground. Some 500 years later, Elizabethans on the island's heights had a grandstand view of the Armada as it sailed up the English Channel. In 1647, Charles I thought he had found sanctuary behind the castle's moated walls; but he was carted off after a year and beheaded.

Queen Victoria and Prince Albert sought another sort of sanctuary: an escape from the constant adulation of their subjects. In 1844 they built Osborne House, their home on the coast near Cowes, where they summered for 50 years. "It is impossible to imagine a prettier spot," the queen wrote to the King of Belgium. "We have a charming beach quite to ourselves — we can walk about anywhere by ourselves without being followed and mobbed."[1]

For over 100 years, the Royal Yacht Squadron has been a mecca to millionaire yachtsmen and royalty. Every August at the famous Cowes Regatta they hoist sails at the world's most prestigious yacht club to ply the waters of the Solent. In this narrow passage between the mainland and the island, schooners and ketches dodge the grand passenger liners steaming into Southampton.

Lord Tennyson composed some of his most famous poems during the 40 years he lived on the island. "The air on the downs is worth sixpence a pint!" he exclaimed.

But the same popularity that inspired Queen Victoria to seek the Isle of Wight as a refuge finally forced the poet to escape back to the

123

mainland. The *"overners"* — day trippers who ferried over in droves — were infringing on his privacy.

World War Two brought new invaders. British radar specialists found the high ground every bit as useful for detecting enemy movements as had their Elizabethan ancestors. The island's cliffs and steep ravines — known as "chines" — provided as ideal a ground for commandos in training as it had for smugglers of bygone days.

One unwelcome overner came from the skies. By mid-1942, the island had suffered its thousandth Luftwaffe raid in the past year. These were the notorious "tip and run" terror attacks. Typically, a pair of Focke Wulf raiders would swoop down under the radar curtain, so low that "they would almost take the top off a telephone kiosk." They would drop a couple of high-explosive bombs on military targets — or on civilian shops and cottages if they could find nothing better — rattle off a few rounds of machine gun fire, again at targets as casual as fishermen in their dories or pedestrians on the High Street — and then run for home.

Despite the deaths and property losses, the courage and good humour of these unique islanders prevailed. The local press reported after one raid that "an elderly woman, rescued from the wreckage of her home, emerged cheerful, despite losing her false teeth. . . . They were later recovered."[2]

In the third week of May 1942, new overners appeared on this much-overrun little island: invaders in khaki with Maple Leaf emblems on their shoulders. The local population, shrunk from its pre-war 85,000 to a mere 10,000 souls, watched in amazement as ferries disgorged 5,000 Canadian infantrymen, signallers and engineers; a tank regiment complete with 58 brand-new Churchill tanks; armoured scout cars, Bren gun carriers and jeeps; light anti-aircraft and field artillery detachments; and thousands of British sailors.

The island was evacuated of all but those locally employed and then sealed: for the next six weeks, no one except a handful of key military personnel was permitted access or exit. Yachtsmen's villas stood empty; offices and houses were deserted. (There were a couple of exceptions: modern-day smugglers such as the enterprising young Canadian woman who somehow managed a short-lived visit to her husband, a major in the Royal Regiment; and two married officers from the Essex Scottish who got ashore one night to see their wives.)

The importance of security was stressed at frequent briefings. "All mail is to be censored within the unit," the Royal Hamilton Light Infantry (RHLI) War Diary noted on May 22. "Strict censorship ordered by Div HQ, as the presence of Cdn troops on Isle of Wight is a matter of security, as is the type of training."[3]

The need for secrecy was underlined in a popular British film that was shown to all the men. *Next of Kin* told the story — very graphically — of the failure of a commando raid and the slaughter of its troops, all because of careless talk. The plot included a somewhat stereotyped young woman of ill repute — a clandestine enemy agent whose assignment was to seduce naïve young officers in order to gather details of forthcoming operations. A briefcase stuffed with top-secret documents was left in a London restaurant with huge consequences. The sobering finale showed the assault troops being greeted with a hail of lead. "They fell in heaps and never stood a chance," one officer in the audience reported. Afterwards, many in the audience remembered how schmaltzy it seemed at the time, and how uncannily prophetic it turned out to be.[4]

The Canadians had no notion that they were being groomed for a specific operation; to them, the Isle of Wight sojourn was just another training exercise, except that there was new emphasis on combined assault techniques.

Although only some 23 miles wide and 13 deep, the tiny island has such a broad range of magnificent scenery that it has always been known as a Britain in miniature. But it wasn't for her beauty that the soldiers sought her out. Her lush, rolling meadows, broad beaches and sheer cliffs offered the troops near-perfect training facilities for combined assault. Soon, booted feet pounded the narrow winding lanes that snaked and dipped across the downs. Tanks were instructed to skirt the ploughed and planted fields where essential crops were growing. Instead, the 40-ton monsters crashed heedlessly through hedges of wild purple rhododendron and verges thick with roses, poppies and marguerite daisies.

Admiral Baillie-Grohman settled his naval staff at HMS *Vectis* in Cowes, the northernmost point of the Isle of Wight "diamond." The heavily guarded naval headquarters had recently been commissioned from the Royal Yacht Squadron (for a rent of one shilling a year). The admiral's flotilla of landing craft and "mother ships" was massing in the Solent, now empty of pleasure boats. Before long there would be 237 vessels bobbing in the Solent harbours: destroyers; LCAs and R boats to carry the troops; LCTs to portage the tanks; and huge numbers of support craft manned by 3,000 British sailors.

Next door to the "fish" was the "flesh." General Roberts' Second Canadian Infantry Division was headquartered in high style in the private and state apartments of Queen Victoria's home at Osborne House. Nearby Norris Castle, where Victoria had summered in her youth, was the headquarters for the 6th Infantry Brigade and the South Saskatchewan Regiment. The former was commanded by Brigadier William Southam, a 41-year-old Toronto publisher; the latter, by Lieutenant Colonel Cecil Merritt. Just a few miles east of Cowes, the Queen's Own Cameron Highlanders had pitched their tents at Wootton Creek. The remaining 6th Brigade regiment, Les Fusiliers Mont-Royal, settled nearby at the Victorian seaport of Ryde.

Across the island in Tennyson country, on the picturesque west coast, Brigadier Sherwood Lett established his 4th Brigade battalions. The Essex Scottish were at Norton in what had recently been a Billy Butlin Holiday Camp. The Royal Regiment of Canada had a spectacular view of the Needles rocks and the lighthouse from their billets at Freshwater. Lord Tennyson's granddaughter who lived nearby would invite them for tea. The Royal Hamilton Light Infantry was billeted at NorthCourt Manor, in the idyllic village of Shorewell.

The Calgary Tanks were fascinated to discover that their training ground was to be the miles of white sand of Queen Victoria's old bathing beach.

Lieutenant Jack H. Dunlap, a troop commander whose tank was named *Bill*, remembered Osborne Beach well. "We were next to Queen Victoria's bathhouse. Every time it rained we took shelter in it. The LCTs would come to shore, and we would take turns getting our tank on and then getting it off. But the navy had no more experience than we."[5]

A typical day, tedious, strenuous and long, was noted in the Calgary Tanks' War Diary.

23 May 42
0600 hours — Embarking, craft afloat
0630 hours to 0830 hours — Cruise
0830 hours to 0900 hours — Disembarking exercise. Craft afloat and withdraw when unloaded
1000 hours to 1300 hours — Gunnery and S.A.T. [Small Arms Training]
1430 hours to 1800 hours — Troop Training exercise.

Evenings, the men would often go through the whole thing again in night conditions, usually in closed tanks. Or they would perform the inevitable maintenance duties.[6]

"That was practically all we did: practise loading and unloading," remembered Lieutenant Ed Bennett, who was crew commander of the tank *Bellicose*. "Once or twice we went to the south coast to practise firing into open seas. On these occasions we saw the infantry on route marches; we were glad we weren't there."[7]

Before the Dieppe raid, an amphibious operation with tanks had never been attempted. It posed interesting new challenges. The men were instructed to render their tanks capable of wading through water up to eight feet deep: no questions asked.

"We had balloon fabric around the turret, stuck on with plastic cement, which we blew off with cordite explosive," Lieutenant Arthur Patterson would later recall. Patterson was crew commander of *Caustic*. "The exhaust pipes were raised straight up four or five feet above the top of the tank. Some had palings* so the tanks would not sink."[8]

Captain Bill Payne developed many of the techniques for watersealing tanks. His testing ground was a school's swimming pool, where he and his crew repeatedly immersed the tanks — at one point dunking Generals Montgomery, Crerar and McNaughton, who had insisted on observing the experiment from *inside* the Churchill.

Another special-purpose device was the new Oke flame thrower. Three tanks were fitted with these.[9]

Few islanders had ever seen tanks before. Now the tranquility of their countryside was disrupted by packs of the steaming, clanking beasts. Sergeant Al Wagstaff, co-driver of *Calgary*, observed that "because the tanks were brand new, we were all trying to put mileage on — driving day and night all over the island to get the kinks out of them."[10]

Les Barton, a local farmer, would recall how he plowed his fields with his three-horse team while scores of camouflaged tanks and carriers streamed past for their morning fill-up at the army petrol pumps. His milk cattle vigorously protested the thunderous vehicles and the pounding small-arms fire.[11]

The infantry battalions, as Lieutenant Bennett observed, had immediately launched into combined assault training of gruelling intensity and urgency. The soldiers found this new regimen fantastic; to the villagers and the tank troopers it was merely awesome. They didn't

---

* Palings, or chespalings, were wooden slats like snow fencing that rolled out and provided a runway of 25 to 30 feet.

yet know it but the army was preparing them for a double-header. They were to carry out two of the most difficult operations of war in a single attack — a commando assault, and from the sea. Nor did they know that the raid was scheduled to go in on June 21, or as soon after as weather permitted. That date was only four weeks away. The men of the Second Canadian Division had to learn and master assault techniques in a fraction of the time that commandos had always been given.

With Double Summer Time in effect, reveille was set at 0500. There would follow 15 or 16 hours of strenuous work. Theo Pearson, a schoolteacher, remembered that

> It became a familiar sight to see squads of Canadian soldiers creeping through gardens and along hedgerows. One morning, after a "battle" in the Freshwater Bay area, they decided to call an armistice, and have their break outside Orchard's Bakery. They bought lots of doughnuts and were about to enjoy them when a "casualty" on a stretcher sat up to take his break. He was told: "You caint do that, Sergeant, you're daid."[12]

The forced march became the first bare-bones challenge of the assault course, as the Queen's Own Cameron Highlanders' War Diary noted: "All coys on speed march, 12 miles in 3 hrs . . ."

Normal infantry pace was two-and-one-half miles per hour. After four weeks of accelerated training on the Isle of Wight, all ranks were required to march (no running) 11 miles in two hours carrying full kit and weapons. They were expected to cover the first five miles in 45 minutes; their gear weighed 50 pounds.

"The training was pretty demanding," reflected Corporal (now Colonel) John Williamson, a section commander with the RHLI. "We learned we could do a lot more than we thought we could."[13]

"At the end of a speed march," recalled Captain Walter McGregor of the Essex Scottish, "one of my lieutenants had blood oozing out the back of his hand, his blood pressure had gone up so high." The man was invalided home.[14]

Along with route march conditioning, the men were taught the dangerous and often frightening art of cliff scaling. The War Diary of the Rileys noted on May 22: "Battalion proceeds on obstacle course where the morning was spent in going through a very tough and difficult obstacle course. This consisted of scaling a cliff, through barbed wire at the top, climbing scaffolding and crawling through culverts, through muddy trenches, over water-filled ditches by swinging from ropes hand-over-hand . . . "

As the men hauled themselves up the bare cliff face, using toggle ropes or scaling ladders, heavy fire was laid down near them by other Canadians manning automatic weapons. Once they had scaled the cliffs they were taught how to get their weapons into immediate action, firing from the hip at the enemy 100 yards away.[15]

All ranks took part. Sergeant Jim Coughlin of the Essex Scottish recalled how marvelous the training was at gelling good teams of men. "You found out the fellow you wanted to be beside — the one you could count on. We learned respect for each other.

"It brought out potential leadership — you'd find your good corporals and sergeants. It also brought out weaknesses in the officers and NCOs."[16]

"Major Norris Waldron, our company commander, was a tough nut," John Williamson remembered. "One day we were cliff climbing. The cliff was forty or fifty feet straight up and we were using grappling hooks. Somebody found he couldn't make it. Waldron said, 'Stand back, I'll do it.' Well, he tried three or four times but he just couldn't manage it. He finally sat on a rock with his head down. A few tears came to the corner of his eye. He was asking the boys to do something he couldn't do himself."[17]

"You were all pretty well dressed the same, had the same type of training. You all had to keep up. You couldn't dodge it," one NCO summed up.[18]

"Lieutenant Colonel Menard O.C. is following every moment of training and encouraging everybody by setting the example himself," Les Fusiliers' War Diary noted proudly about their commanding officer.[19]

There was an isolated instance when a senior officer did try to duck out of a route march by taking a car over certain segments of it. The men never forgot this negative example of leadership, any more than they forgot the positive example of the officer who wept when he couldn't ascend the cliff with his men.

The battalion war diaries reflected other facets of commando and infantry assault training that were begun in earnest in those balmy spring weeks on the Isle of Wight.

25 May, Royal Regiment of Canada: "Street fighting was carried out in the village of Yarmouth, the rifle coys attacking, while HQ Coy and Bn HQ defended the town. Most of the value of this exercise was

lost, owing to the objection of the local people to the use of their back gardens and roofs [by] the troops participating."[20]

A compromise was soon found, as war correspondent Ross Munroe reported in Toronto's *Globe and Mail*: "The infantry worked in a bombed-out village, battling through wrecked buildings and adding to the damage with hand grenades they flung like baseballs. Thousands and thousands of rounds of live ammunition were used in field firing practice."[21]

Les Fusiliers Mont-Royal found it great sport: "C & D Coys went on practice of village fighting and village clearing in West Cowes. 'Blitzed' houses give a very good training ground and we can use *live* ammunition of all kinds."[22]

The men had to master a great number of other new skills in the time available. As well as sharpening village- and street-fighting techniques, they practised assaults on pillboxes, map reading by day and night, accurate grenade-throwing — with live #69 and #36 grenades and smoke grenades — the use of Bangalore torpedoes and other demolitions, mortar firing (both 3-inch and 2-inch), bayonet fighting, and the firing of Bren guns from landing craft.

The Bren was a 28-pound light machine gun that could fire 120 rounds per minute and had an effective range of 500 yards. The Thompson, an American submachine gun known to the Canadians as a Tommy gun, could fire up to 650 rounds per minute but had a much shorter range.[23]

The men were trained in instinctive aiming: that is, shooting from the hip while on the run. Because their weapons were so heavy and because rapid firing was so effective, it was imperative that they learn how to do this.

They learned to cross obstacles of coiled concertina wire. The first man threw himself on the coils of barbed wire; the others ran over his prostrate form. It was not much fun for the volunteers who acted as mats. (The commandos, they discovered too late, always clad their human "mat" in a protective leather coat.)

One June 8, the South Saskatchewan War Diary noted a typical day for the battalion: "HQ Coy on wire cutting, map and compass work. A Coy crossing wire obstacles, climbing and swimming. B Coy assault work and compass march. C Coy unarmed combat. Route march. D Coy route march and lectures on grenades. All coys on night schemes, compass march or crossing wire obstacles. Returning to camp at 0100 hours where they received a hot drink."[24]

On June 10, the Royal Regiment wrote: "The Battalion carried out unit training in the #36 Grenade and the anti-tank rifle, firing from the hip etc. All personnel accustomed to carry pistols were issued with the Sten gun."[25]

The Sten was a new 9-mm machine pistol of British design that was distributed for the first time to Canadian troops just before the Dieppe raid. The riflemen came to call it the "plumber's abortion." It was cheap ($9.00 to produce), crudely made, unreliable, and dangerous to the user. It often jammed, and would go off if dropped. Many soldiers were wounded or even killed by Stens. To make one of them at all battle-worthy required hours of work filing various parts, adjusting and testing.

Lieutenant Tom Taylor, a platoon commander with the Royals, has never forgotten his first exposure to the Sten gun: "One officer on exercises was climbing a fence carrying a Sten when he shot himself in the arm. He ran to the RAP [Regimental Air Post]. As a result, he pumped out blood and lost the use of his arm. That was a great start."[26]

Particular emphasis during training was given to loading and unloading the 33-man LCAs and the 20-man R boats. The LCAs were lightly armoured and offered some protection to troops from small-arms fire; but the flimsy wooden R boats offered none.

All ranks practised the vital skills of clearing the craft as quickly as possible after touchdown, then taking cover and speedily getting their weapons and equipment into play to attack and knock out enemy strongpoints.

In its War Diary, the Essex Scottish recorded one of these essential pre-raid practices: "4 June: Exercise WINDSOR 1 carried out with L.C.A. boats. Attacks and withdrawals were carried out with dispatch. Commanding Officer and Adjutant were forced to swim for it when Beach Officer decided the boat they were in was a casualty. Troops were pleased with the incident. All ranks swam with full equipment using 'Mae Wests.' "[27]

The Cameron Highlanders were not so amused. Due to low tide, their disembarkation took place 200 yards from shore, which meant that they had to wade ashore through waist-deep water. They later reported that "the shorter men had a thorough dunking. One Company Sergeant Major stepped out of his boat and disappeared beneath the waves and was unceremoniously towed the rest of the way by his taller companions."[28]

The training was tough and performed under the pressures of time constraints, but the officers and men enjoyed the challenges and the sense of purpose to it all. They discovered that the beauty of the island was not necessarily limited to its scenery; a seemingly endless parade of lovely local women patriotically made every effort to make the Canadian visit a pleasant one. The Starboard Club in Seaview became a popular drinking hole for the officers and their ladies.

Private Norman Partington of the RHLI Carrier Platoon recalled, "I met some very nice people there, and kept in touch. We were young enough to enjoy it. Jesus! The pubs! There was one in Shanklin for civilians. I think I was the only Canadian to get in there. I was invited by a lady who was married to a commander in the navy. I used to send her cigarettes. She would keep them under the counter and sell them — I guess it was small-time black market — and keep the money for me, so when I went there I had plenty of money.

"We all had lots of cigarettes. A guy my father worked with used to send me three hundred cigarettes twice a month. Plus I got a thousand a month anyway from my company. They cost $2.50 for one thousand and $1.00 for three hundred in Canada. But in Britain they had great bartering value. You may not have had cash but you sure had tangible assets!"[29]

For additional funds, to augment their pay of $1.30 a day, some of the men tried a bit of moonlighting.

"There was a woman who had a goat, name of Larry," Partington related. "She was a market gardener. We used to go there evenings, though we were dead beat, and work for her in the garden until dark. We got ten shillings an hour. We were only on field allowances and didn't have any money otherwise."[30]

Although it was officially frowned upon, the men liberated some of the island's livestock and poultry to supplement their basic mess rations. Trooper Percy Aide of the Calgary Tanks' B Squadron recalled the time "we picked up a calf. It disappeared one night — no one could find it. One of the cooks butchered it and it was cooked and eaten by morning. We were never caught."[31]

Besides a little carousing and minor larceny, all ranks enjoyed playing sports. Baseball and touch football — both novelties to the islanders — were very popular with the men. Inter-battalion and inter-company games and sports days were regularly staged.

While infantry and armoured personnel trained — and occasionally played — at frantic pace, another key support arm, the Royal Canadian Engineers, was also working hard to problem-solve obstacles that might be expected on amphibious attacks.

Here, much reliance had to be placed on intelligence summaries detailing the Dieppe topography and defences, and defining any problems that might be encountered. These reports were disseminated regularly from Combined Headquarters to Second Division Intelligence who in turn, with the objectives disguised, passed them on to the units.

The beach assault party, under command of Major B. Sucharov, and the demolition party, under Lieutenant Colonel L.F. Barnes, CRE (Commander Royal Engineers), had key assignments in what they still thought was going to be a major training exercise. Sucharov's task was to "get all troops, stores, tanks and other vehicles from the point of touchdown by the naval craft onto, across, and clear of the beach area, and ultimately see to the reembarkation of the vehicles."[32]

The demolition party was responsible for clearing minefields and other obstacles.

The technique was this: the engineers drew up a list of targets from the descriptions of beaches and obstacles in the intelligence summaries. Then they researched and experimented with the best methods of attacking them. Mock-ups of each obstacle were constructed; exhaustive technical data was collected. "During the preparations, additional intelligence kept coming in," the sappers noted. "This often called for more experiments and changing of methods." Only after all the data had been compiled and all the methods finalized were teams of sappers selected and trained, each for its own separate tasks.[33]

After intensive study of available intelligence, their calculated assessment was that the beach in the exercise for which they were training consisted of loose, soft shale or pebbles in a gradient of 1 in 30 — quite a gentle slope. They also concluded that there would be obstacles of tubular scaffolding and barbed wire as well as antitank and antipersonnel mines, a two-foot-wide by six-foot-high seawall, another six-foot by six-foot reinforced concrete antitank wall, and reinforced concrete strongpoints.

To each of these targets, teams of men were assigned from the complement of 330 sappers and 86 infantry pioneers who worked with them. Tests on what they were led to believe were comparable beaches — on the Isle of Wight and Dorset coasts — revealed no problems for the tanks in navigating the shingle, the slope, or the low wall. Chespalings designed by Major Sucharov were fitted on several of the tanks as extra insurance. For the high walls, the sappers devised wooden ramps or stairways for the tanks to climb. Each of these ramps was made of some five tons of lumber. A squad of 30 men trained hard to carry these loads an anticipated 30 yards and then to assemble the ramps in an incredible five minutes.

Each target for demolition required careful scientific research as to the weight, dimension, and type of charge best suited to its destruction. For example, to blast through any concrete slabs that might block the routes from the beach to the town, the engineers designed a number of special charges. Each weighed 60 pounds and would have to be hand-hauled several hundred yards across the beaches to be put in place.

The job description of the sappers chosen for these tasks was daunting: each had to be able to carry a 60-pound pack on a six-mile forced march and then perform the required sapper tasks; each had to be well versed in a number of complex technical subjects; and each had to be as skilled as any infantryman in battle drill and weaponry.[34]

While the "fish" and "flesh" were straining to overcome the many problems posed to them, and to achieve new standards of physical stamina, the "fowl" — or a facet of it — paid them a visit.

RHLI War Diary, 10 June: "Thirty paratroops arrived to be inspected by all ranks. Officer in charge explained equipment worn and their method of attack."[35]

The 1st Battalion of the British Parachute Brigade would comprise yet another vital component of the plan. The operational details and destination had not been revealed to the men, but the nature and importance of their task had already been made clear. Near the target were two heavy gun batteries that would be capable of harassing the raid's flotilla. The paratroops were going to jump behind enemy lines to destroy them. "A pretty straightforward and simple operation," they judged.[36]

Finally, on the night of June 11, all the troops boarded landing craft and mother ships for Exercise Yukon. To the men it was just another practice. Its purpose, they had been told, was to rehearse the Second Division in an assault landing in all its elements.

The senior commanders knew more: that it was the final, full-scale dress rehearsal before the Dieppe raid was mounted.

The flotilla, with eight destroyers in support, left the Isle of Wight in the early evening. By 3 a.m. on June 12, it was six miles off the coast of Bridport, Dorset. Yukon called for the division to attack the coast on either side of the town and to advance inland to capture various objectives. The landing was to take place at first light.

The rehearsal was, from Admiral Baillie-Grohman's point of view, "a shocker."[37] The sea was very rough, and many men were seasick. Worse, the naval personnel manning the landing craft made a number of critical navigational errors. The South Saskatchewans were landed three-quarters of a mile from their assigned beach; the same mistake befell the Camerons. Some of the Calgary Tanks were put down one hour late and some were lost and did not land at all. The Royal Regiment came ashore two miles west of their proposed beach.

Montgomery's liaison officer, who was watching, wrote that "the division fell into an indescribable confusion, which was in itself sufficient to throw doubt on the feasibility of the operation, even though there was no enemy present to turn confusion into bloodshed and slaughter."

Unruffled, Montgomery only said that further training and another practice were required before the raid could be launched. ("He did not worry," Rees said. "I almost wished that he would."[38]) A second Yukon was scheduled for June 21, which meant that the Dieppe operation had to be delayed until early July.

On June 19 some 50 additional personnel were attached to the Royal Regiment for Yukon II. These included members of the 3rd Light Anti-Aircraft Regiment and 22 all-ranks from the RCA's 4th Field Regiment. Their task was to take over and operate captured enemy guns.

Yukon II was run on June 23 and came off only "slightly more satisfactory than the first," Baillie-Grohman reported. "But it would have to do. It was my responsibility to land the troops at exactly the right time at the right spot on the French beaches, and I was still not happy about this.

"Fifteen minutes late," Baillie-Grohman noted prophetically, "could mean a disaster."[39]

All of the key players in the Dieppe scenario were standing on the cliff in Dorset watching that rehearsal: the ultimate military authority, General Paget; his designated driver, Montgomery; the senior Canadians, McNaughton, Crerar, and Roberts; and from Combined Ops, Mountbatten and his Naval Advisor, Captain John Hughes-Hallett.

To the latter, the exercise brought a few familiar twinges. Until three days before, Hughes-Hallett had been masquerading as a private soldier with the Camerons. He had shared tented billets and tough training with the Canadians for 11 days, ostensibly to "see what a raid looked like from a soldier's point of view."[40]

While he thought he had taken part anonymously, the Camerons had his number. They "not only admired his fancy underwear but had an unblushing liking for his manner of losing large amounts of money at cards." They added, tongue in cheek, that he was "highly regarded."[41]

Baillie-Grohman caustically dismissed Hughes-Hallett's antics as a "farce": "I told General Roberts quite frankly that I regarded this an insult to the Canadian officers, and I would never have allowed such a performance within my naval command."[42]

Apart from the naval errors, Yukon II was considered enough of an improvement that Mountbatten decided to stage Dieppe on the first favourable date after June 24. Then the weather intervened. Army meteorological specialists reported that they could not foresee suitable tide and wind conditions until early July.

There were still concerns about the naval errors. Both McNaughton and Paget expressed their concerns to Montgomery about these. When Monty reported back to them a few days later, he hinted that the Canadians had expressed other concerns to him: "... certain senior officers began to waver about lack of confidence on the part of the troops," he wrote. "The complaint has been firmly handled."

Montgomery added that he had made arrangements with the navy to correct their problems. He concluded with a enthusiastic postscript, stating that "the Canadians are [first] class chaps. If anyone can pull it off, they will."[43]

Denis Whitaker

We 300 officers of the Second Canadian Division were in for a surprise. On June 27, General Roberts assembled us in a large room at Cowes. This was to be our first briefing about the operation we had spent five weeks training so hard for. We all crowded around a 10-foot-long sand-table model of an unidentified port and coastal area. Everything was in exact scale. The detail was incredible: every street and every house had been reconstructed. The objective was code-named Rutter.

General Roberts told us that in less than a week we were going to form the assault force for a raid on a French port. A couple of officers recognized the coastline, and soon a murmur of astonishment swept the room: "Good God! It's Dieppe!"

Roberts glanced up, furious that security was being so flagrantly breached. He admonished us again not to breathe a word of this outside the briefing room — not even to guess the true destination.

Each battalion was then briefed on its objectives. The RHLI officers were told that along with the Essex Scottish they would make the frontal assault on the main Rutter beach. The Calgary Tanks, along with the sappers, would land in support. The four 4-inch guns on each of four destroyers would be available to provide direct fire support for this frontal attack.

Two flank forces — the South Saskatchewans and the Royals — would land half an hour before the main assault to launch surprise attacks on two of the Germans' gun batteries. These were located on cliff tops overlooking the main attack zone.

The South Saskatchewans and the Royals had key roles. They would depend on darkness and surprise to seize their objectives. No artillery support would be provided for them.

The Camerons would land after the South Saskatchewans had secured their beach. With armoured support they would attack the aerodrome behind the town. Les Fusiliers were designated as floating reserve, to be used at General Roberts' discretion to reinforce success. In the later stages of the attack, they would form a defensive perimeter through which the other units would withdraw.

Along with the flank assaults, the 1st Battalion of the British Parachute Brigade would spearhead the attack. Two companies of paratroops would drop behind Orange Beach at Varengeville, eight-and-a-half miles west of Dieppe, and take out a six-gun battery that was a threat to the naval flotilla. Two additional companies would take out the battery six miles east of the port, near Yellow Beach at Berneval. We were briefed on the support we could expect. The Royal Navy would provide eight destroyers to escort the infantry force and its flotilla across the Channel. With over 800 aircraft committed, the RAF would pulverize the town beforehand. Some would support the infantry, attacking enemy gun positions or providing covering smoke; some would protect the flotilla; most would fight a battle of attrition with the Luftwaffe.

Dieppe was not heavily defended, we were told, and the beaches were suitable for landing tanks and infantry. The entire operation was to be of "two tide" duration, with reembarkation to be completed within 12 to 15 hours of first landing.[44]

The briefing ended. There was an awed silence. The officers reacted with everything from enthusiasm to dismay.

The plan was jigsaw-like in its complexity. Each part relied heavily on the last or the next; if a single part of it failed, the rest could easily disintegrate. It had been designed by Lieutenant Colonel Churchill Mann, GSO 1 (General Staff Officer Operations) Second Canadian Division, who also briefed us. The operation order was an alarming 112 pages long.

Tall, spare, and of considerable wit and eccentricity, Mann was one of the young "comers" of the Canadian Army. He was just 36 years old and had absolutely no operational experience. He had parachuted into senior wartime ranks because of his reputation as a brilliant staff officer and as an even more glittering and innovative planner.

Being totally inexperienced, most of us looked forward to the operation with enthusiasm, and were proud that we had been chosen to carry it out. We had "complete and naïve confidence in its success," as Montgomery's liaison officer, Rees, aptly described it. We had not yet "lost our innocence." How could we, as innocents, tell the difference between folly and brilliance?[45]

The fireplan described by Mann and Roberts seemed massive in scale to tyros like ourselves. The air support? Overwhelming! We all envisioned a town annihilated by bombs, defended by a few quivering Germans of no account. I wasn't alone in my naïve belief that four destroyers, with a total of sixteen 4-inch guns, would obliterate the German defences. We had trained hard; we were confident that we were ready for action — as fit and tough and skilled as a soldier could be. We infantrymen saw ourselves surging onto the beach under the umbrella of thundering naval guns. The Calgary Tanks believed they would swan their tanks across the beaches under that huge curtain of fire. The engineers envisioned their squads swiftly hauling their heavy loads to clear the beach obstacles so that the armour and infantry could get through.

Just as the men had placed their confidence in us, their officers, we in turn placed similar confidence in our senior commanders. We were banking on the fact that all the top Canadians who were commanding the raid — McNaughton, Crerar and Roberts — were gunners with extensive World War One experience.

Were they satisfied that the plan was sound? That their troops had sufficient protection? We counted on it. Or were they, perhaps, the "certain senior officers" whom Montgomery referred to as wavering in confidence?

Without question, we had huge confidence in *each other*. Captain Jim Quinn of the Calgary Tanks described this amazing camaraderie: "Through the training, the process of going overseas, sharing the separation from loved ones, experiencing the exhilarating excitement of the times at first hand, the active and demanding training, all these developed among us a great feeling of affection, trust and pride in each other."[46]

"We were sky-high!" one young officer exclaimed. "There was nothing we couldn't overcome. We'd been told things were going to be easy. One of the jokes in our platoon was, 'We're going to save all our pennies for the French kids when we get over.' "[47]

General Roberts may have just been trying to bolster our courage — and his own — when he assured us that the operation would be simple: "a piece of cake," he said. I remember it so clearly because of a quip my good friend, Lieutenant Jack Prince of the Essex Scottish tossed off. Jack leaned over and whispered to me, "A funny fucking piece of cake!"

———

On July 2, the men of the Second Canadian Infantry Division strode confidently up the ramps of their assault craft. Another damned exercise, they grizzled. Only after they were sealed aboard were the men finally briefed by their officers: at last, the Canadians were getting into action. They would sail that night for Dieppe.

The vigil began. Riding at anchor on the Solent, the 5,000 soldiers and 3,000 sailors by turns sweated, swore, and gambled on the roll of the dice and the upswing of the barometer. A southwest wind was blowing away their chances to fight.

It would be five days before their fate was decided.

CHAPTER

11

THE DISINTEGRATION

The "boys" had started "fiddling Dieppe away." The original Rutter plan was disintegrating. But even as the Canadian troops on the Isle of Wight were training for the raid with all their enthusiasm, pride and "naïve confidence" in its success, Rutter's flaws were becoming obvious and alarming.[1]

Yet the operation still forged ahead.

"No one drew the logical conclusion that Rutter was no longer feasible as a serious operation of war," Rees wrote. "Henceforward it could only be an expensive and murderous laboratory experiment."[2]

One by one, senior field commanders were getting the unshakeable notion that Rutter was being pushed relentlessly towards its conclusion by a powerful unseen force.

Phrases like "for political reasons" and "from the highest quarters" and "the prime minister is determined to go ahead" were used with increasing frequency to thrust aside objections that the plan was irreparably flawed.[3]

"I believe that the operation would have proceeded even if the troops had been asked to land with no better weapons than their bare hands. . . ," Rees concluded.[4]

Bit by bit, it was coming to that.

Originally the Rutter plan contained six key safeguards to ensure its success. First, as the Canadian officers had been told in their briefing, bombers would devastate the town and completely demoralize its defenders, smashing their gun posts and making them incapable of sustained defence. Also, immediately prior to the attack, a direct strike by medium and fighter bombers would help to knock out the enemy artillery batteries on the east and west headlands overlooking the main beach.

The second safeguard, and perhaps the most important, was fire support from naval guns. The troops assigned to attack the main beach would land under a powerful umbrella of gunfire from the escort destroyers.

The invaders were also counting on close support from the next pair of components: that there would be tanks to shepherd in the assault troops on the main beach and that, beforehand, paratroop forces would already have taken out the heavy coastal-gun positions that could menace the flotilla.

The final two elements were two crucial suppositions: that the assault would take the Germans by surprise, and that the enemy defences were weak.

One-half hour ahead of the main attack, the two flanking battalions would land silently in near-darkness, seize the beach, scramble up the cliffs, climb the heights beyond them and eliminate the enemy gun positions on the headlands that dominated the main Dieppe beach. Both battalions were assured that they could rely totally on surprise. They would need no supporting fire. The German defences, described by Casa Maury as puny, would crumble under the onslaught of the infantry's pre-dawn surprise attack.

But one by one, these six safeguards were being eroded. The plan that was predicated upon all the available supports of modern warfare was regressing to the primitive tactics of pre-World War One.

Even while the thousands of Canadian troops waited anxiously in their cramped assault boats; while the 500 paratroopers sealed at their base mused, "At bloody last, this is it"; while RAF ground crews were working feverishly to tune up 800 planes, and 1,000 pilots and air crew waited for their summons; while 2,000 naval personnel manning 237 ships and landing craft scanned the horizon expectantly — Rutter was collapsing.

The safeguard that had given this operation much of its credibility from the outset — that it would be supported by heavy bombers — was about to be snatched away. The original Rutter plan had called for an air bombardment "in maximum intensity by 150 bomber sorties": for a high-level attack against the town, and a low-level one against the headlands, seafront and beaches.[5]

On April 25, Mountbatten, chairing a planning meeting, had emphasized how important it was that "bombing does take place even if visibility conditions do not allow accurate identification of targets."[6]

In fact, on May 30 Churchill had personally waived a previous interdiction against bombing French targets, making a special exception in the case of Dieppe.[7] Yet six days later, in a cloud of contradictions and illogical assumptions, the bombing was cancelled.

Rees attended the meeting at which the plan for heavy bombers was scuppered. He summed up the events: "The original intention of the plan approved by the Chiefs of Staff had been that the bombing of Dieppe during the hours of darkness preceding the landing should be so devastating in its effect that any opposition would be merely nominal.

"Then, at a planning conference, Admiral Mountbatten, handsome and breezy, like Brighton at its best, announced that Mr. Churchill had decided that, for political reasons, it would be inexpedient to undertake the bombing of Dieppe.

"In effect, it knocked the bottom out of Rutter."[8]

Accounts of and explanations for this decision are hazy and contradictory.

On June 5 (presumably *after* Mountbatten had first announced Churchill's "political" axing of the bombing), a meeting was held at Combined Ops' Richmond Terrace headquarters. Two of the Rutter force commanders, Air Vice Marshall Leigh-Mallory and General Roberts attended, as did planning staff from Home Forces and Combined Operations planning staff. With Mountbatten in America trying to persuade Roosevelt that a cross-Channel operation was not feasible, Lieutenant General Montgomery was in the chair.

Leigh-Mallory stated that since the plan for heavy bomber sorties was "not overpowering," it might only serve to put the Germans on the alert. He therefore proposed that the high-level bombing of Dieppe be eliminated from the plan in favour of bomber raids on towns and aerodromes some distance away.[9]

Leigh-Mallory did not explain how his originally promised air support of "150 bomber sorties in maximum intensity" that had been a basic part of the plan from its inception, had mysteriously changed — in his casual turn of phrase — into a "not overpowering" force — one that was passed off as being more bother than it was worth.

He also added that chances of the bombers even hitting Dieppe — let alone hitting the specific targets on the headlands and the buildings along the front — were small.

He did not explain how a bombing plan that had been enthusiastically endorsed as necessary and feasible in May could by June be considered to offer little hope of even hitting the targets.

The next curious conundrum appears in General Roberts' reaction to the bomber withdrawal: strangely, he made no comment. "The minutes of the meeting of 5 June make no reference to General Roberts' views on the air bombardment," Canadian historian Colonel Charles Stacey reported.[10]

Yet the Combined Operations official after-action report stated that the high-level bombing was abandoned because of the "strong opinions" held by Roberts and Leigh-Mallory.[11]

Unexplained was how Roberts' so-called "strong opinion" was not recorded anywhere in the minutes.

Later, other excuses for removing the heavy bomber support appeared. For example, it was suggested that the bombers might miss so small a target in a night attack and that most of the bombs would fall inland or in the sea. There might be problems getting the tanks through the rubble in the streets. Possible casualties to French civilians would be unacceptable. It was even suggested that Roberts was reluctant to protest in case his objections jeopardized the operation and put him out of a job.[12]

The Rutter commanders also learned that the medium bombers had been so reduced in number and in air time over the target as to be of little use. These bombers were to have assisted the advance infantry units by knocking out the headland batteries. At a meeting chaired by Air Vice Marshal J.M. Robb, Deputy Chief of Combined Operations, it was decreed that the 20 low-flying Blenheim bombers "cannot be used later than 30 minutes before civil twilight. This only leaves 5 minutes for low bombing, from 0430 to 0435."[13]

Denis Whitaker

Five minutes was mere tokenism: a long cry from "maximum intensity." Of 2,600 sorties by all aircraft on that day, only 62 were by medium bombers.[14]

With one crucial element of the plan eliminated, there were still five to go. There were in particular the naval guns.

The next crippling blow, then, was the realization that the naval support would be completely ineffectual. Stephen Roskill, the official British naval historian, voiced a shrewd criticism of the planners. He pondered why "the decision to cancel the bombing did not lead to a demand to increase correspondingly the naval support gunfire."[15]

But the reverse was the case. There would be no capital ships — battleships or cruisers — allocated in support of the Rutter raiders. Eight Hunt-class destroyers were assigned, but these were a bit of a joke in naval circles, being scoffed at because of their smaller-than-normal size. Four of these were designated for other support tasks. Even the four remaining had only the most casual of instructions: "Naval forces *may* [authors' emphasis] be required to give close support to the assaulting troops."[16]

In any event, even if the destroyers had been tasked to provide integral close support for the assault force, their guns were too few on a six-mile front, and far too dispersed and lightweight in calibre to be of much value.

When Rear Admiral Baillie-Grohman arrived from the Middle East at the end of May to take up the appointment as Rutter's naval force commander, he saw the operational plans for the first time. He immediately spotted its flaws. The military plan had mushroomed into more than 100 pages of dazzling and inflexible detail. The author, Lieutenant Colonel Churchill Mann, was notorious for his almost obsessive attention for minutiae. This time he had outdone himself.

The Admiral was a seasoned salt. The veteran commander's impatience with inefficiency was legendary. While in the Middle East, he had organized and completed the rescue of 55,000 British troops in Greece who were under immediate peril of being overrun by the Germans.

A tough and unyielding man, Baillie-Grohman was obviously unimpressed with the plan he saw. At this point, although bomber support had not yet been withdrawn, there were still glaring inadequacies.

The photo reconnaissance pictures of Dieppe that he was studying underlined the perils of attacking this objective. A line of sheer, unscalable cliffs dominated this sector of the French coast. The town itself straddled a broad valley formed by the River d'Arques. Twin headlands rose some 200 to 300 feet on either side of the port — obvious danger points.

From the moment they would land on the main Dieppe beach — a mile-wide area that fronted the small town of 25,000 — the two battalions of infantry and their supporting tanks would be in enemy gunsights. The powerful German anti-aircraft guns and heavy mortars known to be entrenched in the heights, and the machine guns installed in pillboxes and buildings along the front, would mow down the attacking force — unless they were silenced. Should the troops manage to land, they would not get very far. A concrete seawall was at places seven feet high and four feet thick and topped with barbed wire. With no apparent breaches, it would block any attempt by the attackers and their armour to advance into the town.

The planners had assigned two battalions to neutralize the headland batteries on the east and west flanks, 30 minutes ahead of the main landing. But this was no solution: the cliffs loomed high above the narrow shale beaches and there was only a slim cut through which the attackers could escape the beaches and climb to the heights.

Apparently no one had asked how those foot soldiers would get ashore, scale the cliffs, and knock out the defenders on the headlands, all in 30 minutes, when they had no umbrella of covering fire and when German machine guns and shore batteries were trained on their every move. Those flank forces would be defenceless.

Impossible! Baillie-Grohman thought. And after they failed, how in hell, he wondered, would the *main* body of soldiers attack the town in broad daylight with minimal support fire if those enemy defences in those cliffs had *not* been neutralized?

"My first reaction to the plan had been that there was no battleship to provide covering fire for a frontal attack," the Admiral later recalled. An intensive umbrella of fire support could force the Germans to take cover; they would be unable to man their weapons. Baillie-Grohman turned then to the naval fire-support plan. "Totally inadequate!" he snorted moments later in disgust. "Six destroyers with 4-inch guns are very unlikely to be able to knock out artillery batteries on the headlands."

With decades of experience, he well recognized the seriousness of the omission.

> Between 1921 and 1934 I took part in *many* Combined Operations exercises ... and always, heavy gun support had been presumed.
> Montgomery then spoke up and drew my attention to the heavy preliminary air bombing in the plan, which could take the place of heavy gunfire.
> I thought a battleship should be included. I had in mind the recent bombardment of Bardia, in which my ship the *Ramillies* had taken part, which had shown me conclusively the tremendous effect of battleship fire on cliffs and elsewhere.[17]

He might also have been recalling reports of Mountbatten's first Combined Operations raid just a few months earlier at Vaagso, when a cruiser *was* made available. Its 6-inch guns provided "accurate and effective bombardment under cover of which the landing craft were able to approach to within 100 yards of the landing places before it was considered necessary to cease fire." If a cruiser had been such an obvious factor in the success of that operation then, why were they resisting it now?[18]

At his first meeting with the force commanders, Baillie-Grohman asked Mountbatten, "Could you not provide a battleship or at least a couple of cruisers to assist troops on shore?"

"Don't raise this point now," Mountbatten told him. "See me privately after the meeting."

Later, in Mountbatten's office, Baillie-Grohman was told that the Admiralty had been approached but that the idea had been turned down "in the highest quarters."

(Baillie-Grohman has always been convinced that the prime minister constituted that "highest quarter.")

"Then how can you countenance going in on a frontal attack without support?" Baillie-Grohman asked indignantly.

"Mountbatten told me he had not wanted the frontal attack plan either," Baillie-Grohman reported. "He said he had been keen on going in on the flanks and had fought hard for it. But the army had insisted on the frontal attack and they had got their way because, after all, it was a military matter."

Fresh warnings of pending disaster awaited the admiral after the fateful 5 June meeting: "Soon after my arrival at Cowes I received a curt signal to the effect that preliminary air bombardment was cancelled.

"So there we were left, without heavy [naval] gun support or preliminary bombing.

"The only gun support for the troops attacking would be from the little 4-inch guns from a few destroyers wallowing about in the sea," Baillie-Grohman summed up bitterly. "When I protested by signal and asked if, failing a battleship, we could have one or two cruisers, the reply was that none was available, and that we must 'depend on surprise.'"

Admiral Baillie-Grohman had issued insistent warnings to the military that the operation was "extremely hazardous." He had been snubbed for his efforts. "The dice were loaded against us . . ." he wrote.

Canadian born himself, the admiral was deeply sympathetic to the Canadian troops and pessimistic about their chances. But he came to the bitter conclusion that he could do no more.

"The project was now a child of the Prime Minister, and it would certainly go ahead, one reason being the hope that it could relieve pressure on the Russian front," he concluded.[19]

———————

Denis Whitaker

A postwar tale circulated by Mountbatten was that Admiral Pound had turned down the request ("Battleships by daylight off the French coast? You must be mad, Dickie.") Years later, Captain Hughes-Hallett acknowledged that a battleship "could have operated in the Dieppe area during the first two or three hours of the operation without undue risk, and would probably have turned the tide in our favour."[20] However, after the disastrous loss of two battleships in the Far East a few months earlier, the Admiralty was understandably reluctant to involve capital ships in a daylight operation in the narrow English Channel.

Until the raid began, few of us at the sharp end had been in a position to appreciate the ineffectiveness of those little Hunt-class destroyer guns. We were too inexperienced. We'd been told in our briefings to expect heavy supporting fire that would neutralize the enemy. We thought, four destroyers assigned to the main beach? That'll knock 'em out! Instead, we would go in naked. Christ! Those guns were peashooters. They had little effect on the enemy.

The main attack from Puys to Pourville covered a front of six miles. Of the eight destroyers, two were allocated to division HQ and were unable to fire their guns for fear of disrupting radio communication. Two were responsible for flank protection of the flotilla. That left four ships — and sixteen 4-inch guns — for fire support for our main attack. These guns were to provide 10 minutes of support on the main beach prior to our landing, followed by 15 minutes on the headlands. Then presumably they were on call to the one artillery FOO (forward observation officer) who was sent in with each battalion. So a total of 16 guns was all we had — useless!

Vice Admiral D.W. Piers of the RCN confirmed to me that *it was a known fact in 1942* that the supporting fire from the Hunt-class destroyers could not effectively engage dug-in enemy gun positions such as were located on Dieppe's east and west headlands. And worse, because of the flat trajectory in which their shells would travel, they had no chance of hitting any targets on the headlands.[21]

Military specialists were warning that the battleplan was becoming a formula for disaster. All admonitions were shrugged off with vague references that the plan was being driven ahead at "a higher level" for "political reasons." At no time did Rutter's senior planners respond directly to the need to compensate for the lack of naval or bomber support.

Brigadier (then Lieutenant Colonel) Stanley Todd commanded 4th Canadian Field Artillery Regiment. He was instructed to send 16 gunners into the attack. Their objective was to man the enemy's French 75-mm guns on the headlands after the infantry had captured them, supposedly to ward off any subsequent German counterattack.

Todd disclosed a disturbing story in a recent interview. "The CRA [Commander Royal Artillery] of 2 Canadian Division, Brigadier Tees, told me he had learned that the Dieppe operation was going to take place without artillery support. We discussed the situation and decided to try to devise a method to supply an artillery regiment for this show. We put in an appeal to Combined Operations Headquarters that in our opinion an operation of that magnitude *would not succeed* unless the infantry had at least a call on heavy close support. We were flatly rejected. The plan was adhered to.

"We decided then that the raid was a political deal from start to finish," Todd said emphatically. "The whole plan was pretty well cut and dried. Roberts was given an operation that included certain elements and then it was decided on a higher level that he must do without those elements.

"He was given a fait accompli and had little choice or little option but to do what was required of him.

"We can only presume that McNaughton and Crerar were given the same menu and it was table d'hôte. They would have said to McNaughton, 'Here's a raid that we've designed. If you want it, take it; but there's no choice about it.' "

Todd's conclusion: "The whole thing originated among Roosevelt, Churchill and Stalin. If it hadn't been for those three men there never would have been a raid at all."[22]

Analyzing the raid more than 30 years later, Professor John P. Campbell of McMaster University wrote on a similar theme: "It was politically important for want of a Second Front to try to placate Stalin with a show of offensive activity."[23]

Todd and Brigadier Tees were not the only senior officers to express concern about the plan. Brigadier Sherwood Lett, who commanded the Fourth Canadian Infantry Brigade, also registered complaints with General Roberts: "Brigadier Southam, commanding Sixth Brigade, and I did express some apprehension when we learned that the preliminary bombardment was not to go on; and Colonel Andrews, commanding Calgary Tanks, was with us on that occasion." Lieutenant Colonel Labatt had also concurred. But they, too, concluded that "it was all pretty well cut and dried and handed to us in an operation order."[24]

But still, the plan supposedly contained other important safeguards: there were the airborne troops, and there were the 58 new Churchill tanks with their 2- or 6-pounder guns to give supporting fire to the infantry as they fought their way into the town.

Then these two vital elements disintegrated.

The airborne troops were essential. They would launch twin surprise attacks from the rear to capture the heavy coastal guns at Bernaval and Verangeville. Yet parachutists and glider troops were so heavily dependent on good weather and clear visibility that the entire operation could be stalled if conditions were not exactly right.

While the Rutter force waited for five hot, breathless days on the Solent, crammed and wretched on their assault craft, the troops cursed the imbecile commanders who kept postponing the attack because of bad weather. "You never had better water in your bathtub!" snorted Major McCool indignantly.[25]

But meteorologists were warning of quite a different picture of the weather over France. Their reports kept the airborne grounded and effectively put the whole operation on hold.

Also waiting impatiently on the assault boats were the officers and men of the Calgary Tanks, whose Churchills had been so painstakingly fine-tuned and rehearsed for their role as the muscle of the main beach attack.

All their efforts were about to be sabotaged as well.

Since the main reason for cancelling the bombing was to get the tanks onto the beach and into the town, one would imagine that there would have been a great deal of effort at senior levels to ensure that the tanks *did* get into town.

The tank commanders were becoming increasingly concerned that without supporting fire, the tanks would be shot up by enemy antitank guns before they got through the beach defences. Viscount Antony Head, a senior staff officer at Combined Ops, recounted how he had complained to Montgomery that "the plan to land tanks on the beach without prior bombardment was fundamentally unsound."

Montgomery had dismissed him with the comment that he was "talking nonsense."[26]

The appeal for fire support would go unheeded. Clearly the pressure from the top was too great to allow any interference. The raid was committed and had to go ahead.

Was there ever a chance the tanks would have succeeded? Calgary Tanks trooper Stan A. Kanik, a geological engineer, later discovered that the tanks "were doomed to failure before we even loaded them on the LCTs in England." The composition of the famed white cliffs of southern England and northern France was such that tanks could not run on the main Dieppe beach.

"The white cliffs are composed of siliceous chalk, interspersed with chert lenses and beds," Kanik noted. "During erosion, the chalk is dissolved in the water and carried away, while the chert remains on the beach and undergoes constant erosion, forming well rounded and extremely hard stones." What the tankers *weren't* apprised of was that the entire main beach at Dieppe was composed of these "chert stones, boulders and rubble" which were deposited by tides at an "angle of repose" of 15 to 20 degrees.

"Secondly, these rocks extended many metres in depth, so vehicles cannot dig down to a solid base for traction. When a tracked or wheeled vehicle tries to climb up this slope, it immediately digs itself down; when the tracks are turned to either side, the stones roll in between the drive sprocket and track." The pins holding the track links give way and the tank is disabled.[27]

Combined Ops' intelligence section ignored several obvious sources of information that would have provided a more adequate description of the topography of the beach. Travel guides would have pointed out that the chert formations at Dieppe were a unique feature. For centuries, tides up to 30 feet had poured over the beach, mounting the large chert pebbles and rocks into steep cairn-like formations. As well, books on the manufacture of the special porcelain found in that particular area of Normandy were available. There were prewar geological surveys to study, and oblique aerial photos that could have been requested.

The Americans sent frogmen to Pacific beaches by night for preliminary reconnaissance prior to such an assault. A few days before the Dieppe attack, RHLI Intelligence Officer Major Richard McLaren attended a pre-Dieppe conference at which someone asked for more detailed information on the composition of the beach. Oh, we're sending a party over by night to investigate, the group was told. Later, they were assured that the investigation had confirmed that the beaches were suitable for tanks. (There is no other evidence that in fact this scouting party had actually been sent.)[28]

Most of the intelligence information about the specific topography of the Dieppe beaches was based on the analysis of photographs — amateur and aerial — in an attempt to determine the size of the boulders on the beach.

"A photograph of a family group picnicking against a breakwater was the only basis from which to calculate the slope of the beach which tanks would have to climb," confirmed British intelligence historian F.H. Hinsley.[29]

Agents from the Central Photographic Intelligence Unit knocked on doors all over England, unearthing scores of scenic postcards and candid snaps of Granny and the kids enjoying a summer vacation on Dieppe's beaches. If the beach was good enough for Granny, it would seem, it was good enough for the 58 Churchill tanks that would have to navigate its steeply graded and rugged surface.

"The larger pebbles and boulders in all this region will consist of chalk which may be expected to provide a good grip for tracked vehicles," the intelligence section dutifully and erroneously reported.[30]

Engineers and tank commanders were told to expect a gentle slope in a gradient of 1 in 30, comprising loose, soft "shale" or "pebbles" — a far cry from the gradient of 1 in 4 of iron-hard rock that was waiting for them on the Dieppe beach.

The Yukon trials to test the tanks were held at Pevensey Bay in Sussex and later at West Bay, near Bridport, in Dorset. In both places, the terrain was supposed to be — but was not — similar.

The conclusion was reached that as the tanks had manoeuvred with ease in these trials, and without throwing their treads, there would be no problems on the Dieppe beaches.

Whitaker Commentary

The intelligence reports had not adequately described the topography. The terrain was not similar; the tests were farcical. We recently examined the beaches in both centres of Dorset and Sussex where the Calgary Tanks trained, and where Operation Yukon rehearsals were staged. In neither place were there the slippery, rounded oversized stone formations — many were rocks the size of baseballs — that were characteristic to that part of Normandy. Dorset had *shale*. Dover's beaches, had they troubled to look, had *chert*.

This surface wreaked much havoc with the tank treads during the raid. It became the tankers' first enemy at Dieppe: their tracks spun in it, became clogged with it and sank into it.

One officer, Marcel Lambert, reported that he "landed with Churchill tanks on a beach quite unlike the ones on which he had been training in England, that simply broke up the tracks of the tanks."[31]

As an after-action German report aptly, and tragically, described it, "The shifting shingle on the beach proved a perfect obstacle, into which the tanks sank easily."[32]

Irresponsible intelligence marked several other aspects of the proposed tank attack: "Did anyone ever inspect the switch-back road from the beach area to the top of the plateau and then to the airport?" Kanik asked. "There is no way a Churchill tank could have navigated [it.]" On the way, the tanks would have to pass under a narrow archway. "A small explosive charge would have collapsed the structure and blocked our exit back to the LCTs."[33]

The seawall was earmarked as a potential problem to tanks. Sappers were given the task of blowing breaches through it or erecting timber staircases over it. They were required to manhandle 60-pound packs of explosives and six-by-six planks across the open beach.

Without strong fire support to keep enemy heads down, how did the planners imagine that the sappers would get through the concentrated enemy fire on the beaches with their heavy loads in order to achieve their objectives? Most would be killed or wounded before they got near the wall.

Then there was the fifth element to safeguard the mission: surprise — the hope of catching the enemy off-guard.

When Admiral Baillie-Grohman signalled a strong protest about the puny naval gun support for the troops, he was told he must "depend on surprise."

This was clearly nonsense. The admiral warned Mountbatten that "the doubtful possibility of surprise [was] making this attack an extremely hazardous one."[34]

Colonel Stacey agreed, as did Admiral Roskill: "Even if the flank attacks caught the enemy unprepared, the town's defenders were bound to be fully alerted before the main assault was launched."[35]

American military commander Lieutenant Colonel Charles Schreiner Jr. recently posed the chilling question: Why, after the bombing was cancelled, was the timing of the landings "never changed to ensure surprise for the main assault? It was scheduled to take place a full thirty minutes after the initial commando landing — plenty of time for the Germans to come to a full alert."[36]

As these eminent historians pointed out, the enemy would hardly ignore the advance warnings of the earlier flank attacks and the five-minute pre-assault bombing.

In fact, the senior planners didn't seriously expect surprise to work. While the troops were embarked and waiting to launch the attack, a Combined Operations internal memo dated July 5 coolly predicted that ". . . we must expect all ports on the [French] coast to be alert, particularly after dawn. Tactical surprise will be most difficult to achieve."[37]

Denis Whitaker

So much for the element of surprise. The only hope was that, with half-an-hour lead time, the troops on the flanks could land, and then attack and neutralize the dangerous gun positions on the headlands before we landed on the main beach. And they would have to achieve all this in 30 minutes, in the semi-darkness, without being observed and challenged and without any covering fire.

It had to be a ridiculous long shot.

The Germans *knew* that we would attack the French coast. They were on the alert. The British and American political leaders had announced the fact twice: once in April after the Modicum agreement and again in that dangerous proclamation that Molotov persuaded Roosevelt and Churchill to sign: "The joint Russo-British communiqué on the 11th June had trumpeted to the world the need for a 'Second Front,' " Admiral Roskill pointed out.[38]

Previous raids would have put the enemy on his guard. Historian John Campbell, a specialist in Dieppe intelligence, wrote: "If the good soldier Haase, guarding a sensitive stretch of the Channel coast not long after the commando raid on St. Nazaire, wasn't thinking in terms of an imminent British landing, then he surely should have been."[39]

History has proven him correct. Rutter was planned for the first favourable day after June 24, depending on weather and tide conditions. Sixty miles away, Major General Haase, commanding the German defences at Dieppe, had only to study the same weather and tide conditions to predict an attack. This had become second nature for both sides for two years.

Haase ordered a special state of readiness between June 25 and July 10. He might never have imagined that the British would be stupid enough to attack frontally, with armour, in broad daylight; but he surely knew an assault of some sort was a possibility.

"In fact," Admiral Roskill noted, "on the 25th/26th of June the artillery in the Dieppe area remained limbered up all night. . . . The Germans had put two and two together."[40]

Finally, all that was left of the operation's six essential safeguards was the assurance that Dieppe was only lightly defended.

What if there was no bombing to soften the enemy, no naval fire support, no airborne troops to wipe out the coastal batteries, no effective tanks on the main beach and no surprise element to emasculate the headland defences? Would it really matter?

The planners had been told that the port was guarded by a small force of "low quality" troops with weak defences.

The welter of misinformation about the enemy that was handed down to the commanders would prove to be the most dangerous element of all. *Four times the number than was expected, and much more than four times the strength, were dug in, on full alert and waiting for the Rutter assault force.*

The plan, denuded of all is essential elements, still forged ahead, pushed, as it is now generally acknowledged, by the heads of state of Great Britain. Why did these men; astute in the art of war, not rescue the project? Why did they not order in a battleship, or reinstate the massive bombing raid?

Was it because naval resources were limited, and bombing not yet accurate enough to do real damage? Partly so. It *would* have been helpful, but mad, to send a battleship into Channel waters, an easy target for German subs or aircraft. It *would* probably have been futile to plan a bombing raid when there was every indication the bombers would miss their targets.

Were they also influenced by their Mediterranean ambitions, and the worry that the inevitable killing of French civilians would kill their chances of getting cooperation from the Free French Government in North Africa?

Or was it that they misjudged that fine line they were treading? Were they gambling that the raiders would somehow pull off a "limited success"? Enough of a show to impress upon Roosevelt and Stalin that a sincere effort had been made, but not enough that the Allied focus would be distracted from the Mediterranean. Did they underestimate Dieppe's capacity for disaster?

Two Canadians may have stumbled on the real answers — but no one was listening to them.

When Brigadier Stanley Todd and CRA of Second Canadian Division, Brigadier Tees, put in an appeal to Combined Operations headquarters for increased fire support, they were "flatly rejected." They decided then that the raid was a political deal and that Roberts and probably McNaughton and Crerar had no choice but to execute the plan "as is," despite its flaws.

As they concluded "if it hadn't been for those three men [Roosevelt, Churchill and Stalin] there never would have been a raid at all."[41]

———

What was Montgomery doing all the while? We come to the most mysterious question of all, the "Monty Conundrum" — why did he display such inexplicably poor military judgement in these critical few weeks?

The strangest aspect of all — and one that was completely out of character of the outspoken General Montgomery — was that the army chief did not himself express similar premonitions of doom about the operation to his bosses: Paget, at Home Forces, or General Brooke, the CIGS and head of the army. He had poured over the plans; he had talked to the commanders on the Isle of Wight a number of times. He had been made aware of their grave concerns.

Why did Montgomery, the responsible military authority for the Dieppe raid, allow the support to be withdrawn and why did he go along with the denuded plan?

It was a mystery to his liaison officer as well. "I was surprised," Goronwy Rees noted, "that the Army Commander should be so little perturbed about the risks of the operation. It was, he implied, an operation that had been decided on by the Chiefs of Staff . . . for reasons with which he was not concerned.

"He did not worry. I almost wished that he would."[42]

CHAPTER

12

THE MONTY CONUNDRUM

In a sense, Montgomery set himself up to take the rap for the final Dieppe plan. Even back in 1942, Lieutenant General Bernard Law Montgomery was considered "an efficient little shit."[1]

Before he became the celebrated Monty who commanded the Eighth Army to its great victories at El Alamein and beyond, before he took to wearing two cap badges when everybody else wore one, and before he gained huge popularity by leaping dramatically onto jeep hoods to hail his troops, his eccentricities had made him a legendary and formidable figure.

His peculiarities terrified many of his junior officers, as well as some who were not so junior. "He's just a bit mad," a recent arrival at his headquarters would be cheerfully informed.

Montgomery set the pace as an ascetic and expected his staff to follow suit. "He's death on smoking," the newcomer would be warned. A delicious morsel of gossip, perhaps apocryphal, made the rounds that one day Montgomery and Crerar were driving together to a meeting.

"Do you mind if I smoke, sir?" Crerar asked politely, lighting up a cigarette.

"Not a bit!" Montgomery replied crisply, at the same time ordering his driver to stop. He then sprang from the vehicle.

". . . As long as I am not in the car!"

Sheepishly, Crerar butted out.

"He's big on physical fitness," the neophyte officer would learn. Soon he would find himself devoting his Wednesday mornings to mandatory pre-breakfast cross-country sprints in the company of a sorrowful lot of other puffing, out-of-shape confrères.

"And he likes showing off," the Monty-explainer would add. He could have cited a recent example of Montgomery's notorious egotism; deciding that he rather fancied himself as an army commander, he created the army and awarded himself the title. It happened like this:

In early 1942, Montgomery's command extended to the British and Canadian divisions in southeastern England. This arm of General Paget's Home Forces was known as South Eastern *Command* — until Montgomery took over. Soon afterwards, an order under the signature of B.L. Montgomery stated that henceforth it would be known as South Eastern *Army*, with Monty himself to be acknowledged as army commander.[2]

Although Montgomery didn't attend many Dieppe planning sessions at Richmond Place, he kept a watchful eye on the operation through his liaison officer, Major Goronwy Rees.

Rees's first encounter with his new boss was memorable, not for Montgomery's appearance, which was unremarkable — "narrow foxy face, long nosed, sharp, intelligent, tenacious . . . very bright and clear blue eyes . . . a small, light, spare body" — but for what the bedazzled young L.O. termed his "queer trick" of repeating a word for emphasis — sometimes maliciously.[3]

One of Montgomery's first targets in their initial conversation was Lord Louis Mountbatten, whose spotty naval career and chaotic way of doing things horrified the orderly general. "A very gallant sailor," he sniped sarcastically. "Had three ships sunk under him. *Three* ships sunk under him. (Pause) Doesn't know how to fight a battle."[4]

However, the skill of the man never lagged behind his eccentricities; Bernard Montgomery was a superb field commander and a brilliant tactician — the best, many said, of World War Two.

Monty swept aside tired old tactical doctrines and tired old commanders, and from those cobwebs spun a modern army that refused to be defeated. "He singlehandedly changed the course of British military technique," wrote his biographer, Nigel Hamilton.[5]

That being so, Hamilton wondered how "a man who would become renowned as one of the most thorough and professional military commanders of the century allowed himself, willingly, to be sold a plan which was both beyond the abilities of his limited forces to fulfill, and which grievously underrated enemy resistance."[6]

But was Montgomery actually *sold* a plan? There is indisputable archival evidence that in fact he was not *sold* anything. In fact, he either suggested or actively promoted the changes to Rutter that resulted in so many casualties on Dieppe's beaches.

Montgomery had studied the battle plan for Dieppe. Nothing escaped his sharp eye. Why did he not point out the two obvious defects

— first, that on the dates selected, an alert enemy would be waiting, and second, that there was not nearly the weight of fire power laid on to deal with them.

Ziegler hypothesized that Montgomery was counting on "surprise and weak defences."[7] Yet he of all commanders was perfectly placed to predict exactly what the enemy must be doing. For two years, the Allies and the Axis had been perched on opposite chalk cliffs, glaring at each other across the narrow expanse of the English Channel. Their plans to keep each other out were almost identical.

The Canadian sector under command of Montgomery's South Eastern Army (SECO) had been earmarked as the "most likely" for German attack. SECO and the Canadian commanders had been repeatedly warned that "the enemy may attempt raids . . . when weather and tide conditions are suitable."

A British defensive blueprint, "Plan to Defeat the Invasion," had been drawn up on December 15, 1941. It decreed that "every battery will be sited so that a practicable hostile landing beach is within its range. There will be no withdrawal in any circumstance . . . all ranks must be determined . . . every German who sets foot in this country must be killed."[8]

On Montgomery's instruction the Canadian defenders had mined the beaches and erected antipersonnel and antitank barriers all along the coast. They had used the caves that pockmarked the English cliffs as weapon blinds.

As Nigel Hamilton pointed out, Bernard's own instructions relating to the defence of South Eastern Army's coastline, with clear-cut orders on states of readiness of coastal batteries, the manning of radio location units, all-round wiring-in of strong points, and constant rehearsal of counterattack operations, could hardly have left him in any doubt that his equally professional counterparts across the Channel would be similarly trained to repulse enemy raids.[9]

Yet Montgomery and Paget failed to draw the logical conclusion that the Germans most probably would have adopted the same defensive safeguards with the same determination.

As the D-Day for the raid drew nearer, Montgomery was also informed by British intelligence that powerful German reinforcements had been moved to France from the Russian Front. One of their most battle-sharp tank units was now just 40 miles from Dieppe.

So Monty *knew* that the Germans would be waiting — and that they would be far more formidable than the Canadians had been led to expect. Why did he remain silent? He finally did admit to Crerar —

weeks after he had learned of the enemy reinforcements — that he was "beginning to get unhappy about the long time on shore" and that it was starting to look "dangerous."[10]

Denis Whitaker

It is ironic that by Monty ignoring these obvious realities, the very Canadians who had been manning the defences on one side of the English Channel should now be decimated by identical German tactics on the other side.

The men who for many months were charged with mounting the defences questioned why the planners ignored the obvious: "When the tide was right and the moon was right, we doubled the sentries, we doubled the alert, we doubled everything," recalled Lieutenant J.S. Edmondson of the South Saskatchewan Regiment. "The Germans are just as smart as we are. If the tide is right and the moon is right and everything is right for us to go, they're going to double theirs. Now how do you think we can gain surprise?"[11]

The second defect in the plan that Montgomery continued to ignore was that it lacked sufficient fire support. General Sir David Fraser, the eminent militarist and historian, who himself was once a Vice Chief of the Imperial General Staff, told the authors that: "Montgomery always had terrific emphasis on well coordinated and massive fire support. This marked Monty's entire career. His acceptance of the Dieppe plan is very mysterious."[12]

When I commanded the RHLI in the fighting in northwest Europe in 1944 and 1945, I fought in the 21st Army Group for nine months under Montgomery's command. Monty's insistence on providing devastating fire power in frontal attacks was well known.

At El Alamein on October 23, 1942 — just two months after the Dieppe raid — Montgomery's Eighth Army artillery opened fire on enemy batteries with more than 1,000 field and medium guns. "The effect was terrific," Montgomery wrote.[13]

Later in the war, in Operation Veritable (the Battle of the Rhineland) in which I was involved, Montgomery's 21st Army Group laid on an attack over exactly the same width of front — six miles. This time, instead of the 16 puny guns of Dieppe, we had 1,334 guns. Instead of the 10 minutes of fire support at Dieppe, the Veritable force had three hours of fire to soften up enemy defences.[14]

There were other inadequacies with the fire plan that experienced gunners like General Brooke, General Roberts or a skilled tactician like Monty should have spotted and corrected. There was only one FOO assigned per battalion. How was he supposed to stand on the beach and direct destroyer fire onto the headlands when he had no observation of where the shells were landing? It was an impossible assignment anyway to ask a man to stand in the open on those beaches under intense fire and achieve anything. (Only one FOO of the six was not killed or taken prisoner, and that man was wounded twice.)

D-Day, also under Monty's direction at 21st Army Group, saw the leading wave of troops disembark and force its way ashore "supported by naval bombardment and air action and by the guns, rockets and mortars of close support craft." Later, 720 guns supported Operation Totalize (an infantry-cum-armour attack by Canadians astride the Caen-Falaise Road on August 7, 1944), during which 200,000 rounds of ammunition were used.[15]

The most incomprehensible feature is that Monty himself had insisted on the changes to the original Dieppe plan that made intensive fire support imperative. He proposed the switch from a flank attack that could have caught the enemy by surprise to a frontal assault that would inevitably expose the infantry to frontal and enfilade enemy fire. Then he chaired the meeting at which the fateful decision was made that robbed the raiders of their heavy bomber support.

While denuding his troops of air support, he was doing nothing at all to increase fire cover from other sources. Admiral Baillie-Grohman was deeply critical of Montgomery's role.

> I cannot imagine how Lieut. General Montgomery could ever have approved the altered plan for the frontal attack on Dieppe, supported only by the little 4-inch guns of a few destroyers. Montgomery went through World War One, where it was learned the hard way that a frontal attack on an enemy position required hours, sometimes days, of the heaviest preliminary bombardment. Yet he did approve the plan, as did COHQ and the other Canadian Generals who had been through World War One.[16]

In later years, Montgomery would always deny that he had insisted on the crucial and damaging switch to a frontal attack. Details about the planning of the raid and its adaptation from mini to mighty were not recorded until some months after the raid was finally staged. That documentation relied to a large extent on after-the-fact and unsubstantiated personal recollections, and hence its credibility is suspect.

Many meetings went unrecorded, their minutes lost, distorted, or destroyed. His biographer, Hamilton, claimed that Montgomery burned all documents related to the operation.[17]

In his unpublished memoirs, Captain Hughes-Hallett wrote of the friction between the military (Montgomery) and the navy (Mountbatten and himself). The controversy concerned the navy's push for a flank attack and the army's supposed insistence on a frontal one.

Hughes-Hallett claims he argued that

> the major problems and uncertainties of an invasion could be tested equally well by avoiding an initial frontal attack. The risk to the troops . . . would be a great deal less.
>
> [Montgomery] said that if we could only allow the troops ashore for a maximum of fifteen hours, then it would be impossible for the flank brigades to work around and reach Dieppe from the landward side in enough time . . . even if there were no Germans to oppose them. He pointed out that the only way the town and seaport could be captured quickly was to deliver a frontal assault and take it by coup de main [surprise action].[18]

Monty later insisted that he had "no recollection of having said that," and maintained that, on the contrary, he saw the flank attacks as "essential."[19] These widely divergent versions of the debate have never been resolved.

The result of this debate is clear, however: the plan was subsequently amended to incorporate the crucial frontal attack. Operation Rutter was approved as follows: The principal body of troops, supported by tanks, would land on the main beach in front of Dieppe. Airborne troops would assault the heavy gun batteries at Berneval and Varengeville, east and west of the town. Infantry units would land on the flanks just before the main force and attack the gun batteries on the headlands overlooking the town. A heavy air bombardment of maximum intensity and a flotilla of 237 ships would support the operation.

Whitaker Commentary

The "Monty Conundrum" is a mystery that has never been solved or even properly addressed. The *real* mystery to us does not centre on who did or did not attend which meetings or approve what plans.

The unanswered question is, why would an experienced commander like Montgomery go along with the final Dieppe plan? The switch from a flank attack — that could catch the enemy by surprise — to a frontal assault — that would inevitably expose the infantry to frontal and enfilade enemy fire was disastrous. From the first meeting at Richmond Place in April until its final execution on August 19, it remained "Monty's plan." For two months, in his capacity as commander of the South Eastern Army, he nurtured it, attended its meetings, talked to its commanders, and watched its rehearsals. He was — as General Swayne of Home Forces noted — the "man in command of the operation."[20]

Even though he was in the Western Desert by the time the raid was staged, the plan he had created and set into motion remained the plan of attack. As Crerar himself wrote, "There was no change in the Montgomery plan of June and that of the operation actually carried out (except the elimination of the Parachute troops)."[21]

Even more mysterious was Montgomery's uncharacteristic silence in the face of such a flawed concept as Rutter. He snubbed any outside protests from other commanders. As General Sir David Fraser recently pointed out, he did not even use the avenues available to him to protest the glaring lack of massive fire support. These were, Fraser pointed out, avenues he used frequently and comfortably. "Monty had a close association with the DMO [Director of Military Operations] and he had lines of communication to the war office. He could have made pleas to correct a bad situation if he thought the support provided to his soldiers was inadequate. He would have made that point very forcibly to the powers above."[22]

It was *so* uncharacteristic that one must dig deeper for an explanation. Since he could not have been counting on surprise, and knew his fire support was not strong, he must have put his reliance on the fact that the enemy was weak. That would account for Monty's strange about-face just before Rutter was due to be mounted. Even after the shambles of the Yukon rehearsal, Montgomery fairly exuded confidence. Just a few days later, he wrote a troubled letter to Crerar suggesting they reduce the time ashore because of the danger posed by the "now confirmed" presence of the German tank division.

Terry Copp, Canadian professor of military history, argues convincingly that, in mid-1942, the British armies were not yet trained or equipped for *offensive* action. "No one had thought through problems of fire support for infantry in ordinary battles, never mind assault landings. It was only after the first El Alamein that 8th Army gradually reverted to the principles of an artillery based battle doctrine."

Copp contends that the new lessons of the Desert War were not implanted in England until early 1943, and cites an article, "The Barrage is Back," that was published at that time in the *Journal of the Royal Artillery Corps*.[23]

The planning for the Dieppe raid therefore conforms to the prevailing ideas about the importance of surprise, speed, mobility and the crucial role of tanks. The principal military commanders involved — Montgomery, Brooke, McNaughton, Crerar and Roberts — apparently gave their approval to the Dieppe plan because they believed that surprise rather than artillery support was the key element, and they believed the raid would succeed.

Perhaps two well-respected British historians should have the last word. From Philip Ziegler: "Possibly it was word from the top; it would have gone ahead on a political basis."[24]

And from General Sir David Fraser: "Monty might have been told that Dieppe had a strong political imperative behind it and therefore it must go through. I think that there must have been an ordinance from above that the operation proceed. Churchill could have said, 'Dieppe is strategically and politically important to the war. It must go ahead. Commitments had been made at a high level.'

"That is understandable and defensible."[25]

PART

5

JULY 1942

CHAPTER

13

RUTTER: A DIRECT HIT

Boredom and frustration marked the five days of waiting it out on the Solent to go into action. Roughly 8,000 men were jammed onto vessels intended for one overnight journey, with food and provisions scaled to the short term.

The Rutter commanders had decided that the operation would take place on "the first favourable date between 3/4 July and 8/9 July," Each day brought fresh disappointment as the southwest winds over France continued to blow too strongly for glider or paratroop landings.[1]

The troops on the LCTs soon wearied of their compo rations. As one soldier recalled, these consisted of "hard tack, cans of stew, bacon (mostly grease), and margarine (just like rock); as well as tea, hard candies, powdered milk and eggs and tins of Woodbine cigarettes."[2]

For security reasons, the men on the mother ship had to stay below. Worse, on the LCTs the navy had slung tarpaulins across the decks to disguise the cargo of tanks, carriers, and sweltering soldiers. Frank Volterman, a medical sergeant with the Royal Hamilton Light Infantry, recalled the discomfort the men experienced spending five days on a LCT: "We were so confined we could only walk a few steps. With the roll of the boat, the men were throwing up. The heads were clogged; the air became fetid."[3]

Living conditions on the LCTs were extremely uncomfortable and the food and water were both "inadequate" observed John Hughes-Hallett, who was on board. Nevertheless, "not a single grumble was heard." After a few days, the men were given strictly regulated recreational breaks on shore.[4]

Mountbatten and Roberts paid morale-boosting visits to the troops. The men were permitted to write one letter home, which would be censored and posted after the operation. They were bemused by the pocket-sized escape kits issued to each officer. To a young lieutenant earning $5.00 a day, the wads of French francs — each officer was issued 5,000 — seemed stupendous. The same kits also contained a silk map of France, a tiny compass, and a small saw embedded in rubber, about the length of a lead pencil.

The spectre of battle hung over their heads. "Maps were distributed of the area to be raided, namely 'Dieppe France,' " the Camerons noted in their War Diary. "The officers explained every detail concerning our own Bn. [battalion] and a general description of the other units' tasks. Soon every man knew his own particular job and started to make sure of his equipment."[5]

The riflemen worked hard over their Sten guns, filing and coaxing them into maximum efficiency. They sharpened knives and bayonets and then primed the grenades, inserting the lethal detonators so they were ready for action.

Despite the general optimism, there were the occasional dour faces. The navy had dropped troops down at the wrong places in the two rehearsals; would it happen again in the raid? The price in real battle for those navigational errors would be high casualties.

Lieutenant Ed Bennett of the Calgary Tanks remembers that "after the briefing, we all had apprehension. But there were hardly any questions. We were all in shock. I thought that we in the tanks might be okay, but remembering the film *Next of Kin*, when the troops on a raid were slaughtered, I thought that might happen to some of the infantry. For the tanks, I knew where I'd end up: our troop was supposed to get way out on the high ground beyond the airport. I doubted we would go that far. But I knew we'd be the last to withdraw if it was successful."[6]

With increasing trepidation, Major Forbes West of the Royal Regiment of Canada had examined the German machine gun post dominating the cliff above their designated landing place. "Looking at the model in Cowes, it seemed we would be enfiladed by enemy fire one hundred yards before we got to land. I wondered how a shell fired from the destroyer's four-inch guns at sea could possibly come down over the edge of the cliff where it would hit anything. I said to the British gunnery officer next to me, you've either got to shoot this thing through the cliff or it won't come down until it gets to Paris. He said he'd have to go and look up his range tables. That was the end of that.

"But my commanding officer, Lieutenant Colonel Hedley Basher, had come up with a suggestion which he made to General Roberts. He said, why don't we put a six-pounder gun on an LCT and blow that machine-gun post off the face of the earth and *then* go ashore. He was told to shut up and mind his own business."[7]

———■———

Meanwhile, Churchill and Brooke had arrived back in England on June 27th. They faced not only the "beautiful row" Churchill expected in the House of Commons, but also a worsening war situation and a monumental workload.

A 10-day backlog of military and political affairs had accumulated while they were in Washington. Churchill had to prepare for the Commons debate on the vote of censure in the House, the second demonstration of lack of confidence in the management of the war that year. The debate was scheduled for July 1 and 2, four days away. He had already decided on his political strategy: he would deliver the concluding speech — 9,000 words of passion and eloquence. The timing for that two-hour address was precise: "He didn't want to finish a moment before time, so no one else would be able to cap his remarks!" his secretary said. In the interim, Churchill himself should have to write it.[8]

There were also considerable problems on the war front. By June 30, the North African situation had become even more critical: Rommel's aggressive advance after his triumph at Tobruk had brought him to within 60 miles of Alexandria. In desperation, Churchill cabled the 8th Army's headquarters: "Egypt must be held at all costs"; the troops must fight "as they would if Kent or Sussex were invaded."[9]

On top of that was the uncertainty about the outcome of the Washington conference. The bad news from Egypt made Operation Torch, the North African invasion, all the more imperative. Had they succeeded in persuading Roosevelt and Marshall to drop their dangerous insistence on Sledgehammer?

The priority that Churchill and Brooke placed on the Dieppe operation as their last hope against the threat of Sledgehammer is clear from their actions on their return. Despite all the pressures on them, internal and external, one of their first acts after returning to London was to call a meeting of some of the principal Dieppe planners for June 30.

"The meeting took place in the Cabinet Room and oddly enough, Mrs. Churchill was also present in the room," noted Captain John Hughes-Hallett. More oddly, none of the force commanders was present. Mountbatten and Hughes-Hallett were there representing Combined Operations. Besides Churchill and Brooke, General Ismay and Brigadier Hollis attended for the Chiefs of Staff Committee. The group reviewed the Rutter plan carefully.

"In the course of the discussion Mr. Churchill turned to me and asked whether I could guarantee success," Hughes-Hallett reported. Hughes-Hallett's reply: "Every ship might be blazing within fifteen minutes of H-hour."

"The CIGS interrupted and told me not to reply. If he or anyone else could guarantee success, he said, there would indeed be no point in doing the operation. No responsible general will be associated with any planning for invasion until we have an operation at least the size of the Dieppe Raid behind us to study and base our plans upon.

"Mr. Churchill at once agreed that if that were Alanbrooke's considered view we must go forward. He would ask Mr. Attlee to inform the Cabinet and he would inform the King."[10]

On July 5, while the Rutter force continued to wallow on the Solent, Montgomery woke up to a threat that should have been made apparent to him for some weeks: the Germans' 10th Panzer Division — one of the Wehrmacht's most powerful tank formations — had been transferred from the Russian Front, and was now in Amiens, less than 40 miles from Dieppe and "at full strength."[11]

Belatedly, Monty started to get a little worried.

He wrote to Crerar the same day.

My dear Harry: Rutter is postponed for 48 hours and, if conditions are favourable, will take place on Wed. 6 July. This continued postponement makes the time on shore very long. This begins to be dangerous, in view of the presence of a German armoured division at Amiens — which has now been confirmed.

Therefore, if the operation takes place on 8 July, it will be done all on one tide. . . . I am quite happy about this speeded-up plan. I was beginning to get unhappy about the long time on shore vide para 1.

If the weather does not allow the operation to take place on 8 July, it will have to be cancelled.

Yrs ever,
Monty[12]

Even for Montgomery, this was an extraordinarily understated way to bring attention to the fact that the enemy had massed a fully reinforced and battle-sharp armoured division within striking distance of Dieppe.[13]

Through Ultra, M.I. 14, and other overt intelligence sources, Churchill, Brooke, and the Chiefs of Staff had been able to track almost every move made by German units. They had learned on May 11 that there was "great activity on coastal defences as a precaution against possible British raids."[14]

As early as May 26 they had been alerted to the 10th Panzer Division's arrival in France. There were "certain indications of the presence of armoured troops in the neighbourhood of Dieppe," the intelligence report of that date warned. The presence of the 10th Panzers in Amiens had been confirmed on June 23 and again on June 30.[15]

Yet in May and June, the Second Canadian Division commanders at the sharp end were still being fed the nonsense that there was a weak German force of "low-category troops" manning poor defences.

It was June 30 before the Canadians — always the last, it seems, to be apprised of vital intelligence — were alerted: "The [10th Panzer] Division is in a position to reinforce Dieppe in about four hours," Lieutenant Colonel Church Mann signalled. "The Division is considered up to strength and has enjoyed a period of two months' rest."[16]

It took Montgomery a full five days to respond to the threat, as evidenced in his letter to Crerar. He changed the raid from two-tide to one-tide — in other words, from fifteen hours to six hours' duration.

But that still left the force vulnerable to the forward elements of the deadly panzers.

Fresh concerns erupted at the Chiefs of Staff level. They had got wind that there might have been grave security leaks about Rutter. While Churchill and Brooke were away in Washington, the Chiefs demanded that Mountbatten tell them why the airborne commander had insisted on an early briefing of some 60 personnel including glider pilots and paratroops, as well as the RAF pilots who would transport them. Mountbatten was able to reassure them; they decided there was "no need for security reasons to cancel the operation."[17]

A few days later, on June 29, Air Vice Marshal Leigh-Mallory also began to sense pending disaster. For the first time since he had been appointed force commander, the idea that there might be "relatively high" pilot casualties seemed to penetrate his thoughts.

"We can be well satisfied if our losses do not exceed, say, 60 to 70 pilots and 120 Spitfire aircraft," he predicted (with an accuracy that was almost eerie) to his boss, Air Marshal Sir William Sholto Douglas, Commander-in-Chief of Fighter Command. This was an alarming and unprecedented number, higher than in any previous operation of the war, and, understandably, Leigh-Mallory was very worried.

His boss was not. Douglas's response was cool: "In view of the importance of the op we must be prepared to accept this possible scale of cas. I certainly do not propose to call the op off."[18]

———————

As the date of the raid neared, the force commanders and divisional and battalion commanders showed increasing concern. Ominously, the anxiety was rising in another quarter as well: in Berlin, among the German High Command (OKW or Ober Kommando Wehrmacht).

Hitler had taken seriously the Anglo-American Second-Front proclamation that Molotov had lobbied so hard for in early June. He told his general staff that they must assume that the Allies were going to make landing attempts in the west in order to relieve the Russians. The Fuhrer responded swiftly to that threat. By mid-June he had appointed Field Marshal Gerd von Rundstedt — whom he considered "the ablest of Germany's generals" — to become Commander-in-Chief West, with 30 divisions under command from Holland to the Spanish border.

"Invasion unlikely in 1942 though large-scale raids probable," an intercepted Wehrmacht intelligence report of June 30 warned tersely. "Coastal defences increasingly strengthened."[19]

———————

While the English were worrying and the Germans were anticipating, the senior Canadian commanders were getting into something of a row with their British counterparts. The underlying cause was scarcely new: General McNaughton was bristling again over the Canadian identity. The immediate provocation was the discovery on July 1 that no Canadians — not even himself or Crerar — had been invited to join the exclusive group of senior officers of the three services at No. 11 Fighter Group at Uxbridge, the command base for the Dieppe operation.

Actually, in the weeks since Crerar and Simonds had manoeuvred the Canadian forces into the Dieppe operation, McNaughton had worked steadily to put out the fires that Crerar had lit under the British. Perhaps because they resented being pushed so hard by the Canadians, the British military had been making life extremely difficult for McNaughton. (Brooke, in his private moments, thought the Canadians were "touchy and childlike."[20])

The army chief had been put firmly in his place early on, in April. After committing the Canadians to the Dieppe raid, he innocently enough voiced his desire to have a "close and intimate liaison with the Combined Operations staff." "Oh, no," replied General Paget's Home Forces headquarters. Direct liaison would "create many difficulties and misunderstandings"; the general must go through Home Forces rather than communicate directly. McNaughton had made another request: that he be placed on the list for intelligence distributed by the War Office, Home Forces and Combined Operations. Home Forces again said no. It would be "most undesirable" for the Canadian army to receive communications directly from Combined Operations: Home Forces would give the Canadian Corps and the Second Canadian Division "such information as they require."[21]

Undoubtedly, this obstructionism was a major reason why the Canadians' access to key intelligence was so limited throughout the Dieppe operation.

McNaughton then had to fight to see a copy of the outline plan for the raid. On May 5 he was moved to comment that "in future Combined Operations involving Canadian troops, the outline plan should be placed before me before submission to the Chiefs of Staff Committee."[22]

In an effort to sort out the Canadian position, McNaughton demanded that a formal chain of command be established running from GHQ Home Forces to SECO to First Canadian Corps to Second Canadian Division — that is, from Paget down to Montgomery then to Crerar then to Roberts.

Finally, even Crerar suffered some nit-picking obstructionism at the hands of the British. On July 3, McNaughton wrote to Paget stressing the importance of including Crerar with the Uxbridge group, "to maintain the proper channel of command for the Canadian units involved."[23]

The lofty refusal that came on July 4 infuriated the proud Canadian. "Actually, there is no room for any more at the Group Headquarters ... it was agreed with Leigh-Mallory that the only people who should be there should be Montgomery and Mountbatten ... it would be wrong for Harry Crerar to go there. There can only be one man in command of the operation."

At 1600 hours on the same day, Crerar and Montgomery had it out. The Canadian forces were not going to be absorbed into the British army, Crerar insisted. "National [Canadian] policies and Imperial Constitutional relations" were at stake, he added.

He capped his remarks with a less-than-subtle threat: if SECO didn't back down and include the Canadians at the command post during the raid, he and McNaughton would raise the issue at the "highest political levels."[24]

In effect, he was saying, "no representation, no troops." Montgomery could have seized this squabble as a legitimate excuse to cancel; instead, he gave in. Crerar and McNaughton got their invitation to the "party."

If Montgomery *had* been looking for an excuse to cancel the operation, he now had one. This was the day before his letter to Crerar voicing his concern about the 10th Panzer's proximity to Dieppe. Instead, he meekly acquiesced to Crerar's threats.

———■———

Churchill and the Chiefs had been eyeing each 24-hour postponement with increasing dismay. The first delay was reported to the prime minister on July 3 — the day after he handily defeated the vote of censure 475 to 25.

Is there no way around this weather problem? he asked Mountbatten's deputy chief, Air Vice Marshal Robb. Churchill had of course been apprised by British intelligence that the enemy was expecting a raid. He knew of the recent order to the Luftwaffe to mount an air reconnaissance vigil over the south coast of England to detect signs of any massing of assault craft. Each hour or day that the Dieppe flotilla remained at anchor in the Solent invited detection by the enemy; the assault would then have to be disbanded.[25]

On July 6, Mountbatten himself took the news to the Chiefs of Staff of yet another postponement, to July 8. This would be the last possible day that the tides would permit the raid. Mountbatten detailed for them the "various minor alterations to the plan" — chiefly, Montgomery's proposal to condense the time ashore to a one-tide raid to avoid confrontation with the enemy armoured division. The Chiefs examined the revised plan and again formally approved it. They also agreed that should Operation Rutter not take place as now proposed, the force should be dispersed and Mountbatten *"should consider remounting it at a later date."*[26]

Surely there is no stronger evidence than this that Churchill and the Chiefs of Staff were absolutely determined and committed to mount the Dieppe operation. Dieppe had become a vital element in their struggle to persuade the Americans to accept their North African strategy.

Finally, a Luftwaffe pilot managed to achieve what Churchill, the Chiefs of Staff, Monty and the Canadian commanders had not even been tempted to try: the cancellation of Rutter.

Luftwaffe pilot Erich Schwarz had been assigned to routine air reconnaissances over the Portsmouth-Southampton sector and the Isle of Wight. In recent weeks his missions had been unproductive and monotonous.[27]

He had seen little of interest: no loaded transports, no fuel depots, no troop ship. Just a few farmers with horse-drawn plows getting an early start on a warm summer's day, and one or two fishing dories, which offered a bit of sport to the airmen.

He swooped in under the radar screen toward the Isle of Wight, wing tips almost skimming the wave caps, and circled round the western end of the Solent at Yarmouth Roads.

There, below him, was Christmas in July: the harbour dotted with ships, hundreds of them, anchored haphazardly around the port. Schwarz noted the date and the target position in his log: 0615 hours, July 7. Enemy identified.

He wagged the wings of his Focke-Wulf 190 at the remaining three fighter-bombers in his flight and led a second run at the tantalizing objective. Each plane aimed its machine guns and 20-mm cannon at the flotilla.

Seconds later, the 190s' high-explosive bombs — each plane carried one — smashed through the *Princess Astrid*, piercing her decks but exploding harmlessly in the water. Then the H.M.S. *Princess Josephine Charlotte* was hit, creating serious damage in the engine room. Asleep below-decks were 500 men from the Royal Regiment of Canada. By a miracle, only four were slightly injured. Private Joe Ryan of the Royal Regiment later recalled that "it was a hot night and we were sleeping on the deck. We had thousands of rounds of ammunition piled up. The bomb skidded right down the side of one guy, burned his leg, then slid across the deck into the water and exploded."[28]

The "tip and run" chance raid punctured not only the two troopships but Combined Ops' last hopes of launching Rutter. A scurried effort was made to find alternative shipping for the troops, but the delay was the final last blow to the raid. "On the way to Cowes, the regimental column was halted by a dispatch rider, who ordered it to return to camp," the Royal Regiment reported. "Weather conditions were still bad, and the tides were now unfavourable.

"The operation against Dieppe had been cancelled."[29]

Denis Whitaker

The military objectives bear scrutiny. The Rutter assault was saddled with some ludicrous tasks in addition to the more legitimate ones. When the raid was transformed into a "one-tide" operation of six rather than 15 hours, these tasks were never amended.

Even the tactical objectives never were very convincing. Was there any real expectation or desire or even *need* that they be achieved? Yet these objectives were not reduced by half or even adjusted when the assault's duration was halved.

The Royal Regiment of Canada was to be Rutter's linchpin. The raid's success depended on the Royal Regiment quickly knocking out the enemy's headland defences. If they failed, the two battalions coming ashore on the main beach would be caught in a murderous crossfire.

Their objectives were the most unrealistic of all.

In 30 minutes, the four companies of the Royals, each with 100 men, had first — while under intense enfilade fire — to secure a bridgehead on the narrow beach of the resort village of Puys, eliminating the coastal defences that dominated the landing site from concrete fortifications. Then, while still under fire, they had to force their way over a 12-foot seawall surmounted by triple concertina barbed wire and scale the sheer 200-foot cliff — a monumental task in itself.

The Royals' next immediate sub-objectives covered an area of over three square miles. There were nine of these. They included the elimination of the following: four light anti-aircraft positions, all dug in, wired, and defended by crews of 8 to 10 men; one heavy anti-aircraft battery, probably of four 75-mm guns, also dug in, wired, and defended; and one four-gun artillery battery in concrete emplacements. In addition, they had to take out a number of machine gun positions as well as a German barracks.

All in 30 minutes, before the main assault.

"One of our tasks was to collect samples of French bread," recalled Major Forbes West of the Royals. "Another was to blow the barrels of some anti-aircraft guns, and then we were also supposed to release French prisoners from a jail.

"Now what lessons of war are to be learned from those three things?"[30]

Other battalions listened in amazement as some of their objectives were listed. There were some that seemed reasonable: Luftwaffe papers, pamphlets, codebooks, and secret files were to be brought back from the aerodrome. The coastguard house, prison, barracks and Palais de Justice were to be captured and searched. The radar station equipment was to be a particular focus of attention.

But some objectives bordered on the ridiculous, given the six-hour deadline and the fact that the assault force would in all likelihood be under fire. Twelve hotels (ranging in size from 40 to 150 rooms) were to be thoroughly searched for "military papers." Military passes were to be recovered from the Gare Maritime. From the local post office, naval and military papers, address lists, and civilian and military rubber stamps and passes were to be brought back. As well, troops were to obtain a record of telephone subscribers.

More lessons of war?

"It is astonishing that the British should have underestimated our defence, as they had details of most of it from air-photos," the German commander of the 81st Corps observed after the raid. "*Equally striking is the short time in which they expected to carry out the operation.*"[31]

CHAPTER

14

CHILD OF CHURCHILL

The cancellation of Rutter on July 7 posed a serious setback for Churchill and the Chiefs. They had promised Roosevelt and Stalin a super-raid and now they had nothing to deliver. Worse, earlier that same day they had formally tabled their final decision that Sledgehammer was not feasible.

Now Churchill delivered the two-fisted blow to Roosevelt. Dieppe had been cancelled by weather; Sledgehammer had been axed by the COS: "No responsible British General, Admiral or Air Marshal is prepared to recommend 'Sledgehammer' as a practicable operation in 1942 . . ."[1]

Sledgehammer, Churchill explained again, was too chancy to provide a permanent lodgement. This operation against France in 1942 would be sacrificial. As well, a failure would so deplete the Allied military strength and equipment that it would jeopardize the 1943 assault on France (Roundup) that the Americans so badly wanted.

"French North Africa is by far the best chance for effecting relief of the Russian front," Churchill added.[2]

To no avail, he and Brooke had tried to talk Washington out of a Channel attack. The British were faced with a two-horned dilemma: they would alienate their American allies if they did not mount Sledgehammer — and they would be throwing their fighting force into useless slaughter if they did.

The British would have to conjure something up to pacify the Americans. Since it was going to be impossible to create another super-raid from scratch that summer, they had no alternative but to remount the old one — Dieppe. Here, ready-made, was the assault of "limited scale" that Marshall (via Britain's U.S. representative Field Marshal Sir John Dill) had said would satisfy the Americans and Russians.[3]

According to General Ismay, Churchill had been "bitterly disappointed" at the cancellation of Rutter, and was "prodding" for its resurrection. The Chiefs were pushing not only for the remount but also for the operation to be planned in such a way that it would not be vulnerable to postponements again.[4]

So it was no coincidence that six days after Sledgehammer was cancelled, the Dieppe raid was remounted. "In discussion with Admiral Mountbatten," Churchill wrote, "it became clear that time did not permit a new large-scale operation to be mounted during the summer, but that Dieppe could be remounted (the new code-name was "Jubilee") within a month, provided extraordinary steps were taken to ensure secrecy. For this reason no records were kept."[5]

Rear Admiral Baillie-Grohman would note caustically that the project, "was now a child of the Prime Minister [which] would certainly go ahead, one reason being the hope that it could relieve pressure on the Russian front."[6]

Churchill may have adopted the child, but it was only after "profound deliberation" that the still well-oiled and smooth-working Chiefs of Staff endorsed the adoption papers.

"Churchill was aware of the plans," Sir John Peck acknowledged, "because for very good strategic reasons he wished to mount raids . . . *provided that* the C.O.S. decided that the risks inevitably attached to any such operation were justified."[7]

Captain Hughes-Hallett observed in a postwar speech that "The most remarkable fact about the Dieppe raid was that it did take place. Credit must be due to the 'constancy of purpose' of the Prime Minister, Mountbatten, Leigh-Mallory and Roberts. Nothing was put in writing, but General Ismay informed the Chiefs of Staff and the Prime Minister. They gave verbal approval."[8]

Even before the cancellation, the Chiefs of Staff had kept their options open by approving Mountbatten's formal suggestion on July 6 that consideration be given to remounting Dieppe should it be called off by weather. Roberts had complied, and warned the men to be discreet when Operation Rutter was cancelled: "I ask you to say nothing . . . because if you do not there is always the possibility that we may be able to do it at a later date."[9]

The next major challenge was to produce a plan that was as close as possible to the original. As time did not permit locating and fully briefing fresh troops or commanders, the same units would have to be employed to whatever extent was possible. No additional training or rehearsals could be permitted. Because of the extremely tight security measures, the men would be assembled at the last minute from their various posts. With no warning, they would be taken to the assault craft and mother ships, which would have been dispersed to a variety of ports rather than gathered in the Solent.

The Jubilee plan, as General Crerar described it, remained "Montgomery's plan."[10] So carefully, in fact, was the child cloned from the parent that on several documents the Jubilee name, when it was formalized in late July, was simply written above the crossed-out Rutter. Other documents simply stated, "Jubilee is Rutter."[11]

Yet another challenge was to make certain the raid would not be subject to cancellation by detractors or by the elements. Weather and the "finicky airborne" had forced Dieppe's cancellation in July. Rutter wasn't the first operation that had been called off because the "whole series of tides, moon, winds and clouds" did not reach the extremely high standards demanded by the airborne forces. The planners had noted even before the cancellation that "the use of paratroops makes the operation particularly sensitive to weather. These troops should be excluded or given a role not vital to the operation as a whole."[12]

The airborne had to go — written out entirely from the Jubilee plan. This was to be the only change in the battleplan itself. Two troops of commandos — Nos. 3 and 4 — were substituted for the paratroops. They were assigned the airborne objectives: to destroy the artillery batteries on Dieppe's extreme flanks. Because the commandos were both skilled and experienced in amphibious operations, they were permitted to make their own plans. Just check them out with General Roberts, they were told.[13]

At Richmond Terrace, detractors were suddenly appearing from surprising directions. The first was Montgomery himself. On June 30 he had enthused that the operation had "good prospects of success." Just over a week later, he changed his mind with startling abruptness, recommending to General Paget that for security reasons the operation with Dieppe as the target should be cancelled "for all time." If another raid was mounted, the objective should be anywhere but Dieppe because of possible German foreknowledge.[14]

Some years later he capped the turnabout when he said, "I had never been happy about this difficult operation being done by such inexperienced commanders and troops. Bravery is no substitute for battle experience." Clearly, by then he had forgotten his letter of July 1,

1942, in which he raved about the Canadian troops: "First-class chaps. If anyone can bring it off, they will."[15]

The one factor that might have transformed an enthusiastic Montgomery into a reluctant dissenter in a bare week was his realization of the presence of the German armoured division near Dieppe. It was one thing to risk a poorly supported surprise attack against a weak enemy and an ill-defended target; it was a far different thing to pit those same troops, with the same support, against the armoured might of 10th Panzer Division, which was battle-sharp and up to strength and equipped with several hundred of the powerful Mark III and IV tanks.

It is not known whether he expressed his concerns about enemy reinforcements to his superiors, Brooke and Paget; but since British intelligence was disseminated first to Brooke and then down to Home Forces — Montgomery and Paget — there can be no doubt that the COS had been just as aware of the danger, and for a longer time.

Montgomery had to go. His recommendation that it be cancelled marked him as a potential troublemaker against the smooth remounting of the raid.

Paget eased him out by creating a new chain of command that bypassed him altogether, appointing McNaughton instead as responsible military commander. Montgomery then cleared his desk of Operation Rutter, burning all relevant documents — which was an extraordinary and highly unprofessional act — and retreated to his South Eastern Army duties.[16] He spent the last weeks of July in England and Scotland observing training exercises. The suggestion has sometimes been made that he resigned from Rutter to take command of the Eighth Army in North Africa; actually, he had not even been short-listed for the command at that time. (This was "the strangest omission of the war," according to his biographer.) It wasn't until the Eight Army's incoming commander, Lieutenant General W.H.E. Gott, was killed in an air crash in August that Brooke proposed Montgomery for the post. On August 10 Monty flew to North Africa — where the Allied victory at El Alamein would make him Britain's most famous soldier.[17]

He left behind a damning legacy: the "Monty plan" for Dieppe.

The Canadians were now in control of the tactical running of the operation. Paget had given Montgomery's job to McNaughton, who promptly delegated that role: "I ask[ed] General Paget to agree to General Crerar being named as the responsible military officer to coordinate." The chain now ran this way: Paget to McNaughton to Crerar down to Roberts.[18]

However much he delegated responsibility, Paget was still the man at the top on the army side. As per the directive issued on March 21 and redefined on May 5, Paget had absolute responsibility over the military aspects of any raid. An outline had first to be presented to him showing "the object of the raid, the place, objective, approximate duration, approximate strength of military forces involved, and any obvious naval and air implications." If he approved, Paget would then assign the troops and appoint a commander. Mountbatten was still responsible to the Cabinet for the raids and for the combined training but Paget — no matter how strenuously he delegated or distanced himself — was clearly the military head man. He was only accountable to the Chief of the Imperial General Staff: that is, to Brooke. These two men therefore can never escape the ultimate responsibility for planning and executing the Dieppe raid.[19]

Admiral Baillie-Grohman had to go. His agitation for greater naval support had been a thorn in the planners' sides all along. Then on July 9, he authored a post-mortem critique of Rutter, which was endorsed by the remaining two force commanders, Roberts and Leigh-Mallory. While the critique stressed that "this is not a criticism of the planners in any way," it noted that Combined Ops had failed to produce a joint appreciation for the three services before handing on the outline plan for Rutter. This had made it "far more difficult for us to get into the planning picture. There was . . . nothing to guide us on certain points," Admiral Baillie-Grohman pointed out.[20]

This was probably the result of the sudden force-feeding of the Dieppe operation caused by the Modicum commitments in April. The last-minute inclusion of large numbers of infantry and armoured troops had resulted in the lack of clearly defined objectives and intentions pointed out by Baillie-Grohman.

It seemed highly likely that Baillie-Grohman would have caused even more commotion when the operation was remounted. It was equally likely his superiors knew it. He was posted elsewhere at very short notice — to Admiral Bertram Ramsay's staff — and was clearly relieved that he was not asked to take the command again. "I am very doubtful if I could have agreed," he later said.[21]

No doubt under his influence, Ramsay followed up two weeks later with a letter to Mountbatten expressing dissatisfaction over several aspects of the current raiding program. Mountbatten wrote in reply that "at the Chiefs of Staff and War Cabinet I was instructed to push on hard with large scale raids." He added that there were "political reasons" why he was "certain they will not cancel."[22]

Captain Hughes-Hallett replaced Baillie-Grohman. Mountbatten confided to him that "much as I loved Tom Baillie-Grohman, I felt you would be a far better Naval Force Commander and persuaded the P.M. and COS to agree to this."[23] Although Hughes-Hallett's rank was somewhat junior to that of the other force commanders — a naval captain is equivalent to a full colonel — his broad familiarity with the plan closed the gap with officers two ranks his senior.

Heeding Churchill's warning about tight security, Jubilee was cloaked in whispers. The wall of secrecy that had been raised around the operation was one of the highest of the war, and some very unorthodox measures were taken to prevent the enemy from learning of it. Fears of a leak were well founded. After locating and bombing the flotilla in the Solent, the Germans undoubtedly were aware that the British were up to something. A complicating factor was that the thousands of Canadian infantrymen who had been trained for Rutter had been released from the Isle of Wight. Many had been given a week's leave and so had plenty of opportunity to explore the pubs that would loosen their tongues.

In all matters dealing with Jubilee, no minutes would be kept. As the official Canadian historian discovered, no entries concerning the raid appeared "after 8 July and before 19 August except two (10 and 11 July) which appear to treat the matter as closed. There is no planning outline for Jubilee."[24]

During July and August, only key insiders were aware that the raid had been remounted. McNaughton was given a list of those who were on the "need-to-know" roster: "it numbered at this time only 20 names including the Chief of Combined Operations himself and the other members of the Chiefs of Staff committee."[25]

The Chiefs of Staff Committee — Brooke, Portal, Pound, Mountbatten and Ismay — knew; but Brooke's Vice-CIGS, General Nye, did not. From Combined Ops, besides Mountbatten, Hughes-Hallett knew, but not the principal COHQ staff officers. The COHQ intelligence officer, Casa Maury, knew; but not any member of any of the various British intelligence services. From South Eastern Army, only Montgomery and Rees knew. From the RAF, Leigh-Mallory knew, as did his boss, Douglas. Eisenhower knew, but his London staff were completely in the dark. Among the Canadians, McNaughton, Crerar, Roberts, Mann, and the principal staff officers knew; but the commanding general at Canadian Military Headquarters in London did not know, even though he was expected to provide all post-battle hospitalization services.

The second floor at 1A Richmond Terrace was set aside for force commander meetings, and no other personnel were permitted on that floor. By July 16 the date had been set. On meteorological advice, the only possible dates were August 18 to 23, or September 1/2 or 6/7.

Jubilee was rarely referred to even by its codename. When the Chiefs of Staff officially approved Hughes-Hallett's appointment as naval force commander, they referred to Jubilee as the "next big raid" — there being no other big raid developed to the stage where commanders might be assigned. "I received official confirmation on July 20 in the form of a minute from the COS committee," Hughes-Hallett recalled.[26]

"I hereby detail you as the responsible military officer for operation _____," McNaughton cautiously wrote to Crerar. He otherwise referred to Jubilee as just "J _ _ _ _ _ _".[27]

In a letter to General Brooke on July 30, Mountbatten made an unusual break in this silence by stating outright, "We had a meeting of the Force Commanders of 'Jubilee' today." Mountbatten apologized for taking up the CIGS' time on the eve of his departure for Cairo, and then reminded him, "As you know, this operation is being mounted in rather peculiar circumstances to preserve complete security."

Mountbatten then asked Brooke to arrange that escape kits for the officers be delivered to the troopships prior to the raid. As this request would have to be referred to other branches, Mountbatten cannily produced a convenient cover-up for Brooke: "I enclose a separate letter suitable for passing on to those who will have to take action, which does not refer to any particular operation."

The implication of this letter was that Brooke, far from being detached, was heavily involved in organizing Jubilee. The fact that the escape kits were in fact delivered is evidence enough that Brooke acted on the letter.[28]

Professor F.H. Hinsley, author of the official history of British intelligence, also noted the extreme secrecy surrounding Jubilee: "In giving approval to the final plan on 12 August the Chiefs of Staff referred to it only as the 'future raiding operation.' "[29]

One important inclusion on the "need-to-know" list were the American president and his key commanders. Eisenhower, who was highly enthusiastic about Jubilee, visited Combined Ops and wrote to Marshall as early as July 11 that "the British have decided not repeat not to withdraw special landing craft from training and raiding operations." (This is clear evidence that even then there was every intention of remounting Dieppe.) "These craft," Eisenhower continued, "would be used for the conduct of raids on an increasing scale in size and intensity. I have given assurance of our keenness to participate . . . and am very hopeful that not only our 1st Ranger Battalion, but other units . . . can gain this experience during the summer."[30]

At last, here was an opportunity for at least some American soldiers to meet Roosevelt's imperative that American soldiers be "blooded" in action against the Germans. Two weeks later, by Special Order No. 13, the 1st Ranger Battalion was officially ordered by Brigadier General Lucian Truscott to report to Commando HQ in Scotland for Combined Ops training.[31]

When only 50 Rangers were earmarked for the Dieppe raid, Roosevelt himself intervened.

> After being informed of the decision to raid Dieppe, [Roosevelt] insisted for reasons of politics and prestige that a United States military contingent participate in the assault. When his request reached London, however, the British General Staff resisted it. Their reasons were that the few American units in Britain at the time were green troops, and so it was decided to take along a token number of Rangers to gain combat experience.[32]

Also to accompany the raiders would be 20 all ranks of No. 10 (Inter-Allied) Commando. Of these, 15 were French and would act as guides and interpreters. The remainder were Sudeten Germans — anti-Nazis with intelligence missions who would certainly be shot if captured. Another volunteer was Flight Sergeant Jack Nissenthal, a radar specialist who would raid the German radar complex. His bodyguard — 10 men from the SSR — were told that under no circumstances was he to be taken prisoner. Finally, there were the war correspondents, covertly assembled and briefed to cover their first battle.[33]

On an afternoon in late July, Shimi Lovat was crouched in the ruins of Dundonald Castle on the southwest coast of Scotland, firing tracer down the hill at his attackers. Lieutenant Colonel the Lord Simon Fraser Lovat M.C., chief of Clan Fraser and commander of No. 4 Commando, had nothing more on his mind that July day than some serious commando training — and a spot of salmon poaching afterwards in the rivers of the Clyde Valley.

His brigadier approached. "Can you climb cliffs?" he demanded.

Less than 48 hours later, the tall young battalion commander with the striking good looks was at Richmond Terrace, glowering at the frivolity for which COHQ was well-known — and being eyed appreciatively by some of the silk-stockinged hangers-on. No. 4 Commando was going to Dieppe.

The objective assigned to Lovat's commando — who were replacing the paratroops — was the six-gun battery at Varengeville, some 1,200 yards inland behind the cliffs west of Dieppe. It could menace the entire flotilla, he was told. Much was going to depend on his men taking those guns out.

Lovat had just two weeks to come up with a plan of attack, and then train his men for it. Like Baillie-Grohman, he was not impressed with Jubilee's battleplan. But he, at least, was able to wrest some compromises from the planners to protect his men from the worst of it. "I came out strongly against the infantry's late start, and a daylight attack," he recalled. The concessions he won were that: "First, we would land before daylight; second, each Commando would be independent, fighting its own way." He would, he conceded, report back when the job was done.

Having managed to disassociate his commandos almost entirely from Jubilee's bosses, Lovat moved his unit to Weymouth and flung it into intensive preparations. Toiling day and night, Lovat and his second-in-command, Major Derek Mills-Roberts, drove their men ferociously. This was *their* training scheme for *their* battleplan.

They practised landing and disembarking in their LCAs, under fire, with smoke, in darkness. They practised what they would do if their LCAs were sunk. They learned "every fold and feature" of the ground they would cover. They tested and retested every weapon, fired grenades and mortars until the air was blue, and blasted endless holes through barbed-wire barricades with Bangalore torpedoes. They staged eight rehearsals right up to the eve of the assault, until every man had his tasks perfectly memorized. The Canadians forming the main raiding force were not permitted pre-Jubilee rehearsals, and had to depend on a mere two practices, Yukon I and Yukon II, two *months* before the raid.

Lovat's greatest worry was that he had to depend on the navy to set his force down on the correct landing place. Poor navigation by naval reserves during the rehearsals with the Canadians had many units deposited on the wrong beach and many minutes late. This, he figured, would spell "lost surprise and sitting ducks over open sights." The commandos were scheduled to land 10 minutes before daybreak — a vital 10 minutes if they were to escape observation by enemy machine gun posts. He asked for, and got, the best navigator the navy could supply.[34]

No. 3 Commando, under the command of Lieutenant Colonel John Durnford-Slater — nicknamed "Torchy" for his red hair — was training nearby at Seaford with a similar objective: to take out the six guns of the "Goebbels Battery," which was east of Dieppe at Berneval. Durnford-Slater had the bad luck to be assigned wooden R boats, or LCPs — "landing craft personnel" — for the entire Channel crossing (instead of transferring into them at the French coast.) His men rehearsed for the raid by cramming onto the flimsy R boats and circling the Isle of Wight all night.[35]

The Americans' 1st Ranger Battalion, officially activated on June 19, 1942, had been undergoing training at the commando centre in Achnacarry in Scotland for the past month. The 488 enlisted men, all ranks, endured training with live ammunition and grenades that was so "rigorous and realistic" that by July 17 one man had drowned and three had been wounded — by bullets or grenade fragments.

On August 1, six officers and 45 men from the Rangers were attached to No. 3 and No. 4 Commando and to units of Second Canadian Division for specialized training for Dieppe.[36]

The Canadians, for their hard training on the Isle of Wight, had received an unexpected bonus — a week's leave, which they enjoyed with their typical high spirits.

———

Denis Whitaker

A few men, including the irrepressible brothers Partington, and the battalion welterweight boxing champion, Private Bill Grant of the RHLI Carrier Platoon, married English brides during their leaves.

Many junior officers sought less sober pursuits in London's West End. Polly, the head bartender at the American Bar downstairs in the Park Lane Hotel welcomed us as if we were long-lost friends. Every noon, a bunch of us met there: Jack Taylor, Sparky Bell, Squeak Wright and Jack Doyle — he with the gorgeous Mexican wife Movotia — and drank double scotch-and-sodas (two and sixpence each) until closing: 2 p.m. Doyle was a big, handsome Irish professional fighter with curly black hair and a magnificent tenor voice that had earned him the nickname "the Irish Thrush." Being Irish, he felt no obligation to join the forces. His wartime contribution to the morale of young officers was his club in Soho, the Swizzle Stick. It opened every mid-afternoon just as the other pubs and bars were closing. This guaranteed that the double scotches would flow without interruption until well into the night.

On July 25 the battalion moved to a tented location on the grounds of Arundel Castle, the Duke of Norfolk's huge estate near the Sussex coast. Here we were involved in a series of "bussing and debussing" exercises in full battle order. These were designed to test our speed at loading and unloading personnel from trucks. We would take off across country, each man taking the equipment that he would normally carry on an actual operation: his weapon (which could be a rifle, a Bren or Sten gun, a Tommy gun, or an antitank rifle) and several hundred rounds of ammunition, as well as grenades, smoke bombs and, in some cases, Bangalore torpedoes. These were long, narrow tubes packed with explosives that we used to blast though wire obstacles.

We returned by evening to the pleasant grounds of Arundel, with its many agreeable distractions.

The duke had a magnificent herd of deer of which he was particularly proud. The mysterious disappearance of one of them caused a fair uproar, with the furious Norfolk descending on our battalion commander, who ordered a full-scale investigation. The culprit was never found, nor was the deer, but it is a fair guess that many a Riley had his first taste of venison that night. As one of the Partington brothers later indignantly commented, "Well, they can't expect *Canadians* not to hunt!"

The American Bar was soon replaced by the Arundel Arms, a charming, beamed, Tudor pub in town; and by the Three Crowns at nearby Angmering-on-Sea, where we spent many amusing hours with the Crazy Gang, the popular British comedians who played the Palladium.

On August 4, the battalion commanding officers were informed, in strictest confidence, that the raid was being remounted. One week later the company commanders were briefed. It must have been tremendously difficult for them to return to camp and pretend all was normal, while knowing that in a few days we would be in action. It must have been even more dismaying that, unlike the commandos, their men would receive only a rudimentary briefing, and only while at sea on the night of the attack. There would be no sand-table models for them, no chance to study "every fold and feature" of the ground and memorize their objectives, no opportunity to test the weapons that were still in crates waiting to be packed aboard. There were some new men who had just joined their battalions that month; these reinforcements had missed the training on the Isle of Wight. They had never heard of Dieppe.

They soon would.

———— ▬ ————

Strangely, the August 18 charts of the remounted operation, detailing the length of time the force would stay ashore at Dieppe, had reverted back to the original 15-hour, two-tide format — almost as if there was no longer the threat that the 10th Panzer Division was a mere four hours from Dieppe.[37]

Quite the reverse. "This begins to be dangerous," Montgomery had written to Crerar on July 5, while informing him that Rutter would go in on one tide because of the danger of a counterattack by the 10th Panzers.[38] Paget and presumably his army commander, Montgomery, had known of the Panzers' presence in northern France since May 18. That it had been brought up to strength and moved to within 40 miles of Dieppe had been confirmed in another report dated June 23.[39]

But by August 18, the situation had become many times more desperate. British intelligence by then had learned that the 10th Panzers had moved even closer, to Flixecourt, halfway between Amiens and Abbeville. Their report also verified that "this Division is a first-class fighting formation and up to strength in men and equipment." The 10th Panzers had a formidable reputation: they had led the German armoured thrust across France in 1940 and then fought on the Russian Front for over a year. Four hours, it was again calculated, was "the shortest time in which advanced elements of this Division could arrive at Dieppe."[40]

The Panzers were not the only serious menace. The Chiefs of Staff had by this time received yet more ominous intelligence: two German S.S. divisions — General Sepp Dietrich's crack Division Leibstandarte S.S. Adolf Hitler, described as a "highly mobile division of experienced troops," and the S.S. Division Das Reich — had been abruptly withdrawn from Russia in mid-battle and posted just 50 miles from Dieppe.

On July 6, at a critical point in an attack on a Russian objective, Hitler, alarmed enough about his western flank, had ordered Colonel

General Franz Halder to transfer one of his key divisions of the First Panzer Army from the Russian Front to the Channel. Halder was outraged that Hitler would snatch one of his few reserve divisions in mid-battle from the front, and saw this as one more indication that the Fuhrer's anxiety over his western flank was increasing hour by hour.[41]

Beset by "disappointment and apprehension," Halder lamented in his diary: "the Fuhrer refuses . . . to release S.S. Leibstandarte Adolf Hitler which would be of considerable value for First Panzer Army's attack."

The S.S. Division order cited "the area Dieppe-Le Havre" as among the coastal region's most threatened.[42]

On top of that, M.I. 14's intelligence summaries had been issuing warnings as early as April 13 of an "increasing German preoccupation with coastal defences." Its report of May 11 advised that the "Germans are showing keen interest in Channel coast."[43]

By mid-July, British intelligence had also reported the presence of a special flak formation, "Flak Division der Landesbefestigungen Ober-West." By August 3, M.I. 14 was asserting that the number of divisions in France had risen from 25 to 27—and this was not counting an enemy paratroop division that had just been posted to Normandy. "This suggests an increased concern with coastal areas, probably due to fear of Allied operations."[44]

"Estimated total of 450,000 to 500,000 German troops in France," stated a War Office Report. All leaves in France were cancelled until end of August.[45]

The appointment of the veteran Field Marshal von Rundstedt as Commander-in-Chief West spoke volumes about the extent of Hitler's panic. He had been warned to expect raids and he was well prepared.[46]

The Chiefs had also learned that Albert Speer, Hitler's brilliant architect and minister of war productions, had recently been placed in charge of building coastal defences. His intention was clear: to accelerate construction of the Atlantic Wall fortifications. "Extensive scheme of coastal fortification underway," British intelligence stated tersely.[47]

This alarming intelligence about the proximity of strong enemy reinforcements and the strength of his defences caused the raid to be finally reduced to a one-tide operation. However, no fundamental changes were made that would offer the fighting force more protection or support. Churchill and the Chiefs of Staff remained insistent. Dieppe must be pushed forward to its conclusion.

15

TWO-TIERED INTELLIGENCE

The Dieppe raid — now codenamed Jubilee — was remounted and moving ahead full tilt, despite the fact that the plan's flaws were becoming increasingly apparent. That short distance between the Cabinet War Room on Great George Street and Combined Operations Intelligence at 1A Richmond Terrace was now proving a long mile in the communications deficiency between the two offices.

There was a two-tiered disparity between the sophisticated intelligence techniques used by Churchill and the Chiefs at the top compared to the clumsy procedures available to the planners at the sharp end.

What *was* Hitler's defensive ability on the French coast? Churchill and the Chiefs had access to a number of sources of strategic intelligence that were certainly not always available to the Dieppe planners.

From Ultra, and from the M.I. 14 files summarized and updated every week, Brooke, Churchill, the Chiefs and various senior military commanders could learn the exact disposition of many of the German forces in Europe and Africa. This included the enemy order of battle, and his strength in men, tanks, guns and aircraft, as well as close estimates of supply positions in fuel and ammunition, and his plans and movements on a day-to-day basis.

In August 1942, for example, Churchill was able to give Stalin the precise number of German divisions in France: "exact information about the number and character . . . there were 25 German divisions, nine of which were of the first line."[1] While the *source* of this intelligence had to be strictly guarded, the *content*, its source camouflaged, could be disseminated more freely.

Yet just a few hundred yards away, Casa Maury's unit did not even know the name of the enemy division that had been posted at Dieppe for some two years. This gives truth to the contention of historian

Walter Scott Dunn that "the British possessed far more information than was released to their own forces."[2]

Churchill had access to Ultra, Britain's magic window into the heart of the Wehrmacht. At Combined Ops, meanwhile, some especially dangerous assumptions were often based upon vacation postcards and old Brownie snaps from family photo albums. Its best information came from topographical sources (ISTD: Inter-Services Topographical Department at Oxford), or from photographic sources (PR or Photo Reconnaissance at Buckinghamshire). These agencies themselves warned that they were "never entirely complete or absolutely accurate."[3]

Through the mechanical genius of the Enigma machine, British intelligence could intercept and decipher enemy signals transmitted in code by wireless telegraphy. The signals were received at the British Intelligence Government Code and Cypher School at Bletchley Park, an ugly, sprawling estate some 50 miles north of London.

The Victorian gargoyles that adorned Bletchley's brick exterior belied the austere nature of the work within. A number of hastily erected Nissen huts scattered across the estate's broad lawns housed some of the brainy young men and women who deciphered, transcribed and disseminated the signals.

Hitler's insistence that he be kept constantly informed had become a huge asset to his enemies. From the earliest days of the war, German military commanders had been required to send daily situation reports to Hitler's OKW (Ober Kommando Wehrmacht) in Berlin. Fortunately for the Allies, these coded reports were often sent to the German High Command by wireless telegraphy, which was the one communication system that Ultra could intercept and decode.

Signals sent by land-line — that is, by telephone or telegraph — were beyond its scope. In more remote campaigns, where communication by telephone was difficult, or at sea, where it was impossible, reliance on wireless telegraphy was almost universal and Bletchley was able to intercept and decode these signals. As a result, Churchill knew Rommel's reported petrol deficiencies in North Africa almost down to the last litre and his troop disposition down to the last corporal. By early 1942, Enigma was intercepting 39,000 signals each month from all war theatres. Of these, 25,000 were from the German army and air force, the rest from the navy.[4]

The system of distribution initiated in the summer of 1940 was fully in place and running without a hitch by 1942. Ultra had come of age, so top-secret that only Churchill, Roosevelt and their Chiefs and key staff knew of it. A condensed analysis of Ultra information was fed to senior army, navy and air force commanders and their chief staff officers on a strictly controlled "need-to-know" basis. Usually only four or five at each headquarters were permitted any access to this top-grade intelligence.[5]

Churchill depended heavily on the messages that Bletchley Park sent to him (always in a locked yellow box) at Number 10 Downing or at Storey's Gate, where his underground war rooms were located. He referred to Bletchley's staff, who worked there for so many years in strictest secrecy, as "the geese who laid the golden eggs and never cackled."

"Where are my eggs?" he would demand playfully each day.[6]

Being privy to Ultra's secrets was rather like playing poker with all the hands visible only to oneself. The trick was to use the information without revealing to either opponents or friendly players that their hands were being observed.

A dramatic example of this was Churchill's stoic acceptance of the huge outrage directed at him by the British Parliament — and people — in February 1942, when the two large German battleships *Scharnhorst* and *Gneisenau* made their impudent escape from Brest to Kiel through the Straits of Dover.

Throughout his entire lifetime Churchill could never reveal — even to most of his closest associates or his family — that far from being despondent over that incident, he had been elated. For he had learned through Enigma decrypts that the ships had been damaged by mines laid by the British navy the day before. "This will keep them out of mischief for at least six months," he exclaimed to Roosevelt.[7]

Although the British refused to divulge to the Russians the fact that they had broken the high-grade German codes, Churchill was able to give Stalin specific warning of the massing of German troops on the Russian border just before Hitler launched Barbarossa. He masked the existence of Enigma by resorting to phrases such as "a well-placed source in Berlin" or "a most reliable source," and by withholding details such as unit identifications that would have tipped his hand.[8]

In contrast with their wealth of knowledge of enemy strength in North Africa and Russia, the Chiefs of Staff were concerned that because the telephone was more prevalently used in Europe, "Detailed intelligence was in short supply for north-west Europe, particularly in relation to the enemy's Army strengths and ground defences." In mid-April the Chiefs issued special instructions to their intelligence agencies to "focus a spotlight on Europe."[9]

Whatever their concern, the Chiefs were hardly in a famine. Contemporary historians still debate how much of Enigma's high-grade intelligence on western Europe was available. Unfortunately, and incredibly, the extent of high-grade intelligence emanating from Europe and particularly from France during this period cannot be confirmed. Even 50 years later the British Cabinet was *still* refusing to give historians access to any Ultra files dated prior to 1943.[10]

However, it is known from available intelligence summaries that armoured units were identified in the Dieppe area in May 1942. Since the Wehrmacht began using wireless transmissions for the first time in France "in Dieppe, Rheim [sic] and St Malo" at that time, and since armoured headquarters often used the Enigma machine for high-level communications, the Chiefs' information relating to these armoured units probably came from Bletchley.[11]

One of Ultra's most renowned specialists, Ralph Bennett, who was a duty officer at Bletchley's Hut 3, and later wrote *Ultra in the West*, recently pointed out another, more oblique way in which Ultra was used to track enemy dispositions in France: "At that time we were getting a great deal from the Russian front. If a unit disappeared from the front, it was a fair inference that it was going west. By its non-appearance in countries such as Poland or Italy we could by elimination quite easily confirm its presence in France."[12]

Bennett's supposition that accurate intelligence on German troop dispositions in France was available in 1942 can be confirmed by studying the weekly intelligence summaries known as the *Martian Reports*, as well as data from low-grade sources. These often included "paraphrased or disguised" Ultra information — again, cloaked in such phrases as a "secret" or "a reliable Polish or French source."

The M.I. (Military Intelligence) information that was released weekly to Brooke and the Chiefs was detailed and accurate. It was in its distribution that the hard-earned intelligence went awry.

The *Martian Reports* were prepared by General Paget's Home Forces headquarters. A "most secret" War Office report stated, with reference to the entire Channel coast, that "G.H.Q. Home Forces will be responsible for collating detailed information, and will be the accepted authority on all other intelligence matters." It further ordered that GHQ provide the information to the War Office and War Cabinet sections "without request." But subordinate operational commands, such as Combined Ops and the Dieppe force commanders, received it only "when required."[13]

The man who bore the ultimate responsibility for the military mounting of the Dieppe raid — General Paget at Home Forces — was on the receiving end of every shred of top-level intelligence. But ridiculous as it seems, the system did not allow him to voluntarily share it with the Combined Ops planners or the force commanders who needed it most. This was to backfire badly.

One of the reasons for this was that the British army as an institution had always been handicapped by internal rivalries between service arms. Another was the "If you don't ask you don't want" rationale between the various intelligence units.

In the months preceding the mounting of Rutter and the remounting of Jubilee, the Chiefs of Staff, War Cabinet, military intelligence and Paget's Home Forces headquarters had been told repeatedly that the enemy forces were making major changes to their coastal defences. The Joint Intelligence Sub-committee (JIC) had warned the Chiefs on July 20 that "all ports are especially strongly defended. Defence of the coast will pivot on ports which will probably be converted into quasi-fortresses with all-round defence." The committee specifically warned them of the presence of hundreds of machine guns and flak batteries.[14]

They *knew* that battle-sharp tank units and two of the Wehrmacht's toughest S.S. divisions were being moved to the west, despite the fact that they were some of the few battle-worthy reserves available and were badly needed on the Russian front.

They *knew* that Hitler was beefing up his already "bristling" Channel coast defences, which Churchill described as the "steelbound fortified coasts of France."[15]

And they *knew* that Germany's most experienced and wily general officer, von Rundstedt, had been appointed to command the Wehrmacht defensive armies in the west.

When Churchill and the Chiefs of Staff (which committee included Mountbatten) approved the Dieppe plan, they were in a position to evaluate the strengths and weaknesses of both sides. They were aware, at least in general terms, of the scope, offensive strength, supporting arms (including the paucity of fire support from the RAF and the Royal navy) and the numbers and experience (or lack of it) of the assault force.

Therefore, they must have known that the Dieppe assault forces would be outnumbered and — in terms of experience — outclassed by the German defenders. They would encounter beaches that were heavily fortified and strongly defended by an enemy force whose ability to counterattack was terrifying. No wonder the commander of the German 81 Corps was baffled that the British so underestimated his defences. Such chaos at intelligence sharing and evaluating could not have occurred in disciplined Wehrmacht ranks.[16]

Whitaker Commentary

Lord Lovat, commander of No. 4 Commando at Dieppe, believed that British intelligence "either lacked reliable agents or seriously under-estimated German High Command." He cited as one intelligence blunder the lack of warning that Haase held cyclist reserves behind the town. It was this reserve that counterattacked the Canadians at Pourville.[17]

Although the Chiefs had been briefed on an ongoing basis since May that the 10th Panzer Division was three to four hours from Dieppe, they approved the raid in June and July and they approved a remounted raid again in July and August of "two-tide" or 15-hour duration. This put the assault force dangerously close to the German Panzer reinforcements. But the transformation to a "one-tide" assault of six hours just before Rutter, and again just before Jubilee, still committed the Canadians to be very much within striking distance of the deadly Panzer forces.

It was not until late June that the Canadian army was informed of the Panzers' presence. There is nothing to indicate that anyone in-formed the Dieppe raiders subsequently of the dramatic increase in enemy strength on the coast.

Why, with their proven knowledge of the bristling defences of the Iron Coast, did Churchill and the Chiefs not impart a warning to the raiding force? Why did they not cancel the operation? Or did their commitment to Roosevelt and Stalin to mount this raid make this impossible?

The Allies may, as Lovat noted, have had few agents in France, but there was another source of intelligence that M.I. 14 could have tapped: first-hand reports were available from American newsmen, who had been relatively free to roam Nazi-occupied France for two years after their British and Commonwealth colleagues had been expelled.

On Thursday, August 20, 1942 — the morning after the raid — *The New York Times* published an uncannily detailed and accurate description of the German defences at Dieppe.

Under the by-line of a "military observer" named Glen Stadler, the UPI article stated that the troops

> must have been met with a murderous crossfire from batteries emplaced in the beaches and cliffs, judging from an unauthorized inspection I made of that area last year.
>
> I have seen beaches bristling with machine guns, backed by small and large cannon concealed in caves in the hillsides and on hilltops commanding the sea.
>
> On the shore road from Havre to Dieppe . . . I studied the system of spacing guns within range of one another to cover the coast and catch any invasion force with a withering crossfire.[18]

How did a New York newspaper scoop the world with its story? How did UPI know more about the Germans' Channel defences than the men who would assault them?

Its source was one of several reports filed by Americans, such as 30-year-old Stadler, who had been assigned to UPI's Paris bureau in 1939. Although the Nazis did not permit correspondents to travel more than 30 miles outside Paris, Stadler and his colleagues made several unauthorized trips to the "Iron Coast" or Zone Interdit.

In December 1941, Germany declared war on the United States. Stadler was arrested, as were UPI's European manager, Frederick Oechsner, and other fellow reporters. They were all held in custody in Berlin until their repatriation in May 1942.

Upon release, they were debriefed in London by British intelligence and later, by the OSS in Washington. Obviously, UPI had the information on file and simply updated it for the story of August 20.

Their observations of the Channel fortifications and, in particular, the information that the enemy had turned the caves into gun positions were thus available to the British and American intelligence agencies months before the Dieppe raid.

The American military historian Alfred Vagts wrote, "It must have been known in London that the town of Dieppe, together with its inhabitants, was nothing but a camouflaged, or reconverted German waterfront fort, with numerous buildings turned into blockhouses and emplacements for machine and other guns."[19]

If it was known in London, New York, and Washington, then why was none of this information available to the men who would fight the battle?

Stadler and Oechsner and their colleagues were repatriated just after the top-priority command from the Chiefs of Staff to "focus on Europe."

It is beyond comprehension that British intelligence did not file their routine but important debriefing of the American reporters, and that the intelligence units responsible for evaluating the Dieppe operation did not, just as routinely, pick up that report — assuming it was available to them.

Obviously, intelligence distribution was two-tiered; the Dieppe planners who so dangerously underestimated the German defences were not supplied with accurate intelligence by the senior staff at Home Forces.

———————

The planners can be forgiven for believing the intelligence given them by their own headquarters that they would confront a weak enemy. Admiral Baillie-Grohman had been extremely disturbed by this: "It seems to me that everything being planned was based on this assumption and if it were wrong the results would be terrible."[20]

Combined Ops' intelligence section misidentified the German division defending the sector. It listed the force as the "not up to full strength" 110th Infantry Division, although Dieppe had been held by Major General Conrad Haase's 302nd Infantry Division since 10 April 1941. COHQ also wrongly located its headquarters: it was not in Arques-la-Bataille, as was indicated (and assigned — or misassigned — as a battle objective for the raiders), but in Envermeu, six miles east. All of this is of less importance than COHQ's apparent ignorance that for over a year, the defenders had been aggressively constructing concrete fortifications to transform Dieppe from a sleepy fishing village into a *Stutzpunkt*.[21]

Having erred on the identification of the enemy, COHQ consequently erred as well on his strength and capability of reinforcements. Rather than the token resistance the raiders had been led to expect, the German defenders were a formidable force.

Defences, they said, were "not heavy." The town was held by "low-category troops amounting to one battalion, with 500 divisional or regimental troops in support, making no more than fourteen hundred men." The enemy, they said, was "second rate," possibly with a company of Local Defence troops (men forty to forty-five years old), and there were not likely to be any first-line troops in the Dieppe area.[22]

As for reinforcements, within eight hours an additional 2,500 Germans could be brought from greater distances (Rouen and the east) comprising divisional infantry and two "raw" armoured divisions. The British intelligence update in August increased the prediction of defenders to 1,700, but reduced the expectation of reinforcement within eight hours to 1,600.[23]

In actual fact, von Rundstedt, concerned because "the Russians were pressing strongly for a Second Front," had ordered that the 302nd Division be reinforced on July 10 and again in August. This meant that Dieppe was now defended by three battalions totalling 3,500 men, with large corps and army reserve battalions on hand. And those potential reinforcements, far from being "raw," were seasoned veterans from the Russian Front: Leibstandarte S.S. Adolf Hitler, S.S. Division Das Reich, and a parachute division. Most ominous of all was the presence, less than four hours away, of the powerful 10th Panzer Division.[24]

Denis Whitaker

We were all very shocked to meet a well-prepared, well-trained and well-armed enemy waiting for us on the Dieppe beaches on the morning of August 19. We had been told that the German defences were weak. I am convinced that our commanders in the battle had been led to believe this as well. Lord Lovat agrees:

> Did Ham Roberts know what he was up against before starting? I suggest the answer is no. Merritt [Lieutenant Colonel Cec Merritt, C.O. of the South Saskatchewans] confirmed that, prior to departure for the operation, he knew little about the Germans, or how their general was likely to react.[25]

This could explain why General Roberts said encouragingly to us in our briefing that unfortunate phrase that was to haunt him all his life, "Don't worry, men, it'll be a piece of cake!"

The caves that punctuated the face of Dieppe's cliffs were an obvious cache for weapons. Even Churchill's wife, Clementine, warned him about their possible threat. He recalled, "One night when I was talking about this business beforehand to Mrs. Churchill (who spent several years of her youth at Dieppe), she spoke about those caves and said what a help they would be to the enemy. I have seen them myself when landing at Dieppe. The whole cliff is pockmarked."[26]

The UPI correspondents had accurately reported that the sheer cliffs above the town were honeycombed with caves. As well, Dieppe's topography was quite similar to some stretches of the English coast, where caves and tunnels also studded the chalk cliffs. South Eastern Army used these caves to advantage as encased gun positions; it took little imagination to conclude that the Germans must be doing the same. Combined Operations' intelligence section had in fact noted their existence east of the harbour, but surmised that they were used as a store for 2,300 torpedoes.[27]

Whitaker Commentary

Oblique aerial photographs would have shown the caves quite clearly and at least hinted at what they were concealing: the lethal machine guns that would end up annihilating the Canadians. The Air Ministry received several advance requests for these photographs. One Combined Ops planner, Major Walter Skrine, signalled on April 17 that "Oblique air photos will be required," followed by a more urgent plea on May 1 for "absolute priority" for oblique photos. But no authorization for them was given to the Photo Reconnaissance Unit prior to Rutter. The only useful oblique photographs — of the harbour and east cliff — arrived, belatedly, on August 10. None had been taken of the west cliffs.[28]

Lord Lovat considered that the intelligence, based as it was on air photographs, was "inadequate," and that the photos themselves were useless: "Such pictures failed to show tunnels were being dug into the chalk headlands covering the sea front and principal landing places; or the anti-tank guns that could rake the town esplanade; all skilfully concealed in daylight."[29]

Baillie-Grohman, Rutter's naval force commander, had nothing but disdain for the intelligence provided to the navy prior to that earlier plan: "Even such a small item as a good picture of Dieppe and the coast I could never obtain from [Casa Maury] in time for distribution before the raid [Rutter] was [scheduled to be] on, in spite of my urgent demands, even though I had often seen such pictures displayed in our railway carriages!"[30]

Once again, we see this strange refusal to heed the experts. Specialists from the artillery, the armour and the infantry had tried to issue warnings, and been brushed aside. Now their own intelligence men were alerting them to danger, and were being ignored.

Wing Commander Douglas Kendall, who commanded the Allied Photographic Interpretation Centre at Danesfield Hall in Medmenham, Buckinghamshire, confirmed to us that he delivered a warning that apparently went unheeded: "We reported at the time that ground sources indicated there were guns in those tunnels. We couldn't identify the size or calibre. We also reported guns on top of the headlands."[31]

Major Reginald Unwin, Staff Officer Intelligence, First Canadian Army, was another seasoned intelligence expert who had cautioned the senior officers about the caves' possible contents. He was convinced they were treacherous gun positions.

When the operation was remounted, Unwin and the intelligence officer assigned to the force commanders' headquarters, Captain Ernest Magnus, reported to Jubilee's temporary offices at Port Southwick in Postsmouth. There, in one of the fort's myriad tunnels, the pair set up office and tackled Jubilee's "massive volume" of information.

"Unwin was a most experienced man; he was quite a lot older, he'd been in the First World War," Captain Magnus recalled. "[He] wrote his appreciation; I wrote mine. We then compared notes. And we were pretty similar in our ideas: that the defences were extremely strong, particularly on the east headland. [That's] where those caves were, where Combined intelligence claimed there were torpedo heads.

"Both Unwin and I were very dubious about those reports. In fact . . . we felt convinced that there was artillery in those caves.

"We were pretty well pooh-poohed, even though we said that it's the sort of thing the Germans would do, [that the guns] are brought out at night and taken back in the morning, so you never see them on air photographs.

"Unwin put in his appreciation. He was a very cautious man. He felt that there was too optimistic a view on the [German] defences. His appreciation went up and probably went through various staffs.

When it came back many parts were deleted, other parts had been added in. Unwin was rather upset about this and so was I."

Unwin, appalled that his warnings should be covered up, did the only thing left for him to do: he refused to sign the report.

Magnus felt compelled to make his protest as well. "I did a very unforgivable thing. (Had I been a career officer it would have been the end of my career.) I took our original appreciation to Roberts, over the head of Church Mann. Roberts was at the end of the tunnel; Mann's office was in front. I watched for my opportunity and as soon as Mann came out I knocked on the door and went in. This was on the day before we went in [to Dieppe] on the 19th.

"Roberts said, 'There's nothing can be done about this. The show must go in.'

"The next day I went down to Newhaven to get onto the LCT. Unwin came down with me. I stepped onto the landing craft, turned around and saluted him . . . I was very disappointed at that time. I never expected to come back. It seemed to me pretty hopeless."[32]

The report, with Unwin's forebodings edited out, formed part of the Confidential Book (the operation order) that was issued to commanders before the raid. By written report and photographs it detailed Dieppe's topography, military objectives, the enemy's order of battle and rate of reinforcement, and the town's defences. It showed artillery installations, machine gun posts, roadblocks, antitank emplacements, pillboxes and beach defences.

But, as Major S.R. Elliot of the Canadian Intelligence and Security Association observed in 1981, "despite its apparent wealth of information the document is remarkable for its many omissions."

Elliot pointed out that the Confidential Book made no attempt "to locate in detail the infantry positions." It also "seriously underestimated the numbers of guns. The known characteristics of certain guns, together with a knowledge of the order-of-battle and the equipment in use, should have enabled COHQ certainly, and Second Division possibly, to make a more detailed evaluation of the number of, and threat posed by, the weapons deployed."[33]

———————

Omissions in providing the force commanders with a true picture of German strength and defences were glaring, yet they have been brushed aside to some extent by the official historians. Colonel Stacey claimed, mildly as was his manner, that the "planners underrated the influence of topography and of the enemy's strong defences in the

Dieppe area." His British counterpart, Professor F.H. Hinsley, is equally bland: although he does acknowledge that "too little care was given to the problem of the caves," he ignores the crux of the matter — that the men of Dieppe were annihilated on the beaches because of the guns in those caves.[34]

Without fire support, without effective backup of tanks, without even the element of surprise, and with completely unrealistic objectives and dangerously inadequate intelligence, the raiders went in, as Major Rees predicted, with little better support than their bare hands.

The serious concerns of a number of senior naval, military and gunnery experts were dismissed. Baillie-Grohman learned that the prime minister was "quite determined to go ahead" and that "the project was now a child of the Prime Minister." Mountbatten was advised "in the highest quarters" that Churchill intended to proceed with the raid no matter what the objections — nothing, he was told, could dissuade the prime minister. Major Rees was told that for political reasons Churchill had decided it would be inexpedient to undertake the bombing of Dieppe.

With the promised heavy bombing cancelled, General Roberts was seemingly brainwashed into going along with a much weakened version of the original plan. A battleship was never even requested, despite Baillie-Grohman's urgings that, *always*, heavy-gun support was presumed in amphibious assaults; and despite the well-understood fact that supporting fire from the Hunt-class destroyers could not effectively engage dug-in positions like the ones at Dieppe.

When Brigadier Lucian Truscott, an American officer who officially witnessed Jubilee, pointed out the "ineffectiveness" of the 4-inch destroyer guns, he was told that "it was realized that such support was inadequate, but that it was the only solution possible since cruisers could not be risked in such restricted waters."[35] Stacey confirmed that a request would have been hopeless, but Captain Hughes-Hallett later contradicted this. A battleship, he said, "could have operated in the Dieppe area during the first two or three hours of the operation without undue risk, and would probably have turned the tide in our favour."[36]

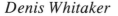

Denis Whitaker

Only a handful of us escaped that rain of fire to reach the town, and none, except 4 Commando, achieved the assigned objectives. But, here again, the inadequate dissemination of intelligence could have been a key factor to even worse disaster. Had the Canadians managed to establish a foothold on the beaches and reach the town, they would very likely have been annihilated by any one of the three battle-sharp armoured S.S. divisions in the region.

German reinforcements from 10 Panzer Division reached Dieppe at the moment of the Canadian surrender.

The lack of intelligence is therefore important, not just in the sad outcome of the soldiers' valiant try, but in any examination of why Churchill and the Chiefs of Staff did not warn the Canadians of the enemy strength that awaited them in Dieppe.

Personally, after hearing the opinions of so many men, I think Lord Lovat was correct when he contended that "the raid had to go ahead for higher political considerations, and I have little doubt that the prime minister's order to proceed was mandatory, and the reasons compelling."[37]

CHAPTER

16

DEATH OF SLEDGEHAMMER

Washington was in shock.

The news that Churchill and the Chiefs had reneged on their Sledgehammer deal wiped out all of the warmth and sympathy that had crept into the Anglo-American relationship following the Tobruk crisis. The recess from acrimony had lasted a mere two weeks; now the two sides were at odds again.

The British were up to their old double-dealing tricks, the American Chiefs of Staff thought wearily. By backing out of Sledgehammer, they were in effect squelching the "second front now" movement that had gained such popular support with the American media and public.

The United States was still totally opposed to a North African invasion. In their view, Operation Torch violated the principle of concentration of force agreed upon by the two nations in 1941; it was obviously just more of the British "periphery-pecking" that General Wedemeyer had so caustically criticized.[1]

Despite Churchill's reassurances, Marshall was convinced that the North African venture would kill the other vital half of his Modicum proposal: that is, the massing of American troops in England (Bolero) and the subsequent invasion of France in 1943 (Roundup). It was, in short, another frustrating betrayal.

Marshall had reason to be suspicious. Churchill would not dream of admitting as much, but the British joint planning staff had secretly advised him that if he did launch a North African campaign, there would be no possibility of amassing the necessary logistics to open a cross-Channel front — not for at least two years, 1944 at the earliest.[2]

In his crusade, Marshall had an ally in 63-year-old Admiral Ernest King, Roosevelt's chief of naval operations. King had a strong voice in U.S. strategy-making. He jealously defended his seniority — and America's priority — in the Pacific war. King had only one idea: to transfer operations to the Pacific. With the Japanese threatening Australia, many factions supported the rationale behind his campaign for a military offensive in the Pacific — at the expense of the war against Germany. King had emotional reasons too: "I fought under the goddam British in the First World War and if I can help it, no ship of mine will fight under 'em again," he grumbled.[3]

Marshall was also backed by the older and possibly even crustier Henry Stimson, who was Roosevelt's Secretary of War. On July 10, the 72-year-old Stimson referred to this "staggering crisis" in his diary.

> They are seeking now to reverse the decision which was so laboriously accomplished when Mr. Churchill was here a short time ago. I found Marshall very stirred up and emphatic over it. He is naturally very tired of these constant decisions which do not stay made. This is the third time this question will have been brought up by the persistent British and he proposed a show-down . . . As the British won't go through with what they agreed to, we will turn our backs on them and take up the war with Japan.[4]

Incensed, the American Chiefs approached Roosevelt with a formal ultimatum — what Marshall called his "showdown" strategy: if the British would not guarantee decisive action against the Germans in Europe in 1942, the Americans should ignore the Atlantic war. Instead, they should "turn to the Pacific and strike decisively against Japan." This move would be "highly popular" with the American people, Marshall insisted — with an eye to Roosevelt's chronic concern about the pending Congressional elections in November.[5]

"Roosevelt's main hurdle," historian David Eisenhower explained, "was maintaining congressional support for Europe First through the off-year elections. Without an operation of some kind against the Germans, the election might become a referendum on Europe First."[6]

Another factor that must certainly have influenced the president's emphasis on "Europe First" was the knowledge that Germany — not Japan — was developing atomic capabilities that had to be stopped.

Britain's representative on the Joint Chiefs of Staff in Washington, Field Marshal Sir John Dill, warned Churchill about this powerful opposition to his strategy. He stressed to the prime minister that he must convince the Americans of his intention to fight the Germans "at the earliest possible moment" this year, "even on a limited scale."[7] Churchill wondered if Dill's message bore Marshall's imprint: Whitehall wags, aware of Dill's close association with Roosevelt's Chief of Staff, since taking up his Washington post, had been whispering that Dill was "going native."[8]

Like a sharp volley at Wimbledon, the strategic ball slammed across the Atlantic carrying the bad news about Sledgehammer and Rutter. Immediately, the Americans slashed it back. Marshall's response was bitter: he threatened to abandon the "Germany First" strategy. The players seemed tireless at thwarting each other.

At the height of that acrimonious week in July, the Dieppe raid was remounted. This decision to restage the operation, coming as it did immediately after the United States threatened to pull out of the European war, has led many historians to view the two events as being less than a coincidence.[9] Although the question is still hotly debated, many now agree that when they were deciding to resurrect Rutter, the Chiefs must inevitably have entertained some notion that here was that ready-made assault of the limited scale which Marshall — via Dill — had just assured them would placate the Americans and Russians.

Marshall's vitriolic reaction — in particular, his threat that the Americans might pull out and let Britain fight Germany on its own — staggered the British. The American Chief of Staff seemed unbending in his insistence on cross-Channel action that year. Intriguingly, several of the U.S. Chiefs were soon seen with a book published in 1926, *Soldiers and Statesmen*, under their arms. It was a critique of Churchill's controversial strategies at Gallipoli. Marshall had somewhat snidely unearthed it and was handing it around. He sent a copy to Dill with Chapter Three highlighted, in which the author emphasized the importance of concentrating on the decisive point.

The British prime minister had obviously underestimated the American president. Those cozy fireside chats at Hyde Park in June had clearly not persuaded Roosevelt to override the authority of his Chiefs of Staff.

While the White House shook with fury at this renewed British betrayal, yet another crisis was in the making. On June 28 the Germans had reopened their long-dreaded eastern offensive. By mid-July the Wehrmacht's massive Army Group South, comprising some 280 divisions, was overwhelming the Russian army in its advance towards Stalingrad and the northern Caucasus: "10,000 men [are] being sacrificed each day on the Russian front," Stalin informed Churchill.[10]

To Marshall, this was precisely the emergency for which Sledgehammer had been designed. Unless an operation against France —

even a sacrificial one — was staged quickly to divert part of the German powerhouse, the Russians were doomed.

Covertly, the British agreed with the prognosis — but not with the cure. The Chiefs had already been warned by the War Cabinet's Joint Intelligence Sub-Committee that it might be "touch and go" on the Eastern Front as to "which adversary collapsed first." On July 19, the British Joint Planners predicted "the possibility of Russian defeat."[11]

Meanwhile, Hitler's obsession with Germany's vulnerability on its western flank had caused him to move several experienced divisions from the Russian Front to the French coast to counter the expected second front. Britain now faced two life-threatening perils. *If* — or as it now seemed, *when* — the Russians were defeated, the Germans would be in a position to pitch their entire might against Great Britain. And *if* the Americans backed out on their European commitment as well, the British might well be invaded and overrun.

Churchill's task would have daunted a lesser man: he was fighting to keep two allies from defecting. First, he had to keep America's energies, resources and manpower onside and in direct support of the British. Second, he had to convince Stalin to stay in the fight when the Russian was brooding that Britain was breaking her promise to launch a second front.

If that weren't formidable enough, Churchill had then to convince both Roosevelt and Stalin of the merits of a campaign in French North Africa. At the time, neither Russia nor the United States showed any interest in a Mediterranean strategy. Nor did they see any reward in one. Opening up the Mediterranean would clearly help Britain to keep her empire, but it would do little to draw German troops from the Russian Front. In Marshall's view, Torch would only dilute the slender resources of both countries.

Churchill needed a miracle and it would have to be of his own making. He later wrote, "During this month of July, when I was politically at my weakest and without a gleam of military success, I had to procure from the United States the decision which, for good or ill, dominated the next two years of the war."[12]

Meanwhile, in Washington, Roosevelt was having none of Marshall and King's less-than-subtle proposal to blackmail the British with a threat to abandon them in Europe. He firmly scrawled "not approved" across the upper-right-hand corner of their showdown memorandum. That would be like threatening to "take up your dishes and go home," he replied. He directed them to return to England and reach immediate agreement with the British. Sledgehammer must be "pushed with utmost vigour," whatever the danger of a Russian collapse. If Sledge-hammer truly proved impossible, then the Chiefs would have to decide on "another place for U.S. troops to fight in 1942."[13]

Roosevelt cabled Churchill on July 15: "Marshall, King and Hopkins leaving for London at once."[14]

On Saturday, July 18, the Americans' Boeing Stratoliner landed secretly at Prestwick. The party was met by the prime minister's train. To Churchill's chagrin, the visitors disdained their British host's invitation to spend the weekend at Chequers and instead went directly to London to work out their strategy for the coming meetings.

They established their headquarters at Mayfair's elegant Claridge's Hotel where they immediately set up a message centre and telephone scramblers. A U.S. army sentry was posted at every door — except, typically, Admiral King's. *He* insisted on having a marine.[15]

Along with Eisenhower and the rest of the London-based American Service Chiefs, the delegation toiled long into the nights, keeping two stenographers busy, while they worked on a position paper for Marshall to present to the Combined Chiefs of Staff. "The prize we seek is to keep 8,000,000 Russians in the war," they argued. The North African assault won't help the Russians; it will only anger them that we have broken our promise. Sledgehammer at least will give them a psychological boost.

Eisenhower emphasized that the delegation keep in mind Roosevelt's suggestion to the British in June: that they regard a cross-Channel operation as a "sacrifice landing" to help the Russians.[16]

During the following nights, room service at Claridge's served seemingly endless cups of coffee and whiskies-on-the-rocks to the fourth-floor team. There must have been some juicy below-stairs gossip about the comings and goings in the 16 rooms the Americans had taken over. At one point an American officer phoned down, "Send someone right away!"

An amused butler found a room full of acrid smoke. Eisenhower's naval aide, Commander Harry Butcher, had tried to cook dehydrated chicken soup over an alcohol burner for his boss. "The alcohol burned black and sooty, and we had to shut it off," he confessed ruefully. "With hurt pride over my poor results, I had humbly to ask room service to prepare our soup. This, with bread and butter, was all we had for dinner, but it was probably the best we've had in London."[17]

During the opening stages of the conference, the hotel's morning staff would watch the squad stride confidently out of the hotel and climb into American military vehicles. By evening, the staff would watch them re-enter the lifts, drained and silent in their fatigue and discouragement. Late into the night the friendly American general with the wide grin and the strange drawl from a place called Abilene, Kansas, would still be holding vigil over a desk piled high with papers.

After five days, the mood subtly changed. The American general no longer grinned; the whiskey flowed more vigorously.

Finally, on Wednesday, July 22, the delegation's mood hit rock bottom. The debate had foundered. Hopkins, doodling on a scrap of paper, summed it up: "Br, say no, we say yes." And later, "I feel damn depressed."[18]

Marshall cabled Roosevelt. It's a deadlock, he reported. The goddamned British won't budge.

The next morning, while still awaiting Roosevelt's response, Marshall asked Eisenhower to make one last stab at finding a compromise. Eisenhower stared at his desk. "I hardly know where to start," he muttered dispiritedly. This "could well go down as the blackest day in history."[19]

All his work over the past year had come to nothing. Inevitably, the deadlock meant the postponement of the invasion of France until 1944. By evening, however, he and his team had pounded out another 11-page proposal — and an idea that was a strategic sizzler. Neither side, Eisenhower pointed out, liked the other's recommendation. Neither side would give in. So why don't both sit tight, with the Americans sending a token force of perhaps one armoured division to Egypt to back up the British Eighth Army? At the same time the Anglo-Americans would concentrate all their resources and energies on launching a really strong and effective Roundup/Bolero — a 1943 invasion of Europe.

Marshall was still leery of committing American troops to British command, and not in the mood to make concessions. He flatly turned down Eisenhower's compromise recommendation; he did not even bother to refer it to Roosevelt for consideration. Sledgehammer had been his baby from start to finish, nourished on the political pablum of New World jealousies and Old World imperialism. He was not going to let go of it.

American historian Stephen Ambrose has termed Eisenhower's last-ditch proposal an "intriguing alternative to the over-all strategy of World War II" and one that has largely been ignored by other historians over the years. Marshall's rejection, Ambrose believes, was "a crucial one: the only chance the British and Americans had of winning the war sooner was to mount the cross-Channel attack earlier," he judged. "The risks would have been greater but so would have been the rewards."[20]

The final decision, with the "amateur" Roosevelt firmly overriding his professional advisors, was to stage the North Africa operation. Torch was "full speed ahead."[21] Brooke, who well remembered Admiral King's "tremendous influence" with Roosevelt, noted that "for once, Roosevelt went against him, and King openly sulked for the rest of the conference."[22]

The death of Sledgehammer had been slow and painful. Many scars were left. F.H. Hinsley, the British historian, has written that "the U.S. authorities had virtually agreed to the abandonment of Sledgehammer on 14 April."[23] This is not accurate, as we have seen. This most controversial of operations first came under fire in April and May, when the Chiefs expressed serious doubts about it — albeit largely to themselves; it was severely wounded in June when Churchill finally voiced these doubts to Roosevelt, and on its deathbed in July.

The Americans' support of Sledgehammer was based on other factors besides strategy: they expected it might fail and regarded it as a possible and necessary sacrifice. "The Russian situation is at least sufficiently critical to justify any action on our part," Eisenhower wrote. "Unsuccessful attack may depress and discourage the Russians — but this should convince them that we are trying to assist."[24]

As well, Sledgehammer had become a valuable insurance policy in their anti-Churchill vendetta against the prime minster's "wild diversionary efforts" at dispersement.[25]

The British motives in foisting the North African campaign on the Americans that year were equally devious. They had snatched up Torch at the last minute, mainly to break the Americans' obsession with Sledgehammer. Major General Sir John Kennedy, who as Britain's Director of Military Operations exercised overall supervision of every plan, admitted as much, and added that when the American delegation came to London in July, the British had no intention of pushing Torch on them. Kennedy himself was quite lukewarm about that operation and had not even prepared an outline plan for American participation.

"We had not meant to press [Marshall] to adopt the 'Torch' plan," Kennedy explained. "The North African project had come up for decision rather unexpectedly." All that the British really had in mind by July was to keep American troops massing in Britain for some future unspecified purpose.[26]

Brooke's sudden change of mind concerning Torch is convincing evidence that, at least in July, the proposal was more of a diversionary tactic than a serious enterprise. The CIGS had been against Torch in June, considering it premature; yet three weeks later he was promoting it vigorously to Marshall. Such "wavering" was uncharacteristic of this totally consistent man, according to Sir David Fraser.[27]

Although the British Chiefs had always seen Torch as an essential precursor to an invasion of Europe, they were not agreed that the timing for it was opportune. They *were* agreed that it would be unthinkable to imperil the lives of hundreds of thousands of men — not to mention all their planes and ships and other logistics — in order to support the Sledgehammer folly.

"The policy of raiding seemed the only alternative that both Britain and the United States could agree upon in 1942," concluded Lieutenant Colonel Charles Schreiner of the U.S. Marine Corps, College of Naval Warfare.[28]

Dieppe, General Fraser believed, thus became "the only substitute for Sledgehammer the British were prepared to consider in 1942."[29]

Whether it succeeded or not at the tactical level, Dieppe would achieve a number of goals. First, it would quiet the clamour of the Americans and Russians for some sort of military action against Germany that year. As Brooke later admitted, it might finally bring home to the Americans "the realities and problems of launching a second front," and bring an end to "their naïve demands for a premature invasion."[30] The contentious issue of a second front would be finally put to rest.

Field Marshal Sir John Dill urged Churchill to weigh the cost of sacrificing British lives by staging Sledgehammer against the worse scenario of seeing Russia defeated. "If the landing ultimately fails tactically but causes diversion from Russian front will it [not] have succeeded?" he asked. But Dieppe offered a much less costly solution. Even if its casualties were high — if it did prove to be a sacrifice — they would be a small percentage of those that could be incurred with Sledgehammer.[31]

Second, Dieppe would satisfy Churchill and Brooke's insistence that an all-out invasion could not be attempted before testing the German Channel defences. That would be like "putting your hand into a bath and seeing how hot it was," as Churchill so pithily described it to Stalin.[32] Roosevelt, too, felt it important to gain battle experience for at least a few of his raw American troops. Looking back, Canadian historians Jack Granatstein and Desmond Morton referred to the "horrible casualties" that Churchill and the Chiefs feared in a cross-Channel invasion. Dieppe, they suggested, might demonstrate "the feasibility or otherwise" of a second front. It would teach valuable lessons for further assaults by sea.[33]

Whatever Dieppe's outcome, it would to some extent appease Stalin. Although a relative pinprick, it could still make Hitler nervous enough to divert more of his troops from his eastern front to protect his Channel flank.

Finally, it would please all three allies by indirectly making a significant contribution to the success of Torch. In the wake of Sledgehammer's demise and Torch's resurrection, Dieppe would take on a new role of becoming a deception plan to divert enemy focus from preparations for Torch. As Mountbatten said, "any good deception would entail the actual mounting of operations."[34]

Canadian publisher Richard Malone, who at the time was a senior staff officer with Montgomery's 21 Army Group, confirmed that the Chiefs' new objective that now justified launching the Dieppe raid was to deceive the Germans about their real intentions in the Mediterranean:

> Following the war I made a point of discussing the subject further with such people as Monty, Brooke, McNaughton, Crerar, Ralston. The real purpose of the raid was deception, to make the Germans believe a full-scale invasion was intended, to hold more German divisions in France and so take the pressure off the hard-pressed Russian armies. Secondly, it was in direct response to the incessant demands of both Washington and Moscow for a second front as early as 1942.
>
> Unable to sell his [peripheral] strategy to the Americans, Churchill compromised by offering to make a raid on the French coast and through deception, threaten simultaneous attacks in Norway and in the Persian Gulf, while the U.S. undertook a landing in North Africa. This was reluctantly agreed to by the U.S.[35]

Persuading Stalin of the merits of abandoning a second front in France in 1942, and dissuading him from negotiating a separate peace with Germany, still remained challenging problems. On July 24th, two days after the demise of Sledgehammer, Stalin signalled Churchill sharply: "I cannot tolerate the second front in Europe being postponed till 1943."

Ambassador Maisky delivered the message himself, and observed its startling effect: "[Churchill] was at once depressed and offended . . . there even seemed to pass through his mind the thought that the USSR might possibly leave the war, because quite unexpectedly he said: 'Well, we've been alone before . . . We went on fighting . . . It is a wonder that this little Island of ours stood up.' "[36]

By then the important steps had already been taken: Sledgehammer axed and Torch adopted. Screened by the deception that Dieppe would offer, and released at last from the pressure to open a second front, the British and Americans were now free to embark on an offensive in a relatively secure zone of war: French North Africa. They were hungry for a taste of success. They had been mired too long in controversy and failure.

Why did the American president defy his Chiefs and come out in support of an operation that had much less appeal? This remains a mystery. Roosevelt's political need to demonstrate to the American voters his determination to fight Germans in 1942 could be one reason.

Records of his secret talks with Churchill at Hyde Park and beyond may someday resolve another.

Had the two men at that time explored the possibility of a trade-off — to a compromise between the American demand for a second front against Germany and the British need for a North African operation? Had Torch and Dieppe become the package deal that finally convinced Roosevelt to back away from Sledgehammer?

In the course of that bitter week in July, those two operations — Torch and Dieppe — seemed to have become *sub rosa* accomplices in the process of killing off Sledgehammer.

PART

6

AUGUST 1942

CHAPTER

17

THE RESTIVE WOLFHOUND

The American terrier that had been yapping at Churchill's heels for four months was now docile with the adoption of Torch. The Russian wolfhound, however, was still snarling and tugging on his lead.

In August, Churchill set off for Moscow to toss a strategic bone or two to the restive nation. It would be an unpleasant confrontation, he feared. Already there was an angry howl coming off the Russian steppes. The goodwill that had been generated by Roosevelt's promise in June of a second front was already vanishing when Churchill cabled Stalin in July to inform him that Sledgehammer had definitely been cancelled. At the same time, the prime minister also broke the news that the Allies were suspending their supply convoys to the Soviets.

Since 1941, British and American convoys had been transporting Western-built weapons, tanks and supplies to Russia. This had been the one measure that all Allies agreed could help to alleviate the Soviet supply crunch. In recent months, however, enemy aircraft and U-boats had been harassing the convoys, inflicting heavy losses of cargo and ships and taking many sailors' lives. On June 27, PQ17, the first joint Anglo-American convoy, comprising 34 merchant ships and 21 escort vessels, sailed from Iceland with 200,000 tons of supplies. When the Luftwaffe discovered the convoy, Admiral Pound panicked at the Ultra warnings that the German battleship *Tirpitz* was within striking distance and ordered the ships to disperse.

Deprived of their escort protection, 23 of these merchant ships were sunk — not by the *Tirpitz*, but by the aircraft and submarines that had been dogging their trail. Only 11, carrying 70,000 tons, survived. Of the 600 tanks in the cargo, 500 were lost. There were few survivors from the arctic waters. The western Allies could no longer justify sending further convoys.[1]

Churchill's signal arrived in Moscow at a time of crisis for the Russians. Ambassador Maisky recorded despairingly in his diary: "26 July: The Fascist hordes are coming nearer and nearer to Stalingrad. Shall we really not be able to hold the Germans off? Will they really, after all, cut us off from the Caucasus and consolidate themselves on the Volga? It seems simply a kind of nightmare out of a horror story."[2]

Stalin's furious reply on July 24 to Churchill's cable reflected the Soviets' bitterness that Sledgehammer had been cancelled. Stalin felt that Russia was being abandoned by her allies and insisted yet again that his country would not tolerate a postponement of the second front in Europe.[3] This cable is what prompted Churchill to pay a conciliatory visit to Stalin — a man he had never met.

Brooke had already arranged a trip to the Middle East. Some weeks before, he had made up his mind to go to Cairo. As commander-in-chief of the army, he felt it was imperative to sort out the evident problems of command that were at the core of Britain's Middle East crisis.

He had expected to deal with this crisis on his own, without Churchill. "The old ruffian is quite jealous that he is not coming along with me!" he had confided somewhat snidely to his wife. His hopes in that regard turned out to be premature. Churchill contrived to tag along, suggesting that the pair combine efforts and jointly visit Cairo first and then Moscow.[4]

On August 2, the prime minister and his official party climbed aboard an unheated Liberator bomber for the first leg of their journey. Churchill's personal physician, Lord Moran, recorded that "Two mattresses had been dumped in the after-cabin. I passed the night in comfort. The P.M. was less happy; he dislikes draughts — and after all, it was a rather feckless way of sending him over the world when he is approaching his seventieth year." [5]

Despite the tightest security, Berlin had learned of the visit and was trumpeting the story. Churchill, much miffed, sent a cable to Ismay: "German wireless announcement re visit to Moscow odd and disquieting as more important matters may leak. Please make searching inquiry with object of future security for our plans."[6]

This was the second of some 247 cables that Churchill would transmit to London during his 21-day trip, which was coded Operation Bracelet. An elaborate distribution system was established before he left: "Signals from London will be classified 'Tulip' and addressed to the Commander-in-Chief Middle East. Signals originating from Bracelet party will be classified 'Reflex.' "[7]

Churchill and Brooke knew that the Dieppe operation was about to be launched. The combined plan for the raid had been signed on July 31, just two days before they left London. On the same day, Brooke had arranged that escape kits be delivered to the assault units before they embarked for France.

There was a strong likelihood, therefore, that Jubilee (or Rutter as several documents still called it) would be mounted in their absence. But no one could give them an exact date. It all depended on the weather. The predicted meteorologist dates were August 18 to 23 or September 1 to 2 or 6 to 7.[8]

When Churchill left on his extended trip, he stipulated that *all* his messages to London which referred to the Dieppe raid should be seen by two men only: Ismay and Hollis. Communications of a more general nature would be disseminated more broadly, for example, to the men standing in for Churchill and Brooke. These were the deputy prime minister, Clement Attlee, and the vice-CIGS, Lieutenant General Archibald Nye. In other words, Attlee and Nye, who were not on the "need-to-know" list, were not to be informed about the Dieppe operation.[9]

When they arrived in Cairo, the travelling party found the troops "dispirited, baffled and defensive in their outlook; the command was disjointed and leaderless." So noted Lieutenant General Sir Ian Jacob, military assistant secretary to Churchill's War Cabinet, who was serving as Churchill's private secretary on the trip. "I doubt whether anyone who was not there can have any idea of the amazing impact of Churchill's presence on the morale of the troops," he observed. The arrival of the 100 American Sherman tanks that Roosevelt and Marshall had offered following the Tobruk crisis was also a substantial morale-booster.[10]

Churchill astounded Brooke by offering him the Middle East command. The Eighth Army was still reeling from its defeat in Tobruk and needed a strong overall commander. Brooke was sorely tempted to accept but turned it down with "bitter despair." He wrote wistfully in his diary that "During the last 9 months with Winston, I had repeatedly longed to be my own master, to escape from the terrific burden of C.I.G.S. work in war, and to return to the open air again to exercise command in the field. [It was] the finest command I could ever hope for."

Brooke denied himself the opportunity because he believed that he could exercise more control over Churchill than could anyone else: "He had grown to have confidence in me and I found he was listening more and more to any advice I gave him."[11]

On Wednesday, August 12, the prime minister embarked for Moscow. It was a flight of ten-and-one-half hours, with a switch at Teheran to a Russian plane. Brooke, travelling separately, arrived the next day with Jacob.

On the evening of his arrival, Churchill had a four-hour preliminary session with Stalin. He immediately launched into his twofold mission: to persuade the Soviet dictator to abandon his pressure for a second front in France that year; and to reconcile him instead to the new Allied North African strategy. Churchill felt that the whole course of the war depended on his success in the Kremlin talks.[12] Many historians today would agree.

The initial two hours of discussion were "bleak and sombre." So he described them in a cable to Attlee and the COS the next morning.

Stalin told him of the terrible plight of his armies. Churchill sought to reassure him with an account of all that his allies were doing to help Russia. He described the massive RAF bombing raids on Germany. He then talked about Torch, the proposed operation against North Africa in 1942. He reminded Stalin of Operation Roundup, which would be "a very great operation in 1943."[13]

(On Roundup, Churchill was being disingenuous; he had been secretly advised by the Joint Planning Staff that an invasion would not be possible until 1944 if he persisted in launching Torch. North Africa had to be regarded as "an alternative and not an addition to Round-Up.")[14]

To make his point, the prime minister sketched the body of a crocodile to represent German-occupied Europe. The attack would be more successful against the "soft underbelly" (through Italy via the Mediterranean) than against the snout (northern France).

Then Churchill explained that the shortage of landing craft had brought about the cancellation of Sledgehammer; and that the same shortage precluded a second-front invasion across the Channel that year. The minutes of this summit meeting reveal just how much Churchill relied on the Dieppe plan as a bargaining tool in persuading Stalin to accept Torch: it enabled him to soften the "no" with a "but" — the "but" being the fact that the British were launching a raid on France — "this month," he told Stalin, "if the weather is favourable." It would be "on a large scale in order to seek information and to test the German resistance. We might lose as many as 10,000 men on this operation, which would be no more than reconnaissance," Churchill added.

The raid would also serve as a deception tactic, in that it would keep the enemy focus in France on the alert and mask the preparations for Torch.

> Our aim was to pretend that we were going to strike at the Pas de Calais. Every day the Germans could for themselves see preparations which suggested this. It was of the utmost importance that nothing should be said or done to indicate that we were not going to attack Hitler in France. At the present moment there were 350 German bombers waiting to resist our landing when it came. Hitler would remove these for work elsewhere if he had the least idea that we were not going to make a landing.

The Soviet premier seemed mollified. "By this time," the minutes noted, "Stalin was very cheerful." Churchill cabled Attlee, "He knows the worst, and we parted in an atmosphere of goodwill."[15]

It was not to last. The second meeting of the two men was at 11 p.m. on Thursday, August 13. This time, Brooke and Jacob were present. The British delegation filed into a Kremlin meeting room. Brooke noted to himself that the sparsely furnished hall was more like a "station waiting room." Stalin, the British foreign office chief Sir Alexander Cadogan would report, was in "a mood of obstinacy and truculence." He thrust an *aide-mémoire* at Churchill. It was an angry rebuttal of the previous day's talks and a reiteration of his unyielding demand for a second front in 1942. Stalin became rude and insulting; he sneered that the British were holding off because they were frightened of the Germans and accused them of going back on their word. "When are you going to start fighting?" he scoffed. "Are you going to let us do all the work whilst you look on?"

These two leaders are "poles apart as human beings," Brooke mused. "I cannot see a friendship developing between them such as exists between Roosevelt and Winston."[16]

In a fury, Stalin pointed out to Churchill that all the best German troops were tied down on the Eastern Front and that "only negligible forces, and the poorest, too, are left in Europe." He added that conditions were favourable now for opening a second front. They might not be so optimal if they delayed until 1943.[17]

The "violence of Stalin's attack was stunning to the British Prime Minister," one diplomat noted. Yet, after his initial recoil, Churchill fought back. Brooke later recounted admiringly how:

He crashed his fist down on the table and poured forth one of his wonderful spontaneous orations. Stalin stood up sucking at his large bent pipe, and with a broad grin on his face stopped Winston's interpreter and sent back through his own: "I do not understand what you are saying, but by God I like your sentiment."[18]

The third confrontation between the two leaders, on August 14, took place in much more elaborate circumstances: at a magnificent banquet for 100 Russian, British and American military and political figures. Stalin, Jacob recalled, was dressed in a

lilac-coloured tunic, buttoned up to the neck, his cotton trousers stuffed into long boots ... Every five minutes throughout the dinner we were drinking somebody's health ... Every time, Stalin made a speech of three or four sentences, and then wandered round the table, clinking glasses with the men whose health he had proposed, and cracking jokes with Molotov. Meanwhile, the Prime Minister was left rather high and dry, with no one to talk to.[19]

On the final evening, Saturday, August 15, the two men were to meet alone with only their interpreters. Churchill, "decidedly upset" by the talks thus far, had been inclined not to attend the banquet or the concluding meeting. "However, he swallowed his feelings," Jacob recalled.[20]

Throughout the talks, Churchill had kept his cable link to London filled with increasingly urgent exchanges. For example, he had cabled Attlee on August 13, pleading for fresh information about whether there was any possibility of renewing the PQ convoys. He was sure the subject would come up in the next meeting, and he wanted to be armed with suitable ammunition.[21]

On the morning of August 15, anticipating another difficult encounter, Churchill cabled Ismay for more vital information on the proposed raid against France that he could use to counter Stalin's expected attack on him.

Clearly, the impending Dieppe raid had become a powerful element in these high-level talks. Churchill was obviously counting on it to placate the Russians. But after building it up to Stalin, he then naturally became concerned that the raid might run into more weather delays. Another cancellation would seriously damage his negotiations with the Russians.

"What is the position about renewal of Rutter?" Churchill had demanded.[22]

Ismay's immediate reply was reassuring: "Jubilee, which is renewed Rutter in all essential features, is due to be carried out First Light 18 August. If weather unfavourable 18th August, operation can be launched any subsequent day up to 24th August inclusive."[23]

Churchill's cable of August 15 has been cited by historian Brian Villa as evidence that in mistaking the codename of the raid, the prime minister was "ignorant of the decision" to remount the Dieppe raid.[24] The authors believe that a more reasonable explanation is the fact that the new codename "Jubilee" had not been assigned until a few days before Churchill's departure for Cairo and Moscow. He had examined and discussed the plan by its old name "Rutter" for two months; his calling it by its old name was an understandable lapse in the throes of a busy departure and the intrusion of other state matters during his trip. Already, in a period of less than two weeks in Cairo and Moscow, the cable was the 99th he had sent to London, and the reply was the 145th received.[25]

At the final British-Soviet meeting on August 15, Stalin had reverted to his stark uniform and grim demeanour. Again, he launched his incessant, repetitious demands for a second front. Churchill could now give the Soviet leader details about the Dieppe raid with more confidence.

> In order to make Germany anxious about an attack from across the Channel, there will be a more serious raid in August, although the weather might upset it. It will be a reconnaissance in force. Some 8,000 men with 50 tanks will be landed. They will stay a night and a day, kill as many Germans as possible and take prisoners. . . . They will then withdraw. . . . The air must be fairly clear to enable fighter protection to be given and the sea not too rough to enable the men to be landed. The object is to get information and to create the impression of an invasion. Most important, I hope it will call forth a big air battle.[26]

Churchill explained that instead of Sledgehammer, the Allies would make two efforts: Dieppe — the raid on France, which would "create the impression of an invasion" and, by this diversion, make Germany anxious about an attack; and Torch, the North African invasion, which would be the real second front for 1942.[27]

At first Stalin worried. "Won't the Germans broadcast the failure of the British attempt at invasion [when they withdraw from Dieppe]?

But he soon grasped Churchill's real intentions behind this new Mediterranean strategy and reassured himself: "Dieppe will be explained by Torch. If Torch succeed[s], then everybody will understand."

This remark, Churchill said, "showed Stalin's quickness of mind in that he connected the two things."[28]

General Jacob agreed that Dieppe was to some extent a sop to Stalin. "Stalin knew that the real thing was in Africa but Dieppe would keep the [Germans] warm."[29]

Clearly, the British had succeeded in mollifying Stalin, and the evening that had begun so gloomily spun into a seven-hour marathon. "Why do you not come over to my apartment in the Kremlin and have some drinks?" Stalin asked. There, they were greeted by a "handsome red-haired girl who kissed her father dutifully." An improvised supper appeared, along with a lavish assortment of drinks and wines. At 1:30 a.m., a now-jovial Stalin attacked a suckling pig with great enthusiasm. It was another hour before Churchill could finally take his leave. "When saying good night, [Stalin] told the prime minister that he was a rough man and begged that his roughness should not be misunderstood."[30]

At 3:15 a.m., exhausted, Churchill returned to his quarters at State Villa No. 7. He bathed and lay down on a sofa. The flight back to Cairo would leave at dawn. Jacob came into his bedroom and sat nearby as Churchill lit a cigar and began his account of the evening.

"The Prime Minister was very tired," Jacob noted, "and lay talking with his eyes shut. Nevertheless, he was very satisfied with the way things had gone."[31]

The next day, in a cable to Roosevelt, Churchill summed up the conference by declaring that Stalin had "swallowed this bitter pill" of Sledgehammer's cancellation. Churchill's obvious triumph was that the plans for Dieppe and Torch had made it go down a little easier.[32]

Denis Whitaker

August 18, 1942, Arundel Castle, Sussex:

At two p.m., an orders group was called for the Royal Hamilton Light Infantry. All officers were assembled at the battalion headquarters tent. The commanding officer, Lieutenant Colonel Bob Labatt, announced that we would be proceeding on Exercise Ford. *Another* mobile training scheme! we thought. The 551 men and 31 officers of the Rileys were ordered to parade in full marching order with all weapons and a full complement of ammunition. Transport would arrive at 4 p.m. I was put in charge of leading the column by motorcycle the 42-mile route via Chichester to Southampton — and God help me if I lost the way again!

We returned to our tents to assemble our gear and regrouped in time to see 28 three-ton lorries roll into the assembly area outside the gates of Arundel Park. The convoy had orders to proceed at 15 miles per hour; no stops were permitted.[33]

Just short of our destination, we were met by an escort of military police who led us to the Southampton docks. There, much to our surprise, was the *Glengyle*, our old friend from the Isle of Wight. We were escorted up the gangplank. Could it be that Dieppe had been revived? General Roberts had hinted back in July that this could be a possibility.

After the ship was loaded and sealed, we were briefed. This *was* it: Dieppe. The plans for the infantry units were identical to Rutter's; the only change was that commandos had been substituted for paratroops. My own assignment was altered: I would command the battalion headquarters protective platoon, to be established at Eglise St.-Remy in the town of Dieppe. The carriers would be taken in by my second-in-command, Lieutenant Joe Pigott.

Problems immediately arose. Owing to normal attrition, some five to ten percent of the men were new to the battalion. They had not trained with us on the Isle of Wight. They had never practised assault landings, never learned street fighting, never scaled cliffs. Further, the special weapons, like the recalcitrant Sten that we had spent weeks honing and coaxing into maximum performance on the Isle of Wight, had all been withdrawn after the cancellation of Rutter. We glared helplessly at their replacements: they were still in crates, packed in heavy grease — the guns had never even been fired! How could they be perfected in the few hours we had before going into battle? Tomorrow at dawn we would be fighting for our lives with them.

As we sailed out of Southampton harbour that evening, there was absolute silence except for the swishing sound the *Glengyle* made as she slid through an almost perfectly calm English Channel. We spent the time we had left cleaning weapons, priming grenades, distributing maps and escape kits, and briefing the troops on their tasks. We did our best to prepare them, but the feeling of optimism many of us had shared before Rutter was now being replaced by apprehension.

The same scene was being played across Southern England: elements of the Second Canadian Infantry Division were being assembled at Portsmouth, Southampton, Newhaven, Shoreham, and Gosport, and loaded aboard the 237 ships and landing craft of what would be the Dieppe flotilla. In a latticed summer house in Bath, war correspondents and broadcasters were assembled, briefed and whisked to Southampton, where they would be spirited aboard General Robert's command ship, the *Calpe,* or onto the various assault craft.

A day earlier Lieutenant Jack Dunlap, a troop commander with the Calgary Tanks, was driving his tank south through the New Forest toward Southampton when he was pulled over by his squadron commander. "I was told to dismount and go into an air raid shelter at the side of the road. Major Page said, 'We're going back into Dieppe.' That was it." Within hours, Dunlap was loading his tank on one of the 24 tank landing craft that would carry them across the Channel.[34]

Montgomery's liaison officer, Goronwy Rees, who had special permission from Monty to join the mission, boarded H.M.S. *Garth* — one of the eight Hunt-class destroyers that had been allocated to the raid — in the company of an American journalist. Already briefed, Rees's mind was on a book of Sickert paintings of Dieppe that he had come across at his club at luncheon that day. He knew that in a few hours he would be looking at the same scenes himself, no longer softly pastel and gentle. He suddenly felt a "violent sense of nausea and disgust at the business of war and of nostalgia for the days of peace."[35]

Lieutenant Dan Doheny RCA, a junior liaison officer, hitched a ride to Portsmouth in a three-ton supply truck. "My driver, a good North Country boy, must have realized something was up. The more so as I had my side arms revolver, a Sten, tin hat and equipment with me. The ships, too, were sealed with sentries at every gang plank." Doheny slipped the lad a package of cigarettes and admonished him not to say a word. "I never says anything to nobody of what I sees or does," the driver replied cheerfully. "I didn't tell him that when he arrived back [at camp] he would be sealed up for 48 hours," Doheny noted.[36]

Brigadier Churchill Mann, the deputy military commander, embarked on H.M.S. *Fernie*, making sure that the thousand-and-one details of his operational plan had been attended to — even to ensuring that carrier pigeons had been stowed in the hold against the event that all other means of communication broke down.

Several platoons from the Essex Scottish, believing they were on yet another exercise, left some of their weapons and ammunition behind. They were forced to borrow 20 Tommy guns and ammunition from the ship's stock after their craft — the converted ferryboats *Prince Charles* and *Prince Leopold* — sailed. The machine-gunners of the Toronto Scottish discovered too late, while setting up their weapons in the bows of their assault craft, that they had no tracer bullets. These were essential in helping them zero in on their targets. The Camerons found their equipment dumped in a pile, the explosives unlabelled, the Stens still thick in grease. Because only the C.O., Lieutenant Colonel Gostling, and a few of his officers had any experience with Stens, the soldiers spent most of the crossing attempting to clean and to familiarize themselves with the weapon — all in the dark.[37]

Aboard the *Prince Albert*, the officers of Lovat's No. 4 Commando had a pre-dawn breakfast of stew, for which they were charged an outrageous thirteen shillings and fourpence. "The stew needed more salt but no one reached for it and we ate in preoccupied silence," Major Derek Mills-Roberts recalled. Lieutenant Colonel Torchy Durnford-Slater's No. 3 Commando was to have hardtack, free, while contorted into one of the 32 wooden 20-man R boats. The U.S. Rangers aboard squirmed uncomfortably on the hard benches, confined even more by their bulky life jackets.[38]

The Royal Regiment of Canada embarked two of its companies aboard the *Queen Emma,* the remaining two on the *Princess Astrid.* Edward Force — comprising three platoons of the Black Watch (Royal Highland Regiment of Canada) and some artillery personnel under command of Captain Ray Hicks — sailed on the *Duke of Wellington.* The Black Watch, whose assignment was to protect the Royals' left flank, had not had any Isle of Wight training either. While the ship was still in port, one young Jock began priming grenades with more enthusiasm than skill. One of these exploded, killing the soldier and wounding 18 others. The corporal in charge of moving the casualties ashore returned too late; his ship had sailed without him.

There were grim coincidences everywhere. A trooper in the Calgary Tanks named Charlie Rodgers had been trained for the assault as a gunner in Lieutenant Bennett's tank. He was replaced at the last moment when the original gunner came back from hospital unexpectedly. Bennett's tank would suffer direct hits. Both he and his gunner would be taken prisoner.

RHLI company commander, Major Norry Waldron, returned to camp from a course just in time to take command of his company for the raid. He would be killed leading the survivors of his company through a gap blown in the wire barricade on the beach.

There had been no intention of permitting the battalion's padre, Honourary Captain John Foote, to accompany the raiders. "I know what's in the wind, Bob. I want to go," he insisted to his reluctant C.O., Bob Labatt. After the battle, Foote, just as stubbornly, would refuse to be evacuated from Dieppe; instead he would stay with "his boys" in POW camp.[39]

The C.O. of Les Fusiliers Mont-Royal, Lieutenant Colonel Dollard Menard, had told one of his officers, Major Paul Savoy, that he was too old for the raid. Under pressure, Menard relented. With the rest of his battalion, Savoy took communion in a Sussex schoolhouse and then climbed aboard his battalion's ship. He would die moments after he touched down on the shores of Dieppe's main beach.

The Queen's Own Cameron Highlanders of Winnipeg, complete with the battalion piper, Lance Corporal Alec Graham, crossed in R boats. Graham was to pipe his unit ashore. He would still be clutching his bagpipes when he was captured some hours later.

The South Saskatchewans, who would precede the Camerons onto the Pourville beaches, were luckier: they crossed in destroyers, only climbing aboard the LCAs 10 miles or so offshore.

Across Sussex, the Second Canadian Infantry Division battalion areas were by now almost abandoned. The few light-duty personnel remaining at them had been told that the men were off on a two-day exercise.

At the Riley headquarters, the officer left behind was my close friend, Captain Jervis O'Donohoe, the assistant adjutant. Jervis stood at the gates to see us off.

The next time I saw him, 32 hours later, he was standing rooted at the same place, tears streaming down his face, as the small straggle of weary and begrimed infantrymen who had survived Dieppe filed silently in. The one officer in the battalion who had come through the battle without being wounded, killed, or captured, hugged him, weeping freely. That officer was myself.

Back in Cairo, on August 17, Churchill sent another anxious cable to London, again with distribution limited to Ismay, and specifically *not*

to the deputy prime minister, Clement Attlee, the Vice-CIGS, Lieutenant General Archibald Nye, or any other member of the Chiefs of Staff or the Defence Committee.

"Please report if and when Jubilee takes place," Churchill urged.[40]

In reply, Ismay cabled twice with further updates on the raid: "18 Aug/42: 'Owing to weather, Jubilee postponed 24 hours ie to First Light Aug 19.' " And later that day, "18 Aug/42: 'Weather sufficiently good. Jubilee has started'."[41]

Fifty years later, General Jacob described to the authors Churchill's anxiety about the pending Dieppe raid: "Churchill took a deep interest in all the details of military operations. He certainly talked to the commanders and heard all about it. It was the kind of thing he was so keen on; he was all for keeping up the battle and not letting the Germans settle down in peace. Brooke would also be very involved. After all, he was head of the army and all operations were under his control."[42]

When Jacob returned to Cairo with Churchill and Brooke, he recalled how excited the prime minister was about the raid. "Churchill was aching for news of Dieppe. He sat up half the night waiting for it."

An extract from the August 19 entry in Jacob's unpublished diary confirms this. "During the day the news of the Dieppe raid had been coming in. We found that the Prime Minister had not been able to contain himself any longer, and was ringing up from the Western Desert for news. Fortunately a communiqué had just come in, which we were able to give him and later a signal from home arrived."[43]

Churchill and Brooke were elated when they learned that the raid had at last been mounted.

Their euphoria would quickly vanish.

CHAPTER
18

THE BEACHES OF HELL

0347 hours: A starburst splintering the night marked the beginning of
the end for the Dieppe raiders.

As Admiral James had feared when he twice so urgently signalled
Calpe, the section of the flotilla carrying Lieutenant Colonel
Durnford-Slater's No. 3 Commando had been intercepted by the
German convoy: a tanker and its escort of some six armed E boats.
Suddenly there was a burst of machine gun and pom-pom fire. Flares
exploded in the sky and searchlights pinned down the hapless men as
they were strafed by 40-mm Bofors fire. In the brief but violent
firefight, serious damage was incurred by escort craft of both sides,
and casualties were severe. Six of the 23 wretched wooden R boats
were sunk, and the steam gunboat carrying their commanding officer
was hit and disabled. The rest of the landing craft quickly dispersed;
only six had escaped intact. For the assault force, the worst news was
that "the entire coast defence system was alerted."[1]

0440 hours: The second-in-command of No. 3 Commando, Major
Peter Young, swiftly took charge. With only his single boatload of
men he headed for the designated landing place, arriving — ironically — five minutes early, thankful that there was still near-darkness.
Young's objective — to take out the heavy, six-gun battery at
Berneval, eight miles east of Dieppe — would require a strong force
of commandos, not the remnant he had left.

"There I was with eighteen men when I should have had one
hundred and fifty," Major Young recounted. His first priority was to
get his men up 100 feet of sheer cliff, barricaded by barbed wire.

"We had no Bangalore torpedos to blow holes through the first thick
coil of barbed wire, but fortunately the Germans had strung the wire
on pegs all the way to the top of the cliff. We started up one side. I
fell off. We tried the other side. I got part way up, pulling myself up

on the wire, hating it, using the only foothold we had — the German pegs. My rifle fell to the crook of my arm. I swung away from the cliff. I thought, 'Oh Christ, if I fall off this time I won't have the guts to start over again.' My toe stuck in a cleft and up we went. In twenty minutes we were at the top."[2] Their hands and clothing ripped by the sharp barbs, Young led his men inland across a narrow gully to the German battery.

0440 hours: Tugboat 32 with navy pilot Hederich and the tug commander, Sonderfuehrer (Boatswain) Achtermann, had been standing off Dieppe port since 0400 hours, waiting to escort the expected German convoy into the harbour. A few minutes earlier, the signal station had reported to the port commandant that a naval engagement was in progress about four nautical miles to sea. Then the commander hear motor sounds. Towards 0445 hours they saw destroyers and several other vessels at a distance of one-and-one-half nautical miles: the expected convoy, they reasoned.

Wait! . . . This may not be our convoy! the commander thought. He gave orders to make for port. As the unknown vessels approached, the signal station flashed the recognition signal to challenge them. There was no response. The alert was sounded.[3]

0445 hours: The officer in charge of the barrage force, 3rd Battery, 302nd Artillery Regiment, gave the immediate order to commence firing.

0500 hours: Taking shelter in a tall cornfield, Major Young and his band of 18 men peered down through their binoculars at the coast. To their relief, they saw five more commando R boats bearing in on their landing place. With his wireless destroyed, Young decided to go forward towards the battery and rendezvous there with the other section. But would they make it in time to lay on the attack before the Germans — now obviously alerted — overran them all?[4]

Within 10 minutes, the German garrison at Berneval battery was manning every gun at the strongpoint. An urgent call for reserves was sent out to the 302nd Division. Major von Blücher, commander of the 302nd antitank and reconnaissance battalion, ordered three companies forward.

At Puys, where the Royal Regiment of Canada were coming into the attack, Hauptmann Richard Schnösenberg, C.O. of the 3rd battalion, 571st Infantry Regiment, satisfied himself that every man was at his post.

Surprise on the eastern flanks of the attack — No. 3 Commando and the Royal Regiment of Canada — was now lost. Unaccountably, to the west of Dieppe the alarm had not yet been sounded. Here, there was still a chance.

0453 hours: West of Dieppe, Lieutenant Colonel the Lord Lovat, commanding officer of No. 4 Commando, was nearing Varengeville and the stretch of coastline above which lay his objective — Hess Battery.

As No. 4 Commando's landing craft sped in towards shore, Lovat heard distant gunfire from the east. They were a mile offshore when the lights from the harbour lighthouse were suddenly doused. Tracer bullets began to sketch erratic lines across the sky.

He realized in dismay that No. 3 Commando's attack at Berneval was probably under fire; but with luck, the Germans would not spot his men under the shadows of the cliffs six miles to the west of Dieppe.

Shimi Lovat was an experienced and canny warhorse. He had devised his own plan for taking out the battery: like No. 3 Commando, he was going to try a pincer attack. His second-in-command, Major Derek Mills-Roberts, would lead 88 men to a pinpoint target: a cleft in the sea cliffs just below the battery. From there they would surmount the heights and attack frontally with snipers, mortars and machine guns.

Lovat, with the main body of his battalion, would land a mile-and-a-half to the west. Then, in a marathon sprint, he would cut a wide detour through a river valley to take the strongpoint from behind in a hell-bent-for-leather bayonet charge.

Mills-Roberts' men landed dead on schedule. The beach was narrow; the cliff loomed sheer and steep one hundred feet above them. The cleft was jammed with coils of barbed wire. With a Bangalore torpedo they blasted a hole, and then widened the gap with a second torpedo. Singly, they scrambled through, scraping skin and in at least one case, snapping off trouser-holding buttons in the process.

The commandos moved up along the steep sides of the gully to the top and advanced towards the battery. They glanced at their watches anxiously; the sky was growing lighter.

Meanwhile, faces blackened, stocking caps pulled low over their brows, Lovat's detachment of commandos was set to leap from their landing craft the moment they touched the shore. "To run a mile at speed we had to cut down on equipment," Lovat had figured. The commandos went in wearing denim trousers and running shoes. They carried only light weapons: rifles, submachine guns, explosive charges and hand grenades. Lovat had stressed in training for the operation that speed and timing would make or break it. "Certain chosen men wearing leather jerkins literally charged into the wire, rolled about and tried to flatten it," Lovat described. The rest of the unit ran deftly over the backs of their comrades and set off on their race against the clock.

———————

0452 hours: At the moment when the Royal Regiment of Canada was supposed to be setting foot on Blue Beach under cover of darkness, the battalion was still two miles out to sea. General Roberts' worst fears were materializing; naval ineptitude had already got the Royals lost — and late. The man responsible for setting them down accurately on Blue Beach was Lieutenant Commander Harold Goulding. Unlike many of the naval personnel who manned the landing craft, Goulding was a professional naval officer. Yet under his supervision, the LCAs carrying the Royals had one disastrous misadventure after another. First they had followed the wrong gunboat. Then, after wasting valuable minutes regrouping, Goulding unaccountably decided to try to make up time by accelerating the lead boats of the flotilla. This only served to leave behind the slower LCMs, or mechanized landing craft, each carrying 100 men. Finally, his flotilla now dispersed, Goulding made the disastrous decision to almost double the length of his run-in by making directly for the main port first before turning east for Puys — rationalizing that he would thus more easily find the tiny cove.

Undoubtedly it was Goulding's section of the flotilla that had turned up unexpectedly at the harbour entrance, and then failed to respond to the recognition signals flashed at them. The Germans — tipped off by this to their presence, and on the alert anyway because of the German convoy scare — immediately switched on their searchlights and opened fire.

Captain Hughes-Hallett's official report about the navy's efforts to land the Royal Regiment at Puys would attempt to cover up the error. It would be the first of several naval cover-ups. He noted (falsely) that "the landing was delayed for 15 minutes on account of time lost when the boats were forming up."[5]

The truth of the disaster was revealed in the report by the Royal's commanding officer, Lieutenant Colonel Douglas Catto. He compiled his report September 13, 1942, with the help of officers and representatives of the 159 imprisoned men of the Royal Regiment at Oflag VIIB POW Camp in Germany. Catto stated that the first wave was actually *35 minutes* behind schedule, with the following assault wave reaching the beach nearly *one hour* late.[6]

Because of Lieutenant Commander Goulding's erratic decisions that morning, the Royals touched down on Blue Beach at Puys in broad daylight, stripped of the element of surprise that was to give them that vital edge over a well-entrenched defender.

0500 hours: At Puys, peering intently through his binoculars, Hauptmann Schnösenberg saw "a big shadow looming out to sea in the mist." These were the first boats of our convoy coming in, he thought.

Then the fog lifted a little and he saw the Union Jack hanging on the mast. "I said, 'It's the English! Fire!' In the moment when I gave the order to fire, I saw the whole beach. They came swimming along like little ducks, *nicht wahr*, hundreds of landing craft." Schnösenberg's troops immediately sounded the alarm, manned their gun positions, and commenced firing according to their pre-determined defensive tasks.[7] The Canadians were literally mowed down as they poured onto the beaches.

Of the two Canadian infantry battalions scheduled to mount pre-dawn surprise attacks on the flanks, only one — the South Saskatchewan Regiment — landed unopposed, on time, and in near darkness. That was at Green Beach at Pourville. Initially, they caught the Germans off-guard. SSR troops stormed the beaches, scaled the seawall and entered the village. Major Claude Orme's C Company quickly took its objectives on the hills to the west and sent back the success signal: "Sorry."

"The code word meant we were on the objective," he noted. "It was to be the only success signal sent to command ship, besides Lovat's, in the entire operation."[8]

But even the SSRs did not get off scot free from naval blunders: part of the battalion was landed on the wrong, or west, side of the River Scie. This was to have a critical effect on the entire assault.

From his bunker near the castle on the west cliffs overlooking Dieppe, the commander of the 75-mm gun battery, Lieutenant Wilhelm

Freiderich Schlie, heard the alarm and started sprinting towards his observation post, dressing as he went. He gasped at the sight of the hundreds of boats carrying the main assault group. "I pushed my helmet on and ran, still wearing sandals. The infantry battalion commander, Capt. Ullrich said, 'The English are there! You must shoot barrage fire (*Speer-feuer*) instantly!' As my eye became accustomed to the dawning, dusky light I saw all over the sea, points, little points. I said, amazed, 'My God, are *all* those English?' Ullrich said, 'Now quickly . . . this is getting serious.' "[9]

0510 hours: On 4 Commando's front at Varengeville, Mills-Roberts heard a shattering noise. The six-gun battery "Hess" — the commando objective — had opened fire on the British flotilla at sea. The guns had to be silenced. But it would be 50 minutes before Lovat's men rounded the valley to get in position behind the battery for the attack.

"I had to improvise as fast as possible," Mills-Roberts recalled. Abandoning stealth, his men raced behind him through the wood towards the battery. Their first mission was to shoot the German sentries in the flak tower; for this, they had to find a vantage point for their snipers. "I could see the German gun crews. In number one gun there was even a cook wearing a cook's hat. Our sniper got himself into a comfortable position at a barn window overlooking the guns. He seemed to take a long time and we waited, noticing the beautiful day, the bees buzzing.

"The rifle cracked; it was a bull's eye . . . rather like shooting a member of the church congregation from the organ loft."[10]

Mills-Roberts quickly moved up his mortar and antitank detachments to silence the enemy machine guns that had turned their fire on the intruders. Sergeant Major Dunning scored a lucky shot with his 2-inch mortar: the bomb hit the ammunition dump. The big guns fell silent as the Germans rushed to extinguish the fire. But the commandos had only a temporary advantage. They still needed Lovat with the main assault force. Where was he?

By now the alarm had been raised in Pourville as well. At Green Beach, the remaining companies of the SSR that had been set down on the wrong side of the River Scie found that they would first have to penetrate the village and then cross the river by a narrow bridge that was under heavy enemy fire before they could begin their assault on their objectives on the headlands. In minutes that bridge was carpeted with dead and wounded men; the advance of the South Saskatchewans came to a halt.[11]

0507 hours: Meanwhile, the Royal Regiment's first wave of infantry was still 1,000 yards off-shore and hopelessly, disastrously late. Their orders had been to land at 0450 — 30 minutes ahead of the landing on Dieppe beach — in order to knock out the guns that would be such a hazard to the main assault on Dieppe. Instead, the Royals came in 5 minutes *after* the main landing. Because the landing had been intended for darkness and surprise, no fire support from the British ships had been laid on. But as they approached the shore, they were now in daylight, and immediately came under heavy fire.

The assault craft scraped bottom several yards offshore. The bow doors opened. This was a signal the Germans on the headlands had been waiting for: their machine guns opened up with an intense crossfire. The men were cut down even before they reached the beach. Dead and wounded piled up in the doorways and ramps of the LCAs. Other wounded men struggled in the shallow water. Many were drowned. The seawall was only 40 yards away, but no more than 15 of the first wave of 150 men reached it.[12]

Goulding pulled back out of range of the enemy fire. His first signal back to the flotilla — which could charitably be described as a huge understatement — read: "Landing effected with slight casualties and no damage to craft."[13]

It set the stage for the next calamities to come.

0515 hours: Action on the main Dieppe beach was just beginning. As the landing craft approached, the skies erupted. The umbrella of fire cover that would keep the enemy heads down during the vulnerable moments when the raiders approached shore was right on time. A squadron of Hurricane fighters screamed down on the enemy defences. Four more followed in swift succession, cannons blazing furiously. At the same moment, the 4-inch guns from the four Hunt-class destroyers opened up on the beach.

Ten minutes later, the promised strike was all over. At the moment when the 1,113 riflemen from the Rileys and the Essex Scottish touched down on the main beach, the Hurricanes turned for home, and the destroyers' guns fell silent. Was this the "maximum bombing" that the men had been led to expect? It didn't begin to do the job. The

4-inch guns were as effective as pea shooters on the defended port. And where were the tanks?

0523 hours: The RHLI and Essex Scottish landed at main beach just three minutes late.

Captain Denis Whitaker, Platoon Commander, Royal Hamilton Light Infantry (RHLI): "As our LCA moved toward shore, the sun was just rising and I could see the dim outline of the buildings along the Dieppe front. We cruised on; the shore came into focus.

"We looked at one another. Something was terribly wrong. Everything was intact! We expected a town shattered by the RAF's saturation bombing the previous night. We thought we would see a lot of damage to the seafront buildings from the shelling. There was no sign of bombing. The window panes were glittering, unbroken, in the reflections of the sun's first rays.

"Half-standing in the centre of the bow of the boat, I was able to peer over the top of the ramp. Smoke had been laid down to mask our approaches. Now, through wisps of smoke, I could see the rocky beach backed by the sea wall, the buildings and hotels on the far side of the green esplanade, and the casino immediately ahead on the right. That was White Beach, my battalion's objectives. Off to the left, at Red Beach, where the Essex were headed, the jetty jutted out some two hundred yards. A high cliff blocked our view towards Puys.

"On the right flank, the west headland loomed darkly. An awesome-looking castle crowned its heights. The west cliffs were dotted with caves. They would be ideal locations for defensive weapons, I thought fleetingly. What frightened me most was the way the headlands on both sides were wrapped around the beach. Enfilade fire from both flanks could make it a terrible killing ground.

"I wondered about the Royals at Puys and the South Saskatchewans at Pourville, whom I assumed had landed half an hour before us. Had they been able to clear the guns from the headlands on both our flanks? If not, we were in deep trouble. Achieving their objectives, even with darkness and surprise to help them, would have been tough.

"Our objectives looked tough as well. Major Bud Matchett, who commanded the Rileys' B Company, had to clear the casino, climb the hill through the town, and then knock out or capture all the enemy positions, including a hotel, a post office, and Gestapo Headquarters. Bud Bowery's D Company was to climb the cliff and take the castle, afterwards hooking right to the west headland to destroy the anti-aircraft and artillery batteries before they began firing on the troops on the main beach. Then he had to make contact with the South Saskatchewans.

"Some objectives for two small companies, each with only one hundred men! The other units had similarly unrealistic assignments.

"When we were about a hundred yards from shore, my worst fears were realized. Enemy machine gun bullets smashed against the sides of the LCA, or cracked just over our heads. The smoke screen laid down on the headlands by the Bostons and Blenheims had quickly dissipated. The Hurricane attack — a single swipe — had only had a momentary effect, now lost, of subduing the German fire. Where was that weak, demoralized enemy with puny weapons that we had been told was defending the town? Dieppe was a fortress, and the Germans were obviously ready and waiting. Fortunately, the armoured sides of the LCA repelled small-arms fire, so we had no casualties at this point.

"The craft drove onto the beach. My stomach jumped up to my throat. This was it!

"The ramp dropped. I led the thirty odd men of my platoon in a charge about twenty-five yards up the stony beach. We fanned out and flopped down just short of a huge wire obstacle. Bullets flew everywhere. Enemy mortar bombs started to crash down. Around me, men were being hit and bodies were piling up, one on top of the other. It was terrifying."

Corporal John Williamson, RHLI: "Being so green, we had loaded ourselves down with so much ammunition we could hardly walk: besides tommy gun ammo, I had a couple of hand grenades and two mortar bombs. When the craft hit the beach, I stepped off and fell flat on my face in the bloody water. I struggled to get up, but with all this ammunition, as well as my battle dress and heavy, hobnailed boots, I was weighted down. If we had to cover any distance, I would have serious problems. Tracer started coming at us even before we got to shore. We said, what the hell goes on? This wasn't supposed to happen. Then I was hit. Soon there was only one man left in our platoon who was not killed or wounded."[14]

Lieutenant Lou Counsell, Platoon Commander, RHLI: "I saw the cannon fighters going in to attack shortly before the RHLI touched down. We were all a little disappointed by the smallness of the air support. The junior officers and men had not been informed that the bombing attack had been cancelled. You felt let down."[15]

Counsell led his men up the beach, stopping to cut the wire. At that moment, he was hit. He lay on the beach, severely wounded, for 12 hours before the Germans found and captured him. He was a reluctant eyewitness to the destruction of his platoon: D Company was virtually wiped out within minutes of landing. Its commanding officer was killed and most of the remainder were cut down by the relentless hail of fire from the guns on the west headland — the guns that were his company's impossible objective.

Private Al Richards, RHLI: "17 Platoon next to me was carrying their Bangalores like everyone else on top of the landing craft. Something hit them and the Bangalores went off. There were only two men who got off that craft."[16]

One of these survivors, Lieutenant Fred Woodcock, was blinded for life.

Captain Denis Whitaker, RHLI: "My platoon's first task was to blow a gap through the wire obstacle with a Bangalore torpedo. It was a huge, thickly-coiled roll of concertina wire, almost as tall as I was and about seven feet deep. Corporal Jack Brabbs and Private Bill Grant bravely crawled up to the wire and pushed the torpedo in place. Suddenly George Naylor yelled, 'Bill's been hit!' He was dead, shot in the head. (Bill had been in the regiment since 1926 and had married an English girl just a few weeks before.) Jack Brabbs took over and the wire was blown, but his elbow was shattered by rifle fire. By this time several of my men had been wounded."

Corporal Jack Brabbs, RHLI: "The guys helped me back from the wire. I got near a tank but it was drawing all sorts of fire. My lips were smashed by pieces of stone that shattered when hit by bullets or mortars."[17]

Lieutenant John Gartshore, RHLI: "I got into the casino after being hit in the arm. I couldn't crawl, the wall was so low. So I pushed myself along on my back. At the casino I decided to go on. But when I got up I passed out. Even our own tanks were firing on the casino; they kept firing until they ran out of ammunition."[18]

Captain Denis Whitaker, RHLI: "Our main task as battalion headquarters protection platoon was to get into town to the St. Remy Church, where we were to prepare and set up defences for a battalion headquarters. This was where our commanding officer, Lieutenant Colonel Bob Labatt, along with five or six of his headquarters staff, would control the battalion battle. His signallers had to establish communications with the companies; on another radio net they would send reports back to brigade and through them, to General Roberts at Division HQ on the *Calpe*.

"The machine gun fire was intensifying. Mortar shells were falling all around us and snipers were hitting the men with deadly accuracy. Much of this fire was coming from gun positions in caves we didn't know existed.

"This was the enemy that had been described to General Roberts as '1400 poor quality German troops.' We'd gone in naked, with very little fire support. The naval guns had lifted after ten minutes, but they hadn't made much of a dent anyway. For some reason, the navy had insisted on carrying a high percentage of ineffective armour-piercing instead of high-explosive shells. And the Hurricanes had done little damage before they left. We couldn't figure out why the Churchill tanks that were supposed to land with us and give us cover still hadn't arrived."

Private Ian McDonald, Essex Scottish Regiment: "We thought that, with all the naval firepower, there would be nothing left on the beach and it would simply be a walk-through. But about three seconds after landing we saw that the shelling had done no damage to the German positions."[19]

0520 hours: The Essex Scottish had come in at the same time as the Rileys on the east half of the main beach. They weren't lucky enough to have a casino on their front. It at least offered the Rileys some protection from bullets and mortar bombs. The Essex got across the two wire obstacles and reached the seawall that formed the near perimeter of the esplanade. By this point their casualties were about 30 to 40 percent.

Major Jim Green, Essex Scottish: "In my company area, the sea wall was low where the shale [chert] had piled up against it, and there wasn't much cover. We tried to get up into the town along the cover of the wall but that was not possible because there was a trench full of Germans dug into the esplanade who just mowed our people down."[20]

Three times, the Essex organized a valiant charge across the flat, featureless esplanade that separated them from the town. Three times, they were repelled, with devastating casualties. All they were able to do after that was keep on firing from behind the sea wall at the still faceless enemy.

0535 hours: "Doug touched down 0535." This signal was dispatched by Captain G.A. Browne, a forward observation officer attached to the Royal Regiment. Browne, who landed at Blue Beach in the second wave with the C.O., Lieutenant Colonel Doug Catto, had managed to maintain some communication with the destroyer, H.M.S. *Garth*, for two hours. Strangely, General Roberts on the *Calpe* was not receiving any information from his units. For reasons that no one has ever been able to deduce, Roberts was being isolated in a vacuum of silence.

The first signal that was relayed to him was at 0620, when he was erroneously informed by an unknown source — later believed to be Germans breaking into his radio net — that the Royal Regiment had not landed. The decisions he would make, based on that intelligence, compounded the disaster horribly.[21]

The second wave of Royals coming into Puys faced beaches strewn with bodies of their comrades. They had no chance at all.

Major Forbes West, Royal Regiment of Canada: "When the navy landed the second wave of the Royal Regiment forty-five minutes late — and in daylight — the Germans by then were able to fire accurately at very close range, instead of merely firing bursts in the dark. We were enfiladed from less than one hundred yards. Within ten or fifteen minutes of landing the signallers had all been killed. I was left without any means of communication. We were massacred by a machine gun in a German tank turret beside the house that used to belong to Alexandre Dumas.

I couldn't help but remember, when we were first briefed for Rutter, my C.O., Hedley Basher, had asked the artillery to put a six-pounder gun on a LCT and blow that thing off the face of the earth before we went ashore. He was told to shut up and mind his own business."[22]

Private Ron Beal, Royal Regiment: "I got out in six feet of water. There were a lot of dead lying right at the shoreline. I got over them, halfway up the beach, and I dropped. Run and drop, run and drop. This was my training. Machine gun fire was bouncing off the stones. I made it to the wall on the second try." Beal then peered cautiously around him. What he saw filled him with dread. Puys was a fortress.

"At the top of the hill was a house. Halfway down was a pillbox set on a track [with a] 360-degree arc of fire to it. Then at the base was a heavy gun emplacement with machine guns. Straight ahead was barbed wire. In behind the barbed wire were some trenches with machine guns and halfway up the right flank was another machine gun emplacement. Out on the extreme right cliff was another pillbox."[23]

A few of the naval crews on the LCAs showed undue haste in offloading the troops — some into fairly deep water — or in backing off before all the men had disembarked.

Lance Corporal W. Duggan, B Coy, 10 Platoon, Royal Regiment:
"The LCA did not beach but was within twenty-five yards of the
beach. The men had to swim in about seven feet of water to reach
shore. We rushed out of the craft with our mortar, which was on a
dolly and weighed about four hundred pounds. When we hit the water
the dolly sank instantly. We struggled to move it. Many of the
detachment disappeared and I found myself alone trying to pull it onto
the beach."[24]

Private J.E. Creer, A Coy, Royal Regiment: "We tried hard to get
a Bangalore torpedo up on the wall to blow the barbed wire but it
seemed hopeless. Just as Mr. Patterson got up on the ladder he was
hit. Private Graham tried it and he was hit the same way. Just then,
Private Stevenson shouted at me that he was hit. He was lying behind
his gun with no protection around him at all, but he kept shouting,
'Fight! Keep fighting!' "[25]

The third wave coming into Puys, comprising three platoons of the
Canadian Black Watch under command of Captain Ray Hicks of the
Royals, was put down under the cliff at the eastern end of the beach.
Not one man escaped the murderous fire to return to England.

Private Reg Hall, Black Watch Regiment: "After we landed, we all
dashed off in a hail of bullets for the cliff. The three chaps in front of
me went down within a few yards. We huddled under the cliff on the
starboard side. We could see the German machine guns on top of the
cliff because it was kind of horseshoe-shaped. There were German
snipers on the top throwing potato mashers [grenades] and sniping at
us. That's where the majority of casualties came from, the grenades.
The fire was so heavy we couldn't do anything except take shelter."[26]

*Lieutenant Walter Höpener, 12th Field Company, 571 German In-
fantry Regiment, Puys:* "As the landing ramps fell and the attackers
sprang firing onto land, they met the destructive fire of the two heavy
MGs. An inferno began which was to last almost three hours. In our
command post, two young soldiers who had only been here a few days
threw up constantly — it was their first action.

"We were amazed at the attacker, who fought with bravery and élan
against an opponent who could not be seen. Nobody thought of giving
up. Taking effective cover behind their dead comrades, they shot
uninterruptedly at our positions. Thus with their bodies these dead
soldiers provided their comrades with the last service of friendship."[27]

—■■■■—

0600 hours: The South Saskatchewans units who had been landed on the wrong side of the River Scie were now struggling to get a foothold on the bridge. Beyond it lay their main objective: the guns on the east headland that were causing such terrible casualties to the Rileys and to themselves. The SSRs' commanding officer, Lieutenant Colonel Cec Merritt, walked out on the bridge and, ignoring the hail of fire, waved his helmet and yelled to his men, "Come on over! There's nothing to it!"[28]

Crossing in his wake or underneath by the girders, the men followed Merritt in a charge against German MG posts. "It was his very audacity that took Jerry by surprise," his adjutant, Lieutenant "Buck" Buchanan said. But with no communication to allow them to call down accurate fire from the destroyers, and with such a severe shortage of mortar ammunition that it was exhausted in the first 10 minutes, the Saskatchewans were unable to make significant progress. They had only rifles and machine guns to defend against the heavy German mortar shelling. Any attempt by A Company to ascend the east headland and capture the radar station with the Canadian radar expert, Flight Sergeant Jack Nissenthal, was thwarted by determined enemy defenders.

0600 hours: When the Queen's Own Cameron Highlanders of Canada surged onto Green Beach 40 minutes after the South Saskatchewan attack, they expected to make an unopposed landing against a quelled enemy. But the Germans were far from subdued. Instead, the determined defenders greeted these new invaders with a rain of fire. One of the first victims was the Camerons' C.O., Lieutenant Colonel Alfred Gostling.

Private Herbert Webber, Cameron Highlanders: "Our first casualty was C Company's sergeant major. He got hit right in the head and was killed instantly. It was through him that Colonel Gostling was killed. He looked over and saw that the CSM was hit but he didn't know he was dead. He stood up and yelled, 'Stretcher-bearer, stretcher-bearer!' Just then he was shot."[29]

Major Andy Law immediately took command.

The riflemen had been heartened by the courage of the piper Corporal Alec Graham, who steadfastly played the bagpipes during the last twenty-minute run-in to shore. The strains of "A Hundred Pipers" would inspire many a young soldier to fighter longer and harder that day.

The Camerons' assignment — as unrealistic as were the other units' — was to pass through the SSR and capture and destroy the aerodrome at St. Aubin. Following this, they would capture the German divisional headquarters, mistakenly believed to be at Arques-la-Bataille, six miles inland. To achieve all this, they were planning to connect with a unit of Calgary Tanks.

There was a laundry list of other, smaller objectives, some quite ludicrous.

Lieutenant Tom Melville, Cameron Highlanders: "My platoon was to go through the woods and find an anti-aircraft gun and bring back its sights. I thought, this is ridiculous. Don't they know what an ack-ack gunsight looks like?"[30]

Because the South Saskatchewans had been unable to clear Pourville or its headlands, and because the Calgary Tanks were still pinned down on Dieppe's main beach, the Camerons would attain none of their objectives that day. To complicate matters still further, the navy had landed them astride the Scie instead of entirely on the left bank. (They had done the same to the SSR.) This split the battalion's three companies. Even so, Law was able to lead the bulk of his men some three miles inland — the deepest penetration made by any force that day.

———————■———————

At 302 Division HQ in Envermeu, General Haase's concern focussed on the threat to his relatively undefended left flank at Pourville. He had been told that British soldiers had forced a landing there. At 0530 hours he had ordered out reserves: a German cyclist platoon, which was on its way to Quatre Vents Farm, and a reserve battalion of the 571st Infantry, whose vanguard detachment of 75-mm artillery was now moving up against the Camerons.

Von Rundstedt had responded swiftly to the emergency, placing the battle-sharp 10 Panzer Division under command of 81 Corps. Its advanced detachment — one reinforced battalion — was at Torcy le Petit, only 14 kilometres south of Dieppe. The remainder was at Flixecourt, near Amiens. It would be some four hours before the entire division could arrive at Dieppe.

How serious was this threat? Haase worried. Was it a full-scale invasion? The second front they had been expecting? Haase decided to have a look for himself. From an observation post on the bluffs — Captain Ditz's "eagle's nest" — Haase and the 10th Panzer commander observed the chaotic battle below. The main beach seemed under control, although enemy patrols had infiltrated the town. Haase had been told that the attack at Berneval was by a small force of commandos. His reserves far outnumbered them and would have no problem in subduing the British. There was no need to order reserves to Puys. The invader there was pinned to the beaches.

No, the danger lay to the west. Battery 813 at Varengeville had been virtually destroyed. Enemy infantry had broken through the perimeter defences at Pourville. But why had the British not yet poured in fresh troops and armour to reinforce their position? he puzzled.

Haase decided that, on arrival, the 10th Panzer Division would deploy directly toward Pourville. "Attack the heights first," he ordered. "Then attack Dieppe from the west and clear out the main beach.

"This enemy must be destroyed."[31]

CHAPTER

19

THE UNSEEN ENEMY

0530 hours: At Dieppe beach, the attack was floundering. Its momentum had been lost during the first minutes when the infantry went in with no armoured, artillery, or air support. In desperation, Lieutenant Colonel Bob Labatt of the Royal Hamilton Light Infantry radioed 4th Brigade headquarters. "Get Johnny forward." This was the agreed code for requesting tank support from Lieutenant Colonel Johnny Andrews' Calgary Tank Regiment.

Labatt couldn't know it, but the main assault was already lost. The failure of the two flank attacks to seize the headland guns had sealed the fate of the 1,100 men battling for a single mile of beachfront at Dieppe. They were being beaten back by an enemy they couldn't even see.

On top of that, the navy reserves had blundered again. Because of navigational errors the three LCTs carrying the first wave of nine tanks and their supporting sappers were 10 to 15 minutes late in landing. During these crucial minutes, the hapless infantrymen had no armoured support and no help from sappers in punching a way through the beach obstacles. Nor were they able to dig slits in the stone beach; they could only wedge their bodies into narrow depressions formed by the tides on the jagged rocks. It was a futile attempt to protect themselves from the shells, bullets, shrapnel and stone splinters that were ricocheting wildly about them. Meanwhile, the delay had given the enemy a chance to recover from the air and naval bombardment and consolidate their defences.

As the first tanks lumbered down the ramps and onto the beach, a huge problem declared itself. The tank commanders and troopers discovered that the beach stones were of an extremely hard mineral called chert. Even worse, this stone was many metres in depth, which meant that no traction was possible for wheeled vehicles. Tanks threw their treads when the stones — some the size of baseballs — became wedged in the sprockets.

Fifty-eight tanks were supposed to land on the main beach, but only twenty-nine did. Of these, twelve Churchills lost their treads on the stone or were disabled by antitank fire. Crews that attempted to dismount and repair the tracks were cut down by heavy fire. Two tanks were mistakenly driven off the LCT ramps into deep water. One commander was drowned immediately. The other was machine-gunned before he reached shore.

The stone, which General Roberts had been assured was "suitable for landing armoured vehicles" knocked out two of the first nine tanks to land that day. Four did manage to climb over the sea wall and get to the esplanade, where the crews' limited vision rendered their guns ineffective against the well-hidden German strongpoints. The second wave came in immediately afterwards. All of its nine tanks landed safely, but, again, only four managed to get over the sea wall and reach the esplanade. The LCTs bringing the tanks to shore came under heavy fire. Several were sunk or beached.

Just half of the 350 divisional assault engineers from three field companies of the Royal Canadian Engineers (7th, 11th and 2nd) plus the 1st Field Park Company, managed to land in assigned groups with the tanks: 71 sappers in beach assault parties and 98 demolition sappers. Their tasks were to manhandle heavy explosives and Banga-lore torpedoes to blast holes in the strong wire barriers, to lay chespal-ing slats under the tank treads, and to haul timber to build ladders to get the tanks over the six-foot concrete sea wall. These men had no protection from enemy fire; they were mowed down mercilessly. The sappers were to suffer 85 to 90 percent casualties that morning — the worst toll of any unit there.[1]

0550 hours: Captain Denis Whitaker, RHLI: "We were pinned down on the beach. As I lay there, one tank a few yards to my right had its six-pounder gun shattered by an enemy solid-shot shell. I was deter-mined to get my men off before the enemy artillery, mortars and MGs annihilated us. The sea wall in front of us was an impossible exit. But to our right I saw the casino — a three-storied white stucco building about fifty yards from the edge of the beach — and thought we might be able to get through it and into the town.

"There was a terrific racket — bullets were whizzing past, shells exploding, men shouting and screaming. I yelled, 'Follow me! Make for the casino!' We laid down two cannisters of smoke and ran like hell. There was a pillbox right in front. Private John Shuart from B Company threw in a grenade to silence it. Then we found a wire entanglement blocking the casino entrance. We cut through that with wire cutters and got inside, entering on the run and firing our Sten guns. Major Bud Matchett had been killed on the way to the casino. His second-in-command, Captain Tony Hill, took command of B Company. The Rileys had now lost three of their four company commanders in the effort to cross the beach.

"The building was filled with Germans — two or three dozen I should guess — many of whom threw up their hands. In the fight that followed, some were shot. A few got away down a corridor. We made our way through what must have been the main salon, although it had no furnishings and had been partially destroyed by the Germans. At the east side of the building, we were able to look out a window and see down below us a row of slit trenches filled with German infantry.

"With the aid of a Bren gun, and an antitank rifle wielded by Private Tommy Graham, we took them by surprise and cleared up this position."

0630 hours: Captain Denis Whitaker, RHLI: "We jumped out the window and made our way through the slit trenches over the bodies of the enemy to a low wooden shelter. As we arrived here, a heavy concentration of mortar bombs came down on us. They had got our range from the headlands. We flung ourselves down on the cement floor and discovered to our chagrin that the whole shack had been used as a latrine. It was impossible to move, as the mortaring continued without interruption; we lay in this crap for twenty or thirty minutes, feeling great revulsion for every German alive!"

0603–0630 hours: Calgary Tank Regiment: The next waves of tanks came in. By now, 16 had made it to the esplanade; none had been able to get past the huge concrete roadblocks blockading the streets leading into the town.

Lieutenant Ed Bennett, Commander No. 10 Troop, Calgary Tanks: "We were hit coming in by a gun at the end of the jetty. The shell exploded one of the cylinders on my tank that held the hydrogen. I was standing on the back just behind the turret, looking to see whether we would go to the right or to the left and I got caught in the blast. I lost my hair and scorched my face and got some shrapnel in my eye. I kept going until my eye closed up."[2]

0630 hours: Captain Denis Whitaker, RHLI: "When the mortaring let up, I decided to try to get across the 150 yards of the esplanade and into the town. Running and zigzagging like mad, with bullets hitting the ground all around me, I made it. On the town side of the esplanade I crouched by a low wall with tall iron pickets on top. Again a machine gun got my range. Bullets hit the wall in front of my head and right under my stomach. I got out of there in a hurry, running along the wall to an opening which led to the town, and got into a building through a window. By this time there were only a few men with me from my platoon, including George Naylor and Al Reiger, although there were a few, like Lieutenant Dan Doheny, from other units."

0635 hours: Private K.C. (Casey) Lingen, B Coy, RHLI: "When I left the casino, I joined up with Captain Whitaker and some of his boys. After we got to the wall, a Jerry MG started to fire and splattered the wall above our heads. We dashed to the left into a couple of cleared Jerry pits and started to fire [at them] but without success. Then we saw a tank cruising up and down the road in front. One of the boys waved to him and pointed towards the Jerry."[3]

That tank proved to be Captain Bennett's.

0700 hours: Lieutenant Ed Bennett: "All three tanks in my squadron, Beefy, Bloody, and Belicose, got up on the esplanade. We saw Canadian troops taking cover beside the Casino. Two of them pointed to us to go over towards a small building on the esplanade that had some low trenches connecting with it. The Germans started to run out of the trenches and we had a field day. After that we went right down to the end of the esplanade in front of all the hotels and buildings, along Maréchal Foch Road, thinking we might be able to get through some of the side streets."[4]

0700 hours: Captain H.H. Ditz, Battery Commander, 302nd German Infantry Division: "The smoke from our shells mixed with the artificial smoke so that soon the whole valley of Dieppe lay under a white carpet out of which the houses appeared like shadows. Enemy aircraft had damaged our whole communications network. The same thing happened to all five batteries.

"I looked on the beach; the artificial fog [was] growing thinner. The picture which presented itself could teach any man what fear means. The beach was strewn with infantry equipment: machine guns, packs, grenade throwers, munitions. . . . Two whole regiments were clinging tightly against the concrete wall, seeking protection from our artillery fire and from the machine gun fire of the beach company, and tank upon tank stood at the water's edge. Everywhere along the whole strand our shells were exploding, their effect multiplied ten times by the exploding of the stone splinters.

"On the green grass between the concrete wall and the edge of town, where the beach company had dug out their trenches, tanks were twisting and turning . . . trying to get through into the town. Well, they could try forever! The commander of our division had closed all the streets leading from the beach to the town with a tank-proof concrete wall."[5]

0700 hours: THE CASINO HAS FALLEN.

This report, received from the Royal Hamilton Light Infantry, left General Roberts in a dilemma. He was in a virtual void of silence, having had no really solid information since the assault had been mounted an hour-and-one-half before. He had conflicting information about the Royal Regiment and believed they had not disembarked at Puys.

He had not heard from No. 3 Commando at Berneval, although Goebbels Battery had been blessedly silent. Nor had he any word from Lovat's No. 4 Commando. All he knew of the South Saskatchewans and Camerons at Pourville was that they had landed. He had only indirect communication with the Essex Scottish. His one link with the main assault group was through the principal military landing officer, Major Brian McCool. To relay a message, McCool would periodically dash across the beach, dodging enemy fire to get to the Calgary Tanks' signals officer, Major Gordon Rolfe. In this way, Rolfe in his damaged scout car, *Hunter*, and McCool, maintained what radio communication there was throughout the battle, and until both men were taken prisoner.[6]

Roberts' main concern at this point was to knock out the devastating fire on the east and west headlands. The 61 sorties the Boston medium bombers had flown against the enemy positions on the two headlands had not been successful. It was obvious there had been no direct hits. (Only 12 craters with any relation to either target were later detected by air recce. As one historian noted, "Machine gun nests in the face of the fortified headlands were totally unsuitable targets for cannon-fighters or fighter-bombers."[7])

It was vital that Roberts commit his one floating reserve, Les Fusiliers Mont-Royal, wherever he could reinforce success. But where best to do this? He pinned his hopes on the optimistic reports that the main beach assault was going well. If the Rileys had captured the casino, by now he guessed they must be in the town.

Then a cryptic message from the Essex Scottish that they had reached the town led Roberts to believe that the entire main force had broken through the German defences. In those critical minutes, baffled and confused by snatches of conflicting reports, General Ham Roberts lost control of the battle.

Tragically, the valiant efforts of a handful of men had become distorted in the ensuing signals. There *had* been a small handful of Essex get into the town of Dieppe, as had groups of Rileys. Essex CSM Cornelius Stapleton, with a group of fourteen men, had charged over the wall and found their way into town. For over an hour they roamed the streets, wreaking havoc with pockets of enemy; but they had returned to the beach when their ammunition was depleted and they realized that no other Essex Scottish had gotten over the wall.

Sergeant Dave Hart, 4 Brigade Signaller: "Our problem was trying to get communications through. I passed the message that got garbled: ONE MAN IN THE ESSEX SCOTTISH HAS PENETRATED THE TOWN. Unfortunately, [Brigadier] Church Mann took this to mean the entire battalion of Essex Scottish had penetrated the town."

Meanwhile, Roberts had no inkling that the Essex had been pinned to the beach, unable to manage any offensive action, or that they had sustained 75 percent casualties in the first hour. Based on the information at hand, he made the fateful decision to focus his remaining reserves on the headlands that had so bedeviled him. He sent word for the Royal Regiment — whom he believed were somewhere offshore — to join the Essex and try to get through the town and up the east cliffs. The signal was, of course, never received by the beleaguered Royals. Roberts then sent in his last reserves, the FMR, to the main beach with the same mission.

Hart had realized the message had been garbled and that the whole operation would be jeopardized if this misinformation was acted upon. He tried to get back to Mann. Too late, he was told. They're committed.[8]

0724 hours: Operation Jubilee log: JOE BEING SENT IN TO FRED: The FMR were ordered in to reinforce the Essex Scottish. The most tragic error of that tragic day had now been made.

Lieutenant Dan Doheny RCA; Liaison Officer, Second Division Headquarters, H.M.S. Calpe: "Information about the battle was either negligible or not being passed around. I gathered from General Roberts it was proceeding satisfactorily and it was just a matter of time before the town was in our hands."

Doheny's original task was to go ashore for administrative purposes as soon as the town had been secured: "to drive a colonel around and maybe have a couple of beers," the 27-year-old Montreal lawyer noted sardonically. Now this was changed. "Get ashore and find out what is happening," he was instructed.

Doheny jumped aboard a motor launch as it was pulling away. He was perched up in the bow, enjoying the warm sun, when he realized they were in the midst of FMR assault boats heading into shore. "I transferred over to Lieutenant Colonel Joe Menard's R boat. We had just formed up and started in when the first shell fell in the middle of the flotilla. I was quite surprised but thought it must be some inland battery firing at us. Then shells began to fall so close I expected a direct hit any minute."

The moment the boat touched shore, Doheny leaped off and took cover behind a tank. He saw a friend, Lieutenant John Counsell, and learned for the first time the true situation. " 'It's an awful F.U.,' Johnny told me. 'They were waiting for us. They knew we were coming.' " Then, in another whine of bullets, Counsell slumped over, shot in the back. Doheny did what he could for him, and then sprinted up to the casino to join the party of Rileys just as it was heading out across the esplanade toward the town.[9]

As the FMR burst through the smoke screen in their 26 unarmoured R boats, the commanding officer, "Joe" Menard, urged them on with victory shouts of "show 'em what French-Canadian boys can do!" But the assaulting force was met with a renewed frenzy of fire, focussed entirely on the helpless men. Some of the boats were sunk on their way in. Others dispersed, a few landing at the Essex's Red Beach. Most of the troops were set down at the far western end of the RHLI's White Beach. Les Fusiliers charged bravely off their craft, firing from the hip; but they were soon pinned down by the same unseen enemy that had trapped the Essex Scottish and RHLI.

Corporal Robert Berube, HQ Coy, FMR: "There were twenty of us in the R boat. When we came out through the smoke and onto the beach, only seven got across. The rest were all killed. We just stayed on the beach. You moved and you'd had it."[10]

The group at the western end of the beach, taking cover below the headlands, was torn to pieces by dozens of grenades tossed down from the clifftop. In all, 119 men were killed. Menard was wounded five times and evacuated, unconscious.

0730 hours: "Sorry." Roberts received this second — and last — victory signal of the day. The first had come from a company of South Saskatchewans on the west bank of the Scie. This time it came from Lord Lovat's No. 4 Commando at Varengeville.

While Mills-Roberts' snipers and mortars had achieved great success against the six-gun battery, the killing blow was to come from Lovat's main body of commandos. They completed their wide detour on the run and in perfect time. At 0628 hours, precisely on schedule, a squadron of Hurricanes armed with cannons, swooping dangerously low, blasted the battery. Lovat's unit attacked in their wake. His 164 ferocious, bayonet-slashing commandos swarmed over the stunned German battery crews. Within 10 minutes, the garrison was demolished. Captain Pat Porteous, although wounded, led one group in a final charge across open ground swept by machine gun fire, and captured the battery. He was later awarded the Victoria Cross for this action.

At 0730 hours, bearing their wounded, No. 4 Commando reembarked. Twelve men had been killed. The message to Roberts added, with a forgivable note of bravado: "Every one of gun crews finished with bayonet. OK by you?"[11]

0745 hours: At Berneval, 14 miles east of Lovat's unit, Major Peter Young and his small band of No. 3 Commando fired three white Very lights — the withdrawal signal — to Lieutenant Commander Henry Buckee RN, commanding the LCA that had brought them in three hours before.

When Young realized that the Germans had been alerted to their attack, and that the additional 120 or so men from No. 3 Commando that he had seen coming in late would not be able to help him, he decided to go it alone. He knew he had no hope of capturing and destroying the battery, which was his battalion's assignment. But he could at least keep the battery silent for as long as possible. So he and his 18 men tackled the 350-man Goebbels Battery, peppering it with so much small-arms fire that it did not fire at the flotilla during the attack. "In an hour-and-a-half, we fired one hundred rounds of rifle shot per man," he noted. "There was not much ammunition left." One of the big German guns finally swung 180 degrees around and began bombarding them, but as it could not depress its barrel sufficiently, its shells sailed harmlessly over their heads, landing "somewhere in France."[12]

When the Germans mounted a counterattack against them, Young prudently withdrew. The commandos — by then back on the beach with the enemy at its heels and bullets coming uncomfortably close — were whisked off by Lieutenant Commander Buckee. Young's band had taken only one casualty during its remarkable exploits.

The other section of 3 Commando's pincer attack was not as lucky. Because of the earlier attack by the German convoy, the five boatloads of men had landed late and in daylight at the second Berneval beach. They found an alerted enemy waiting for them. Although they fought their way toward the battery, the Commando was soon surrounded by vastly superior numbers of Major von Blücher's reinforcements. The raiders were forced back and trapped on the beach with no option but to surrender. The Germans reported 82 prisoners taken. Among those killed was Lieutenant Edwin Loustalot of the U.S. Rangers, the first American of the war to lose his life in land fighting against the Germans.[13]

———

0700 hours: General Roberts summoned Lieutenant Commander Goulding to the *Calpe* to investigate the puzzling silence from the Royal Regiment. As he arrived, by coincidence, a signal from the Royals finally reached Roberts via the *Garth*: FROM BLUE BEACH: IS THERE ANY POSSIBLE CHANCE OF GETTING US OFF? Roberts immediately instructed Goulding to evacuate the Royals.

When Goulding's motor launch approached the beach, heavy fire opened up and he retired. At 1145 hours, Goulding finally contacted the *Calpe* — his first communication since being sent out to Blue Beach at 0700 hours to evacuate the Royals: COULD NOT SEE PROVISION [position?] BLUE BEACH OWING TO FOG AND HEAVY FIRE FROM CLIFF AND WHITE HOUSE. NOBODY EVACUATED.[14]

0700 hours: The situation on Blue Beach was desperate. For close to 30 minutes, Lieutenant Colonel Douglas Catto, the Royal's C.O., had lain prone on top of the 12-foot seawall, struggling to cut through the dense tangle of barbed wire that blocked his battalion's escape from the hell of Puys beach. A young lieutenant, Bob Stewart, crawled up with his Bren gun to give covering fire. Machine guns peppered the men relentlessly while Catto painfully cut through to the last strand of wire.

Rallying some 20 officers and men, including artillery forward observation officer Captain George Browne, Catto led the way through the gap they had made. Lieutenant Stewart, now severely wounded, continued firing to cover their escape. "He must have been out of his mind with rage," recalled one soldier. "I remember him getting hit in the legs but still standing up, cursing and swearing."[15]

As the men moved up the cliff, they met two young officers from the Royals who had somehow managed to get across the beach, over the wall and up the cliff earlier, and now had an extraordinary story to tell:

Lieutenant Thomas L. Taylor, C Coy, Royal Regiment of Canada: "As we touched down, we heard a sound you could never forget: a tremendous 'rat-tat-tat' as blistering volleys of machine gun bullets raked the armoured door of my LCA. That gun was trained directly on us. The naval commander wanted to know why I was not getting out — he said he had to get back to England! With that, the fire switched and out we went. There was no hesitation by the troops who followed me. However, only ten of us made it to the wall.

"As I reached the wall, a Bangalore torpedo had just blown a gap through the wire and there was a ladder at the wall. I think it was [Captain] Gus Sinclair who made the hole, but he was killed right afterwards. Then I was through the gap with five men. We scrambled up the cliff through a defile that at least gave us some protection from the guns on the west, but not from the east. One of my men — he'd always been a bit of a rebel — stopped halfway to light a cigarette and that's when he got it. The others, who were more disciplined, made it up.

"At the top of the cliff I met Lieutenant Sterling Ryerson. We were the first two of the regiment to gain the high ground. Sergeant Edward Cole joined us shortly afterwards. We put a machine gun emplacement out of action in the first house on the right. We went in with our Stens firing and Ryerson got three Germans. I guess we were on the cliff for more than an hour, but as no one seemed to be coming up, we went part way down. There we met the C.O."[16]

Joining forces, the handful of men moved up the cliff on the west side, attacking and clearing enemy from several positions before heading towards the battery on the west headlands that was to have been their main objective. Catto hoped to touch base with the Essex Scottish, not realizing that they, too, had been trapped on the beach. German patrols by now combing the area left them no alternative but to hole up in a small inland copse. Meanwhile, the gap had been sealed by enemy machine gun fire, cutting Catto off from his men on the beach.

Private Ron Beal, Royal Regiment: Beal, a stretcher-bearer, was trying to do his job in impossible conditions. "About fifty percent of the battalion, three to four hundred men, were against the wall. There were wounded men out on the beach calling for help. At this point, no one was venturing out there. Anything that moved, they just opened up everything. Machine gun fire was bouncing off the stones. I ran out of bandages, ran out of morphine."[17]

One landing craft managed to get in and try to evacuate the troops. Overloaded and under heavy fire, its doors could not be closed because of the dead piled on the ramp. It finally capsized and sank, with its captain and crew killed. A pitiful handful of Royals swam out to other boats and escaped the beach: 209 men died on it.[18]

0817: The *Calpe's* log noted, "Have control of White Beach." Armed with yet another piece of misinformation, Roberts now decided to reinforce what he believed was the success of the Rileys on White Beach: he ordered the Royal Marine Commandos to assist in seizing the east headlands. As they approached shore, their commander, Lieutenant Colonel Joseph Phillips, quickly grasped the true situation. Leaping to his feet, in disdain of the enemy fire, he turned and waved, "Back! Back!" to his men in the craft following him. The 200 Marine Commandos in the craft behind him turned back in time as Phillips fell mortally wounded. But 66 others who preceded him were killed or captured.[19]

0830 hours: The remnants of the Royal Regiment of Canada surrendered.

Private Reg Hall: "All of a sudden a German officer came along the beach carrying a white flag. He said, 'It's all right boys, put down your arms and your ammunition.' Then we all marched out."[20]

0835 hours: 571 Regiment report: "Puys firmly in our hands. Enemy has lost about 500 men prisoners and dead."

0830 hours: Captain G.A. Browne, RCA: "Catto and I went to the cliff edge to see if we could see anything." All they could see was a pall of smoke over the main Dieppe beach. They heard the occasional sound of firing. From the Royals at Blue Beach there was only silence. The realization sank in: the battle was over.

"A few minutes later, we heard the Royal prisoners being marched along the road."[21]

0835 hours: White Beach: Lieutenant Colonel Johnny Andrews, C.O. of the Calgary Tanks, had come in earlier and been unable to land when the ramp of his LCT had become blocked. He anxiously radioed his signals officer, Major Gordon Rolfe: "Is it worthwhile my coming ashore?" Rolfe replied that it was pretty bad but that he was needed. Andrews' last signal was, "About to beach. Be seeing you. Cheerio."[22]

Brigadier Sherwood Lett; Commander, 4th Canadian Brigade: Brigadier Lett "We had very heavy casualties on the LCT, including myself. Colonel Andrews said goodbye and pulled off. But the chains on the ramp of our landing craft had been shot away, so the ramp went down to the bottom and Colonel Andrews landed in nine or ten feet of water. All I could see was his pennant at the top. He bailed out and swam to a small landing craft and was taken aboard, but in a few minutes it was set afire and we did not see him again."[23] (Johnny Andrews was machine-gunned in the water. His body was never recovered.)

Although he did not land, Brigadier Lett was severely wounded, he continued to issue orders from his stretcher on the LCT.

0900 hours: Les Fusiliers Mont-Royal radioed the command ship: IN SEVERE DIFFICULTY, MUST BE TAKEN OFF OR WILL BE WIPED OUT.

0905 hours: They radioed again: COMPLETELY SURROUNDED.

Not long after that, a German patrol climbed stealthily down a track in the cliffs and demanded the surrender of FMR. In all, 344 officers and men of that battalion were marched off the west beach at gunpoint. They left behind over 100 of their comrades, dead and dying.

CHAPTER

20

VANQUISH

0940: VANQUISH 1100 HOURS. This withdrawal signal was sent to all assault forces.

1000 hours: Captain Denis Whitaker, RHLI: "I realized that it was pointless to proceed any further into the town as it appeared that the commanding officer and the bulk of the force had been unable to get off the beach. The overpowering enfilade fire from the west flank had pinned the men to the ground. Any movement brought instant death in the form of sniper or machine gun fire.

"There was no alternative but to return to the casino. We dashed across the esplanade, dodging back and forth to avoid the fire that was coming from the area of the castle. Arriving safely back, I found many of my battalion friends, including Major Harold Lazier, Captain Tony Hill, Lieutenants Johnny Webster and Bill Currie, and Company Sergeant Major "Lucky" Stewart, as well as Lieutenant Dan Doheny. They were holding about twenty German prisoners, one of whom told me they'd been waiting for us for a week. Whether this was true or not I do not know. But they were certainly ready when we landed.

"Tony Hill had led the only small group that got into the town. He told me an amazing story about going with eight or nine men into a theatre near the church, where he found an elderly Frenchwoman nonchalantly counting money."[1]

Captain Tony Hill, RHLI: "It really was quite funny to see this one Dieppoise counting last night's receipts in the middle of all this — guns going off everywhere — when we walked through. She paid no attention, no attention whatsoever. Then we went to a rendezvous at the church. But we had nobody to rendezvous with. The rest of the company was still on the beach. So we went back to the casino."[2]

1015 hours: Captain Denis Whitaker, RHLI: "Word came that an attempt to evacuate us would be made at 1100 hours. We organized the casino as an all-round defensive position and arranged to lay a smoke screen with canisters to cover our withdrawal when the boats came in. Then we settled down to wait."

Private Johnny Shuart, RHLI: "When the LCAs came in, the riflemen went first. Private Moody stayed on with me to man the Bren gun and feed me mags as we fired at the enemy."[3]

1030 hours: With almost all their ammunition used up, the remnants of the Essex moved back to the water's edge. This provoked the Germans into laying on an increased attack of shelling and dive bombing, causing many new casualties and preventing the landing craft from getting in, or getting off.

(Of the 553 officers and men of the Essex who embarked for Dieppe, 530 were casualties — 382 as prisoners of war. Only 51 returned, and half of these were wounded. There were just two officers left in the battalion.)[4]

Lieutenant Wilhelm Freiderich Schlie, Commander, German 75-mm gun battery: Schlie's task during the attack was to direct artillery fire. His "eagle's nest" on the cliff top overlooked the invaders on the main beach and, later, the LCAs coming in to evacuate them.

"At first it looked very threatening as we saw so many tanks coming towards us. But then we saw that the tanks couldn't advance and the soldiers couldn't get any further. Gradually, from the German side, reserves came through. Then we noticed they were trying to re-embark those people who were still on the beach. We naturally kept shooting as long as they were in range."[5]

Major Richard McLaren, Intelligence Officer, RHLI: "From our Battalion HQ, to the left of the casino, I could see a German artillery officer on the cliff. He would raise his arm. Every time the boats came in, his arm would drop and down came the shells."

(Even before the Germans took him prisoner, McLaren felt their intrusion. His no. 14 radio set wasn't very functional, but it did carry jazz from a German dance band!)[6]

On White Beach, RHLI Padre Captain John Foote had moved calmly throughout the entire terrible morning searching out the wounded and carrying them to Captain Wes Clare's makeshift Regimental Aid Post behind a LCT that had beached broadside. It, at least, offered some protection from the fire. The injuries were appalling: men had limbs turn off, muscles spilling out of their thighs, guts being stuffed back into stomachs, ears ripped off, eyes blinded.

When the LCAs came in for the withdrawal, the burly padre lifted many wounded lads into his arms and carried them out to the waiting craft. But he refused all offers to be evacuated. "My place is with my boys," he said. One hundred and ninety-seven of "his boys" from the Rileys died on the beach that morning; 175 more were marched off with John Foote to spend three wretched years in prisoner of war camps.[7]

1000 hours: By now, many of the tanks had returned to the beach. Although most had been immobilized by damage from shellfire or the chert, they continued to function as pillboxes, firing until their ammunition was spent.

Lieutenant Jack Dunlap, Calgary Tank Regiment: "We received a call for all tanks to return to the beach, to be prepared to lay down a smoke screen to cover the landing of evacuation boats. Because my three tanks were to be part of the rear guard that day, I think my crews knew that their chances of leaving the beach were minimal. As the boats appeared, they came under very intense fire. There was a rush of men for the boats. Some were swamped by too many men, sunk by gunfire or forced to turn back with partial loads. Casualties on the beach and in the water were unbelievable."

Men like Dunlap stayed back in their tanks, providing continuous fire to cover the evacuating troops. For this reason, only three men from the Calgary Tanks who had landed got back to England that day.

The 157 tank troops who spent the next three years as POWs would have time to reflect that during training, they had been given no landing practice on chert beaches (such as the one at Dover). Nor had they received any training in close-quarter street fighting, which they would certainly have encountered had their tanks been able to get off the beach and into Dieppe's narrow streets.[8]

Lieutenant Dan Doheny: "I think one of the biggest mistakes of Dieppe was that they relied too much on the tanks. It was the first time that Churchill tanks had been employed in the war. Certainly, someone should have known that the stones on the beach would upheave the tracks."[9]

———■———

1000 hours: The Luftwaffe — the entire German air strength in Western Europe, comprising some 945 aircraft from bases in Holland and France — began crowding Dieppe's airspace. This is what the RAF fighters had been waiting for — the day they could entice the Luftwaffe into the air and destroy it.

Lieutenant Wilhelm Freiderich Schlie: "From the German side came aircraft. Then came more [British] air attacks. They were very unpleasant. I was on the bluff, about sixty metres over the sea. They came lower than we were, perhaps thirty to forty metres high. Then in the last moment before the bluff, firing from every valve, they made *schuup*! like a jump, and flew over us, just over our heads."[10]

Throughout the day, in the RAF briefing rooms at Tangmere, Biggin Hill, and a number of other fighter bases near the south coast of England, several hundred fighter pilots downed mug after mug of tea as they waited tensely for their flights to be called into action. As their names were posted on the board, the white-faced pilots pulled on helmets and gloves and bolted for the landing strips. They knew that their time over the target would be limited to just a few minutes — even less, if they didn't conserve petrol by flying at low revs. Their adversary, based nearby, would have all the time in the world. It could be murderous.

1000 hours: Flying Officer Jack Godfrey, RCAF: In a letter to his wife, Godfrey would describe that day: "We waited around about two hours and finally the call came through. We were to escort Hurricane bombers on a low-level attack on gun positions to the left of the town. . . . Of all the jobs, this was the worst. We took off at 10 o'clock . . . and flew over the water at about twenty feet above the waves, cruising quite slowly at about 200 mph. [The point of this was to conserve fuel.]

"We hit the coast flat out [going] inland about three miles, weaving amongst trees. I don't think I was more than five feet from the deck. The lower you are, the safer, because they can't see you coming.

"At the top of the rise was a big flak position. All hell was breaking loose. There were heavy ack-ack guns and I don't know how many machine guns. The next thing I saw was the tail of John's kite just blow away and the fuselage break in two right behind the cockpit. I don't suppose poor John even knew he was hit before it was all over."[11]

In the early hours of the assault, six squadrons had orbited overhead. Their role then was primarily to protect the flotilla. At 0715 hours, No. 403 Squadron of the RCAF, flying Spitfire VBs, claimed six enemy fighters, but lost three of its own. The pilots of two of them (one the son of the Canadian Minister of Agriculture) collided after shooting down an Me 109.[12]

On his third patrol of the morning over Dieppe, Squadron Leader L.V. Chadburn, commanding No. 416 Squadron, was credited with a probable on a JU 88. His squadron was attacked by about fifteen FW 190s, and claimed to have shot down three enemy.[13]

The peak period for both sides was during and after reembarkation, when nine RAF and RCAF squadrons were engaged. They also laid smoke to get the attackers on and off the beaches, and protected the flotilla on its homeward voyage.

Before the Dieppe attack, the troops had been briefed that they would have close support from the air. The RAF, they had been told, had ready an armada of two fighter-bomber squadrons (Hurricanes) and five medium-bomber squadrons, as well as over 60 fighter squadrons. Yet entreaties from the desperate men trapped on the beaches that specific enemy gun positions be taken out seldom brought an effective response. This was the fault not of the brave and tireless RAF and RCAF pilots and crews, but of cumbersome communication. By the time the requests were relayed back and a squadron dispatched, 86 minutes would have lapsed.[14]

Pilot Officer "Duke" Warren, 165 Squadron, described an attack that was typical of dozens that morning: "We spotted a German Dornier 17 at one thousand feet and dived to attack it. The enemy aircraft dove to port. I got in an attack closing to from one hundred and fifty to fifty yards. Strikes were seen on the port engine, which burst into flames. The Dornier continued to dive but very soon the crew bailed out and it crashed in the sea near Dieppe Harbour."[15]

1100 hours: The LCAs, covered by naval fire and RAF fighters, and shielded by smoke laid down by the aircraft and ships, started for the beaches. From the cliff tops, the Germans poured fire on the men trying to evacuate, and on the naval crews in the boats. Very few craft, if any, reached the Essex on Red Beach. Twenty-three officers and 359 men of that battalion — two-thirds of the attacking force — waited in vain. They were finally taken prisoner. One hundred and twenty-one men died on the beaches, or of wounds after being captured.[16]

1100 hours: Red Beach: Brigadier William Southam, 6th Brigade Commander, spoke to a young corporal: "Try to get away," he said urgently. "Burn your papers right here and now. Then get away if you can."

The corporal lit a match and burned his intelligence papers, wondering if he should do the same for the brigadier's.

"He had an army-type briefcase," Lance Corporal Lecky recalled, "one that hooked onto your belt, and he had laid it on the fender of the scout car. Then after we were prisoners I found out that they had captured his operation orders."[17]

Two thousand Canadians who were to spend the next three years in German POW camps were manacled for 409 days because a brigadier ignored the same advice he had given to a corporal. The orders had stated that captured Germans were to be shackled. On finding these papers, the enemy retaliated in kind.

1100 hours, White Beach: Captain Denis Whitaker, RHLI: "The worst part was the dash for the boats amid a hail of bullets and mortar or shell fire. Apart from trying to help the wounded, it was every man for himself. I expected every step to be my last. I waded until the water was chest deep before reaching a LCA. We helped the wounded aboard and then helped each other. The boat started forward with the ramps still down. Water rushed in. They finally raised the ramp. I yelled, "Bail with your helmets!" I saw one of my men, Al Reiger, swimming. We passed beside him and I reached out and grasped his hand. But I couldn't hold him. He slipped from my grasp. I didn't know what happened to him. I assumed that he drowned because he was never heard of again. The helmsman would not go back for him — that was to me very disturbing."

Corporal Jack Brabbs, RHLI: "I got on one of the boats and I wasn't doing too bad until someone climbed over the side and jumped on my arm, my wounded arm. I passed out. When I came to, I was the only one alive on the boat and it was sinking. A flak ship came along. They picked me up, and I was on my way back."[18]

Lieutenant Jack Dunlap, Calgary Tank Regiment: "When no more boats were seen to be coming in, the gunfire dropped off and became desultory. The whole beach and shoreline were a shambles of broken bodies, beached boats, derelict tanks. We observed troops surrendering west of our position, a movement that gradually swept down the beach towards us. Further resistance seemed futile. As the German troops appeared in our sector, we raised our hands in the traditional manner and gave up."[19]

1100 hours, Green Beach: Evacuation of the Cameron Highlanders and South Saskatchewans from Pourville was complicated by the low tide and the particular topography of Green Beach. The LCAs remained several hundred yards out, and the troops had to wade or swim through intense German fire. Enemy snipers had a field day picking off the floundering men, many of whom were already wounded. Lieutenant Colonel Cec Merritt and Major Claude Orme coolly set up a makeshift rear-guard defence in a small bandstand near the shore, and with a couple of machine guns and a few grenades, kept enemy heads down long enough to cover the evacuation.

Lieutenant Buck Buchanan, South Saskatchewan Regiment: "Being prairie guys, very few fellows could swim. Merritt could swim. [Major] Jim McRae said to him, 'Come on, get the hell out of here.' But Merritt, he was a bulldog. These were his men. He was only a young fellow and this was such a disaster, he must have been torn to pieces inside. He started off but then he said, 'Oh God, my job is back there,' and he swam back to the beach. So he stayed there, same as Padre Foote.

"This has always been a little bit of a tender point with those of us on the Dieppe raid: who got back, and who stayed behind as prisoners."[20]

The South Saskatchewans left 84 dead on Green Beach; 89 more, including Merritt and 8 other officers, became POWs.

The Victoria Cross — the highest battle honour — was awarded to Colonel Merritt and to RHLI Padre John Foote, who both chose to stay with their boys.

Back in the wooded copse, the Germans prodded the bushes to find Major Andrew Law and his small band of Camerons. Corporal Alec Graham laid down his Sten gun and rifle—and his bagpipes. Never again in history would a Canadian Scottish battalion be piped into an attack.[21]

He had given 19-year-old Sergeant (later Lieutenant Colonel Marcell C. Swank of the U.S. Rangers the most inspiring moment of his young life: "There, in the early morning light, with streamers flying from his bonnet, braced magnificently against the cabin of one of the neighbouring craft, stood a Scottish Highlander playing 'The 100 Pipers.' "[22]

1220 hours: Captain Hughes-Hallett signalled, NO FURTHER EVACUATION POSSIBLE, WITHDRAW.

Throughout Vanquish, the naval officers and ratings conducted the withdrawal with unbelievable dash and courage. Under devasting fire, they fearlessly brought their LCAs and LCMs in to the beaches time after time to rescue the men of Second Division infantry units. Some of the craft were sunk by shell fire. Some craft were swamped, but still the navy persisted in their efforts to evacuate the maximum number despite the horrendous casualties.

1300 hours: VANCOUVER. With heavy heart, General Roberts signalled this code word that ordered the entire naval force to head back to England.

1308 hours: From the beaches of Dieppe, over 2,000 men watched the last British vessel disappear over the horizon; 1,874 of these were

Canadian. The remainder were commandos or personnel from the Royal Navy. Sapper Lieutenant W.A. Millar of the Royal Canadian Engineers' 7th Field Company signalled; . . . OUR PEOPLE HAVE SURRENDERED.

1337 hours: The log of the 571st German Infantry Regiment would read, "Pourville firmly in our hands."

1358 hours: After firing 7,458 field rounds, the German artillery fell silent. The battle for Dieppe was over.

1620 hours: Lieutenant Colonel Doug Catto and his incredible band of 20 men were still under cover in the woods. Catto had seen his Royals — whom he had commanded for a bare two months — destroyed in *minutes.* He resolved to formally surrender. He sent off his unwounded of the group with their escape kits and then strode toward the cliffs.

Lieutenant Tom Taylor, Royal Regiment: "Late in the afternoon, it was agreed we should all make our way as best we could into the country in pairs. Unfortunately, the woods were surrounded and we fell into enemy hands before we had a chance to escape."[23]

Hauptmann (Captain) Richard Schnösenberg, Commanding Officer, 3rd Battalion, 571 Infantry Regiment: "Officially, I accepted Colonel Catto's surrender. Unofficially, I spent some time with him in my command post."

The two men shook hands before Catto marched off to POW camp. The German expressed great sympathy and admiration for his adversary: "Colonel Catto did not overcome the shock of Dieppe. On his first action he lost his whole regiment in two hours. He saw that it was over, that there was nothing more to win. Still, he became the front fighter of his regiment. He was captured at the furthest forward position. I characterize this affair as the last knightly encounter with the enemy on the field of battle."[24]

The Germans were not inhumane in their treatment of the prisoners captured on the beach, but they would allow only a few men to go back and rescue some of the wounded still lying on the beach. At mid-afternoon, the tide — a 22-foot surge — came in. Many drowned who might have survived their wounds. Others, who managed to crawl to higher ground, bled to death.

At Tangmere and Biggin Hill that night, weary airmen silently lifted their beers to toast the 60 pilots and 106 aircraft that had been lost during that day's work. It had been the biggest single-day air battle of the war, and the bloodiest. It was fortunate, perhaps, that they were unaware of the prediction made by the air force fighter commander, Air Vice Marshal Leigh-Mallory: His casualty estimate had been eerily accurate: he had predicted 60 to 70 pilots lost, and 120 Spitfires shot down. His superior, Air Marshal Sir Sholto Douglas, had chided him for "worrying too much."[25]

———■———

Steaming into Portsmouth later that afternoon, a slightly drunk and vastly relieved second-in-command of No. 3 Commando, Major Peter Young, perched barefoot on the deck, singing hilariously off-key — quite oblivious to the dignitaries lined up to greet the man behind one of Dieppe's few successes.

———■———

The 1,874 Canadian officers and men who were captured at Dieppe became prisoners of war at Oflag VIIB at Eichstatt, or at Stalag VIIIC. On October 8, 1942, after a special roll call, Dieppe prisoners were marched through the village and up a steep path to the nearby Schloss Willibaldburg Schloss, where their hands were tied with ropes. This was in reprisal for the threat — discovered by the Germans in the captured orders that Brigadier Southam had neglected to destroy — to tie up German POWs.

Sapper Lieutenant W.A. Millar later became known as "the Canadian Escape King." His first attempt, on June 3 and 4 of the following year, was through a 120-foot tunnel. Of the 65 men who escaped that night, six, including Lieutenant Millar and Lieutenant Colonel Merritt, were Canadians. They were all recaptured and sentenced to 14 days' solitary.[26]

A few escaped successfully. The forward observation officer attached to the Royals, Captain G.A. Browne, escaped from a train bearing Canadians to POW camps in Germany. He made his way to Barcelona, where he wrote his report on January 18, 1943.

———■———

In the village of Winona, Ontario, two weeks after the raid, the stunned residents read the casualty lists in the newspaper, column after column. Awakening, like the rest of Canada, to the extent of the disaster, they realized for the first time how it affected their small hamlet.

They had no young men left. Every single lad of the town of fighting age had been killed or taken prisoner in one short morning.

CHAPTER
21

RUN FOR THE HILLS

On August 20, a sweltering day in Cairo, Churchill and Brooke learned of the disastrous casualties at Dieppe. Almost 4,000 Canadians and British had been killed, wounded or taken prisoner. Two-thirds of the Canadian force was destroyed.

Neither man could allow the personal sorrow they felt to let them lose sight of the fact that the raid had achieved many of its goals. Lord Moran, who was in Cairo with the pair when they received the signal, noted in his diary: "The P.M. will not hear of the word 'failure.' The casualties were heavy but the results were important."

Brooke, on hearing the first reports, blurted out the ultimate judgement: "It is a lesson to the people who are clamouring for the invasion of France."[1] That he had averted a premature second front would be considered his finest contribution towards victory in the entire war. The Allies had learned unequivocally of the German defensive strength on the Continent. Stalin was now silent and subdued. Roosevelt was firmly focussed on North Africa.

But what of relations with Canada and the rest of the British Commonwealth? If word got out that Churchill had used Dieppe as a political pawn, it would be suicidal to Commonwealth relations. Could the British afford to alienate their allies who were bearing so much of the burden in fighting, in war production and in provision of training facilities? Unjust though it might be, were they not likely to be accused — again — of using Commonwealth troops as cannon fodder? "I have long feared the dangerous reactions on Australian and world opinion of our seeming to fight all our battles in the Middle East only with Dominion troops," Churchill had written.[2]

And so the great cover-up began.

"Explain," said the prime minister on August 29, 1942, *ten days* after the Dieppe raid. "Explain how the military side of the Dieppe raid was planned."[3]

"The time has now come when I must be informed more precisely about the military plans," said the prime minister on December 21, 1942, *four months* after the Dieppe raid. "Who made them? Who approved them? What was General Montgomery's part in it? And General McNaughton's part? What is the opinion about the Canadian generals selected by General McNaughton? Did the General staff check the plans? At what point was V.C.I.G.S. [the Vice Chief of Staff] informed in C.I.G.S.'s absence?"[4]

"How did this all go?" said the prime minister in August, 1950, *eight years* after the Dieppe raid, "Surely the decision could not have been taken without the Chiefs of Staff being informed. If so why did they not bring it to my attention?"[5]

———

Although many of the Dieppe records have been lost, removed or destroyed, or are still — even in 1992 — sealed from the public by Cabinet order, enough documentation has survived to make a convincing case that Churchill, Brooke and the Chiefs of Staff were in every way aware of the key operational details of the raid and in fact pressed hard for its execution.[6]

Their subsequent efforts to feign ignorance and innocence do not hold up to evidence gleaned in a month-by-month chronicle of their actions and comments during the build-up to Dieppe.

On May 13, 1942, following what Professor F.H. Hinsley described as a "long study," the Chiefs officially approved Dieppe's Outline Plan.[7] Ten days later, according to Philip Ziegler, Churchill, Brooke and Mountbatten spent three hours discussing the Dieppe raid and the prospects for invasion. Then, at the beginning of June, Churchill again considered the plan and personally waived the restriction against bombing the area.[8]

Admiral Baillie-Grohman gave an account of his efforts in June to get a battleship for the raid. He was told that the Admiralty had been approached but that the idea had been turned down "in the highest quarters" — which, he was convinced, meant Churchill — and that the prime minister intended to proceed with the raid no matter what the objections.[9] On June 24, at a War Cabinet meeting, the Chiefs again examined the operation. A lengthy debate followed as to whether the premature briefing to the airborne had compromised it.[10]

Churchill, Brooke and Ismay, meanwhile, were in Washington and discussed Dieppe with Roosevelt and his Chiefs. (Mountbatten had informed them of the raid in a visit earlier in June.) Roosevelt insisted "for reasons of politics and prestige that a United States military contingent participate in the assault."[11]

Captain John Hughes-Hallett later narrated the events of a meeting on June 30 when Churchill and Brooke studied the Dieppe plan with Mountbatten and himself. Also present were Generals Ismay and Hollis, the two high-level staff members who would be singled out again in August as the sole recipients of information from Churchill and Brooke — then in Moscow and Cairo — on the mounting of the Dieppe raid. Brooke stressed to Churchill the necessity of a raid as a prelude to an invasion.[12]

At the July 6 meeting of the COS, Mountbatten sought permission to shorten the duration of the raid from two tides to one, and explained "various minor alterations to the plan." The minutes reveal that after the Chiefs gave detailed examination to the Dieppe plan, they agreed to the proposal.

They then suggested that Mountbatten "should reconsider remounting it at a later date" if bad weather continued to force cancellation. This is surely strong evidence of their determination to launch the raid.[13]

Churchill described the remounting of the raid in his World War Two history, *The Hinge of Fate*:

> In discussion with Admiral Mountbatten, it became clear that time did not permit a new large-scale operation to be mounted during the summer, but that Dieppe could be remounted (the new code-name was "Jubilee") within a month, provided extraordinary steps were taken to ensure secrecy. For this reason no records were kept.[14]

The July 20th COS meeting approved Captain John Hughes-Hallett as naval force commander for "the next large-scale raiding operation" — Dieppe being the only large-scale raiding operation at this advanced stage of planning.[15]

Correspondence on file from Mountbatten to Brooke dated July 30 reinforced the fact that Brooke, as head of the army, was closely involved:

> I must apologize for taking up your time on the eve of your departure [for Cairo] but we had a meeting of the Force Commanders of "Jubilee" today and the question of the issue of escape outfits to the troops taking part was raised.
>
> As you know, this operation is being mounted in rather peculiar circumstances to preserve complete security and there are therefore great objections to adopting our normal procedure [in] issuing these outfits.

Significantly, Brooke responded to the request for escape kits. They were delivered to the officers aboard the assault boats on the eve of the raid.[16]

On August 12, the Chiefs recorded two debates. Sledgehammer was still technically dragging on. The Chiefs' first discussion centred on this "future operation."

Next, still cloaking all references to the Dieppe raid in tightest secrecy, they formally approved "the outline plan for a future raiding operation." This was as close as their minutes ever came to mentioning the forbidden "Jubilee" or "Dieppe." In the absence of Churchill and Brooke, Portal took the chair and the Vice-CIGS, General Nye, represented Brooke.[17]

The five cables between Churchill and Ismay from August 15th to the 18th clearly demonstrate that although Churchill and Brooke were out of the country, they were very much aware that the raid was imminent. Churchill and Brooke took pains to ensure that their cables to London would be seen only by Ismay and Hollis, with the acting prime minister (Attlee) and the Vice-CIGS (General Nye) specifically omitted. This is conclusive evidence of the tight security surrounding the Dieppe raid. Ismay and Hollis were among the very few included in the "need-to-know" group.[18]

The August 19th entry in General Jacob's diary emphasizes the prime minister's keen involvement following his trip to Moscow. Churchill, he said, was "aching for news of the Dieppe raid."[19]

Almost before the pall of smoke had lifted from Dieppe's beaches, the principals concerned took off for the hills. "Suddenly everybody seemed to be withdrawing from responsibility," Martin Gilbert considered. "It's like that quotation of Churchill's: 'they all gang up together, like doctors in a case that has gone wrong.' "[20]

The search for a scapegoat began. Mountbatten was the principal target. But he had no intention of shouldering the blame. Churchill and the Chiefs of Staff had given the raid their blessing, he insisted. Therefore, the responsibility was ultimately theirs.

Their first attempt to implicate Mountbatten took place at a dinner party one Saturday night at Chequers, the prime minister's country residence. There, less than two weeks after the Dieppe raid, Brooke confronted the Combined Ops chief over his role in planning it. Angrily, Mountbatten threatened to force an inquiry if Brooke did not retract his accusations:

August 31, 1942.

Dear C.I.G.S.:

I was absolutely dumbfounded at dinner last Saturday at Chequers, when you made your very out-spoken criticism of the manner in which the Dieppe raid was planned. . . . The prime minister sent for me on the terrace and said, 'I heard C.I.G.S. complaining that the planning was all wrong for the Dieppe show; what did he mean?' I replied: 'It was planned in accordance with the Chiefs of Staffs [sic] own instructions.'

Mountbatten went on at length to explain how the plan had evolved, including Paget's and the Canadians' involvement:

General Montgomery attended all the principal planning meetings and personally supervised the Military Plan while General Roberts was preparing it. I left General Montgomery an absolutely free hand. A telegram to General Montgomery would confirm this.

. . . After the first attempt was abandoned, I obtained the concurrence of C.-in-C. Home Forces, and C.-in-C. Portsmouth, to be the final authority to mount and launch the operation. The Chiefs of Staff approved. From beginning to end the army were given complete freedom.

. . . I should very much hope that after reading the account of the planning arrangements for Dieppe . . . you will feel able to withdraw your criticism and assure me that the planning was, in fact, done with due regard to the Army's special responsibilities.

If, however, you should still feel that the arrangements for planning were unsatisfactory, I should have no option but to ask the Minister of Defence for a full and impartial inquiry into the planning and execution of the raid and the conduct of all concerned."

Brooke accepted the explanation and, as is obvious by Mountbatten's follow-up letter of September 4, retracted his criticism. In the letter, the Combined Operations Chief thanked Brooke for his "extremely friendly reception" when the two men met to discuss the issue, and for "the personal confidence which you expressed in me by saying that you would allow the existing [command] arrangements to stand."

Mountbatten consequently withdrew his threat of asking for an inquiry.[21]

On December 23, 1942, Churchill and the Chiefs tried again to deflect public criticism aimed at them, especially from Canada. The Chiefs of Staff held an informal investigation into the "security aspects" of the raid. This was possibly at the instigation of General Nye, the Vice-CIGS, who had expressed indignation that he was not on the need-to-know list prior to the raid.

They asked Mountbatten the key question: had he withheld information from them that the Dieppe raid was to take place? The minutes show that he responded forcibly, reminding the Chiefs that "the necessary people had always been informed." On the particular occasion of Dieppe, however, he had received special instructions from the Chiefs of Staff that only certain individuals were to be informed of the intention to remount the operation. He had been compelled, in fact, even to mislead his own staff on this occasion."

The outline plan, Mountbatten reminded them, had been initiated by Combined Operations headquarters in April 1942 and approved at a May 13 Chiefs of Staff committee meeting.

Because of the extreme level of secrecy surrounding the remounting of the raid, however, when the Chiefs gave authorization on August 12, the Vice-Chief, Nye, "was not specially informed of the operation."[22]

Again, the Chiefs dropped their inquiry. The minutes show no protest or disclaimer. As Fraser and Gilbert point out, if Mountbatten's statement to the Chiefs had *not* been accurate and truthful, they would have denied it vehemently and taken him to task at the meeting: ". . . The COS would have had Mountbatten's blood."[23]

———————

Initially, Churchill was very open about his involvement. On September 8, three weeks after Dieppe, he informed the House of Commons that he "gave his sanction" to the raid which he "personally regarded

. . . as an indispensable preliminary to full-scale operations."[24] But within a short time, he was strenuously disclaiming knowledge of the operation. He persisted in this attitude for eight years. Finally, in 1950, he acknowledged his responsibility.

Dieppe was not the first time that Churchill had feigned ignorance of a major catastrophe, or the first time he had been caught out in attempting to avoid responsibility and possible censure. Historian A.J.P. Taylor cites a parallel episode that occurred after the fall of Singapore in 1941, when Churchill cast the blame on his senior staff for his own mistakes.

The historian wrote: "[Churchill] said at one point that he did not realize the weakness of their Singapore defences: 'I ought to have asked; my advisors ought to have told me.'

"Well," Taylor said, "I am sorry to say that the records show his advisors told him, and Churchill pushed their warnings aside."[25]

Sir William Deakin, who served as personal assistant to Churchill while he was writing his memoirs, agrees that Churchill's statements were an attempted cover-up. "Churchill was so inclined, as he had been after Trondheim in 1940 and after Singapore."[26] Churchill's physician, Lord Moran, recalled the prime minister's tendency to what he called "Black Dog" — Churchill's own term for the fits of depression that might last for months. "You have fought against it all your life," Lord Moran had commented to his patient. "You always avoid anything that is depressing."[27]

Churchill's first concerted effort to distance himself from the operation was in December, 1942. Pretending ignorance, he attacked the plans, asking Ismay, "Who approved them? At first sight it would appear to a layman very much out of accord with the accepted principles of war to attack the strongly fortified town front without first securing the cliffs on either side. I was not consulted about the resumption as I was away. . . . I think I had already started for Cairo and Moscow."[28]

Churchill was forgetting that when he was in Moscow with Stalin, and later when in Cairo, he had urgently cabled Ismay in London as to when the raid would be launched. His instructions about the top-secret distribution of the signals — limited to Ismay and Hollis — were a clear giveaway of his close involvement. He was also perhaps not aware that careful minutes had been kept of all his conversations with Stalin about Dieppe one week before it was mounted. According to the official interpreter's transcript, Churchill informed Stalin that "there will be a more serious raid in August. It will be a reconnaissance in force. Some 8,000 men with 50 tanks will be landed."[29]

By 1950, when he was writing volume four of his memoirs, Churchill could not avoid addressing the issue. He again tried to disassociate himself from it. This time, other factors were influencing his run for the hills. He was feeling the pressure of deadlines and a coming election. At 76, he was unwell. He had suffered cerebral damage following his first stroke in 1949, and this affected his memory.

As one of his century's most highly paid and prolific writers, Churchill had mastered how to get his works onto the marketplace in maximum speed and efficiency. All that had really changed as he had grown older was his increasing dependency on his aides: the recollections of some and the literary skills of others.

It was not a unique circumstance that by then Churchill relied on others to contribute segments of chapters to his memoirs. Almost all his work was researched and drafted by one expert or another. Increasingly, as he aged, Churchill's role was as master editor. His technique was to quiz the specialists in the particular subject he was tackling, delegate the writing of it and fine-tune the finished product.

In these postwar years, Lord Ismay had become his surrogate memory, the essential back-up to Churchill's sometimes failing one. When he came in his memoirs to recounting his critical trip to Hyde Park and Washington in June 1942, he could not even recall its highlights. He had to ask his old friend Ismay, "What was my main purpose in crossing the Atlantic at this time?"[30] Ismay's subsequent responses became the foundation of Churchill's chapter on his meetings with Roosevelt and their importance in the development of grand strategy.

In the same way, he could not recall the events preceding the Dieppe Raid — traumatic as they had been at the time. Again he turned to his long and trusted associate.

Ismay gently reminded him that he, Churchill, had been fully aware of the raid. "My recollection is that you had approved the raid in principle before you left for Cairo, but that the decision to launch the operation was taken after you had left. Mountbatten certainly pressed hard for it, but he did not have the deciding voice."[31]

Ismay drafted an explanatory paragraph. He proposed that Churchill insert it in the chapter:

"Before I left England, I had approved an operation against Dieppe and I anxiously awaited news. Accordingly, I telegraphed to General Ismay, 'Please report if and when Jubilee takes place.' "[32]

Being forced to accept the direct responsibility for this operation obviously did not sit well with Churchill. His dilemma was that the account had to reflect well on himself. But it still had to produce for posterity — and the prickly Canadians — a reasonable explanation about the Dieppe raid.

Churchill had dropped a telling clue or two that clearly revealed his foreknowledge. He remembered talking to his wife about the raid before it was mounted, and he remembered describing it to Stalin. "One night when I was talking about this business *beforehand* to Mrs. Churchill, she spoke about these caves and said what a help they could be to the enemy," Churchill reminisced.

If he had not been consulted about the raid, he could hardly have chatted with his wife about the dangers of Dieppe's cliffs in a military operation. Churchill himself had pencilled in the word "beforehand" into the text after it was typed. Nor could he have described it in such colourful terms to Stalin just a week before the raid was launched: "It [Dieppe] was to be like putting your hand into a bath and seeing how hot it was."[33]

He grasped the same lifeline he had after Singapore: someone else to take the blame. "My advisors ought to have told me," he said then of the Singapore fiasco. "Why did they not bring it to my attention?" he protested eight years later about the Dieppe raid.

Churchill instructed his ghost-writer to insert in the Dieppe draft: "On the initiative of Admiral Mountbatten, the project was revived."[34] But — as he had in his fiery retort to the Chiefs of Staff in December, 1942 — Mountbatten still refused to become such a convenient scapegoat.

Mountbatten highlighted the three fundamental facts that Churchill could not escape: "You were (as ever) the moving spirit. You and the Chiefs of Staff went into the revived plans carefully." And thirdly, "there were no written records because you and the Chiefs of Staff agreed to this on account of the extraordinary secrecy."[35]

To everyone's relief, Churchill backed down and accepted his responsibility in the affair. A less controversial version — drafted by Mountbatten in consultation with a number of his then associates in Combined Operations — became the substance of the *Hinge of Fate* account of the Dieppe raid. "After the Canadian authorities and the Chiefs of Staff had given their approval I personally went through the plans with the C.I.G.S., Admiral Mountbatten and Captain Hughes-Hallett."[36]

—■—

Whitaker Commentary

Churchill's statement that he and the Chiefs were not informed of the raid, were not responsible for it, or even aware that it was to be staged, is not credible.

Churchill and Brooke *approved* the raid — they *wanted* it — and they gave their word to Roosevelt and Stalin that it would take place.

Yet it has inspired one historian to hypothesize that the Dieppe operation was launched on the whim of their junior member, Mountbatten, without the approval or authority of the remaining three Chiefs or the prime minister.[37]

In our opinion, the system would never have allowed this to happen.

It must be remembered that as well as serving as prime minister, Churchill was also the minister of defence. He bore, as General Jacob describes it, the responsibility for conducting the military side of the war. This would certainly include so major a raid as Dieppe. As well, Brooke was the commander-in-chief of the army. No military operation could have been mounted without the knowledge and approval of both men.[38]

Both contemporary and later evidence confirm that the Chiefs of Staff were a highly organized, effective and smooth-running machine of four skilled militarists, led by a minister of defence who was at once brilliant, mercurial and impetuous.

The Chiefs were what Ismay termed "magnificent watchdogs." They had in place a system of checks — some formal, some relying on a quiet word over a discreet brandy. These ensured that Churchill's brilliance was kept in harness, or in Lord Ismay's words, that "his conceptions were militarily practical and desirable and that the necessary resources were available." As an intermediary, they had that marvellous "oilcan-smoother," Ismay, whose integrity has never been questioned.

Their principal weapons were a discerning eye and a sharp and ready tongue. Silent brooding was not their style. Meeting once or twice daily, they had ample opportunity to air their concerns — and none was reticent. When they disagreed, they "argued themselves into agreement."[39] They had similar checks and rechecks on proposed combined operations.

It was Martin Gilbert who pointed out a frequently overlooked fact: "Churchill or the Chiefs of Staff could have cancelled the raid anytime in August, right up to the day it was mounted. The fact that they didn't means they accepted it."[40]

Gilbert has spent more than 20 years meticulously researching the Churchill papers, to which he has exclusive access. He is the author of an eight-volume official biography on Churchill. In a recent interview with the authors he stressed how carefully the Chiefs assessed the practicality of every last one of Combined Operations' proposed raids.

"The Chiefs of Staff became involved in cancelling operations that in their opinion were not feasible operations of war," he explained. "At every point it was open to the joint planners or the Chiefs of Staff to say 'It isn't on'; or 'This is not going to be a successful operation; it is not realistic.'

"I've *never* come across a plan they disapproved of which went ahead," Gilbert stated.[41]

Sir John Peck, Churchill's wartime secretary, supports Gilbert on this. Although his recent comments to the authors were directed specifically to the Dieppe raid, they can be construed as a general commentary on how tightly the Chiefs controlled *all* military operations:

> Between the planning and final execution of Dieppe . . . the fighting in N. Africa had taken a critical turn for the worse and it is important to realize that the decision to go ahead with the raid after the postponement, the risks of leakage, the option of sending troops to N. Africa etc., was only taken after profound deliberation by the chiefs of staff, force commanders etc. It was emphatically not a case of Churchill pressing on with a pet project in the face of military opposition.[42]

British naval historian Stephen Roskill concurred that "The final decision to remount the operation was taken by the Prime Minister in consultation only with Admiral Mountbatten, the Chief of Combined Operations."[43]

From April until August 1942, the only major raid that survived the elements and the close scrutiny of the Chiefs was Dieppe — a raid that for any number of practical reasons was unsound. The topography alone made its success extremely unlikely. So did the fact — which the Chiefs had already gleaned from Ultra and other sources — that the Germans were accelerating the build-up of their Channel defences and moving in trained divisions. It was common knowledge that the

Germans expected a raid. Even if they hadn't been expecting one, when the British discovered that the Germans had successfully intercepted Churchill's high-security telephone link with Roosevelt during May and June of 1942, they must have known that Hitler was aware of some of their intentions.

Mountbatten had introduced the Dieppe project as a dress-rehearsal for the [Sledgehammer] invasion. Since the Chiefs privately had strong reservations against Sledgehammer, the idea of letting Dieppe serve as its substitute must have been both obvious and persuasive.

Having approved it, could they possibly have been unaware that the raid was on? Ziegler thinks not: "It was not physically possible that the raid could be staged without authorization by the Chiefs of Staff. There were 237 ships and over 800 aircraft involved. The First Sea Lord and the Commander of the Royal Airforce would never allow their forces to be used without consent. Besides, Mountbatten never stuck his neck out." Neither, unnecessarily, did Churchill. So why, Ziegler wondered, would Churchill use the phrase "I reviewed the plans" if he had not done so?[44]

The opinions of men like Gilbert, Fraser, Peck and Ziegler are impressive. The Chiefs accepted Mountbatten's formal explanation in December 1942, without any word of doubt or criticism, just as Brooke had evidently accepted his explanatory letter three months before.

If Churchill and the Chiefs had disagreed with the way Mountbatten handled the Dieppe Raid, they would have found a way to express it. Instead, they continued to promote him to even greater honours. In October 1943 they appointed him Supreme Commander in South-East Asia — not bad for a 43-year-old naval officer who in two years had risen from a destroyer captain to commodore, then to Commander Combined Operations, and a little more than a year later to overall command of Britain's operations in South-East Asia — and then Viceroy of India, First Sea Lord and finally Admiral of the Fleet.

Surely if Mountbatten had lied to the Chiefs and concocted the story of their authorization, he would have been publicly denounced and would have never received the honours that accrued to him.

Churchill and the Chiefs' ready acceptance and continuing endorsement of the Dieppe plan suggests one of two things: either the plan was deemed practical and workable — which is doubtful — or the Chiefs broke an ironclad rule and approved a flawed plan on the grounds that it had become an essential element to the grand strategy of 1942 as, in General Fraser's words, "a sop for those who wanted action in 1942 and a substitute for Sledgehammer."[45]

We believe that Lord Lovat was justified when he said, "Mountbatten was told by Churchill that he had to do something to satisfy Molotov. . . . Mountbatten got his orders from above. I think that must be true."[46]

Then there was General Sir Alan Brooke. After his one spontaneous "that-will-show-them" outburst in Cairo, Brooke maintained a resolute silence about the raid for the rest of his life. But as CIGS at the time the raid was mounted, he could hardly plead ignorance, especially in the face of overwhelming evidence. Brooke was too astute a general officer not to know what his armies were up to. He was, after all, their commander-in-chief. Home Forces, who were in charge of the military planning of Dieppe, came directly under his command. McNaughton and Crerar were in London all summer, and must have discussed the raid privately with him.

In addition to the several planning meetings he attended, there was the letter Mountbatten wrote him on July 30 requesting escape kits. And there was the trip to Cairo and Moscow where he and Churchill received Ismay's cables informing them that Jubilee was being mounted in the next few days.

Either man — Churchill as head of state and minister of defence, or Brooke as head of all military forces — had only to cable a single word back to London to stop the operation. That word was "no." But their task in Moscow was to sell Torch and Dieppe to Stalin as a substitute second front. They could not afford to back out.

"Brooke was obviously apprised of and *au fait* with Dieppe," General Fraser concluded. "He was a delegator who would approve of overall plans but would not interfere regarding detail. Churchill loved detail and he loved to interfere; but would not overrule Brooke."[47] Ziegler concurs that Churchill and Brooke clearly bore the responsibility for mounting the raid, and that it was a political decision. "Churchill made a commitment to Stalin: the raid was going to go, even though they expected heavy casualties."[48]

In *his* rush for the hills, Mountbatten blamed Home Forces and the military planners, claiming he had no authority over the operation:

"Dieppe was planned by the army. . . . It was they who decided to throw overboard my idea of the enveloping movement. If my plans had been used . . . they'd have been attacked from the back . . . we'd have overrun them. It's heartbreaking. . . . If I'd been in charge of the operation, it would have been a very different story.

"I suppose I could have cancelled the operation but then we would never have learned the lesson."[49]

Actually, the man-on-the-spot who could have cancelled Dieppe was Hughes-Hallett. His cover-up is the most sinister of all. He has never satisfactorily explained why the urgent signals warning him of the inevitable collision with the German convoy were not dealt with — or even passed on to Roberts.

Crerar's post-Dieppe protest about this to the Chief of Combined Operations, Lord Mountbatten, elicited the reply that signals *had been received* by Hughes-Hallett at about the same time as the signals sent by Admiral James, with the same warnings of the imminent presence of a German convoy. But the CCO said *that* convoy was a *different* convoy and "had nothing to do with the German vessels met at 0350 hours." The fact is, German records reveal there was only one convoy in the area: the one that disrupted the Dieppe flotilla and destroyed any hope of a surprise attack.[50]

That whole vacuum of silence, out of which Ham Roberts tried futilely to conduct a battle, smacks of the same suppression of information. There was no absence of radio signals from the Dieppe beaches to the destroyers. There was just an absence of signals to reach General Roberts.

"The most remarkable fact about the Dieppe raid was that it did take place," Hughes-Hallett wrote of the revival of the operation. "Credit must be due to the 'constancy of purpose' of the prime minister, Mountbatten, Leigh-Mallory and Roberts. Nothing was put in writing, but General Ismay informed the Chiefs of Staff and the prime minister. They gave verbal approval."[51]

The "credit" — if that is the word — belongs to Hughes-Hallett. Had he heeded the radar warnings, Dieppe would not have taken place. The question has been raised more than once: was this more instruction from the "highest quarter"? Were Mountbatten and Hallett ordered to push the raid to its conclusion, no matter what?

———

Curiously, General Paget has also maintained absolute silence on the subject. Yet from its inception, he had been as close to the planning of the raid as anyone. As principal officer responsible for all military content for raids on France, it was his specific duty to ensure the military part of the plan was sound. He had attended Rutter's Yukon I rehearsal on June 11. After Yukon II, he wrote to Montgomery detailing the deficiencies revealed in the exercises. Monty responded at length in a reassuring reply.[52] Paget then became embroiled in the to-and-fro of trying to keep Crerar from joining the senior British officers at Uxbridge the night Rutter was to be launched. He had argued that "the only people who should be there should be Montgomery and Mountbatten . . . it would be wrong for Harry Crerar to go there. There can only be one man in command of the operation."[53]

When Montgomery was replaced, Paget formally designated the military line of responsibility on July 17 to become: Paget–McNaughton–Crerar–Roberts. Again, inescapably, Paget had top billing.[54]

All the delegating in the world could not exonerate him as the man who bore the ultimate responsibility for the military side of the operation: both of Rutter and the renewed Jubilee. Yet he did not raise any kind of official protest when the raid was remounted, despite the fact that Monty had recommended against it. He did not even step forward afterwards and acknowledge his role.

———

Montgomery ran faster and farther than anyone.

Paget had delegated to him the authority in the military planning of the Dieppe project. Yet Montgomery later maintained, "I wasn't responsible. I couldn't give any orders. I could go to meetings but I couldn't give any orders."[55]

Before Rutter, Monty had enthused that "the Canadians are first-class chaps. If anyone can pull it off, they will."[56]

But after-the-fact, he said, "Home Forces should never have allowed inexperienced troops to take it on. I should have been more emphatic. I did protest verbally; I think I should have protested vehemently and in writing. But I didn't, so I suppose I must bear certain responsibility."[57]

After Rutter was called off, Montgomery didn't challenge the *plan itself* when he recommended cancellation. He challenged the *target*. Although, years later, he emphasized repeatedly his stance that Dieppe should be cancelled "for all time," he was not being completely truthful. What he actually said was, change the venue: "If it was considered desirable to raid the Continent, then the objective should not be Dieppe."[58]

There being no protest from its author about inadequate fire support, that same "Monty plan" continued to be the formula for Jubilee. With the exception of deleting paratroops and adding commandos, it remained the same even after Montgomery had been let off. The fact that he was in Cairo on August 19 does not make him any less culpable for Dieppe's faulty design. Regarding the Monty conundrum, Ziegler muses, "It is difficult to understand why Monty accepted a flawed plan. Possibly it was word from the top; that it would go ahead on a political basis."[59]

General Fraser concurs: Churchill could have said, Dieppe is strategically and politically important to the war. . . . It must go ahead. Commitments had been made at a high level."[60]

———————

Even the Canadians resorted to some political tiptoeing.

The Canadian War Cabinet Committee minutes between July 1 and December 30, 1942, reveal few references to a battle that cost Canada 3,367 casualties. On August 19 there was a terse note: "concerning 5,000 Canadians in Dieppe — report by McNaughton later."[61]

Canadian politicians and military personnel muzzled many of its spokespersons. Think positive — and say little — seemed to be the order of the day.

General McNaughton was one of the few who steadfastly defended the plan and his role in it: ". . . in like circumstances, like background of importance and with like knowledge of what the various possibilities were and the assessment of the risks and so on, I would, if I were in exactly the same position, I'd do the same thing tomorrow. The responsibility for the decision was mine and nobody else's."[62]

Canada's RCAF had 12 squadrons actively involved in the raid. The Canadian Minister of National Defence for Air, the ebullient "Chubby" Power, happened to be in Britain at the time. Through his verbose diary, we get a glimpse of his busy August 20th, the day after the raid. He spent some time comparing Canadian issue army boots to their British parallel (the former were "much better"); he went to a training school, toured the Southampton area, had lunch there at the Royal Plaza Hotel and a mosey through the bombed-out areas of Southampton. As a result, he was two hours late meeting a Canadian squadron leader, commenting that "I only had three minutes to talk with him before the scramble came."

He did chat about Dieppe with two American correspondents and the wife of one British commando. Then he went back to his hotel — apparently never taking the time on that or subsequent days to talk with any Canadian survivors of Dieppe: not in hospital, not in barracks.[63]

A hapless young lieutenant named Burr was quietly reprimanded because a military lecture he gave shortly afterwards at Cambridge created the impression that "the intelligence received prior to the operation was inaccurate."[64]

Brigadier Churchill Mann masked his personal responsibility in a curious way. Montgomery is reputed to have said that "the divisional commander [Roberts] isn't much good, but his G.S.O. 1 [Mann] is a cracker. He'll carry him through."[65] It was this "cracker" who drew up the 120-page Detailed Military Plan that was to cause so many difficulties during the raid. The plan's inflexibility and unrealistic objectives didn't allow the troops an iota of manoeuvrability or initiative when the battle turned against them. Further, Mann had stipulated that the two brigade commanders take a copy ashore — and then ignored Roberts' order countermanding this.

This document, subsequently captured, contained one dangerous clause. Appendix L, paragraph 4, No. B/2 instructed the raiders: "Whenever possible, prisoners' hands will be tied to prevent destruction of their documents." Again, Roberts had objected. Again, Mann had overridden him, apparently on instruction from Mountbatten that this was a routine commando policy. When German captors discovered this order, they vented their anger over it by daily tying up or manacling the hands of the almost 2,000 Canadian prisoners of war. This brutality would last until November 22, 1943 — for a miserable 15 months after their capture.[66]

Mann later contended that leaking this document was intentional — that it was part of some "secret plan" to deceive the Germans into thinking the Allies were training for a cross-Channel invasion. Incredibly, he wrote: "Officers were permitted to carry their orders with them on the operation, as is usual on training exercises, and several (as was intended) left theirs behind upon re-embarkation."[67]

Of all those associated with the planning of Dieppe, General Harry Crerar was the only one other than Brooke to voice the opinion that the raid had a "sobering influence on Allied policies, strategy and

Combined Service tactics." Crerar contended that, had Dieppe turned out to be a "cheap success," it would have resulted in a false appreciation of the problem of invasion. By the raid's failure, in that sense, it made a positive contribution. In other words, strategically it worked.[68]

The pity of it is that the men who made Dieppe happen — Churchill, Brooke and the Chiefs of Staff — felt compelled to mask their accountability for so many decades. Can they really be held up to blame for pursuing a strategy that was successful, no matter how high the cost?

The Dieppe raid did not damage Winston Churchill's political fortunes, nor should it have. He was re-elected prime minster in 1951, and although he resigned his leadership of the party four years later, he was twice more elected to his riding.

Nor was the reputation of any member of the Chiefs of Staff committee or most of the senior commanders involved tarnished by their part in mounting the Dieppe raid. Lord Mountbatten, as noted, went on to greater glory, as did Crerar, Hughes-Hallett, Leigh-Mallory and Montgomery.

The Allies can be grateful to Churchill, Brooke and the Chiefs. Churchill won a truce of sorts with the Russians and a firm entente with the Americans. Brooke's greatest feat, averting a premature invasion, was won on the Dieppe beaches. Both achievements were major factors in winning the war in Europe. If Dieppe was a useful pawn, they played it wisely and well. Nevertheless — as General Sir David Fraser summed up — "It was one of those things that must be done no matter how difficult."

If there had to be an official scapegoat, what better a one than a man of the stature of Major General Hamilton Roberts. He lost his division; he was never again to command troops in the field. He lost the respect of his men. Year after year, on August 19, a small box would arrive in the post for him. Its contents: a small, stale piece of cake — a cruel reminder of his morale-boosting pre-Dieppe comment: "Don't worry boys. It will be a piece of cake."

Roberts bore his assigned role in silence and in dignity until his death. His only comment was "History will exonerate me."[69]

And so it has.

PART

7

AFTERMATH

DIEPPE TO D-DAY

On June 6, 1944, at 0745 hours, the first Allied troops converged in a mass assault on the Normandy coast of France.

By the end of the day, 130,000 troops from Britain, the United States and Canada, along with 20,000 vehicles, were firmly planted on French soil, not to leave until Germany was finally defeated eleven months later.

Brigadier Sir Bernard Fergusson aptly noted that "though there are still some that dispute the value of what was learned on the beaches of Dieppe, they are not to be found among informed persons, or among any who bore high responsibility in the later stages of the war, except for Lord Montgomery."[1]

To illustrate the many and varied lessons that accrued to the Allies as a result of Dieppe, a comparison of the Second Canadian Division's assault on August 19, 1942, with that of Third Canadian Division on June 6, 1944, is essential. This gives the real proof of Dieppe's lasting contributions.

Dieppe: Second Canadian Division led the attack on Dieppe with two brigades forward: a force of some 5,000 men. The assault was against a heavily defended port where enemy gun positions from the high cliffs and headlands completely dominated the landing beaches. The defenders held every advantage.

D-Day: Third Canadian Division led the attack at Juno Beach with two brigades forward. Its 3,000 men went in over open beaches, avoiding the defences concentrated on the many ports that dotted the French coast. The ground was flat, and completely devoid of dominating features.

Dieppe: There was no softening up of German defences prior to the operation by the Allied air forces. The heavy-bomber assault that had been planned was cancelled when the air commander stated that accuracy was so limited that the target would probably be missed, and that cratering could block the advance of armour.

Instead, 10 minutes before the troops landed, 12 close support fighter aircraft laid on a mere 10-minute attack on the enemy beach defences with cannons and machine gun fire. During the battle, there were only 68 sorties by RAF Blenheims and Bostons. These had little effect on German strongpoints.

D-Day: For Overlord, the planners at 21st Army Group prepared a massive Allied bombing attack that would demoralize enemy defences before the seaborne landing. The previous night, to touch off the operation, RAF Bomber Command had attacked with 1,000 aircraft, dropping its heaviest load of the war: 5,266 tons of high-explosive bombs. At dawn, 1,300 Flying Fortresses of the Eighth U.S. Air Force delivered a follow-up massive bombing attack to further reduce the German coastal defences. The effect on morale was huge.[2]

Dieppe: Almost two months before the raid, two rehearsals were staged. The crews operating the landing craft were all green, under-trained ratings from the Royal Navy Voluntary Reserve. They set the troops down late and often miles from their assigned beaches. Some of the tanks never did find their beaches and did not land. The men landed without specific objectives, floundered about for several hours, and reembarked.

The navy's poor navigation had not greatly improved by August 19, and their errors accounted for much of the ensuing disaster. The Royal Regiment of Canada, designated in the linch-pin role to launch a surprise attack under cover of darkness, was set down in daylight and in full view of the alerted German defenders. The first wave was 17 minutes late; the second wave was 45 minutes late. More than half the South Saskatchewan Regiment was put ashore on the wrong side of the River Scie. By the time they fought their way across the river, the enemy had dug in. Their surprise attack on the east headlands became impossible.

On the main beach, the tanks were also landed late, leaving unprotected the infantry force they were supposed to be supporting.

Some success was derived from the experimental shipboard use, for the first time in action, of the RAF radio-navigational aid GEE.

Adapted for the navy, it enabled the troopships to arrive accurately and on time at the designated point where landing craft were lowered for their final assault.[3]

D-Day: After the navy's failure at Dieppe, the slick "J Force" was formed as a permanent unit specializing in amphibious landings. (The "J" in "J-Force" stood for "Jubilee," the unit's origins.) Its sailors landed the Third Canadian Division on the Normandy beaches accurately and on time. The amphibious landing had been rehearsed countless times to fine-tune naval techniques and coordinate them into a cohesive team with the infantry. Two pre–D-Day exercises demanded perfection. "Pirate" was a full-scale affair with supporting arms held in Dorset nine months earlier. "Trousers" — another exercise — was an almost exact duplicate of D-Day, lacking only the invasion's massive bombardment to recreate Overlord.[4]

GEE "provided crucial advantages" to the navy on D-Day. Like "Mulberry," it was in the planning stages when the Dieppe raid was mounted. Even so, the results at Dieppe must have encouraged Overlord's planners to persist in its development.

Dieppe: On the main beach assault, four small Hunt-class destroyers, each armed with four 4-inch guns — 16 in all — provided *all* the supporting fire for the one-mile front — for just 10 minutes prior to the landing.

D-Day: In all, 196 guns from four field regiments, as well as guns from a massive array of naval vessels, supported Third Division's landing on Normandy on a similar frontage. Included were battleships, each mounting 15-inch guns, cruisers carrying 5- and 6-inch guns, and destroyers firing 4- and 4.7-inch guns.

Dieppe: The only possible artillery support for the infantry, at any stage, was to come from a small detachment of the 4th Canadian Field Regiment RCA, which was to take over and fire a battery of French 75-mm guns located on the east headland, if, as, and when it was captured. (A "cockeyed idea!" observed Brigadier Stanley Todd, who commanded the regiment. "The planners, in my opinion, had little knowledge of artillery, and no use for it anyway.")[5]

D-Day: The Dieppe experience persuaded future planners to rely on fire support rather than on surprise. The official "lessons learned" report from the raid stressed above all else the need for overwhelming fire support during the initial stages of the attack: "It is during those vital minutes while troops are disembarking, cutting or blasting their way through wire, clearing beach mines and finding routes over obstacles that the need for close support is at its greatest."[6]

Brigadier Todd, CRA Third Division artillery in 1944, noted wryly that "Dieppe made D-Day easier. The generals were all keen to supply whatever I wanted."[7]

The 12th, 13th, 14th and 19th Field Regiments RCA, each had 24 105-mm artillery pieces mounted on "priests" (Sherman tank chassis). These were carried in on landing craft tanks. The guns were to fire at preselected targets during the run-in. D-Day also saw the first use of LCRs (landing craft rocket). There were eight of these supporting Third Canadian Division. Each carried 1,100 5-inch rockets that blanketed a huge area with a devastating concentration of fire.

"In my fire plan," Brigadier Todd later explained, "the rockets took over when the field artillery finished their firing, and pulled off to let the infantry LCAs pass through. They so timed their volleys to last until the infantry was 500 yards offshore, when they then took over with their own mortars and divisional artillery. The idea was to saturate the beach with fire from the opening by artillery at 10,000 yards out to sea till the lead companies landed."[8]

Dieppe: Only five forward observation officers (FOOs) were attached to the assault force, one to each assaulting battalion. Their task was to direct and control the fire from the destroyer's guns. They had no direct observation of the targets on the headlands whose destruction was an essential element in the raid, and therefore they could not direct accurate fire on them. This greatly reduced the raid's chances of success. Furthermore, the 4-inch guns on the destroyers were of little use as their flat trajectory made them incapable of hitting the Germans' headland batteries.

D-Day: Thirty-nine FOOs directed the fire of the many naval vessels and other close support weapons that took part in the battle. As well, air spotters accurately directed fire from aircraft on targets of opportunity.

Brigadier Todd would recall that "in Normandy, we had major improvements. We sent a FOO and party ashore with the leading companies (about one hundred men) to direct the fire of the battleships and cruisers in support of 3 Division. These were *in addition* to the normal element of FOOs assigned to forward infantry companies."[9]

Dieppe: When the assault force approached the beaches, enemy small-arms fire raked their landing craft. Many of these craft were flimsy wooden R boats that offered no protection against any type of enemy fire. There were no heavily armed support craft.

D-Day: The infantry of Third Canadian Division were carried onto the beaches by landing craft armoured against small-arms fire. R boats were not used. The landing craft were designed for close infantry support as the troops approached the beaches. Ahead of the assaulting infantry was a flotilla of close support landing craft: the eight landing craft guns (LCGs) carried 4.7-inch artillery pieces, the four landing craft support (LCSs) carried automatic cannon, and 18 other landing craft assault fired twenty-four 60-pound bombs.

Dieppe: The enemy defenders experienced little effect from our meagre support fire. Some reported later that they managed to get under cover during the brief moments when they were under bombardment; but that immediately afterwards they were able to man their gun positions and produce withering fire to pin the attackers to the beaches.

The first wave of infantry was stopped mainly by the enemy's accurate small-arms fire. As well, their sniper fire was extremely deadly. There was virtually no supporting fire to help the infantry overrun the enemy's beach defences.

D-Day: As a result of the massive fire support, enemy opposition was effectively neutralized for a vital period that allowed the assaulting Third Canadian Division troops to successfully break through the beach defences. Fieldworks behind the beaches were largely eliminated, wire entanglements were broken down, and the defenders were left in shock by the weight of our fire.[10]

Brigadier Todd would note that at one beach assigned to the British, airborne troops were not able to take out a German battery that completely dominated their beaches with continuous enfilade fire: "After a few futile attempts, the British had to abandon their beaches and come through Third Canadian beaches, which made for a delay and for a while left our left flank open. The point was confirmed that you cannot expect success unless all enemy guns controlling the landing beaches are effectively dealt with."[11]

Dieppe: The German coastal land defences included concrete sea-walls and antitank ditches, as well as wire barricades and many concrete pillboxes. It was the sappers' task to assist the tanks by blowing gaps in them, or by raising wooden barricades over them.

Most of the Churchill tanks were unable to get off the beach as the sappers could not get through the heavy enemy fire to work on the obstacles. In addition, the rucksacks they used to carry their explosives caught fire easily.

The armour was supposed to support the infantry. But the Churchill tanks were, for the most part, ineffectual. Some drowned, some bogged down, others were knocked out because their tracks were broken by enemy antitank weapons or thrown by the chert surface of the beaches. At best, the tanks were reduced to mobile pillboxes. Their guns were 2- and 6-pounders that fired only solid shot.

D-Day: In March 1943, as a direct result of Dieppe, Brooke ordered Major General Sir Percy Hobart, commander of the 79th British Armoured Division, to convert his division into an experimental formation, that would devise and develop a number of specialized armoured fighting vehicles. These became known as the "Hobart Funnies."[12]

Immediate support for the assaulting infantry was provided by the duplex-drive (DD) tanks, which had been developed following careful study of the problems of the Dieppe tanks. The DD tanks were mobile both at sea and on land. Once ashore, their flotation equipment could be discarded, allowing them to operate as tanks. Their 75-mm guns fired the more effective high-explosive shells as well as solid shot.

There were a number of other versions of these Armoured Fighting Vehicles (AFVs). The Flail was a tank that carried rotating chains to explode mines. The Piscine carried a huge bundle of faggots (wooden slats) for filling antitank ditches. One tank carried its own bridge to get vehicles over antitank ditches. Hobart also developed an armoured flame-thrower that could support any infantry attacking fortified positions.[13]

Shortly after the raid, and doubtless with the memory of the 188 sapper casualties from Dieppe on his mind, a Canadian lieutenant named J.G. Donavan offered the suggestion that a tank be modified to carry engineers and their equipment. The AVRE (Armoured Vehicle, Royal Engineers) was the result. This engineer tank carried charges to destroy strongpoints or concrete obstacles such as beach walls — all the tasks that had been tackled at great personal peril, and without success, by engineers on foot at Dieppe. Like its stablemates, this armoured innovation played a major part in the success of D-Day and became an essential spearhead for many infantry attacks for the rest of the war.[14]

Ralph Allen, the Canadian journalist, wrote: "How many lives this Hobart-inspired or Hobart-encouraged menagerie saved before the war was over there is no way of guessing. But they were many more than the lives lost at Dieppe, and according to the impersonal cost accounting of war and in the jargon of military college blackboards, the final verdict may be that Dieppe was a tactical failure but a strategic success."[15]

Dieppe: An important lesson of Dieppe was that no major defended port could be captured quickly or intact. Before Dieppe, there was conflict within British intelligence and planning circles regarding invasion strategy. The *Dewing Report on Invasion* continually stressed the need for capturing a major French port early in a raid or an invasion. Curiously, this report's projection of a German invasion of Britain reflected the reverse. It was considered that German forces would come ashore on various sheltered beaches with lighter defences, with a view to the quick capture of London.[16]

In June 1942, when outlining the objectives for a Channel assault, Churchill wrote that "seizure of at least four important ports must be accomplished. The cost in men and material must be rated very high."[17]

D-Day: The Dieppe experience not only debunked this theory but proved that an assault through a defended port could not succeed without the destruction of the port, which would impair its usefulness when captured. This expedited the development of the artificial Mulberry offshore harbours which proved so successful in the Normandy landings and for logistical support afterwards.

Official Canadian historian C.P. Stacey summed up Dieppe's results in this way:

> I think the most important benefits we got from [Dieppe] were probably ones that nobody expected. That is, it gave the Allied high command quite a new and different view of the assault operation. There's very good evidence that the Dieppe plan was

essentially the sort of plan that the Allied high command entertained and were counting on using in a big invasion operation. It
was just going to be Dieppe on a larger scale and in particular,
yes, attacking ports. That plan was absolutely forgotten after
Dieppe.[18]

Dieppe: Combined Operations intelligence completely underrated the
strength of the defenders and the defences at Dieppe, as well as the
topographical difficulties that would be encountered there. There were
four times more German troops in the area than had been estimated.[19]

Enemy defences were far stronger than anticipated. As F.H. Hinsley
observed, intelligence had relied mainly on photo reconnaissance and
had made no allowance for the limitations of that technique. As a
result, the possible presence of enemy gun positions hidden in the
caves or cliffs of the eastern and western headlands was ignored —
an omission that was to cost the main assault sorely. In the intelligence
summaries, even the identity of the division occupying Dieppe was
incorrect.[20]

D-Day: For Overlord, intelligence about the enemy was accurate and
well defined.

Dieppe: Poor radio communication was a major problem. General
Roberts was completely out of touch with most of his units and could
not properly conduct the battle.

D-Day: Professor Hinsley pointed out that one of the chief lessons of
Dieppe was the need to set up a communications centre, with field
personnel of Sigint (Signal Intelligence) to man it, in a nearby headquarters ship.[21]

Dieppe: Cooperation and communication between infantry and air
was at a primitive level. When ground troops sent out an appeal for
bomber support to take out an enemy position, the request had to be
relayed back to RAF headquarters in England, and then planes were
dispatched. It therefore took some 86 minutes for a bomber to appear
over target.

D-Day: Air-ground communication had improved immeasurably. The
air force liaison officer at each brigade headquarters could call in air
close support to assist the infantry in a matter of minutes.

Dieppe: Infantry objectives were so unrealistic as to be impossible to achieve. The plan had no flexibility.

D-Day: Commanders on the ground had the option of adjusting the battleplan to the current situation. Reasonable objectives were met within the time frame.

Dieppe: The strength of units held back in reserve was inadequate to reinforce success. Only 16 percent of the assault force was held in reserve.

D-Day: The fundamental principle learned from Dieppe was that the "minimum force required for success should be allotted to the assault and the maximum retained as a reserve to exploit a success."[22] The D-Day planners held back 33 percent of their force in reserve.

Dieppe: Hitler was completely taken in by the Churchill-Roosevelt declaration of 1942 about the opening of the second front and by the raid on Dieppe. Despite General Halder's objections, he ordered the transfer of 10 crack divisions from Stalingrad to the West Wall in September 1942. This was the turning point in his campaign against Russia, and in the war as a whole.[23]

D-Day: From the Dieppe raid and the earlier raid on St Nazaire, Hitler concluded that the eventual Allied invasion, when it came, would be launched against a major port. He directed that high priority be given to the planning and construction of port defences, and lowest priority to the open beaches. Hitler also revised his coastal defence strategy. Rather than deploying his reserves as counterattack forces concentrated in pockets some distance behind the coast, he spread them along the Channel. This weakened their ability to counterattack.

This change in defence doctrine certainly helped the Allies during their amphibious assault and during their parachute and glider landings in Normandy.[24]

Official British historians J.M.A. Gwyer and J.R.M. Butler noted that "The Dieppe raid confirmed Hitler in his conviction of the need to prepare against an invasion. A week after the raid he charged Commander-in-Chief, West, to have 15,000 fortifications of a permanent nature built during the winter months. Thus it is probable that the Germans' success in repelling the Dieppe raid influenced their strategy, which proved fatal in 1944, of attempting to hold an invasion on the beaches instead of relying on a mobile reserve."[25]

Dieppe: Hitler was motivated by his success at Dieppe to impose the edict that there be no withdrawal of German forces in battle under threat of death.

D-Day: German forces were forbidden to retreat from Normandy. Instead of withdrawing and regrouping, they were annihilated.

Was Essential Experience Gained at Dieppe?

The raid on Dieppe was the first attempt by the British at an opposed landing since Gallipoli in 1915. (The previous American attempt dated back to the Civil War.) While there was no lack of modern doctrine, it had not been tested under fire. Problems associated with assaulting and seizing a port had to be explored. Techniques for handling a sizable assault fleet, with its new types of assault craft and equipment, had to be tested under actual conditions. The strengths of the German defences had to be probed.[26]

General Theodore J. Conway was an American member of the Dieppe planning syndicate. Immediately after the raid he was assigned to work on plans for Operation Torch with General Lucian Truscott. The outline for Torch, finished in September, was carried back to the United States in several mail bags, each, he claimed, weighing about 50 pounds. "Truscott's experience in Dieppe had a great deal of influence on the North African landings. Dieppe was 'a success' in the sense that we learned many things we couldn't have otherwise learned."[27]

Admiral Roskill noted one direct by-product of Dieppe: "The landing at Salerno in September 1943 might have ended in disaster on a vastly greater scale had not the gunfire of the heavy warships held the ring when there was danger of the enemy breaking through to the beaches."[28]

Churchill believed that the raid "helped to hold troops and resources in the West, which did something to take the weight off Russia."[29]

The prime minister defended the Dieppe raid before the House of Commons on September 8, 1942. He said that he had personally sanctioned the raid because he felt it was absolutely necessary for the Allies to gain information that would be essential to the success of full-scale operations in the future.[30]

The same view was expressed by General Brooke at a meeting at 10 Downing Street on June 30, 1942. He said, "No responsible General will be associated with any planning for invasion until we have an operation at least the size of the Dieppe raid behind us to study and base our plans upon."[31]

Was Dieppe a Failure or a Success?

General Crerar believed that "had Dieppe turned out to be a cheap success, there would have resulted a false and quite inadequate appreciation of the problem of invasion. The 'sobering effects' of the Dieppe operation, in my opinion, have had an important effect on Allied policies, strategy and of course, Combined Service tactics."[32]

Historian Philip Ziegler concluded, "If there had been no Dieppe and the invasion proper had been conducted with similar insouciance, the bloodshed would have been on a scale many times greater, the course of the war might have been turned."[33]

Historian Eric Maguire went one step further; stating that without the experiences of Dieppe, it is unlikely that Overlord would have taken place; and that had it been attempted, it would surely have failed.[34]

From the beaches of Normandy, General Eisenhower signalled Mountbatten: "Except for Dieppe and the work of your organization we would have been lacking much of the special equipment and much of the knowledge needed for the invasion."[35]

On June 10, 1944, six men composed a letter to the former commander of Combined Operations at the time of the Dieppe raid: Lord Louis Mountbatten:

> Today we visited British and American armies on the soil of France. We sailed through vast fleets of ships with landing craft of many types pouring men, vehicles and stores ashore. We saw clearly the manoeuvre in progress and in process of rapid development.
>
> We shared our secrets and helped each other all we could. We wish to tell you of this remarkable technique and therefore the success of the venture has it origin in developments affected by you and your staff of Combined Operations.

The letter was signed by Winston Churchill, Field Marshal Lord Alanbrooke, Field Marshal Smuts, General George Marshall, Admiral Ernest King, and General Hap Arnold. [36]

Denis Whitaker

I am appalled when people with little or no operational experience attempt to dismiss the lessons learned at Dieppe as inconsequential. These lessons, both strategic and tactical, saved countless lives as a result of their far-reaching influence on the success of future operations.

The courage and sacrifice of our men of Dieppe was clearly not in vain. The men of D-Day landed with a strong umbrella of air and artillery support. Their assault equipment — landing craft, armour and weapons — were superb. Their intelligence was accurate.

These assault skills and technical innovations were "bought and paid for" by Second Canadian Division at Dieppe.[37]

EPILOGUE

By the summer of 1942, the war had placed unbearable pressures on Great Britain. She could not boast a single victory in the field. Her far-flung empire was disintegrating, seized piecemeal by powerful Japanese and German forces.

The American Chiefs of Staff were demanding a second front in France in 1942 and were threatening to pull out of the European war to concentrate entirely against Japan if they could not have their way.

The Russians were in imminent danger of being overrun by the Germans. They, too, were demanding a second front in France in 1942. Stalin was accusing the British of being afraid to fight. Even conservative British second-fronters were saying in apology: "We cannot expect the Russians to believe in our sincerity if we only send planes and are not prepared to face casualties comparable to theirs."[1] If the Soviets survived, they were also threatening to pull out, to sue for a separate peace with Germany.

If the American focus shifted entirely to the Pacific and the Germans were released, one way or the other, from their Russian campaign, Hitler would be free to turn all his power against Britain. Without American and Russian Allies to come to her defense, Britain would be dangerously vulnerable to attack. Abandoned, and with only her own flimsy military might, the island would surely fall.

This was the terrible dilemma that faced Churchill and the Chiefs of Staff. Both her Allies saw the U.S.-proposed Operation Sledgehammer — a token invasion of 12 divisions that might at least provide a foothold in Europe — as their best shot at a second front for 1942. They didn't understand that the German forces defending France were too powerful. The Allies would not stand a chance. Brooke, who perceived this clearly, was adamant against mounting a major cross-Channel second front that year.

If Britain complied with her Allies' demands, the bulk of her military and logistical strength could be decimated. But if Britain did *not* stage one, her partners were threatening to abandon her to almost sure defeat.

"By the middle of the year," historian Philip Ziegler observed, "the raid on Dieppe was all that was left to satisfy the Americans and Russians of British aggressive intentions against the Continent.[2]

He could have added that the raid seemed to be all that was left to satisfy the "tragic coincidence" of two sets of vote-getting pressures for a cross-Channel military operation to be mounted. Roosevelt was becoming increasingly insistent that American troops see action against the Germans — before the coming Congressional elections in the fall. The Canadian government and military chiefs were pushing to get their troops into some sort of operation, and had managed to ingratiate themselves to the British in order to be included.

Churchill and the Chiefs came up with a compromise strategy: a large-scale raid against France (Dieppe) to satisfy the second fronters, plus a major operation (North Africa) where they had a chance of success.

The raid on Dieppe thus became the catalyst to resolve their dilemma: a brilliant and desperate scheme devised by Churchill and the Chiefs of Staff — desperate because they had manoeuvred themselves into an impossible corner, brilliant because no matter what the outcome, the dilemma would be resolved. When the raid succeeded, as they expected, her Allies would be appeased and would fall in line with Britain's imperialist plans in the Mediterranean. It would also mask the proposed North African assault, and force Hitler to further reinforce the French coast.

After months of persuasion, they finally sold Roosevelt, and a more reluctant Marshall, on the package. Now they had to sell Stalin. Moscow became the pivot. Churchill's five days in Russia in August 1942, would mark an "important turning-point in the history of the war," as his private secretary, Sir Leslie Rowan, later termed it. "Unless Churchill and Brooke could persuade Stalin that to open up a second front in Europe in 1942 would be a calamity, the whole course of the war would be changed."[3]

In Moscow, after days of bitter quarrelling, Stalin was won over. The deal was made. The Russian leader himself summed it up: "Dieppe will be explained by Torch."[4]

Churchill and Brooke were committed to their strategic gamble. Dieppe had to be mounted — and remounted, when it was aborted the first time. The Chiefs had to walk a fine line between the merits of putting on a battle of significant size to make their point, and the hazards of suffering a costly debacle. Theirs was a balancing act between the necessity of the operation and the possible calamity of its casualties. In the process, did they underestimate Dieppe's capacity for disaster?

Even when the flaws grew more flagrant, and the dangers became increasingly apparent, Churchill and the Chiefs had no choice but to push the raid to its conclusion. Their strategic commitment to Stalin and Roosevelt did not allow them to back down.

They understood the hazards of mounting a frontal attack against an entrenched enemy in a defended port — an enemy that they knew, via high-level intelligence, was growing stronger by the day.

The only chance of real tactical success rested on surprise. Although the tides and weather posted obvious signposts to the Germans, they at least had no inkling that Dieppe was the objective.

No one could have anticipated the problems at the tactical level that sabotaged the raid's chances. The unexpected encounter with the German convoy ended any hope of surprise. The inadequate system of communications and ensuing blackout led General Roberts to lose control of the battle. The inept intelligence created insurmountable difficulties: the erroneous assessment of the topography crippled the tanks, and the stubborn refusal to consider the possibility that machine-gun posts might be hidden in the caves resulted in many of the troops being killed or maimed before they had any chance at all to fight.

The planners had worried about the inexperience of the Canadian infantry and laid on specialized training; they should have concerned themselves as well with inexperienced Canadian and British commanders, whose inflexible operational plan denied any possibility of improvisation.

Why did Churchill and the Chiefs not order in a battleship? Why did they not reinstate the massive bombing raid?

There were valid military and strategic reasons for their failure to act in the face of the plan's disintegration. Hampered by the unsophisticated techniques and doctrines of the day, the army believed that with surprise, speed, mobility — and above all, those all-important tanks — they had provided an adequate plan for the attack.

There was so much to learn about mounting amphibious operations before D-Day could be staged. Gunners were still groping for the best tactical role of artillery. Dieppe itself, followed by Montgomery's El

Alamein victory, would be catalysts in generating greater emphasis on the massive artillery fire as an infantry-support tactic.

Tanks had never before been used in amphibious warfare. The planners somehow believed that they were magical hunks of steel. All they had to do was to get them onto the main beach — and that, after all, was their rationale for a frontal attack — and the armour would somehow cut through all enemy defenses. In their naïvety, they hadn't even worked out how the tanks would survive if they *did* get into the town. The German antitank teams, skulking in doorways and around corners, could easily have knocked them out, one by one. It wasn't until 1944 that the vulnerability of tanks in close combat was seriously recognized.

The mistakes of the planners contributed to the disaster, but they learned from their errors; Normandy is proof of that. The multitude of tactical lessons learned at Dieppe — the need for massive artillery bombardment, improved air-sea and air-ground coordination, improved naval fire support, better employment of artillery, armour suited to the assault, infantry better trained to it, and equipment specifically designed for the task — gave the Allies the edge in post-Dieppe operations.

After the disastrous sinking of the *Repulse* and the *Prince of Wales* and the heavy losses resulting from the PQ 17 and other Murmansk convoy runs, Churchill was bound to agree with Admiral Pound's insistence that no more battleships be squandered from the dwindling British fleet. The narrow Channel waters off Dieppe, with the threats of sinking from submarines or bombers, would have made the venture doubly hazardous.

By the same token, Air Marshals Portal and Harris were equally adamant against using bombers as mere "sideshows" to help the infantry. Their focus was on the millennium raids over Germany; it was tough enough to scrape together 1,000 airworthy bombers without wasting any on infantry raids over France.

The air force would argue with justification that they lacked the technical ability in 1942 to inflict significant damage on precise targets at night. There was only a slim chance that in a night raid over a small objective like Dieppe, the bombers would even hit their targets.

However, the crux of the refusal to provide battleships and bombers probably lay with Churchill and the Chiefs of Staff's fear that massive pounding of Dieppe would result in heavy casualties to the local French population. Churchill and Brooke had skillfully manoeuvred the Allied focus to a Mediterranean strategy. They had guaranteed the Dieppe/Torch second-front compromise to Stalin. Torch's success could be jeopardized if the wholesale slaughter of French civilians at Dieppe cost the Allies the cooperation of the Free French in North Africa. Aboard the *Calpe*, on the eve of the attack, Lieutenant Doheny overheard discussions among senior officers to the effect that American General Mark Clark was at that moment en route to Algiers to make a deal with the French. His negotiations would be jeopardized by the slaughter of innocent civilians.[5]

Why, in the face of intelligence warnings about enemy reinforcements, did they forge ahead with the attack? Churchill, the gambler, took a desperate chance. As the summer of '42 progressed, the commitment he and the Chiefs made to Dieppe and Torch became more and more binding. At the critical Moscow meeting in August 1942 it became irrevocable. *Nothing* must stop it: not even the unexpected appearance of the German convoy that disrupted the timing of flotilla and destroyed the possibility of surprise. This is undoubtedly why the warning signals from Southampton were not divulged to General Roberts, who might have responded by cancelling the raid.

The bottom line is that the gamble worked. Just one week after the raid, Hitler responded by ordering that "15,000 fortifications of a permanent nature" be constructed on the French coast. One month later he transferred ten more infantry divisions from the Russian Front to northern France. The fighter air battle above Dieppe — the largest single-day confrontation of the war, with the greatest casualties on both sides — had a subduing effect on the Luftwaffe. "After Dieppe, there seemed to be a reduction in business," more than one RAF fighter pilot noted from their daily sweeps across the Channel.[6]

Britain and the United States went on to victory after victory, first in the Mediterranean, then in Italy, and finally in Northwest Europe. When the Allies attacked France again, in 1944, this time the British and Americans set the schedule amicably, and this time the timing was ripe. Even then it wasn't easy.

Denis Whitaker

The point of this book is to raise questions, and to satisfy one veteran's quest for the whole story. My hardest lesson from Dieppe, after all my years of careful and sometimes painful research, was in not finding a pat answer for everything. Gaps will always remain in the "how" and "why."

If the Dieppe Raid had worked, it would probably have warranted a half-page entry in history books. It was a small pinprick in a whole catalogue of minor but successful operations that culminated in victory. Even its 65 percent casualty statistic would not have raised alarms. The Commando raid on St. Nazaire, after all, has been judged a success over the years despite the \79 *percent* casualty rate to the Commandos.

Because Dieppe *didn't* work, in the tactical sense, it has been the focus of countless books, articles and untempered debates for fifty years. Much of the controversy has become confused and convoluted. In the scramble to assign blame, the good that came out of the raid has been overlooked.

I am convinced that the raid was conceived and propelled along by Sir Winston Churchill, with the full support of his Chiefs of Staff. These were men burdened with decisions that affected the future of millions of people living in terror and under tyranny. They did their best for us and their best in this instance was brilliant. Dieppe contributed to the defeat of Germany.

At first, the raid would serve as a substitute to postpone the ultimate invasion until the Allied troops were better equipped and prepared. Later, it had an important diversionary role to mask the North African invasion.

The planners did not design the assault to fail; I doubt that it even crossed their minds that it would. It was definitely not staged for glorification of any one individual. I do not believe that Canadian troops were sent to Dieppe just to prove the point that a second front was a dangerous and impossible objective. There was no conspiracy to tip off the Germans that we were coming. We were never, ever, viewed by Churchill and the Chiefs as cannon fodder.

What it comes down to, for me, is that Dieppe was a tragedy but not a failure. It was a strategic success. Canadians are inclined to downplay or dismiss their achievements. This is one reason that the unity of our country is troubled and at stake.

The men at Dieppe fought heroically under impossible odds. Their efforts should not be denigrated. They contributed a great deal towards the ultimate victory. All Canadians can be proud of that.

ENDNOTES

We acknowledge with thanks the following archives, whose resources including Crown copyright material were unstintingly searched and shared on our behalf. Without this cooperation there would be no book.

LONDON, ENGLAND
PRO: Public Record Office
IWM: Imperial War Museum
KC: Liddell Hart Centre for Military Archives, King's College
National Maritime Museum, Greenwich: Baillie-Grohman Papers

OTTAWA, CANADA:
DND: Department of National Defence, Directorate of History
NAC: National Archives of Canada

U.S.A.:
USAMHI: U.S. Army Military History Institute, Carlisle, Pa.
NA: National Archives, Washington

CHAPTER ONE: POINT OF NO RETURN

1. IWM, London. Hughes-Hallett Memoirs.

2. PRO, London. CAB 101/335: Capt. S.W. Roskill. *The War at Sea*, Vol. 2. (London: H.M. Stationery Office, 1956).

3. PRO, London. W.O. 219/1934, Martian Report No. 13. DEFE 2/542: Operation Rutter.

4. PRO, London. DEFE 2/330. Order of the Day 10.8.42.

5. DND, Ottawa. Directorate of History: Interview with Hauptmann Richard Schnösenberg by Dr. McHugh.

6. DND, Ottawa. Directorate of History: Interview with Lt. Walter Höpener.

7. National Archives, Washington. Record Group 332, ETO Historical Division, Administration Files (1942–1946). #491: Address by Maj.-Gen. Roberts at the U.S. Assault Training Center, ETOUSA, 24 May–23 June, 1943.

8. DND, Ottawa. Directorate of History: Interview with Capt. H. Ditz, 302 Div.

9. PRO, London. DEFE 2/330. Captured enemy document circulated by GHQ, Home Forces.

10. Unpublished wartime diary of Lt. Dan Doheny, kindly loaned to the authors. Personal taped interview with Lt. Doheny, Nov. 24, 1990; Dec. 21, 1991.

11. National Maritime Museum, Greenwich. Manuscripts GRO/33: Baillie-Grohman, *Flashlight into the Past*, Vol. II.

12. PRO, London. DEFE 2/552; Col. C.P. Stacey, *Six Years of War* (Ottawa: The Queen's Printer, 1955), 336.

13. PRO, London. DEFE 2/330. Captured enemy document circulated by GHQ, Home Forces.

14. DND, Ottawa. Directorate of History: Interview with Lt. Siegfried Butzert, Grenadier Regiment 571.

15. The Dieppe Raid (Combined Report), October 1942, C.B. 04244.

16. PRO, London. WO 219/1933 Martian Report No. 4. DEFE 2/542: Operation Rutter. IWM, London. Combat Report, Corps HQ, 81 Corps.

17. DND, Ottawa. Directorate of History: 78/52. Letter from Capt. Ron Naler-Tyminski, Capt. of O.R.P. *Slazak*. April 21, 1974.

18. NAC, Ottawa. RG24 Vol. 20488. File 981GN (D13). Report of Port Commandant of Dieppe.

19. PRO, London. DEFE 2/339. Analysis of Preliminary Reports made to C.C.O. by force commanders and their staff on Operation Jubilee, Aug. 20, 1942.

20. NAC, Ottawa. RG24 Vol. 20488. File 981GN (D13). Report of Port Commandant of Dieppe.

21. DND, Ottawa. Lecture Notes. "The Combined Services Raid on Dieppe." IWM, London. Hughes-Hallett Papers.

22. PRO, London. DEFE 2/339. Analysis of Preliminary Reports made to C.C.O. by force commanders and their staff on Operation Jubilee, Aug. 20, 1942.

23. IWM, London. Corps HQ, 81 Army Corps. Combat Report. Aug. 25, 1942. Stacey, *Six Years of War*, 359.

24. DND, Ottawa. COHQ: Letter from Mountbatten to Crerar, Oct. 5, 1942.

CHAPTER 2: SECOND FRONT NOW!

1. Randolph Churchill, *Blood, Sweat and Tears*. (Toronto: McClelland & Stewart, 1941), 353.

2. Norman Longmate, *How We Lived Then*. (London, Hutchinson, 1971), 102.

3. Mollie Panther-Downes, *London War Notes*. (Toronto: Doubleday, 1971), 206. Eric Morris, *Churchill's Private Armies*. (London: Hutchinson, 1986), 240.

4. I.M. Maisky, *Memoirs of a Soviet Ambassador: The War, 1939–1943*. (London: Hutchinson, 1967), 248.

5. Eleanor Roosevelt, *This I Remember*. New York: Harper, 1949), 265.

6. British Newspaper Library: The British Library Reference Division, Colindale, London. (This archive contains newspapers dating back to 1801.)

7. Angus Calder, *The People's War: Britain 1939–1945*. (New York: Pantheon Books, 1960), 278.

8. Personal interview with Elizabeth O'Donohoe, September 7, 1991. British Newspaper Library: *Daily Express*, April 10, 1942.

9. Longmate, 183.

10. Mark A. Stoler, *The Politics of the Second Front: American Military Planning and Diplomacy in Coalition Warfare 1941–1943*. (Connecticut: Greenwood Press, 1977), 41.

11. Panther-Downes, 28.

12. General Heinz Guderian, *Panzer Leader*. (London: Michael Joseph, 1952), 256. Stephen Handelman, *Toronto Star,* June 22, 1991. Maisky, 281.

13. Capt. S.W. Roskill, *The War at Sea*. Vol. 2., 239.

14. Maisky, 250.

15. Liddell Hart Centre for Military Archives, King's College, (KC), London. Alanbrooke 3/A/V. Arthur Bryant, *The Turn of the Tide: 1939–1943*. (London: Collins, 1958), 300, 310.

16. PRO, London. CAB 79/21; WO 106/4175.

17. Maisky, 270.

18. John Colville, *The Fringes of Power: Downing Street Diaries 1939–1955*. (London: Hodder & Stoughton, 1985), 732.

19. Calder. 147–148.

20. John Colville, *Winston Churchill and his Inner Circle.* (New York: Wyndham, 1981), 122.

21. A.J.P. Taylor, *Beaverbrook.* (London: Hamish Hamilton, 1972), 525–27.

22. John Barnes and David Nicholson, eds. *The Leo Amery Diaries, 1929–1945. The Empire at Bay.* Vol. 2. (London: Hutchinson, 1980), 821.

23. KC, London. Alanbrooke 3/A/V.

24. A.J.P. Taylor, *Beaverbrook*, 527.

25. British Newspaper Library, *Daily Express,* April 23, 1942.

26. Calder, 298; Tom Driberg, *Beaverbrook.* (London: Weidenfeld & Nicolson, 1956), 285–86.

27. British Newspaper Library, *London Times*, April 25, 1942. Robert E. Sherwood, *Roosevelt and Hopkins: An Intimate Story.* (New York: Harper, 1948), 533.

28. Harry C. Butcher, *My Three Years with Eisenhower: The Personal Diary of Captain Harry C. Butcher USNR, Naval Aide to General Eisenhower 1942–1945.* (New York: Simon & Schuster, 1946), 23.

29. J. L. Granatstein and Desmond Morton, *A Nation Forged in Fire.* (Toronto: Lester & Orpen Dennys, 1989), 186. "The Case for the Second Front Now." Published by the Quebec Committee for Allied Victory, 1942.

30. PRO, London. AIR 40/1782. "The Russian Front — An Appreciation" by D.D.I.3 (Deputy Director of Intelligence 3), July 29, 1942.

31. *The Leo Amery Diaries,* 799.

CHAPTER 3: CHURCHILL AND THE CHIEFS

1. Lord Hastings Ismay, *The Memoirs of General Lord Ismay*, (Westport, Ct.: Greenwood Press, 1960), 279.

2. Personal taped interview with Lt.-Gen. Sir Ian Jacob, GBE, CB, Woodbridge, Suffolk, May 28, 1991. Sir John Wheeler-Bennett, ed. *Action This Day: Working with Churchill.* Memoirs by Lord Normanbrook, Sir John Martin, Sir Ian Jacob, Lord Bridges, Sir Leslie Rowan. (London: MacMillan, 1968). Gen. Jacob's chapter in *Action This Day* provided valuable insight into the workings of the Chiefs of Staff.

3. Colville, *Fringes of Power*, 752. Astley, Joan Bright. *The Inner Circle.* (London: Hutchinson, 1971), 70.

4. Interview with Mrs. Astley. May 23, 1991. Astley. *The Inner Circle*, 69.

5. Colville. *Winston Churchill and his Inner Circle*, 186. Astley. *The Inner Circle*, 129.

6. KC, London. Alanbrooke 12/X1: Col. John Bevan.

7. David Fraser. *Alanbrooke*. (London: Collins, 1982), 535.

8. KC, London. Alanbrooke 3/A/V.

9. Fraser, 538.

10. KC, London. Alanbrooke 3/A/V.

11. Fraser, 295.

12. KC, London. Alanbrooke X1/4/47–106.

13. Personal taped interview with Anthony Verrier. May 21, 1991. Maj.-Gen. Sir John Kennedy, *The Business of War*. (London: Hutchinson, 1957), 208.

14. Wheeler-Bennett, *Action This Day*. 192. Personal taped interview with Lt.-Gen. Sir Ian Jacob. This view is confirmed by Arthur Bryant in *Turn of the Tide* (page 10): "There is no case on record in which . . . their considered advice on a major strategic issue was overruled."

15. A.J.P. Taylor. *The War Lords*. (London: Penguin, 1978), 77.

16. KC, London. Alanbrooke 10/3/1–13.

17. A.J.P. Taylor, ed. *Churchill Revised*. (New York: Dial Press, 1969), 219.

18. Martin Gilbert. *Road to Victory*. (Toronto: Stoddart, 1986), 229.

19. A.J.P. Taylor, ed. *Churchill Revised*, 59.

20. PRO, London. WO 106/4175, COS 42 46th Meeting(O) 27 May/42.

21. Kennedy, 265.

22. A.J.P. Taylor, ed. *The War Lords*. 89. A.J.P. Taylor, *Churchill Revised*, 54, 213.

23. Alan Moorehead, *Gallipoli*. (Toronto: MacMillan, 1989), 32.

24. Bryant, 302.

25. Robert Rhodes James. *Churchill: A Study in Failure*. (London: Weidenfeld & Nicholson, 1970), 76.

26. Letter to the authors from Sir John Peck, June 20, 1990.

27. Philip Ziegler, *Mountbatten*. (New York: Alfred Knopf, 1985), 169.

28. Personal taped interview with Lt.-Gen. Sir Ian Jacob.

29. KC, London. Alanbrooke 3/A/VI.

30. Personal taped interview with Lt.-Gen. Sir Ian Jacob.

31. Forrest C. Pogue, *George C. Marshall.* (New York: Viking Press, 1963), 263.

32. Ziegler, 167.

33. Sherwood, 526. Jacques Mordal, *Dieppe: The Dawn of Decision.* (London: Souvenir Press, 1963), 57 (quoting Lt.-Gen. Sir Leslie Hollis). Ziegler, 210.

34. William Manchester, *The Last Lion.* (London: Little Brown & Co., 1988), 568.

35. Gilbert, *Road to Victory*, 112.

36. KC, London. Alanbrooke 3/A/V.

37. Personal taped interview with Lt.-Gen. Sir Ian Jacob.

38. *The Leo Amery Diaries*, 814.

39. Col. C.P. Stacey, *Six Years of War.* (Ottawa: Queen's Printer, 1955), 314.

40. John P. Campbell, *Canadian Defence Quarterly,* Vol. 6. No. 1, 1976. 40. The authors are indebted to Professor Campbell for his generosity in sharing with them his expertise in the intelligence factors of the Dieppe Raid.

41. Gilbert. *Road to Victory,* 112.

CHAPTER 4: A MODICUM OF DUPLICITY

1. Peter Simkins. *Imperial War Museum: Cabinet War Rooms*, 46. The Cabinet War Rooms are now open to the public and the audio-visual tour gives a fascinating glimpse of wartime London.

2. David Irving, *Hitler's War.* (New York: Viking Press, 1977). 384; Walter Scott Dunn Jr., *Second Front Now.* (University of Alabama, 1980), 191. (This fact was confirmed to the authors in an interview with Enigma and intelligence expert Mr. Ralph Bennett, May 29, 1991).

3. Sherwood, 529.

4. British Newspaper Library, London. *Express*, April 9, 1942.

5. Ismay, *The Memoirs of Lord Ismay,* 214.

6. Eleanor Roosevelt, *This I Remember*, 173.

7. Richard W. Steele, "Political Aspects of American Planning, 1941–1942." Vol. XXXV, *Military Affairs*, (published by the American Military Institute, April 1971), 69.

8. Sherwood, 521.

9. Thomas Parrish, *Roosevelt and Marshall*. (New York: Wm. Morrow, 1989), 255. Kent Greenfield, *American Strategy in World War II: A Reconsideration*. (Baltimore: Johns Hopkins University Press, 1975), 29.

10. Steele, "Political Aspects of American Planning, 1941–1942," 72.

11. J.M.A. Gwyer and J.R.M. Butler, *Grand Strategy*. (London: HMSO, 1964), 574.

12. Maisky, 268.

13. Albert C. Wedemeyer, *Wedemeyer Reports!* (New York: Holt, 1958), 105.

14. Pogue, 315.

15. Sherwood, 535–36.

16. Stacey, *Six Years of War*, 312. Sherwood, 538.

17. Roger Parkinson, *Blood, Toil, Tears and Sweat: The War History from Dunkirk to Alamein*. (London: Hart-Davis McGibbon, 1973), 392.

18. Gilbert, 89.

19. Parrish, 273.

20. Gilbert, *Road to Victory*, 89. Parkinson, 395. Winston Churchill. *Hinge of Fate. The Second World War*, Vol. 4. (New York: Bantam Books, 1962), 279.

21. Greenfield, 29. Sherwood, 533.

22. Parkinson, 395.

23. Bryant, 299–300.

24. Parrish, 266.

25. Pogue, 317, 320.

26. Personal taped interview with Lt.-Gen. Sir Ian Jacob.

27. Fraser, 248.

28. Wedemeyer, 42.

29. Ismay, 249–50.

CHAPTER 5: A VERY POLITICAL WAR

1. Personal interview with Professor Anthony Verrier in London, England. May 21, 1991.

2. National Film Board: "The King Chronicle," 1988.

3. Granatstein and Morton, *A Nation Forged in Fire,* 11.

4. Directorate of History, Department of National Defence, DND, Ottawa. 1123M2.009 (D10), A.G.L. McNaughton, "Principles of Imperial Defence: A Canadian Aspect," 1927.

5. Malone, 25.

6. KC, London. Alanbrooke 3/A/V.

7. Stacey. *Six Years of War: The Army in Canada, Britain and the Pacific.* (Ottawa: Queen's Printer, 1966), 94.

8. NAC, Ottawa. King Diary, June 10, 1941.

9. NAC, Ottawa. Minutes of the Cabinet War Committee, Vol. 4, C4653A, January 24, 1941.

10. NAC, Ottawa. King Diary, May 20, 1940. C.P. Stacey, *Arms, Men and Governments: The War Policies of Canada.* (Ottawa: Published by Authority of the Minister of National Defence, 1970), 41.

11. National Film Board: "The King Chronicle."

12. Martie Hooker, *In Defense of Unity,* Unpublished Master of Arts Dissertation (History), Carleton University, 1985. C.P. Stacey, *Canada and the Age of Conflict.* (Toronto: University of Toronto Press, 1981), 19, 220.

13. Granatstein and Morton, *A Nation Forged in Fire*, 7. Brereton Greenhous, *Semper Paratus.* (Hamilton, Ont: The Royal Hamilton Light Infantry Historical Association, 1977), 168.

14. Colonel G.W.L. Nicholson, *The Gunners of Canada.* Vol. II. (Toronto: McClelland & Stewart, 1972), 61.

15. Brig.-Gen. S.V. Radley-Walters, "Maj.-Gen. Worthington," *Onward II. History of the Calgary Tanks.*

16. Granatstein and Morton, *A Nation Forged in Fire,* 14.

17. Col. C.P. Stacey and Barbara M. Wilson, *The Half-Million. The Canadians in Britain, 1939–1946.* (Toronto: University of Toronto Press, 1987), 33. R.W. Queen-Hughes, *Whatever Men Dare. Regimental History of the Queen's Own Cameron Highlanders of Canada, 1935–1960),* (Winnipeg: The Regiment, 1960), 47.

18. Nicholson, *The Gunners of Canada*, 54.

19. NAC, Ottawa. RG24, Vol. 14,242. War Diary 14 Army Tank Regt., January 19, 1942.

20. *War Services of Canadian Knights of Columbus*, (Montreal: Gazette Printing Co., 1948), 94.

21. NAC, Ottawa. RG24, Vol. 14,215. War Diary RHLI, December 1941.

22. Lt.-Col. G.B. Buchanan, *MBE, The March of the Prairie Men: Regimental History of the South Saskatchewan Regiment.* (Weyburn, Sask: privately printed, 1957), 8.

23. Sgt. Steve Merrick, "To Die For One's Country," *Onward II. History of the Calgary Regiment.*

24. Greenhous, 170.

25. Buchanan, 10.

26. Brian Nolan, *King's War.* (Toronto: Random House, 1988), 87.

27. Hooker, 94.

28. Stacey, *Arms, Men and Governments,* 149.

29. C.P. Stacey, *Six Years of War,* 243. Hamilton, 477. W.A.B. Douglas and Brereton Greenhous, *Out of the Shadows. Canada in the Second World War.* (Toronto: Oxford University Press, 1977), 109.

30. DND, Ottawa: CMHQ Historical Officer's Report No 70.

31. Buchanan, *Regimental History of the South Saskatchewan Regiment,* 10.

32. Stacey, *Arms, Men and Governments,* 229. Stacey, *Canada and the Age of Conflict,* 350.

33. Stacey, *Canada and the Age of Conflict,* 350.

34. NAC, Ottawa. King Diary, August 21, 1941.

35. NAC, Ottawa. RG2, 7C, Vol. VI, C4654, Minutes of the Cabinet War Committee, 29 October, 1941. Ibid, Vol. IX, C4874, May 1, 1942.

36. Private Collection: "Uncle Harry"; memoirs of his batman.

37. Stacey, *Arms, Men and Governments,* 39–40.

38. *Winnipeg Free Press,* February 18, 1943.

39. Stacey, *Arms, Men and Governments,* 217.

40. Col. C.P. Stacey, *A Date With History: Memoirs of a Canadian Historian.* (Ottawa: Deneau Publishers, 1982), 95. NAC, Ottawa. RG24 Vol. 10,750, File 220 C1.009 (D2): Letter Feb. 5 1942 from Gen. Crerar to Gen. Montgomery.

41. NAC, Ottawa. Operations — Raids. Index to Correspondence.

42. NAC, Ottawa. RG24 Vol. 10,765. "Notes on Conference held on 6 Mar 42."

43. NAC, Ottawa. Hughes-Hallet Papers. MG30 E463, Simonds to Mountbatten, 22 January 1969 and Mountbatten to Simonds, 4 February 1969.

44. Stacey, *Six Years of War*, 329.

45. Desmond Morton, *A Military History of Canada.* (Edmonton: Hurtig, 1985), 204.

46. Stacey, *Arms, Men and Governments, 40.*

47. Douglas and Greenhous, *Out of the Shadows*, 104.

48. Interview with Maj.-Gen. Spry by M.A. Hooker, *In Defense of Unity*, (May 1985), 167.

49. Stacey, *The Half-Million*, 174.

CHAPTER 6: ENEMY ATTACK!

1. NAC, Ottawa. RG24. Vol. 15,215. War Diary RHLI Jan. 2, 1942.

2. R.W. Queen-Hughes, *Regimental History of the Queen's Own Cameron Highlanders of Canada*, 55.

3. Nicholson, 101.

4. Robertson, 58.

5. NAC, Ottawa. RG24. Vol. 15,215. War Diary RHLI March 1942: Exercise Hill.

6. DND, Ottawa. CMHQ Historical Officer's Report No 70. Queen-Hughes, 48.

7. Nicholson, 109–110. Hamilton, 500.

CHAPTER 7: THE FISH, FLESH AND FOWL

1. Gilbert, 88, 89, 92. Pogue, 317–19. Sherwood, 534, 538.

2. Gilbert, 92.

3. Personal interview with Gen. Sir Ian Jacob, May 30, 1991; Personal wartime diary of Gen. Jacob (Military secretary to War Cabinet 1939–1946; Chief Staff Officer, Ministry Defense, 1952). Sent to authors, June, 1991.

4. Ziegler, *Mountbatten*, 183.

5. Stacey, *Six Years of War*, 327.

6. Personal interview with Philip Ziegler, Mountbatten's official biographer. London, May 25, 1990 and May 22, 1991.

7. James Leasor, *Green Beach.* (London: Heinemann, 1975), 9–12.

8. Nigel Hamilton, *Monty, the Making of a General*. (London: Hamish Hamilton, 1981), 518.

9. NAC, Ottawa: RG 24, 10,765 (D129).

10. Interview with Col. Brian McCool by Mrs. Joan Caswell, Trent University, 1981 as part of her thesis. Mrs. Caswell, who is herself blind, is chairman of the CNIB Board of Peterborough, Ontario.

11. Interview with Col. Brian McCool by Mrs. Joan Caswell.

12. Stacey, *Six Years of War*, 329.

13. Ziegler, 164.

14. Baron Simon Christopher Joseph Fraser Lovat. *March Past: a Memoir*. (London: Weidenfeld & Nicholson, 1978), 238.

15. Ziegler, 164.

16. National Maritime Museum, Greenwich, England. Manuscripts: GRO/33: Baillie-Grohman. *Flashlight into the Past*. Vol. II.

17. DND, Ottawa 79/567. Macartney-Filgate Interviews, 1979. Folder #14. Terence Robertson, *The Shame and the Glory*. (Toronto: McClelland & Stewart, 1963), 69.

18. Personal interview with Gen. Sir Ian Jacob.

19. Lovat, 187.

20. PRO, London. DEFE 2/546: "Rutter." National Maritime Museum, Greenwich, England. Baillie-Grohman Papers.

21. KC, London. Alanbrooke 3/A/V.

22. RHLI Heritage Museum, Hamilton, Ontario: C.B. 04244. The Dieppe Raid: Combined Report (October 1942). Stacey, *Six Years of War*, 330.

23. King's College, London. Alanbrooke 3/A/V.

24. Personal taped interview with Brig. P.A.S. Todd CBE, DSO, ED, CD; CCRA 2 Cdn. Corps. 1 Cdn. Army, June 29, 1990.

25. Personal taped interview with Maj. John Roberts, July 30, 1991. Major Roberts, then 22, served through the Northwest Europe Campaign as a battery commander of an anti-tank regiment in 4 Canadian Infantry Division. He fought from France through to Germany.

26. Goronwy Rees, *A Bundle of Sensations*. (London: Chatto & Windus, 1960), 156.

27. Personal taped interview with Lt.-Gen. William Anderson, OBE, CD, RCA, February 24, 1991.

CHAPTER 8: THE MOLOTOV COCKTAIL

1. Maisky, 280.

2. Stoler, 42.

3. Maisky, 262.

4. Maisky, 281.

5. Maisky, 275.

6. Ziegler, 187.

7. Taylor, *Churchill Revised*, 53. Herbert Feis, *Churchill, Roosevelt and Stalin*. (London: Oxford Press, 1957), 46.

8. Gilbert, *Road to Victory,* 113.

9. Stoler, 44.

10. Parrish, 276.

11. Alexander Werth, *Russia at War 1941–1945*. (New York: Barrie & Rockliffe, 1964), 380.

12. Stoler, 47–48.

13. Gwyer and Butler, 618.

14. Stoler, 49.

15. Pogue, 262. Richard W. Steele, "Political Aspects of American Military Planning, 1941–1942."

16. Feis, 67.

17. Gilbert, 119.

18. Parkinson, 419.

19. PRO, London. CAB 120/684; Stacey, *Six Years of War,* 314–15.

20. Werth, 382.

21. Werth, 382, 385.

22. KC, London. Alanbrooke X1/5/107–15.

23. Graham Lyons, ed, *The Russian Version of the Second World War*. (London: Leo Cooper, 1976), 43.

CHAPTER 9: PRECIPICE AT HYDE PARK

1. Sherwood, 442.

2. Taylor, ed. *Churchill Revised*, 164.

3. PRO, London. CAB 120/684. Stacey, *Six Years of War*, 314–15.

4. Sherwood, 363.

5. Martin Gilbert, *Never Despair: Winston S. Churchill 1945–1965.* (London: Heinemann, 1988), 415. Sherwood, 364.

6. Wedemeyer, 105.

7. Churchill, *Hinge of Fate*, 337.

8. Parrish, 284.

9. Pogue, 262. KC, London. Alanbrooke 3/A/V. Wheeler-Bennett, *Action This Day*, 208.

10. Ziegler, 185. Sherwood, 582.

11. Fraser, 246.

12. KC, London. Alanbrooke 10/3/1–13.

13. Gwyer, 624.

14. KC, London. Alanbrooke 3/A/V1.

15. Chester Wilmot, *The Struggle for Europe*. (London: Collins, 1952), 101.

16. Steele. "Political Aspects of American Military Planning, 1941–1942," 71.

17. Gwyer, 626.

18. KC, London. Alanbrooke 12/X1.

19. Wilmot, 635.

20. Personal Interview with Professor Anthony Verrier.

21. KC, London. Alanbrooke 3/A/V. Lord Moran, *Churchill: Taken from the Diaries of Lord Moran.* (Boston: Houghton, 1966), 23.

22. KC, London. Alanbrooke 12/XI.

23. Wedemeyer, 105, 146.

24. Richard Langhorne, ed, *Diplomacy and Intelligence During the Second World War.* (Cambridge: 1985), 222–23.

25. Wedemeyer, 155.

26. Henry L. Stimson, *On Active Service in Peace and War.* (New York: Harper, 1947), 422.

27. Wedemeyer, 132.

28. Wedemeyer, 135.

29. KC, London. Alanbrooke 12/XI.

30. KC, London. Alanbrooke 12/XI.

31. Gwyer, 627. Stoler, 53.

32. Parrish, 286 (McCrea Draft memoirs. FDRL).

33. Parkinson, 430.

34. Ismay, 255.

35. KC, London. Alanbrooke 3/A/V1.

36. Moran, 41, 195.

37. Gilbert, 120. Ziegler, 185.

38. Moran, 42.

39. Ismay, 256; Calder 299.

40. Fraser, 258.

41. Gwyer, 627–28.

42. KC, London. Alanbrooke 3/A/V1.

43. KC, London. Alanbrooke 3/A/V1.

44. IWM, London. Hughes-Hallett Papers, 158.

45. Ismay, 257.

CHAPTER 10: TIGHTEST LITTLE ISLAND

1. Richard J. Hutchings, *This Island: An Illustrated Guide to the Isle of Wight*, 18. The authors are indebted to librarians from the County Reference Library, Lord Louis Library, Newport, Isle of Wight.

2. Adrian Searle, *Isle of Wight at War 1939–1945*. (Wimborne, Dorset: The Dovecote Press, 1989), 68, 69.

3. NAC, Ottawa. War Diary: RHLI. RG24, Vol. 15,215, May 1942.

4. Lovat, 243.

5. Taped personal interview with Lt. Jack H. Dunlap, 6 Troop, B Squadron Troop Cdr. September 1991.

6. PRO. DEFE 2/549. "Training Programme with TLCs," 14 Cdn. Army Tank Bn.

7. Taped personal interview with Capt. Ed Bennett, Calgary Tanks, September 1991.

8. Taped personal interview with Calgary Tank officer, Lt. Arthur Patterson, Troop Cdr, C Squadron, 15 Troop. September 1991.

9. Lt. R.G. Maltby, "Churchills Don't Float", *Onward II: The History of the Calgary Regiment*. Hugh Henry, *The 14th Cdn. Army Tank Regt.*

at Dieppe. Dissertation submitted for a Master of Arts (History), University of Victoria, 1991.

10. Taped personal interview with Sgt. Al Wagstaff, C Squadron, October 1991.

11. Taped personal interview with Mr. Leslie Barton, Shorewell, Isle of Wight, 22 May 1990.

12. Searle, 70.

13. Taped personal interview with Cpl. John Williamson (now Col.), Section cmdr, RHLI, C Coy, 15 Pl. July 1991.

14. Taped personal interview with Capt. Walter McGregor, Essex Scottish. July 1991.

15. NAC, Ottawa. War Diary: RHLI. RG24, Vol 15,215, July 1942. Greenhous, *Semper Paratus*, 184. DND, Ottawa. Report No. 123. Historical Officer, Cdn. Military HQ, Ross Munro, *Globe & Mail*.

16. Taped personal interview with Sgt. Jim Coughlin, Essex Scottish, July 1991.

17. Taped personal interview with Col. John Williamson.

18. Taped personal interview with Sgt. Jim Coughlin, Essex Scottish, July 1991.

19. NAC, Ottawa. War Diary: FMR. RG24, Vol. 17,511, June 1942.

20. NAC, Ottawa. War Diary: Royal Regt. of Canada. RG24, Vol. 17,510, June 1942.

21. DND, Ottawa. Report No. 123. Historical Officer, Cdn. Military HQ, Ross Munro, *Globe & Mail*.

22. NAC, Ottawa. War Diary: FMR. RG24, Vol. 17,511, June 1942.

23. Correspondence with Jacques Nadeau, O. St. J, C.D., FMR, September 23, 1991.

24. NAC, Ottawa. War Diary: SSR. RG24, Vol. 17,512, File 582C July 1942.

25. NAC, Ottawa. War Diary: Royal Regt. of Canada. RG24, Vol. 17,510, June 1942.

26. Taped personal interview with Lt. Tom Taylor, Royal Regt. of Canada, July 1991.

27. NAC, Ottawa. War Diary: Essex Scottish. RG24, Vol. 17,513, August 1942.

28. Queen-Hughes, *History of the Queen's Own Cameron Highlanders of Canada*, 57.

29. Taped personal interview with Pte. Norman Partington, RHLI Carrier Platoon, July 1991.

30. Personal interview with Pte. Partington.

31. Taped personal interview with Trooper Percy Aide, of B Squadron Calgary Tanks. September 1991.

32. *Onward II: The History of the Calgary Regiment.* Henry, *The 14th Cdn. Army Tank Regt. at Dieppe.*

33. PRO, London. DEFE 2/547. "Training of Beach Assault Engineers."

34. PRO, London. DEFE 2/548. "Engineer Training Reports."

35. NAC, Ottawa. War Diary: RHLI.

36. DND, Ottawa 594.014 (D8). Operation Rutter, Detailed Military Plan, 20 June 42. Max Arthur, *Men of the Red Beret, Airborne Forces 1940–1990.* (London: Hutchinson, 1990), 5.

37. Baillie-Grohman, *Flashlight into the Past*, Vol. II.

38. Rees, 156.

39. Baillie-Grohman, *Flashlight into the Past.*

40. IWM, London. "Before I Forget." Unpublished Memoirs of Vice Admiral John Hughes-Hallet.

41. Queen-Hughes, *History of the Cameron Highlanders of Canada*, 60.

42. Baillie-Grohman, *Flashlight into the Past*, Vol. II.

43. Stacey. *Six Years of War.* 334–35. Letter from Gen. Montgomery to Gen. Paget, 1 July 1942.

44. The Dieppe Raid (Combined Report), October 1942. CB 04244.

45. Rees, 151.

46. Capt. Jim Quinn (now Lt.-Gen.). "Some Regimental Notes." Calgary Tank Regt.

47. Taped personal interview with Col. John Williamson.

CHAPTER 11: THE DISINTEGRATION

1. Rees, 151.

2. DND, Ottawa. Interview of Goronwy Rees, CBC "Closeup," 1962.

3. Baillie-Grohman, *Flashlight into the Past*, Vol. II.

4. DND, Ottawa. Interview of Goronwy Rees, CBC "Close Up," 1962.

5. PRO, London. DEFE 2/ 542.

6. PRO, London. DEFE 2/542.

7. DND, Ottawa, COHQ Records Vol. 21 ("Rutter" Vol. I A) 1 June 1942.

8. Rees, 145.

9. PRO, London. DEFE 2/552. Stacey, *Six Years of War,* 336.

10. Stacey, 337.

11. "The Dieppe Raid," Combined Report, October 1942. C.B. 04244.

12. DND, Ottawa. CBC "Close Up." IWM, London, The Papers of Vice-Admiral J. Hughes Hallett. JHH 3/1 Dieppe "Jubilee Papers." IWM, London. Haydon Papers. Draft by Maj. Walter Skrine.

13. PRO, London. DEFE 2/ 542, "Operation Rutter," May 11, 1942.

14. DND, Ottawa. Directorate of History. 75/17. John P. Campbell. "Analysis of Air Operations at Dieppe," 1974.

15. Roskill, 241.

16. "The Dieppe Raid," Combined Report. C.B. 04244. PRO, London. DEFE 2/546, 28 May 1942. Meeting held at Combined Ops. HQ. ADM 179/220, 13 May 1942, "Outline Plan for Operation Rutter." ADM 179/220, 27 June 1942, Operation Order No. 299 (Raid on Dieppe) dismissed the close support role of the covering naval forces.

17. Baillie-Grohman, *Flashlight into the Past*, Vol. II. GRO/30: Baillie-Grohman Papers: "Military Questionnaire on Dieppe Raid with Answers by the General Officer concerning Canadian Forces. Operation Jubilee: Questionnaire for Military Force Commander."

18. IWM, London. "Military Lessons to be Drawn from the Assault on Dieppe."

19. Baillie-Grohman, *Flashlight into the Past*, Vol. II. PRO, London. DEFE 2/546:Dieppe Raid: Operation Rutter. Minutes of the 1st Meeting of the Combined Force Commanders at COHQ, 1st June 1942.

20. DND, Ottawa. Mountbatten speech Sept. 29, 1973. Roskill, 241. Stacey, 398.

21. Personal interview with Vice Admiral Piers, 4 April, 1991.

22. Personal taped interview with Brig. Todd, 29 June, 1990.

23. John P. Campbell, "The Ultra Revelations." *Canadian Defence Quarterly*, Vol. 6, no. 1, summer 1976.

24. DND, Ottawa. CBC "Close Up." Interview of Brig. Sherwood Lett, commander Fourth Canadian Infantry Brigade.

25. Interview of Maj. Brian McCool.

26. Ziegler, 189.

27. "Chert Beach — Alias Dieppe" by Trooper Stan A. Kanik, *Onward II: The History of the Calgary Regiment.*

28. Personal taped interview with Maj. Richard McLaren, RHLI, November 1991.

29. Hinsley, 699.

30. PRO, London. DEFE 2/330.

31. Donald McLachlan, *Room 39: Naval Intelligence in Action, 1939–1945*, 388.

32. PRO, London. DEFE 2/330. "Lessons Drawn from Attempted Enemy Landing at Dieppe."

33. Kanik, "Chert Beach — Alias Dieppe." *Onward II.*

34. Baillie-Grohman, *Flashlight into the Past*, Vol. II.

35. Roskill, 244. Stacey, 398.

36. Lt.-Col. Charles Schreiner, *The Dieppe Raid: Its Origins, Aims and Results.* U.S. Marine Corps College of Naval Warfare. Naval War College Review, May–June 1973.

37. PRO, London. DEFE 2/ 546, Appendix IV.

38. Roskill, 172.

39. John P. Campbell, "Dieppe and German Foreknowledge." (Toronto: Extension Bulletin. A Periodical of the Canadian Forces Extension School. Summer, 1974), 38. Personal interview with Professor Campbell.

40. Roskill, 172.

41. Personal taped interview with Brig. Todd, June 29, 1990.

42. Rees, 157.

CHAPTER 12: THE MONTY CONUNDRUM

1. Stacey, *Date with History*, 235.

2. Rees, 135.

3. Rees, 135.

4. Hamilton, 516.

5. Hamilton, 456.

6. Hamilton, 522.

7. Personal taped interview with Philip Ziegler, Mountbatten's official biographer. London: May 25, 1990 and May 22, 1991.

8. NAC, Ottawa. RG 24, Vol. 10,750. File 220 C1.009 (D3).

9. Hamilton, 521.

10. NAC, Ottawa. RG 24, Vol. 10,750. File 220 C1.009 (D3).

11. DND, Ottawa 79/567. Macartney-Filgate Interview of Lt. J.S. Edsmondson, 1979. Folder #32.

12. Personal taped interview with Gen. Sir David Fraser G.C.B., O.B.E., D.L., May 22, 1991.

13. Field Marshal Sir B.L. Montgomery, *El Alamein to the River Sango.* (Berlin: British Army on the Rhine, 1946), 18.

14. Whitaker, W.D. & S. *Rhineland.* (Toronto: Stoddart, 1989), 47.

15. Field Marshal Sir B.L. Montgomery. *Normandy to the Baltic.* (Germany: British Army on the Rhine. April 1946), 29. Nicholson, 313.

16. Baillie-Grohman. *Flashlight into the Past.* Vol. II.

17. Hamilton, 515.

18. IWM, London. The Papers of Vice Admiral John Hughes-Hallet. JHH 3/1 Dieppe. Jubilee Papers: Unpublished Memoirs of Vice Admiral J. Hughes-Hallett.

19. DND, Ottawa. Directorate of History. CBC "Close Up." Interview with Field Marshal Sir B.L. Montgomery.

20. NAC, Ottawa. MG 30 E 157, Vol. 2. file 958-009 (CD 21).

21. DND, Ottawa. CMHQ Historical Officer's Report #128.

22. Personal taped interview with Gen. Sir David Fraser, G.C.B., O.B.E., D.L.: Vice-CIGS biographer of Alanbrooke.

23. Personal taped interview with Professor Terry Copp, May 1992. Correspondence with Professor Copp, January 1992.

24. Personal taped interview with Philip Ziegler.

25. Personal taped interview with Gen. Fraser.

CHAPTER 13: RUTTER: A DIRECT HIT

1. PRO, London. DEFE 2/546. Minutes of meeting, June 15, 1942, to discuss Operation Rutter.

2. Taped personal interview with Col. John Williamson, RHLI, August 1991.

3. Taped personal interview with Sgt. Frank Volterman, RHLI. September 1991.

4. IWM, London. Papers of Captain John Hughes-Hallett.

5. NAC, Ottawa. RG24. Vol. 17,512. War Diary, QOCH, July 3, 1942.

6. Taped personal interview with Lt. Ed Bennett, Calgary Tank Regiment.

7. Taped personal interview with Maj. Forbes West, Royal Regiment of Canada, October 21, 1991.

8. Gilbert, *Road to Victory*, 140.

9. Parkinson, 433.

10. IWM, London. Papers of Captain John Hughes-Hallett. KC, London. Ismay II/3/260/4aii.

11. PRO, London. WO 219/1933. Martian Report No. 4. June 23, 1942.

12. NAC, Ottawa. RG 24, Vol. 10,750. File 220 C1.009 (D3). Letter from Gen. Montgomery to Gen. Crerar, July 5, 1942.

13. PRO, London. DEFE 2/546. Intelligence Report: Operation Rutter.

14. PRO, London. DEFE 2/542. WO 208/3573. M.I. 14/SIF/19/42.

15. PRO, London. WO 219/1933. Martian Report No. 4 and 5.

16. PRO, London. DEFE 2/548. Operation Rutter, Amendment No. 5, June 30, 1942.

17. PRO, London. DEFE 2/546. War Cabinet COS (42) 188th Meeting. June 24, 1942.

18. PRO, London. AIR 16/760. Actual air casualties at Dieppe were: 106 aircraft, of which 98 were fighters, and 67 pilots dead/missing and presumed dead (Stacey, 388). Leigh-Mallory was close: he predicted 120 aircraft and 60 to 70 pilots.

19. PRO, London. WO 219/1933. Martian Report No. 3, 4, and 5: June 16, 23 and 30.

20. IWM, London. BLM 20/5.

21. DND, Ottawa. CMHQ Reports. Letter from Lt.-Gen. Swayne to Lt.-Gen. McNaughton, April 27, 1942.

22. Stacey, *Six Years of War*, 333.

23. Stacey, *Six Years of War*, 338.

24. NAC, Ottawa. MG 30-E 157. Vol. 2. File 958-009 CD21. Stacey, *Six Years of War*, 338.

25. PRO, London: DEFE 2/542. WO 208/3573 M.I. 14/SIF/26/42, June 29, 1942.

26. KC, London: Ismay II/3/242.

27. PRO, London. WO 208/3573 M.I. 14/SIF/26/42, June 29, 1942.

28. Taped personal interview with Pte. Joe Ryan, Royal Regiment of Canada, September 1991.

29. Maj. Donald J. Goodspeed, *Battle Royal: A History of the Royal Regiment of Canada*. (Toronto: Royal Regt. of Canada Assoc., 1962), 387.

30. Arthur Kelly, "Dieppe." *Hamilton This Month* Magazine, October 1989.

31. NAC. Ottawa. RG24. 10795 225C1.013: Operation Jubilee Detailed Military Plan, 10 Aug. IWM, London. Corps. HQ, 81 Corps. Combat Report.

CHAPTER 14: CHILD OF CHURCHILL

---

1. PRO, London. CAB 65/28. Gilbert, 143. Parkinson, 439.

2. PRO, London. CAB 65/28. Parkinson, 439.

3. Gwyer, 632.

4. KC, London: Ismay II/3/242. Fergusson, 173.

5. Churchill, 444.

6. Baillie-Grohman. *Flashlight into the Past*. Vol. II.

7. Correspondence with Sir John Peck, June 30, 1991.

8. DND, Ottawa 79/567 folder 68. Hughes-Hallett speech at Royal Regiment Dinner. IWM, Hughes-Hallett Papers.

9. NAC, Ottawa. RG24, Vol. 15,215, RHLI War Diary, July 7, 1942.

10. DND, Ottawa. CMHQ Historical Officer's Report no. 128.

11. PRO, London. AIR 16/746. NAC, Ottawa. Vol. 10,795 225C1.013 "Operation Jubilee Detailed Military Plan."

12. DEFE 2/546. Operation Rutter.

13. Lovat, 239.

14. B.L. Montgomery, *The Memoirs of Field-Marshal the Viscount Montgomery,* (London: Collins, 1958), 76.

15. NAC, Ottawa. 220CL.009 D3 #54. DND, Ottawa. CBC "Close Up." September 9, 1962. Stacey, 335.

16. Hamilton, 515.

17. Hamilton, 496, 527.

18. PRO, London. DEFE 2/337.

19. Hamilton, 518. Stacey, *Six Years of War*, 329.

20. Baillie-Grohman Papers. July 9, 1942.

21. Lovat, 273. Robertson, 135.

22. PRO, London. DEFE 2/306. Correspondence Admiral Sir Bertram Ramsay to Lord Mountbatten. July 25 and 27, 1942.

23. NAC, Ottawa. MG 30 E463 Hughes-Hallett Papers.

24. Ottawa. Directorate of History 594.019 (D1) Dieppe 1942. C.P. Stacey. War Diary volumes for Rutter and Jubilee. COHQ.

25. NAC Ottawa. 220 CL. 009 (D3). # 63. MG 30 E133. McNaughton War Diary July 42. RG24, Vol. 10,584. File 215C (D233). PRO, London. DEFE 2/337. Operation Jubilee.

26. Stacey 341. IWM, London. Hughes-Hallett Papers.

27. NAC, Ottawa. RG24 Vol. 10,750, file 220C1.0091031. Letter from Gen. McNaughton to Gen. Crerar, July 27, 1942. Files dated as late as July 31, 1942, handwritten and categorized "most secret," have the original operation name "Rutter" at the top stroked out and "Jubilee" written above it.

28. PRO, London. DEFE 2/550. Letter from Vice Admiral Mountbatten to Gen. Brooke. July 30, 1942.

29. Hinsley, 697.

30. Chandler, 378.

31. PRO, London. DEFE 2/335. Operation Jubilee. COHQ Records. Report by Brig L.K. Truscott Jr.

32. Jerome J. Haggerty, "A History of the Ranger Battalions in World War II." Ph.D dissertation, Fordham University, 1982, 95.

33. Robertson, 137. Jack Nissen and A.W. Cockerill. *Winning the Radar War*. (Toronto: MacMillan, 1987).

34. Lovat, 241–43.

35. Ronald Atkin, *Dieppe 1942*. (London: MacMillan, 1980), 43.

36. Dr. Michael J. King, "Rangers: Selected Combat Operations in World War II," *Leavenworth Papers*, Combat Studies Institute, Fort Leavenworth, Kansas, June, 1985.

37. NAC, Ottawa. RG24. 10795 225C1.013: Operation Jubilee Detailed Military Plan. August 10, 1942.

38. NAC, Ottawa. RG 24, Vol. 10,750. File 220 C1.009 (D3). Letter from Gen. Montgomery to Gen. Crerar, July 5, 1942.

39. PRO, London. WO 219/1933 Martian Report No. 4. WO 208/3573. Summary of M.I. Indications Files: M.I. 14/SIF/20/42 (for week ending May 18, 1942).

40. DEFE 2/542. Operation Rutter. Lovat, 277.

41. PRO, London: WO 208/3573. Summary of M.I. Indications Files: M.I. 14/SIF/31/42 (for week ending 3 August, 1942). M.I. 14/SIF/32/42 (for week ending 10 August, 1942). KC, London. Ismay II/3/ii. Capt. S.W. Roskill, "The Dieppe Raid and the Question of German Foreknowledge." (Appendix 1). London: *Royal United Services Institute Journal.* Feb.–Mar. 1964. Walter Warlimont, *Inside Hitler's Headquarters 1939–1945. (New York: Praeger, 1964), 247–48.*

42. Warlimont, 247–48.

43. PRO, London. WO 208/3573. Summary of M.I. Indications Files: M.I. 14/SIF/15/42 (for week ending 13 April, 1942). M.I. 14/SIF/19/42 (for week ending 11 May, 1942).

44. PRO, London: WO 208/3573. Summary of M.I. Indications Files: M.I. 14/SIF/30/42 (for week ending 27 July, 1942). M.I. 14/SIF/31/42 (for week ending 3 August, 1942).

45. PRO, London. WO 219/1933. Martian Report No. 8, July 21, 1942.

46. PRO, London. WO 219/1933. Martian Report No. 3, 4, and 5: 16, 23 and 30 June. Capt. S.W. Roskill, "The Dieppe Raid and the Question of German Foreknowledge." (Appendix II), Translation of German battle report, C-in-C West, 19 August, 1942.

47. PRO, London, WO 208/3573. Summary of M.I. Indications Files: M.I. 14/SIF/19/42 (for week ending 11 May, 1942).

CHAPTER 15: TWO-TIERED INTELLIGENCE

1. Gilbert, *Road to Victory,* 176–77.

2. Dunn, 187.

3. NAC, Ottawa. RG 24, Vol. 10/766, File 222C1 (D144).

4. Anthony Cave Brown, "C", (New York: MacMillan, 1987), 402.

5. Ronald Lewin, *Ultra Goes to War.* (London: Hutchinson & Co., 1978), 124, 184.

6. Lewin, 64.

7. Gilbert, *Road to Victory*, 56.

8. Personal taped interview with Ralph Bennett. London, May 29, 1991.

9. F.H. Hinsley et al., eds, *British Intelligence in the Second World War*, Vol. 2. (London: HMSO, 1981), 103.

10. Personal taped interview with Mr. Bennett.

11. PRO, London. DEFE 2/542. Operation Jubilee. Intelligence Report, May 26, 1942.

12. Personal taped interview with Mr. Bennett.

13. PRO, London. WO 106/4124, Combined Operations: Security and Intelligence.

14. McMaster University Archives, Hamilton. CAB 79/22. COS (42) 211th Meeting.

15. KC, London, Alanbrooke VI/2: "To President Roosevelt from Former Naval Person," August 26, 1942. Gilbert, 219.

16. IWM, London. Corps HQ, 81 Corps. Combat Report.

17. Lovat, 268–69.

18. *The New York Times*, August 20, 1942. Frederick Oeshsner, *This is the Enemy,* (Boston: Little Brown & Co., 1942), 324), 324. Arthur Kelly, *Hamilton This Month*, Hamilton, Ontario, October 1989 and October 1990.

19. Dr. Alfred Vagts, *Landing Operations: Strategy, Psychology, Tactics, Politics, From Antiquity to 1945.* (Harrisburg: Military Service Publishing Co., 1946), 701.

20. Baillie-Grohman, *Flashlight into the Past.* Vol. II.

21. NAC, Ottawa. RG24. 10,795 225C1.013. Detailed Military Plan. August 7, 1942. C.B. 04244 The Dieppe Raid (Combined Report).

22. PRO, London. WO 106/4196. DEFE 2/542, DEFE 2/550. Churchill, 443.

23. RG24 Vol. 10,765. File 222C1 (128). Operation Rutter, Detailed Military Plan. Information Enemy. June 20, 1942. PRO, London. DEFE 2/544. GHQ/H.F./INT/19 April 1942. C.B. 04244. The Dieppe Raid (Combined Report).

24. PRO, London. WO 219/1933 Martian Report No. 4. DEFE 2/542: Operation Rutter.

25. Lovat, 268.

26. KC, London. Ismay II/3/247/2a, Churchill to Pownall.

27. C.B. 04244 The Dieppe Raid (Combined Report).

28. PRO, London. DEFE 2/550. S.R. Elliot, *Scarlet to Green.* (Ottawa: Canadian Intelligence & Security Association, 1981), 172.

29. Lovat, 268 and 270.

30. Baillie-Grohman, *Flashlight into the Past.* Vol. II.

31. Personal interview with Douglas Kendall, March 11, 1991.

32. DND, Ottawa. 79/567. Macartney-Filgate Interviews, 1979. Folder #70. Interview with Maj. Reginald Unwin, G 3, First Canadian Army.

33. Elliot, 165.

34. Stacey, *Six Years of War*, 398. Hinsley, 700. With respect, Hinsley and Stacey seem to have somewhat underestimated the effect of the poor intelligence on the raid.

35. PRO, London. DEFE 2/335. Brigadier Lucian Truscott report to C.C.O.

36. Roskill, 241. Stacey, 398.

37. Lovat, 277.

CHAPTER 16: DEATH OF SLEDGEHAMMER

1. Wedemeyer, 105.

2. Parkinson, 441.

3. Wilmot, 108.

4. Stimson, 424.

5. Stoler, 55.

6. David Eisenhower, *Eisenhower At War.* (New York: Random House, 1986), 84–85.

7. Gwyer, 632.

8. KC, London. Pownall Diaries. Parrish, 291.

9. Douglas Botting, *The Second Front*, (Alexandria, Va.: Time-Life Books, 1990), 22. Schreiner, A-6.

10. PRO, London. CAB 120/65.

11. Gilbert, 114. Hinsley, 101.

12. Churchill, 376.

13. Parrish, 291–92 (July 15, 1942. PSF [Safe File], FDRL; Draft of FDR substitute memo, "Instructions for London Conference," FDRL.) Greenfield, 30.

14. F.L. Loewenheim, H. Langley and M. Jonas, eds. *Roosevelt and Churchill: Their Secret Wartime Correspondence.* (New York: Saturday Review Press, 1975; DaCapo, 1990), 225.

15. Sherwood, 607.

16. Stephen E. Ambrose, *The Supreme Commander.* (New York: Doubleday, 1970), 71. Ziegler, 185. Sherwood, 582.

17. Butcher, 29.

18. Parrish, 295–96.

19. Greenfield, 30. Ambrose, 73.

20. Ambrose, 75–77.

21. Parrish, 296.

22. KC, London. Alanbrooke 12/XI.

23. Hinsley, 100.

24. Ambrose, 70.

25. Wedemeyer, 135.

26. Kennedy, 261–62.

27. Fraser, 258.

28. Schreiner, A-4.

29. Fraser, 294.

30. Richard S. Malone, *A Portrait of War.* (Toronto: Collins, 1983), 113–15.

31. Gwyer, 632.

32. KC, London, Ismay II/3/247/2a.

33. Granatstein and Morton *A Nation Forged in Fire*, 50.

34. PRO, London, WO 106/4175.

35. Malone, 113–14.

36. Maisky, 293.

CHAPTER 17: THE RESTIVE WOLFHOUND

1. Gilbert, *Road to Victory*, 142. Lewin, 226.

2. Maisky, 291.

3. Maisky, 292.

4. Fraser, 280.

5. Moran, 54.

6. PRO, London. CAB 120/66, Reflex No. 2, 2 August, 1942.

7. PRO, London. CAB 120/65.

8. NAC, Ottawa. RG24: Vol. 10,750. 220CL.009 D3 and RG24: Vol. 10,795 CL.013.

9. PRO, London. CAB 120/65.

10. Wheeler-Bennett, ed. *Action This Day*, 252.

11. KC, London, Alanbrooke 3/A/VI. August 6, 1942.

12. Wheeler-Bennett, ed. *Action This Day*. (Sir Leslie Rowan), 251–52.

13. PRO, London. CAB 120/66, Reflex No. 85, August 13, 1942. PREM 3/76A/11, folio 42-3. Gilbert, *Road to Victory*, 174–75. Reis, 74–75.

14. Parkinson, 441.

15. PRO, London. CAB 120/65: Minutes at the Kremlin on Wednesday, August 12, 1942. PREM 3/76A/12. Gilbert. 181–83. Martin Gilbert's chapter in *Road to Victory* "Moscow, August 1942. 'The ogre in the den,'" quoted extensively in these pages, offers a fascinating and vivid account of Churchill's visit to Moscow.

16. PRO, London, CAB 120/69: "Most Secret Cypher Telegram," Tulip No. 152. Sir A. Cadogan to Foreign Office. KC, London. Alanbrooke 3/A/VI. "Notes on My Life." August 13, 1942. Maisky, 303. Memorandum from Stalin to Churchill, August 13, 1942.

17. Gilbert, *Road to Victory*, 184. "Meeting at the Kremlin." PRO, London, August 13, 1942, PREM 3/76A/12.

18. Gilbert, *Road to Victory*, 186: "Interview of Averell Harriman by Martin Gilbert," KC, London. Alanbrooke 3/A/VI.

19. Gilbert, *Road to Victory*, 191.

20. Wheeler-Bennett, ed. *Action This Day*. (Sir Ian Jacob), 215–16.

21. Gilbert, *Road to Victory*, 183. PRO, London. CAB 120/66, Reflex No. 81, August 13, 1942.

22. PRO, London. CAB 120/66, Reflex No. 99. This signal from Churchill was distributed only to Gen. Ismay and Maj.-Gen. Hollis.

23. PRO, London. CAB 120/69, Tulip No. 145, August 16, 1942.

24. Villa, Brian Loring. *Unauthorized Action*. (Toronto: Oxford University Press, 1989), 33. CBC "The National," 1990.

25. PRO, London. CAB 120/66, Reflex No. 99, Aug. 15. CAB 120/69, Tulip No. 145, Aug. 16, 1942.

26. Gilbert, *Road to Victory*, 198.

27. Stoler, 61.

28. Gilbert, *Road to Victory*, 198. Kennedy, 264.

29. Personal Interview with Gen. Jacob.

30. PRO, London. CAB 120/69. Gilbert, *Road to Victory*, 200.

31. Gilbert, *Road to Victory*, 205–06.

32. Gilbert, *Road to Victory*, 208.

33. NAC, Ottawa. RG24. Vol. 10,795 225C1.013: Operation Jubilee, Detailed Military Plan, Aug. 10. Operation Ford I.

34. Interview with Lt. Jack H. Dunlap, troop commander, 6 Tp, B Squad, Calgary Tank Regt.

35. Rees, 161.

36. Personal taped interview with Lt. Daniel Doheny, January 1992. Personal diary of Daniel Doheny, written in P.O.W. camp following the Dieppe raid, kindly loaned to the authors.

37. Atkin, 63.

38. Lovat, *March Past*, 247.

39. Robertson, 312.

40. PRO, London. CAB 120/67, Aug 17/42. Reflex No. 137. This signal from Churchill was designated for distribution to Gen. Ismay only.

41. PRO, London. CAB 120/69. August 18, 1942: 'Tulip No. 170' and 'Tulip No. 188.' Ismay to Churchill.

42. Personal taped interview with Gen. Sir Ian Jacob, Military Assistant Secretary to War Cabinet 1939–1946, Woodbridge, 30 May, 1991. *Action This Day* (Gen. Jacob), 208.

43. Letter from Gen. Jacob to the authors with extract of unpublished diary June 4, 1991.

CHAPTER 18: THE BEACHES OF HELL

1. PRO, London. CAB 101/335. Roskill, 246. Stacey. *Six Years of War*, 359.

2. DND, Ottawa. Directorate of History, CBC broadcast: "Close Up." 1962:594.009 D/13. Transcript of interview with Maj. Peter Young.

3. NAC, Ottawa. RG24. Vol. 20,488, File 981GN. (D13). Report of Port Commandant of Dieppe.

4. For a detailed account of No. 3 and No. 4 Commando's actions, see: Roskill, 243–47. Stacey, 358–63. Lovat, 247–61 (by Maj. Derek Mills-Roberts). See also: Richard Garrett, *The Raiders: The Elite Strike Forces that Altered the Course of War and History.* (New York: Van

Nostrand Reinhold Co., 1980), 126–27. From the archives of the U.S. Army Military History Institute, Carlisle.

5. Combined Report C.B. 04244.

6. Stacey, 364.

7. DND, Ottawa. Directorate of History 79/567, Macartney-Filgate Interviews, CBC. Interview with Hauptmann Richard Schnösenberg.

8. DND, Ottawa. Directorate of History 79/567, Macartney-Filgate Interviews, CBC. Transcript of interview with Maj. Claude Orme, SSR.

9. DND, Ottawa. Directorate of History 79/567, Macartney-Filgate Interviews, CBC. Interview with Lt. Schlie, Hamburg, 3 February, 1978.

10. DND, Ottawa. Directorate of History, Transcript of CBC broadcast: "Close Up." 1962: 594.009 D/13. Interview with Maj. Derek Mills-Roberts.

11. Stacey, *Six Years of War*, 369–74.

12. Goodspeed, 394–95.

13. Robertson, 267.

14. Personal taped interview with Cpl. (now Col.) John Williamson, RHLI, July 1991.

15. DND, Ottawa. CMHQ Report 128. Interview with Lt. L.C. Counsell by Col. C.P. Stacey, CMHQ, June 6, 1944.

16. DND, Ottawa. Directorate of History 79/567, Macartney-Filgate Interviews, CBC. Interview with Pte. Al Richards, RHLI.

17. Personal taped interview with Cpl. Jack Brabbs, July 1991.

18. Personal taped interview with Lt. John Gartshore, October 1991.

19. Personal taped interview with Lt.-Col. Ian McDonald, September 1991.

20. DND, Ottawa. Directorate of History 79/567, Macartney-Filgate Interviews, CBC. Interview with Maj. Jim Green, Essex Scottish Regt.

21. Atkin, 124.

22. DND, Ottawa. Directorate of History, CBC "Close Up," 1962: 594.009 D/13, interview with Maj. Forbes West. Personal taped interview with Maj. West, July 1991.

23. DND, Ottawa. Directorate of History 79/567, Macartney-Filgate Interviews, CBC. Interview with Pte. Ron Beal, Royal Regt. of Canada. Personal taped interview with Pte. Beal, July 1991.

24. DND, Ottawa. Directorate of History 79/567, Macartney-Filgate Interviews, CBC. Interview with L/Cpl. W. Duggan, Royal Regt. of Canada.

25. DND, Ottawa. Directorate of History 79/567, Macartney-Filgate Interviews, CBC. Interview with Pte. J.E. Creer, A. Coy, Royal Regt. of Canada.

26. DND, Ottawa. Directorate of History CBC broadcast: "Close Up." 1962: 594.009 D/13. Interview with Pte. Reg Hall, Black Watch Regt. of Canada.

27. DND, Ottawa. Directorate of History 79/567, Macartney-Filgate Interviews, CBC. Interview with Lt. Walter Höpener, 571 Infantry Regt.

28. Stacey, *Six Years of War*, 370.

29. DND, Ottawa. Directorate of History 79/567, Macartney-Filgate Interviews, CBC. Interview with Pte. Herbert Webber, Queen's Own Cameron Highlanders of Canada.

30. DND, Ottawa. Directorate of History 79/567, Macartney-Filgate Interviews, CBC. Interview with Lt. Tom Melville, Queen's Own Cameron Highlanders of Canada.

31. IWM, London. Combat Report, 81 Corps. Battle Report C-in-C West.

CHAPTER 19: THE UNSEEN ENEMY

---

1. *Onward II: 14 CATR at Dieppe*, June 1991.

2. Personal taped interview with Lieut. Ed Bennett, commander No. 10 Troop, Calgary Tank Regt.

3. DND, Ottawa. Directorate of History 79/567, Macartney-Filgate Interviews, CBC. Interview with Pte. K.C. (Casey) Lingen, B. Coy, RHLI.

4. Personal taped interview with Lieut. Bennett.

5. DND, Ottawa. Directorate of History 79/567, Macartney-Filgate Interviews, CBC. Interview with Capt. Ditz: Battery Commander, 302 German Infantry Division.

6. Robertson, 323.

7. DND, Ottawa. 75/17. Directorate of History. John P. Campbell, "Analysis of Air Operation at Dieppe," 1974.

8. DND, Ottawa. Directorate of History 79/567, Macartney-Filgate Interviews, CBC. Folder 45. Interview with Sgt. Dave Hart, 4 Bde. Signaller, 2 CID.

9. Unpublished wartime diary of Lt. Dan Doheny. Personal taped interview with Lt. Doheny, November 24, 1990 and December 21, 1991.

10. DND, Ottawa. Directorate of History 79/567, Macartney-Filgate Interviews, CBC. Interview with Cpl. Robert Berube, HQ Coy, FMR.

11. Stacey, *Six Years of War*. 362–63.

12. CBC transcript, "Close Up." 1962. Maj. Peter Young.

13. Garrett, 126.

14. Stacey, *Six Years of War*, 367.

15. Atkin, 125.

16. Personal taped Interview with Lt. Thomas L. Taylor, C. Coy. Royal Regt. of Canada. September 20 and December 21, 1991.

17. DND, Ottawa. Directorate of History 79/567, Macartney-Filgate Interviews, CBC. Interview with Pte. Ron Beal, Royal Regt.

18. Goodspeed, *Battle Royal*, 397.

19. Robertson, 358.

20. Transcript. CBC "Close Up." Pte. Reg Hall, Royal Regt.

21. DND, Ottawa. Battle Report. Interview with Capt. Browne who escaped from the train bearing Canadian prisoners to POW camps in Germany. He made his way to Barcelona where he wrote his report.

22. Stacey, *Six Years of War*, 382. Robertson, 358.

23. DND, Ottawa. Letter to his wife by Brig. Sherwood Lett.

CHAPTER 20: VANQUISH

1. DND, Ottawa. After-action interview with Capt. W.D. Whitaker at CMHQ, London, September 1942, by Col. C.P. Stacey.

2. PRO, London. DEFE 2/339. After-action interview with Capt. Tony Hill, RHLI.

3. PRO, London. DEFE 2/339. After-action interview with Pte. Johnny Shuart, RHLI.

4. 1 Bn. the Essex Scottish Regt., 18.

5. DND, Ottawa. Directorate of History 79/567. Macartney-Filgate Interviews, CBC. Lt. Schlie.

6. Personal taped interview with Maj. Richard McLaren, Intelligence Officer, RHLI.

7. *Semper Paratus*. History of the RHLI, 208.

8. Hugh George Henry (Jr.), *The Tanks of Dieppe.*

9. Personal taped interview with Lt. Dan Doheny.

10. DND, Ottawa. Directorate of History 79/567. Macartney-Filgate Interviews, CBC. Lt. Schlie.

11. Personal taped interview with Flying Officer Jack Godfrey RCAF. Letter written by Senator Godfrey to his wife, Mary, after the Dieppe operation, kindly loaned to the authors.

12. DND, Ottawa. Directorate of History 39-6A. No. 403 Squadron ORB.

13. DND, Ottawa. Directorate of History 43-2. No. 416 Squadron ORB.

14. PRO, London. Air 39/19: "Dieppe, Analysis of Army/Air Support Missions." Annex to DDMC, "Army Air Support and Tactical Reconnaissance During Operation Jubilee." 24 October, 1942.

15. IWM, London. Leigh-Mallory 75/283. Pilot Officer "Duke" Warren, 165 Squadron.

16. 1 Bn. the Essex Scottish Regt, 18.

17. DND, Ottawa. Directorate of History 79/567, Macartney-Filgate Interviews, CBC. L/Cpl. Lecky, QOCH.

18. Personal taped interview with Cpl. Jack Brabbs.

19. *14 CATR at Dieppe.* Personal letter from Lt. Dunlap, December 12, 1990.

20. DND, Ottawa. Directorate of History 79/567, Macartney-Filgate Interviews, CBC. Capt. "Buck" Buchanan.

21. DND, Ottawa. Directorate of History 79/567, Macartney-Filgate Interviews, CBC. Cpl. Alec Graham.

22. Lt.-Col. Edward Smith. *Dieppe.* (Association of the U.S. Army, August, 1977), 27.

23. Personal taped interview with Lt. Thomas L. Taylor, C. Coy. Royal Regt. of Canada, December 21, 1991. Goodspeed, *Battle Royal*, 397.

24. DND, Ottawa. Directorate of History, 79/567 Folder 101. Interview with Hauptmann (Capt.) Richard Schnösenberg, Commander at Puys.

25. PRO, London. AIR 16/760. Letter from Air Vice Marshall Leigh-Mallory to Air Marshal Sholto Douglas, June 29, 1942.

26. Col. A.J. Kerry and Maj. W.A. McDill. *The History of the Corps of Royal Canadian Engineers.* (Ottawa: Military Engineers Association of Canada, 1966), 108–10.

CHAPTER 21: RUN FOR THE HILLS

1. Moran, 73.

2. Stacey, *Six Years of War*, 323.

3. PRO, London. CAB 127/24. Letter from Mountbatten to Brooke. August 31, 1942.

4. PRO, London, PREM 3/256, folio 8. Churchill to Ismay 21 December 1942. KC, London: Ismay II/3/244a.

5. KC, London: Ismay II/3/252a: Churchill to Ismay, August 1950.

6. PRO, London. CAB 79 and CAB 80 were only opened a few years ago. CAB 121 is still closed.

7. Gwyer and Butler, 638. Hinsley, 695.

8. Ziegler, 188.

9. Maritime Marine Museum, Greenwich. GRO 22. Papers of Admiral Baillie-Grohman.

10. McMaster University Archives, Hamilton, Ontario. War Cabinet COS (42) 188th meeting, June 24, 1942.

11. Haggerty, 95.

12. PRO, London. CAB 101/335: Hughes-Hallet Papers.

13. McMaster University Archives. Minutes of COS 64th Meeting, July 6, 1942.

14. Churchill, *Hinge of Fate*, 444.

15. McMaster University Archives. COS 214th Meeting July 20, 1942: "Responsibility for Mounting and Planning Large Scale Raids." IWM, London. Hughes-Hallet Papers.

16. PRO, London. DEFE 2/550. Mountbatten letter to Brooke, July 30, 1942.

17. PRO, London. CAB 79/22. COS (42) 234th Meeting, August 12, 1942.

18. PRO, London. CAB 120/65-69.

19. Gen. Sir Ian Jacob's personal unpublished diary. August 19, 1942. Excerpt kindly loaned to the authors.

20. Personal interview with Martin Gilbert.

21. PRO, London. CAB 127/24. Letters from Mountbatten to Brooke, August 31 and September 4, 1942.

22. KC, London. Ismay II/3/246b. COS (42) 355th, December 29, 1942. PRO, London. CAB 79/22. COS (42) 234th Meeting, August 12.

23. Personal interviews with Mr. Gilbert and Gen. Fraser.

24. Stacey, *Six Years of War*, 337.

25. Taylor, *The War Lords*, 89. Parkinson, 357.

26. Personal interview with Col. Sir F.W.D. Deakin DSO, Personal Assistant to Churchill when writing his memoirs.

27. Moran, 180, 195.

28. KC, London: Ismay II/3/244a, and Ismay II/3/247/2b. Martin Gilbert, *Never Despair: Winston S. Churchill 1945–1965*. (Toronto: Stoddart, 1988), 551.

29. Gilbert, *Road to Victory*, 198.

30. KC, London: Ismay II/3/136b: Churchill to Ismay.

31. KC, London: Ismay II/3/248: Ismay to Churchill, 22 March, 1950.

32. KC, London: Ismay II/3/251/2a. Ismay to Churchill.

33. KC, London: Ismay II/3/247/2a and 2c.

34. KC, London: Ismay II/3/261/4a.

35. KC, London: Ismay II/3/261/2.

36. Winston Churchill, *Hinge of Fate*, 458.

37. Brian L. Villa. *Unauthorized Action*: *Mountbatten and the Dieppe Raid*. (Toronto: Oxford University Press, 1989).

38. Sir John Wheeler-Bennett (ed), *Action This Day*, 192.

39. Kings College, London. Ismay IV/Ala/3/1. Alanbrooke X1/4/47-106.

40. Personal interview with Martin Gilbert.

41. Personal interview with Martin Gilbert.

42. Letter to the authors from Sir John Peck, June 20, 1990.

43. PRO, London. CAB 101/335. Stephen Roskill, *The War at Sea. 1939–1945*. Vol. II. London: 1956. (Confidential Print).

44. Personal interview with Philip Ziegler.

45. Personal interview with General Fraser.

46. DND, Ottawa 79/567: Interview with Lord Lovat, No. 4 Commando commander, 1972. Levat, *March Past*, 277.

47. Personal interview with General Fraser.

48. Personal interview with Philip Ziegler.

49. DND: (Folder 79.) McCartney-Filgate interview with Lord Mountbatten.

50. DND, Ottawa. COHQ. Letter from Mountbatten to Crerar. October 5, 1942.

51. DND, Ottawa. Directorate of History. 79/567 folder 68. Hughes-Hallett speech at Royal Regiment Dinner. PRO, London: CAB 101/335: Hughes-Hallet Papers.

52. Stacey, *Six Years of War*, 334.

53. NAC, MG 30-E 157. Vol. 2, File 958-009 CD21.

54. NAC. RG24. Vol. 10,750, File 220CL.009 (D3): McNaughton Papers July 17, 1942.

55. DND: CBC "Close Up." Interview with Field Marshal Montgomery by Frank Willis, 1962.

56. Stacey, *Six Years of War,* 334–35. Letter Montgomery to Paget July 1st, 1942.

57. DND. CBC "Close Up." Interview with Field Marshal Montgomery, 1962.

58. Field Marshal Sir B.L. Montgomery, *Memoirs of Field-Marshal Montgomery*, 76.

59. Personal interview with Philip Ziegler.

60. Personal interview with Gen. Sir David Fraser.

61. Queens's University Archives. C.G. Powers. Box 38. Ministerial File. War Cabinet Committee minutes, July 1 to December 30, 1942.

62. DND: CBC. "Close Up." Interview with General McNaughton, 1962.

63. Queens's University Archives. C.G. Powers, Box 46: France, 1942.

64. NAC. RG24, Vol. 10,766, File 222C1 (D144).

65. KC, London: LH 15/4/16: *Sunday Times*. 28/7/63: letter to the editor by Goronwy Rees.

66. Robertson, 159–60.

67. McMaster University Archives: *Canadian Defence Quarterly*. Vol. 9, No 1, Summer 1979: "On the Real Purpose of the Dieppe Raid" by Maj.-Gen. C.C. Mann.

68. DND. CMHQ Report 128. Letter from Gen. Crerar to Gen. Kenneth Stuart, May 31, 1944.

69. Personal interview with John Roberts.

DIEPPE TO D-DAY

1. Fergusson, *Watery Maze*, 181.

2. Montgomery, *Normandy to the Baltic*, 53–54.

3. J.R. Robinson, "Radar Intelligence and the Dieppe Raid." *Canadian Defence Quarterly*, April 1991.

4. John Keegan, *Six Armies in Normandy*. (London: Jonathan Cape, 1982), 125.

5. Personal taped interview with Brig. Todd, June 29, 1990. The authors are indebted to Brig. Todd for reading this chapter and offering an invaluable critique. Robinson, "Radar Intelligence and the Dieppe Raid."

6. IWM, London, "Military Lessons to be Drawn from the Assault on Dieppe."

7. Interview with Brig. Todd.

8. Interview with Brig. Todd.

9. Interview with Brig. Todd.

10. Montgomery, *Normandy to the Baltic*, 54.

11. Interview with Brig. Todd.

12. Wilmot, 181.

13. W. Denis and Shelagh Whitaker, *Tug of War: The Canadian Victory that Opened Antwerp*. (Toronto: Stoddart, 1984), 285.

14. Kenneth Macksey, *Armoured Crusader: Major General Sir Percy Hobart*. (London: Hutchinson, 1967), 245.

15. Ralph Allen, *Ordeal by Fire*. (Toronto: Doubleday, 1961), 406–07.

16. PRO, London. AIR 40/2349 C.C. (42) 71, September 12, 1942. Review of Combined Planning Staff of the Dewing Report.

17. PRO, London. PREM 3/333/2.

18. DND, Ottawa. Directorate of History. 79/567 Folder 105. Interview of Col. C.P. Stacey.

19. IWM, London. The Papers of Vice Admiral John Hughes-Hallett. JHH 3/1 Dieppe. Jubilee Papers. "Unpublished Memoirs of Vice Admiral J. Hughes-Hallett."

20. Hinsley, 699–700.

21. Hinsley, 704.

22. Gwyer and Butler, 642.

23. KC, London. Ismay II/3/11. Stacey, *Six Years of War*, 405–06.

24. Lt.-Col. Daniel J. Webb, "The Dieppe Raid: An Act of Diplomacy." *Military Review* LX, May 1980. (U.S. Army Military History Institute, Carlisle, Pa.). Lt.-Col. Merrill Bartlett, *Assault from the Sea: Essays on the History of Amphibious Warfare*. (Annapolis: Naval Institute Press, 1983), 257.

25. Gwyer and Butler, 643.

26. Schreiner, A-5.

27. U.S. Army Military History Institute, Carlisle, Pa. Senior Officers Debriefing Program. Interview of Gen. Theodore J. Conway.

28. Roskill, 251.

29. Ziegler, 192.

30. Stacey, *Six Years of War*, 337. PRO, London. PREM 3/256.

31. IWM, London. Draft memoirs of John Hughes-Hallett.

32. DND, Ottawa. CMHQ Report 128. Letter from Gen. Crerar to Lt.-Gen. K. Stuart, May 31, 1944.

33. Ziegler, 191.

34. KC, London. LH 15/4/16. *The Spectator*. August 23, 1963. (Book review by John Hughes-Hallett.)

35. Ziegler, 191. (The Papers of Dwight David Eisenhower, Vol. III.)

36. Winston S. Churchill, *Triumph and Tragedy*. (Boston: Houghton Mifflin, 1953), 13–14.

37. DND, Ottawa. CMHQ Report 128. Personal message from Gen. Crerar.

EPILOGUE

1. Barnes, 815.

2. Ziegler, 187.

3. Wheeler-Bennett, 251–52.

4. Kennedy, 264.

5. Personal interview with Lt. Doheny. This is confirmed in Dwight D. Eisenhower's *Crusade in Europe*, page 87. (New York: Doubleday, 1948).

6. Gwyer, 643. Stacey, *Six Years of War*, 406. Personal interview with Pilot Officer Barry Hamblin. 242 Fighter Squadron, RAF.

BIBLIOGRAPHY

Allen, Ralph. *Ordeal by Fire*. Toronto: Doubleday, 1961.

Ambrose, Stephen E. *The Supreme Commander: The War Years of General Dwight D. Eisenhower*. New York: Doubleday, 1970.

Arthur, Max. *Men of the Red Beret, Airborne Forces 1940–1990*. London: Hutchinson, 1990.

Astley, Joan Bright. *The Inner Circle*. London: Hutchinson, 1971.

Atkin, Ronald. *Dieppe 1942: The Jubilee Disaster*. London: MacMillan, 1980.

Barnes, John, and David Nicholson, eds. *The Leo Amery Diaries, 1929–1945. The Empire at Bay*. vol. 2. London: Hutchinson, 1980.

Bartlett, Lt.-Col. M. *Assault From the Sea: Essays on the History of Amphibious Warfare*. Annapolis: Naval Institute Press, 1983.

Battalion, The Essex Scottish Regiment. (Allied with the Essex Regiment.) Welland, Ont: Wellington Press, 1946.

Beardmore, George. *Civilians at War: Journals 1938–1946*. London: Murray, 1984.

Beckles, Gordon. *Canada Comes to England*. London: Hodder & Stoughton, 1941.

Bennett, Ralph. *Ultra in the West*. London: Hutchinson, 1979.

Bonham Carter, Violet. *Winston Churchill As I Knew Him*. London: Collins, 1965.

Bryant, Arthur. *The Turn of the Tide. 1939–1943*. London: Collins, 1958.

Buchanan, Lt.-Col. GB, MBE. *The March of the Prairie Men: A Story of the South Saskatchewan Regiment*. Weyburn, Sask: privately printed. 1957.

Burns, E.L.M. *General Mud*. Toronto: Clark, 1970.

Butcher, Harry C. *My Three Years with Eisenhower: The Personal Diary of Captain Harry C. Butcher USNR, Naval Aide to General Eisenhower 1942–1945*. New York: Simon & Schuster, 1946.

Calder, Angus. *The People's War: Britain 1939–1945*. New York: Pantheon Books, 1960.

Campbell, John P. "Dieppe and German Foreknowledge." *Extension Bulletin*. Toronto: Extension Bulletin, A Periodical of the Canadian Forces Extension School. Summer, 1974.

———. *"Analysis of Air Operations at Dieppe,"* 1974.

————. "Dieppe, Deception and D-Day." *Canadian Defence Quarterly,* vol. 9, no. 3. Winter, 1980.

————. "The Ultra Revelations. The Dieppe Raid in a New Light as an Example of Now Inevitable Revisions in Second World War Historiography." *Canadian Defence Quarterly*, vol. 6, no 1. Summer, 1976.

"The Canadians at War, 1939–1945" *Readers Digest*. Montreal, 1986.

The Canadians in Britain 1939–1944. Ottawa: King's Printer, 1944.

The Case for the Second Front. Montreal: Quebec Committee for Allied Victory, 1942.

Cave Brown, Anthony. *Bodyguard of Lies*. New York: Fitzhenry, 1975.

————. *"C"*. New York: McMillan, 1987.

Centans d'histoire d'un regiment canadien-francais. Les Fusiliers Mont-Royal. Montreal: Editions du Jour, 1971.

Chalmers, W.S. *Full Cycle: The Biography of Admiral Sir Bertram Home Ramsey*. London: Hodder, 1959.

Chandler. *The Papers of D.D. Eisenhower. The War Years*. Baltimore: Johns Hopkins University, 1970.

Colville, John. *Winston Churchill and his Inner Circle*. New York: Wyndham, 1981.

Churchill, Randolph. (ed.) *Blood, Sweat and Tears*. Toronto: McClelland & Stewart, 1941.

Churchill, Sir Winston. *The Second World War*. Vol. 4, *The Hinge of Fate*. London: Houghton Mifflin, 1950.

Colville, John. *The Fringes of Power. Downing Street Diaries 1939–1955*. London: Hodder & Stoughton, 1985.

Douglas, W.A.B., and Brerton Greenhous. *Out of the Shadows*. Toronto: Oxford University Press, 1977.

Driberg, Tom. *Beaverbrook: A Study in Power and Frustration*. London: Weidenfeld & Nicolson, 1956.

Dunn, Walter Scott Jr. *Second Front Now: 1943*. Tuseaticosa, Alabama. University of Alabama Press, 1980.

Eisenhower, David. *Eisenhower: At War, 1943–1945*. New York: Random House, 1986.

Elliot, S.R. *Scarlet to Green*. Ottawa: Canadian Intelligence & Security Association, 1981.

English, John A. *The Canadian Army and the Normandy Campaign*. New York: Praeger, 1991.

Feis, Herbert. *Churchill Roosevelt Stalin: The War They Waged and the Peace They Sought.* London: Oxford, 1957.

Fergusson, Bernard. *The Watery Maze: The Story of Combined Operations.* London: Collins, 1961.

Fraser, David. *Alanbrooke.* London: Collins, 1982.

Garrett, Richard. The Raiders. The Elite Strike Forces that Altered the Course of War and History. New York: Van Nostrand Reinhold Co., 1980.

Gilbert, Martin. *Second World War.* Toronto: Stoddart, 1989.

––––––. *Road to Victory: Winston S. Churchill 1941–1945.* Toronto: Stoddard, 1986.

––––––. *Never Despair: Winston S. Churchill 1945–1965.* Toronto: Stoddart, 1988.

Goodspeed, Maj. Donald J. *Battle Royal: A History of the Royal Regiment of Canada, 1862–1962.* Toronto: Royal Regt. of Canada Assn., 1962.

Granatstein, J.L., and Desmond Morton. *A Nation Forged in Fire.* Toronto: Lester & Orpen Dennys, 1989.

Greenfield, Kent. *American Strategy in World War II: A Reconsideration.* Baltimore: Johns Hopkins University Press, 1975.

Gwyer, J.M.A. and J.R.M. Butler. *Grand Strategy.* Vol. III, *June 1941–August 1942.* London: HMSO, 1964.

Haggerty, Jerome J. "A History of the Ranger Battalions in World War II." Ph.D. diss., Fordham University, 1982.

Hamilton, Nigel. *Monty: The Making of a General 1887–1942.* London: Coronet Edition, 1984.

Harris, Sir Arthur. *Bomber Offensive.* Toronto: Stoddart, 1990.

Harrison, Gordon A. *The U.S. Army in WWII: Cross-Channel Attack.* Washington: OCMH, U.S. Army, 1951.

Harrisson, Tom. *Living Through the Blitz.* London: Collins, 1976.

Henry, Hugh George Jr. *The Tanks of Dieppe: The History of the Calgary Regiment (Tank), 1939 to August 19, 1942.* Victoria: University of Victoria, 1985.

Higgins, Trumbull. *Winston Churchill and the Second Front.* London: Oxford University Press, 1958.

Hinsley, F.H. *British Intelligence in the Second World War, Vol. 1 & 2.* London: HMSO, 1979: 1981.

Hooker, Martha M.A. *In Defence of Unity: Canada's Military Policies 1935–1944.* Ottawa: Carleton University, 1985.

Hughes-Hallett, J. "The Mounting of Raids." *Journal of the United Services Institute*. November, 1950.

Hunt, Barry, and Donald Schurman. *Prelude to Dieppe. Thoughts on Combined Operations Policy in the "Raiding Period" 1940–1942*. London: Croom Helm, 1977.

Hunter, T. Murray. *Canada at Dieppe*. Ottawa: Canadian War Museum, 1982.

Ismay, Lord Hastings. *The Memoirs of General Lord Ismay*. Westport, Ct: Greenword Press, 1960, 1974.

Irving, David. *Churchill's War*. London: Avon, 1990.

———. *Hitler's War*. New York: Viking Press, 1977.

James, Robert R. *Churchill: A Study in Failure. 1900–1939*. London: Weidenfeld & Nicholson, 1970.

Johnson, Johnnie. *Wing Leader*. Toronto: Clarke, Irwin, 1956.

Keegan, John. *Six Armies in Normandy*. London: Jonathan Cape, 1982.

Kelly, Arthur. "Dieppe." *Hamilton This Month*. Hamilton, Ontario: HTM, October 1989.

———. "Of Gods and Goblins." *Hamilton This Month*. Hamilton, Ontario: HTM, October 1990. As told to Arthur Kelly by Frederich Oechsner.

Kennedy, General Sir John. *The Business of War*. London: Hutchinson, 1957.

King, Dr. Michael J. "Rangers: Selected Combat Operations in World War II." *Leavenworth Papers*. Combat Studies Institute, Leavenworth, Kansas, June, 1985.

Langhorne, Richard (ed). *Diplomacy and Intelligence During the Second World War*. Cambridge: 1985.

Leasor, James. *Green Beach*. London: Heinemann, 1975.

Lewin, Ronald. *Ultra Goes to War: The Secret Story*. London: Hutchinson & Co, 1978.

Loewenheim, F.L. (ed), Harold D. Langley, and Manfred Jonas. *Roosevelt and Churchill: Their Secret Wartime Correspondence*. New York: Saturday Review Press, 1975.

Longmate, Norman. *How We Lived Then: A History of Everyday Life During the Second World War*. London: Hutchinson, 1971.

Lovat, Baron Simon Fraser. *March Past: A Memoir*. London: Weidenfeld & Nicholson, 1978.

Lyons, Graham (ed). *The Russian Version of the Second World War*. London: Leo Coooper, 1976.

Macksey, Kenneth. *Armoured Crusader: Major General Sir Percy Hobart*. London: Hutchinson, 1967.

Maguire, Eric. *Dieppe August 19*. London: Jonathan Cape, 1963.

Maisky, I.M. *Memoirs of a Soviet Ambassador: The War, 1939–1943*. London: Hutchinson, 1967.

Malone, Richard S. *A Portrait of War 1939–1943*. Toronto: Collins, 1983.

Manchester, William. *The Last Lion: Winston Spencer Churchill Alone 1932–1940*. London: Little Brown & Co., 1988.

Masterman, J.C. *The Double-Cross System in the War of 1939 to 1945*. London: Yale University, 1972.

McLachlan, Donald. *Room 39: Naval Intelligence in Action, 1939–1945*. London: Weidenfeld and Nicholson, 1968.

Mellor, John. *Forgotten Heros: The Canadians at Dieppe*. Toronto: Methuen, 1975.

Mills-Roberts, Derek. *Clash by Night*. London: Kimber, 1956.

Montgomery, Field Marshal Sir B.L. *El Alamein to the River Sango*. Berlin: British Army on the Rhine, 1946.

———. *Normandy to the Baltic*. Berlin: British Army on the Rhine, 1946.

———. *Memoirs of Field-Marshal Montgomery*. London: Collins, 1958.

Moorehead, Alan. *Gallipoli*. Toronto: MacMillan, 1989.

Moran, Lord. *Churchill: Taken from the Dairies of Lord Moran*. Boston: Houghton, 1966.

Mordal, Jacques. *Dieppe: The Dawn of Decision*. London: Souvenir Press, 1963.

Morton, Desmond. *A Military History of Canada*. Edmonton: Hurtig, 1985.

———. *A Nation Forged in Fire*. Toronto: Lester & Orpen Dennys, 1989.

Neatby, H. Blair. *William Lyon Mackenzie King*. Toronto: University of Toronto Press, 1976.

Nicholson, Col. G.W.L. *The Gunners of Canada*. Toronto: McClelland and Stewart, 1972.

Nissen, Jack, and A.W. Cockerill. *Winning the Radar War*. Toronto: MacMillan, 1987.

Nolan, Brian. *King's War*. Toronto: Random House, 1988.

Oeschsner, Frederick. *This is the Enemy*. Boston: Little Brown & Co., 1942.

Onward II: The History of the Calgary Regiment. Vancouver, B.C.: Published by the 50/14 Veterans' Association, June, 1991.

Panter-Downes, Mollie. *London War Notes 1939–1945*. Toronto: Doubleday, 1971.

Parkinson, Roger. *Blood, Toil, Tears and Sweat: The War History from Dunkirk to Alamein*. London: Hart-Davis McGibbon, 1973.

Parrish, Thomas. *Roosevelt and Marshall*. New York: Wm. Morrow, 1989.

Pogue, Forrest C. *George C. Marshall*. New York: Viking Press, 1966.

Queen-Hughes, R.W. *Whatever Men Dare: History of the Queen's Own Cameron Highlanders of Canada, 1935–1960*. Winnipeg: The Regiment, 1960.

Ramsay, W.G. (ed). *After the Battle* Vol. 2, *World War Two—Then and Now*. London: After the Battle Magazine, 1977.

Rees, Goronwy. *A Bundle of Sensations: Sketches in Autobiography*. London: Chatto & Windus, 1960.

Robertson, Terence. *The Shame and the Glory*. Toronto: McClelland & Stewart, 1962.

Robinson, J.R. "Radar Intelligence and the Dieppe Raid." *Canadian Defence Quarterly,* April, 1991.

Roosevelt, Eleanor. *This I Remember*. New York: Harper, 1949.

Roskill, Stephen. *Churchill and the Admirals*. New York: Wm Morrow, 1978.

Roskill, Capt. S.W. *The War at Sea. Vol. II*. London: H.M. Stationery Office, 1956.

———. "The Dieppe Raid and the Question of German Foreknowledge. A Study in Historical Responsibility." Journal of Royal United Service Institute. Vol. CIX February-November 1964.

Schreiner, Lt.-Col. Charles. "The Dieppe Raid: Its Origins, Aims and Results." U.S. Marine Corps College of Naval Warfare. *Naval War College Review,* May–June 1973. 35–41.

Searle, Adrian. *Isle of Wight at War 1939–45*. Wimborne, Dorset: The Dovecote Press, 1989.

The Secret History of World War II: The Ultra Secret Wartime Cables and Letters of Roosevelt, Stalin and Churchill. New York: Richardson & Steirman, 1986.

Sherwood, Robert E. *Roosevelt and Hopkins: An Intimate Story*. New York: Harper, 1948.

Soames, Lady Mary. *Clementine Churchill. By Her Daughter Mary Soames*. Toronto: Houghton, 1979.

Stacey, C.P. and Barbara M. Wilson. *The Half-Million: The Canadians in Britain, 1939–1946.* Toronto: University of Toronto Press, 1987.

Stacey, Col. C.P. *Arms, Men and Governments: The War Policies of Canada.* Ottawa: Department of National Defence, 1970.

————. *Six Years of War: The Army in Canada, Britain and the Pacific.* Ottawa: Queen's Printer, 1955.

————. *The Canadian Army 1939–1945: An Official Historical Summary.* Ottawa: King's Printer, 1948.

————. *Canada and the Age of Conflict.* Toronto: University of Toronto Press, 1981.

————. *A Date with History: Memoirs of a Canadian Historian.* Ottawa: Deneau, 1983.

Steele, Richard W. "Political Aspects of American Planning, 1941–1942." Vol XXXV, *Military Affairs*, published by the American Military Institute, April 1971.

Stevenson, William. *A Man Called Intrepid: The Secret War.* New York: Ballantine, 1976.

Stimson, Henry L. *On Active Service in Peace and War.* New York: Harper, 1947.

Stoler, Mark A. *The Politics of the Second Front: American Military Planning and Diplomacy in Coalition Warfare 1941–1943.* Connecticut: Greenwood Press, 1977.

Stuebing, Douglas. *Dieppe 1942.* Toronto: Clarke, Irwin, 1969.

Taylor, A.J.P. *Churchill Revised: A New and Authoritative Appraisal of his Life and Career.* New York: Dial Press, 1969.

————. *Beaverbrook.* London: Hamish Hamilton, 1972.

————. *The War Lords.* Lordon: Penguin, 1978.

Vagts, Dr. Alfred. *Landing Operations: Strategy, Psychology, Tactics, Politics, From Antiquity to 1945.* Harrisburg: Military Service Publishing Co. 1946.

Villa, Brian Loring. *Unauthorized Action: Mountbatten and the Dieppe Raid.* Toronto: Oxford University Press, 1989.

War Services of Canadian Knights of Columbus 1939–1947. Montreal: Gazette Printing Co., 1948.

Warlimont, Walter. *Inside Hitler's Headquarters 1939–1945.* New York: Praeger, 1964.

Webb, Lt.-Col. Daniel J. "The Dieppe Raid: An Act of Diplomacy." *Military Review*, LX, May 1980. (US Army Military History Institute, Carlisle, Pa.)

Wedemeyer, Albert C. *Wedemeyer Reports!* New York: Holt, 1958.

Werth, Alexander. *Russia at War 1941–1945*. New York: Barrie & Rockliffe, 1964.

West, Nigel. *A Thread of Deceit: Espionage Myths of World War II*. New York: Random House, 1985.

Wheeler-Bennett, Sir John (ed). *Action This Day*. London: MacMillan, 1968.

Whitaker, W. Denis and Shelagh Whitaker. *Tug of War: The Canadian Victory that Opened Antwerp*. Toronto: Stoddart, 1984.

Whitehead, William. *Dieppe 1942: Echoes of Disaster*. Toronto: Nelson, Personal Library, 1979.

Wilmot, Chester. *The Struggle for Europe*. London: Collins, 1952.

Ziegler, Philip. *Mountbatten*. New York: Alfred Knopf, 1985.

ACKNOWLEDGEMENTS

This book could not have been produced without the generous assistance of historians and archivists, friends and veterans.

In Ottawa, we availed ourselves of the enormous resources of the National Archives of Canada and the unfailing help of military archivist, Barbara Wilson. At the Department of National Defense, Directorate of History, historians Alec Douglas, Brereton Greenhous, Steven Harris, and Bill McAndrew generously shared their knowledge and time. In Toronto, the Royal Canadian Military Institute and the Canadian Forces Staff College both opened up their libraries to us, and for their hands-on assistance we thank chief librarians Ann Melvin and Catherine Murphy respectively. The archives of two universities generously allowed us to use their facilities: Queen's in Kingston and McMaster in Hamilton. From these sources we unearthed scores of books, articles and transcripts of documentary films on the Dieppe subject.

Of particular value were the unpublished theses, generously loaned, of Martie Hooker, MA, *In Defence of Unity: Canada's Military Policies 1935-1944*, and of Hugh George Henry Jr., *The Tanks of Dieppe: the History of the Calgary Tank Regiment*. We acknowledge, too, the special help of librarians at the Country Reference Library (Lord Louis Library), Newport, Isle of Wight, the public library of Hastings, West Sussex, and the Centennial library in Oakville, Ontario.

A great deal of assistance was given us by World War II veterans. Many offered helpful insight into the operation. Tom Taylor and Dan Doheny generously loaned us their unpublished diaries, written from a prisoner of war camp following Dieppe. Fellow Rileys Frank Volterman, Jack Brabbs and John Williamson, to mention a few, went out of their way to assist us. Brigadier Stanley Todd CBE, DSO, ED, CD, RCA, and Lieutenant General W.A.B. Anderson CBE, CD, RCA shared reminiscences from senior levels.

Of special note was the assistance given us by Terence Macartney-Filgate, who produced the fine CBC documentary *Dieppe 1978*. One of Terry's most esteemed possessions — a plaque from the German 302nd Infantry Division — bespeaks his even-handed treatment of the battle. Also of immeasurable help were screen writer John Krizanc and *Readers Digest* editor Ken Ramstead.

Terry Copp, professor of military history at Wilfrid Laurier University and author of *The Brigade: The Fifth Canadian Infantry Brigade*

1939–1945 (forthcoming) very kindly read our manuscript and we are the grateful beneficiaries of the many hours he devoted to our project and his many valuable suggestions. For arranging our access to McMaster, and for being an uncomplaining sounding board over the past few years, we thank John Campbell, professor of history at McMaster. Portions of the manuscript were also read by Dr. Steven Harris at DND, by Brigadier Stanley Todd, by Professor Ian Shaw of Brock University, and by Brian Farrell and David Hall, both doctoral students who unstintingly took time from preparing their own theses to help us prepare ours.

Brian Farrell's thesis was curiously parallel in many ways to our own. His ongoing advice and his critique of our chapters were immensely helpful. David Hall was "our man in London," putting in painstaking hours of archival slogging and sifting to assist our work. His skill, his encouragement and his meticulous eye for appropriate sources were invaluable.

London was the Mecca. We returned on three different occasions as each fresh discovery led to the next. As he has for our previous two publications, Rod Suddaby, Keeper of the Department of Documents at the Imperial War Museum, has been of enormous help. We acknowledge, too, the unstinting cooperation of archivists at the Public Record Office in Kew, Surrey, and at the Liddell Hart Centre for Military Archives at King's College where Dr. Patricia Methuen is the able curator.

We were privileged to be received by a number of British scholars and retired military leaders, who gave us invaluable insight and personal assistance. Foremost, we thank Martin Gilbert, Churchill's official biographer. Although he has exclusive access to the Churchill papers, Mr. Gilbert is outstandingly generous in sharing their contents with historians around the world. Martin not only offered us his expertise, which is monumental, but he also introduced us to several associates who proved to be most cooperative, helpful and cordial. Two men were key members of Churchill's wartime offices: Lieutenant General Sir Ian Jacob GBE, CB, was military assistant secretary to Churchill's War Cabinet from 1939 to 1946; Sir John Peck served as his private secretary. As well, Sir William Deakin DSO was Churchill's personal assistant when he was writing his memoirs. Joan Bright Astley was an important key member of General Ismay's staff who ran the War Cabinet Secret Information Centre.

General Sir David Fraser GCB, OBE, DL freely shared with us his vast experience and knowledge of the interrelation of military and government. Fraser was a former Vice-Chief of the Imperial General Staff and, subsequently, the highly regarded biographer of *Alanbrooke*.

Several British historians and authors of outstanding international reputation were most helpful. Philip Ziegler, Lord Mountbatten's official biographer and author of *Mountbatten*, was invariably generous with his time and encouragement. Intelligence specialist Ralph Bennett, who wrote *Ultra in the West*, helped us unravel some of the intricacies of British intelligence. Historian, author and military book critic for the London *Financial Times*, Anthony Verrier, added useful insight. As ever, our friends Major General and Mrs. Barry Lane have outdone themselves in their generosity and support.

In the United States, Lieutenant Colonel Martin W. Andresen and John J. Slonaker again opened the resources of the U.S. Army Military History Institute at Carlisle Barracks, Pennsylvania, to us.

We acknowledge with gratitude the generous assistance of the Canada Council, and the help of historians Desmond Morton, Jack Granatstein, Bill McAndrew and Ron Haycock in recommending us for grants. Thanks go to Alix MacAulay for once again producing an excellent index.

We are deeply appreciative of the ongoing support and patience of our friends and families. To our 10 neglected grandchildren we can only say, we have some catching up to do!

A decade ago, a young woman *did* stand at the railing of the Dieppe-Newhaven ferry, and *did* weep for her father who fought on the Dieppe beach. That woman was our daughter, Martie Hooker. She went on to an outstanding academic and writing career. Martie has been the editor of all three of our publications, drawing from her Masters of Arts background in military history as well as her skills as a writer.

But her Dieppe experience perhaps gave her an inside edge in the dedication and love that she poured into this one.

Oakville, Ontario
1992

INDEX

CANADIAN FORMATIONS

DIEPPE

DATE DUE

MAR 1 5 1994	*1918*	
APR 0 5 1994	*1918*	
MAY 0 5 1994	*4424*	
JUN 1 8 1994	*5098*	
AUG 1 9 1994	*4812*	
MAR 1 4 1995	*5617*	
MAR 0 5 1997	*5364*	
APR 1 5 1997	*4677*	